Communications
in Computer and Information Science   1284

Commenced Publication in 2007
Founding and Former Series Editors:
Simone Diniz Junqueira Barbosa, Phoebe Chen, Alfredo Cuzzocrea,
Xiaoyong Du, Orhun Kara, Ting Liu, Krishna M. Sivalingam,
Dominik Ślęzak, Takashi Washio, Xiaokang Yang, and Junsong Yuan

More information about this series at http://www.springer.com/series/7899

Andrzej Dziech · Wim Mees ·
Andrzej Czyżewski (Eds.)

Multimedia Communications, Services and Security

10th International Conference, MCSS 2020
Kraków, Poland, October 8–9, 2020
Proceedings

 Springer

Editors
Andrzej Dziech
AGH University of Science and Technology
Kraków, Poland

Wim Mees
Royal Military Academy
Brussels, Belgium

Andrzej Czyżewski
Gdańsk University of Technology
Gdańsk, Poland

ISSN 1865-0929   ISSN 1865-0937   (electronic)
Communications in Computer and Information Science
ISBN 978-3-030-58999-8   ISBN 978-3-030-59000-0   (eBook)
https://doi.org/10.1007/978-3-030-59000-0

This Springer imprint is published by the registered company Springer Nature Switzerland AG
The registered company address is: Gewerbestrasse 11, 6330 Cham, Switzerland

Preface

It is not obvious among technical sciences to find a second equally diverse and multidisciplinary one, as multimedia communication technology. The richness of this discipline is rapidly growing, especially when we consider its connection with telecommunications and security challenges. Following a long tradition of MCSS conferences, this year marked the 10th edition and was characterized by a unique diverse set of topics that perfectly illustrated the wealth of issues that are positioned at the center of scientific interest of researchers, who have demonstrated their commitment to this broad area.

Consequently, according to the MCSS conference prerogative, the call for papers was positively received and resulted in these proceedings. The reader will find a discussion of the issues belonging to main topics of the conference such as cybersecurity, multimedia processing and analysis, and systems architectures and designs.

Multimedia surrounds us everywhere. It is estimated that only a part of the recorded resources are processed and analyzed. These resources offer enormous opportunities to improve the quality of life of citizens. As a result, of the introduction of a new type of algorithms to improve security by maintaining a high level of privacy protection. Among the many articles, there are examples of solutions for improving the operation of monitoring systems or preventing threats in the industrial environment.

The important group of issues is the creation of solutions and functionalities into ready-to-use systems. The practical use of research results was discussed during the conference. Connecting them with modern architectures is a natural necessity in the case of future implementations.

A significant part of the MCSS 2020 was dedicated to cybersecurity and, more specifically, to the outcomes of the ECHO EU project "European network of Cybersecurity centers and competence Hub for innovation and Operations."

The Central Competence Hub serves as the focal point for the ECHO Multi-sector Assessment Framework, enabling multi-sector dependencies management, provision of an Early Warning System and a Federation of Cyber Ranges. The Multi-sector Assessment Framework refers to the analysis of challenges and opportunities derived from sector-specific use cases, transversal cybersecurity needs analysis, and development of inter-sector Technology Roadmaps involving horizontal cybersecurity disciplines. The Early Warning System, Federation of Cyber Ranges, and Inter-sector Technology Roadmaps are then subjected to Demonstration Cases incorporating relevant involvement of inter-dependent industrial sectors. The ECHO Cybersecurity Certification Scheme provides a sector-specific and inter-sector process for cybersecurity certification testing of new technologies and products resulting from the proposed Technology Roadmaps.

Additionally, more application related work is also presented at the conference, including solutions supporting the effective analysis for the security of diagnostic and repair work on industrial devices with the use of mobile units and advanced image analysis. Research and development focusing on these issues were performed in the INRED project which has the objective to develop an innovative system supporting employees in the implementation of renovation and repair works industrial diagnostic devices, as well as ensuring a significant increase in work safety with a simultaneous increase in the quality of work.

As the editors, we hope that every participant of this conference, as well as readers of these proceeding, will appreciate the possibility of broadening their knowledge, thanks to the detailed and careful presentation of ideas, methods, and achieved results by the authors. Finally, we would like to turn your attention to the unique environment of the scientific event, which is the millennial Cracow with its unique charm of the autumn.

August 2020

Andrzej Dziech
Wim Mees
Andrzej Czyżewski

Organization

Volume Editors

Andrzej Dziech   AGH University of Science and Technology, Poland
Wim Mees   Royal Military Academy, Belgium
Andrzej Czyżewski   Gdansk University of Technology, Poland

General Chair

Andrzej Dziech   AGH University of Science and Technology, Poland

Program Chairs

Wim Mees   Royal Military Academy, Belgium
Andrzej Czyżewski   Gdansk University of Technology, Poland
Remigiusz Baran   Kielce University of Technology, Poland
Mikolaj Leszczuk   AGH University of Science and Technology, Poland
Andrzej Matiolański   AGH University of Science and Technology, Poland

Executive Committee

Matteo Merialdo   RHEA Group, Belgium
Nikolai Stoianov   Bulgarian Defence Institute, Bulgaria
Marcin Niemiec   AGH University of Science and Technology, Poland
Marton Kis   Semmelweis University, Hungary

Program Committee

Charalampos Dimoulas   Aristotle University, Greece
Hans-Joachim Nern   IMAS Intelligent Media and Systems, Germany
Marcin Niemiec   AGH University of Science and Technology, Poland
George Papanikolaou   Aristotle University of Thessaloniki, Greece
Remigiusz Baran   Kielce University of Technology, Poland
Andrzej Matiolański   AGH University of Science and Technology, Poland
Todor Tagarev   Institute of ICT, Bulgaria
Jan Cimbalnik   International Clinical Research Center, St. Anne's University Hospital, Czech Republic
Pawel Korus   New York University, USA
Luis Angel Galindo   Telefonica, Spain
Miroslav Voznak   VSB-Technical University of Ostrava, Czech Republic
Wim Mees   Royal Military Academy, Belgium
Bozena Kostek   Gdansk University of Technology, Poland

Olaf Maennel	Tallinn University of Technology, Estonia
Nikolai Stoianov	Bulgarian Defence Institute, Bulgaria
Vasilis Katos	Bournemouth University, UK
ChristianmyckMCSS! Kollmitzer	FHTW, Austria
Theodora Tsikrika	CERTH, Greece
Oleg Illiashenko	National Aerospace University (KhAI), Ukraine
Jan Derkacz	AGH University of Science and Technology, Poland
Michał Grega	AGH University of Science and Technology, Poland
Andrzej Dziech	AGH University of Science and Technology, Poland
Pavel Varbanov	European Software Institute CEE, Bulgaria
Michael Cooke	Maynooth University, Ireland
Marton Kis	Semmelweis University, Hungary
David Larrabeiti	Universidad Carlos III de Madrid, Spain
Mikolaj Leszczuk	AGH University of Science and Technology, Poland
Andrzej Czyżewski	Gdansk University of Technology, Poland
Andrzej Duda	Grenoble Institute of Technology, France
Jakob Wassermann	University of Applied Sciences Technikum Wien, Austria
Matteo Merialdo	RHEA Group, Belgium

Contents

Multi-sector Assessment Framework – a New Approach to Analyse Cybersecurity Challenges and Opportunities

Salvatore Marco Pappalardo[1,2,3], Marcin Niemiec[4(✉)], Maya Bozhilova[5], Nikolai Stoianov[5], Andrzej Dziech[4], and Burkhard Stiller[6]

[1] CIRM, Viale Zara 81, Milan, Italy
marco.pappalardo@softwareengineering.it
[2] Software Engineering Italia S.r.l., Via Santa Sofia 64, Catania, Italy
[3] University of Messina, COSPECS, PhD St, via Concezione 8, Messina, Italy
[4] AGH University of Science and Technology, Mickiewicza 30, 30-059 Krakow, Poland
{niemiec,dziech}@kt.agh.edu.pl
[5] Bulgarian Defence Institute, Sofia, Bulgaria
{m.bozhilova,n.stoianov}@di.mod.bg
[6] Communication Systems Group CSG, Department of Informatics IfI,
University of Zurich UZH, Binzmühlestrasse 14, 8050 Zurich, Switzerland
stiller@ifi.uzh.ch

Abstract. This paper presents a new approach to analyse cybersecurity challenges and opportunities, focused on the development of a new risk assessment and management framework. Such a multi-sector assessment framework should be able to evaluate and prioritize cybersecurity risks in trans-sectoral and inter-sectoral contexts. It leads toward proper resource allocations and mitigation actions. To achieve this goal, the analysis of existing risk assessment and management frameworks was performed. Also, an overview on common multi-sectoral technological challenges and opportunities were provided being derived from sector-specific use cases as well as transversal and inter-sectoral challenges and opportunities. As a result of this analysis the architecture of the ECHO Multi-sector Assessment Framework was proposed. The identified technological challenges and opportunities, multi-sector dependencies, and transversal aspects determine the input data for the new framework. The architecture is applicable in healthcare, energy, maritime transportation, and defence sectors, being extensible to others. The framework enables the definition of governance models or the design of cybersecurity technology roadmaps.

Keywords: ECHO project · Cybersecurity · Risk assessment framework · Challenges and opportunities

1 Introduction

Ensuring cybersecurity is becoming more difficult in every next year since new attacks exploiting new vulnerabilities are carried out, while regulatory institutions and

A. Dziech et al. (Eds.): MCSS 2020, CCIS 1284, pp. 1–15, 2020.
https://doi.org/10.1007/978-3-030-59000-0_1

researchers change and improve rules (such as regulations or standards). However, society needs to be prepared to face new cybersecurity challenges. At a national level, there are recognized needs and challenges for personal data protection [1], organisational and corporate cybersecurity [2], and a national cybersecurity system [3].

Unfortunately, threats in cyberspace are not limited to one country or sector. They cross borders and could have devastating consequences at a regional or European level. The European Union recognized increasing threats and challenges by cyberattacks as well as opportunities and advantages in the new information age. In April 2019, the Council adopted a respective regulation – the Cybersecurity Act [4]. One of the cross-cutting measures that the EU has worked on in parallel is cyber defence, where the EU has updated its framework taking into account changing security challenges.

The ECHO (European network of Cybersecurity centres and competence Hub for innovation and Operations) project is one of four pilot projects – including the CONCORDIA project – funded by the European Commission, to establish a cybersecurity competence network [5]. The ECHO project will provide an approach to proactive cyber defence for ensuring the cybersecurity resilience of the EU, using a multi-sector collaboration. ECHO involves thirty industrial and academic partners from Europe and wants to unify currently fragmented cybersecurity efforts across the EU. One of the ECHO outputs – the ECHO Multi-sector Assessment Framework – will enable a multi-sector cybersecurity dependencies analysis.

This paper presents results from the work conducted in WP2 of ECHO. It starts with the analysis of risk assessment and management frameworks. Further, an overview is provided on common multi-sectoral technological challenges and opportunities derived from sector-specific use cases as well as transversal and inter-sectoral challenges and opportunities. As a result of the analysis conducted, the architecture of the ECHO multi-sector risk assessment framework is proposed.

2   Risk Assessment and Management

IT (Information Technology) professionals describe the risk as a threat exploiting a system's weakness and causing an adverse effect [6]. The two main factors of risk include impact (the degree of harm caused by the threat) and likelihood of this threat. Thus, this approach to cybersecurity can support entities in making decisions associated with the security and operational stability of IT environment. Therefore, this overall process is called risk management. Risk assessment – the crucial stage of the risk management lifecycle – performs an assessment of threats in a measurable way and identifies cost-effective actions.

Specifically, the risk assessment process describes the overall process including 3 activities: identify hazards and risk factors that have the potential to cause harm (risk identification), analyse and evaluate the risk associated with that hazard (risk analysis and risk evaluation), and determine appropriate solutions to eliminate the hazard or control the risk if the hazard cannot be eliminated (risk control).

However, different standards can describe and approach this process in different ways. Therefore, the basic risk assessment frameworks and methodologies are overviewed in the following and comprehensively analysed to derive a broadly applicable multi-sector assessment framework [7].

2.1 Risk Assessment and Management Frameworks

The main goal of a risk assessment framework is to serve as an approach for prioritising risks posed to an organisation, thus, enabling a sound decision making in terms of allocation of resources. Applied to the ECHO-network and competence hub, this means that the ECHO Risk Assessment Framework needs to support the evaluation of the cyber incident risk in at least four domains the project covers (healthcare, energy, maritime transportation, and defence). The design of a new framework should be performed in a comprehensive way by tackling vertical (by zooming in on each specific domain) and horizontal dimensions of these domains (by looking at transversal/inter-sectoral aspects, i.e., covering more than one domain). This two-dimensional analysis will track the route to induce innovation in risk assessment activities as well as to identify and isolate transversal, inter-sectoral as well as multi-sectoral elements.

For each domain (vertical path) a specific analysis had been performed to investigate how these four ECHO-domains apply risk frameworks to their key business processes in the light of well-known domain-related storylines. This analysis led to a clear assessment of what needs and basic requirements a modern risk assessment framework for specific domains has. Those gaps identified between the target security and current security levels will represent a clear qualitative metric to understand what is missing in current solutions.

The horizontal analysis is a key added value in today's interconnected and interdependent world. It is also a core part of the vision of the ECHO project: deliver an EU trans-sectoral and inter-sectoral cybersecurity concept and marketplace. The analysis performed here now followed a different path since it defined first what is intended by transversal and inter-sectoral risk assessment. Secondly, it assessed existing risk assessment frameworks in order to verify whether they do cover by design transversal and inter-sectoral risk assessments and also does identify key trans-sectoral and inter-sectoral business processes and security challenges.

2.2 Selected Frameworks

The **ISO 31000** [8] is the international standard that provides a common approach to the management of any type of risk (from strategic to operational risks) and a model, which can be integrated into the business management system. This standard introduces a set of principles and guidelines to help organisations to run a risk assessment and risk analysis. It was developed by a range of stakeholders and is intended for use by anyone who manages risks – not only professional risk managers. It provides a best-practice structure and guidance to all operations concerned with risk management. The ISO 31000:2018 standard defines a family of standards relating to risk management, where the risk assessment is considered crucial. The first step is definition of the organisation's context and the scope of the risk management strategy. Secondly, the identification and development of the risk criteria is necessary. Thirdly, the risk assessment is performed, while being composed out of risk identification, analysis, and evaluation.

The **TOGAF** standard [9] is a framework for enterprise architectures. The TOGAF standard defines risk management as a technique used to manage risk during an architecture transformation project. The risk management process consists of five activities.

- Risk classification: Risks are usually classified in terms of time, cost, and scope, but they could also include contractual risks, technological, scope and complexity, environmental, and personnel risks.
- Risk identification: This process determines which risks may affect the project and describes their characteristics.
- Initial risk assessment: This activity assesses the initial level of risk (e.g., catastrophic, critical, marginal, or negligible) and the potential frequency (e.g., frequent, likely, occasional, seldom, or unlikely).
- Risk Mitigation: The identification, planning, and conduct of actions that reduce risk to the acceptable level.
- Risk Monitoring: The process of tracking risk management execution and continuing to identify and manage new risks.

The **SP 800-30** [10] introduced by National Institute of Standards and Technology provides guidance for carrying out the risk management process. SP 800-30 focuses on the risk assessment component, providing a detailed step-by-step process for organisations. It consists of four steps: prepare for risk assessments, conduct risk assessments, communicate risk assessment results to key organisational personnel, and maintain the risk assessments over time. The methodology is a part of the risk management framework (SP 800-37) and information security risk management (SP 800-39). They allow for addressing of the full risk management lifecycle. The key advantage of SP 800-30 includes flexibility – users can define different algorithms for assessing and combining risk factors that can be applied to different use cases and stages. However, the main drawback covers the definition of likelihood and impact that depend on 'organizational and management inputs'.

MEHARI [11] is a European open-source risk assessment methodology (provided under a Creative Commons License), fully compatible with ISO 27001 and part of the ENISA suggested risk assessment methodologies, including multiple guidelines and manuals. MEHARI is enriched by a risk assessment tool provided as an Excel sheet, which supports the risk analyst though an entire risk assessment iteration. The taxonomy and knowledge base of MEHARI is focused on ICT (Information and Communication Technology) risks, however, no specific sector is targeted. MEHARI is widely used to analyse and treat risks within multiple sectors. It does not take into account inter-sector opportunities and challenges, however, the methodology is generic enough to assess ICT risks from a multi-sector perspective.

MAGERIT [12] is also an open-source methodology for risk analysis and management, developed in 1997 by the Spanish Ministry of Public Administration. It was offered as a framework and guide to the public administration in response to the perception that government increasingly depends on IT for achieving its service objectives. The second version of this methodology was published in 2005. Given its open nature, it is also used outside administrations and can be applied to all companies that use IT systems. It offers compliance with standards as of ISO/IEC 27001/2005, ISO/IEC 15408/2005, ISO/IEC 17799/2005, and ISO/IEC 13335/2004. According to the ISO 31000 terminology, MAGERIT implements a risk management process within a working framework for governing bodies. This process allows for the decision making, taking into account risks derived from the use of IT technology.

2.3 Analysis of Frameworks

The analysis of basic risk assessment frameworks and methodologies helps to choose a proper risk assessment methodology for multi-sector issues. The results of this analysis are presented in Table 1, highlighting that no widely used and well documented methodology explicitly takes into account inter-sector parameters. All analysed methodologies can be applied within the ICT landscape of multi-sector environment, without a specific focus on single sectors and without a clear methodology to develop single-sector focused extensions. Inter-sector dependencies, such as threats and vulnerabilities, are not considered. However, transversal factors, such as policies or regulations, are taken into account within these methodologies, although not always explicitly identified or described in detail. Existing frameworks and methodologies are assessed against the requirements by design the E-MAF is subject to.

The interpretation of Table 1 indicates that the best coverage of requirements is provided by MEHARI and MAGERIT. For other aspects, they seem to be also complementary. However, none of the analysed methodologies provides useful inputs with respect to curricula and training.

3 Cybersecurity Challenges and Opportunities

Modern technologies, new services, and changing user requirements raise both challenges and opportunities, especially in cybersecurity. A challenge is defined as an obstacle or hard task related to technological, organisational, economic, societal, or any other dimension that is difficult to mitigate or to overcome. Usually, the challenge is a result of the current status of dimensions under investigation or due to upcoming advancements/changes in respective fields. An opportunity determines the possibility or chance, which occurs because of a favourable combination of circumstances.

3.1 Technological Challenges and Opportunities

Modern technologies influence our society. However, the process of digitalisation increases the potential impact and likelihood of cyberattacks. Therefore, the awareness of technological challenges and opportunities is crucial. This includes the fact that technologies typically involve multiple sectors, thus, the risk of cyberattacks propagates to different domains and end-users [13].

The starting point to analyse technological factors of cybersecurity is the JRC Technical Report 'A Proposal for a European Cybersecurity Taxonomy' published in 2019 [14]. This taxonomy presents crucial technologies related to the cybersecurity domain, which enhances the development of different sectors. Additionally, research domains are introduced, which represent areas of knowledge related to different cybersecurity facets. These domains cover technological aspects of cybersecurity and can be used also across multiple sectors.

The main research domain which is worth mentioning is cryptology – including symmetric and asymmetric cryptography. The important challenge of symmetric-key cryptography is the secure, light-weight cryptography to protect small, inexpensive

Table 1. Analysis of risk assessment frameworks and methodologies.

SPECIFIC REQUIREMENTS	ISO31000	TOGAF	SP800-30	MEHARI	MAGERIT
Does the methodology enable improvement of multi-sectoral management processes for mitigation of risks?	Medium	Low	Low	High	No
Does the methodology assess transversal and inter-sector opportunities and challenges?	Medium	Low	Low	Medium	Low
Does the methodology enable a transversal vision for security countermeasures?	No	No	No	Medium	High
Does the methodology have been developed in the EU?	Medium	No	Medium	High	High
Does the methodology enable benchmarking initiatives?	Medium	High	No	Low	Medium
Is the methodology clear and well defined?	Medium	Medium	Medium	High	High
Is the methodology open source?	No	High	Yes	High	Yes
Are related taxonomies well defined?	No	High	Low	High	Medium
Are related taxonomies expandable?	No	No	Low	High	High
ECONOMIC FACTORS					
Does the methodology include a risk analysis method based on financial factors?	Low	Medium	No	Medium	High
Does the methodology support risk financing strategies for the residual risk?	No	No	No	Medium	Medium
INNOVATION					
Does the methodology support the provisioning of a selection of roadmaps to reduce the risk?	No	Low	No	High	High
Does the methodology enable/define linkability to tools/ICT products?	No	No	No	Medium	Medium
Does the methodology support the concept of curricula?	No	No	No	No	Low

(*continued*)

Table 1. (*continued*)

SPECIFIC REQUIREMENTS	ISO31000	TOGAF	SP800-30	MEHARI	MAGERIT
Does the methodology support the concept of certification scheme?	No	Low	No	No	Low
Does the methodology identify transversal, inter-sector and specific skills for curricula?	No	No	No	No	No
Does the methodology provide a basis for training programmes?	Medium	No	No	No	Low

electronics or low-powered devices (e.g., sensors). The source of many threats is due to the implementation of cryptographic algorithms since they can work in a different way than standards define them or they may contain backdoors. Other challenges (but also an opportunity) include the post-quantum cryptography, which works on quantum computer-resistant security mechanisms.

The main challenge of asymmetric cryptography involves conditional security. These cryptography algorithms are secure under specific conditions only and are based on the difficulty of specific mathematical problems (e.g., the security level of RSA algorithm depends on prime factorization being computationally difficult as of today). Additionally, asymmetric cryptography is characterised by low efficiency because of long keys and modulo operations. Also, the trust on public keys in a network environment is a crucial issue. Thus, related identities determine the practical security of asymmetric cryptography. Therefore, an appropriate trust model has to be used in practice.

Currently, a strong driver in security-related steps is Artificial Intelligence (AI) and detailed Machine Learning (ML). For such system components, the security and accuracy are a challenge. However, it is assumed to be used to detect cyber threats and risk management, authentication, behavioural analysis, and anomaly detection or cryptography purposes (i.e., to establish a secret key).

Additionally, big data and its mechanisms generate new possibilities for security solutions, however, they also give rise to opportunities for adversaries to access sensitive and personal information. The volume, speed of data generation, and different types of data form crucial challenges. Cloud-based systems can solve some of these problems with processing big data, however, confidentiality or privacy of data sent to the cloud can be compromised. Thus, dishonest cloud data providers can also analyse packets and active connections with users. One of the most critical challenges with Security-as-a-Service (SecaaS) is the necessity of exposing the customer's security policy to the cloud service provider.

Industrial Control Systems – for example, Supervisory Control and Data Acquisition (SCADA) – generate such challenges due to weak security of firmware, non-secured protocols, leaks of security services/mechanisms, out-of-date anti-virus software, or wrong development practices. However, industrial systems supported by a high-level process supervisory management can be also an opportunity from the cybersecurity point of view: the protection by a firewall or Intrusion Detection/Preven-tion Systems (IDPS) or proper isolations from corporate networks used.

The rapid increase in the importance of quantum technology possibly will allow users to improve the security and performance of communication networks and will threaten current security mechanisms at the same time. By means of this technology, entirely new ways of solving problems of cybersecurity are developing – for example, uncovering passing eavesdroppers (quantum cryptography) or using quantum random generators to produce truly random sequences for cryptography purposes. However, the implementation of these solutions in real networks and systems is a challenge.

3.2   Inter-sectoral Challenges and Opportunities

As inter-sectoral challenges and opportunities these ones are considered that are caused by inter-sectoral dependencies. An inter-sectoral dependency is defined as a one-directional or bi-directional relationship between entities across different sectors in order to provide the services properly by each sector. The degree of interdependency of the bi-directional relations is not mandatory to be equal in both directions.

Cyber capabilities are a base of financial, economic, transportation, energy, and defence infrastructure [15]. The cyberspace is recognized as the fifth war domain. The military is a priority target for cyber-attacks because compromising another nation's military through cyber actions is difficult to be traced back to the attacker, or even is impossible. Industrial control systems for water and power networks, as well as for maritime transportation are at the top of the list for cyber-attacks, because a successful cyber-attack against them could have a devastating real-world impact. The healthcare sector is also among the most attacked sectors since attackers have realized the value which patient records have on the black market. Therefore, all considered sectors are high priority victims of cyber-attacks. A number of cybersecurity incidents are due to inter-sectoral dependencies, which either propagate across the sectors or have a cascading effect at the services, provided by the sectors.

Adapting the approach used in the analysis of cross-border (inter)dependencies [16], the inter-sectoral challenges are classified into three main categories.

- Challenges due to common vulnerabilities
  Most of the cyber assets used by the sectors are standardized commercial-off-the-shelf products. Vulnerabilities and attack vectors of these assets are common for all sectors. This allows for the implementation of possible common solutions (opportunities) to mitigate vulnerability exploitation. This category encompasses common technological challenges, which are overviewed in the previous subsection.
  Because AI and ML being identified as the most important enterprise technology of the next decade, followed by cloud platforms and big data [17], major cybersecu-rity challenges and relevant opportunities, which impact all considered sectors, are related to these technologies. Whether through malicious or unintended misuses of AI, potential consequences could be severe when it is applied for attacks on critical infras-tructure, social engineering attacks, attacks on autonomous weapons, attacks targeting the healthcare sector, and data poisoning attacks. Cloud computing and big data are

identified as the next important technology challenges to cybersecurity in these sectors. Exploiting vulnerabilities in IoT technologies is also a challenging cybersecurity issue that crosses all sectors. Other common cybersecurity challenges are related to using legacy systems, unsupported operating systems, and legacy practices.

Alongside technological cybersecurity challenges, within all sectors, human resources challenges are recognised, who are objects to cyber-attacks – leveraging malicious insiders, including corrupted employees, and social engineering. The relevant awareness and education of employees are among the opportunities and countermeasures to address the issues. Lack of regulatory requirements regarding cybersecurity is also reported as a challenge in all considered sectors.

- Challenges due to propagation of cyber-attacks in connected ICT systems in different sectors

This category includes a security incident propagation due to the underlying connectivity of sector communication and information systems. For instance, an attack infecting ICT systems of one sector propagates by infecting connected resources or systems in another sector.

An example of bi-directional interdependencies between smart power networks (smart grids) and consumer communications networks is shown in [18]. Smart grids, in addition to electricity networks, include communication between provider and consumers, intelligent metering and monitoring systems [19]. This allows the spread of cyber-attacks against ICT systems of consumers to be distributed in electricity networks and vice versa.

- Challenges due to dependencies of services in two or more sectors

The ECHO report D2.5 [20] identified the inter-sector dependency between maritime transportation and energy sector services. Because sectors depend on energy sector services, all cybersecurity challenges related to the power grid will affect all sectors, too. The report D2.1 [21] studies inter-sector dependencies and identifies healthcare services dependencies on telecommunications, big data, and navigation services; energy services dependencies on telecommunication services and big data; and maritime services dependencies on space services.

The inter-sector cybersecurity dependencies identified introduce new cybersecurity challenges and open a new way for threats. Therefore, it is important to address those challenges, which arise from inter-sector dependencies identified in definitions of multi-sectoral cybersecurity requirements.

3.3 Transversal Challenges and Opportunities

Not only technological factors influence cybersecurity. Beside technological issues, important role play also transversal challenges and opportunities. These issues are universal and multi-factorial. It is worth mentioning that they do not occur in isolation, but interact [22].

The one group of transversal factors is concentrated on human. Human factors can be divided into the following: cognitive, behavioural, social, psychological, affective, and motivational. Other transversal factors are financial. They can be connected with the financial squeezing or such activities as corporate espionage or active attacks (i.e., ransomware or cryptojacking). An important role also plays the privacy issue – especially related to GDPR (General Data Protection Regulation), i.e., the governance structure for privacy, privacy policy or data privacy operational procedures. Additionally, it is worth mentioning about political factors. This group contains geo-political issues, cyber-terrorism, international relations and such activities as fake news or hacktivism.

One of the main groups of transversal factors is education and training. Employees can receive minimal or partial training in cybersecurity field (inadequate or outdated training) and sometimes they are not informed about the crucial threats. Technical staff can have no basic knowledge of cybersecurity (i.e., applied mathematics, security services, or network protocols) because of the bad recruitment process and shortage of competent people on the labour market. However, technical staff can be well educated but do not have current specialist knowledge related to cybersecurity (i.e. people employed many years ago who have not received training since leaving education). The reason for this condition may be employees' ignorance, false assessment of own knowledge, no possibility of expanding knowledge in the company or bad source of knowledge (i.e. not reviewed documents, not professional e-learning courses).

Education and training also apply to non-cyber staff and it can be a source of transversal challenges. Awareness of basic cybersecurity regulations/policies (i.e., password policy or information security policy) is important. Non-IT staff should be aware that cybersecurity is crucial and they should have even basic knowledge about the company's security policy. However, the reason for lacking basic knowledge is often: no necessary procedures in the company, ignorance and unawareness and lack of early-age education in schools. Even if non-IT employees are aware of cybersecurity issues and they have basic knowledge about the company's security policy, sometimes they do not have the necessary knowledge to effectively protect themselves against attacks (mainly social engineering attacks). The reason can be employees' ignorance or no possibility of expanding knowledge in the company (i.e., no additional training regarding malware types, cyberattack methods, security tools).

4   A New Multi-sector Assessment Framework

The identification of inter-sector, multi-sector, and transversal aspects will build the basis for the further abstraction/extension of the innovative risk assessment and management methodology, which, starting from selected domains, could be easily applied to a wider set of sectors. In fact, ECHO Multi-sector Assessment Framework (E-MAF) provides the means to analyse transversal and inter-sectoral challenges and opportunities and supporting the development of cybersecurity technology roadmaps.

E-MAF will leverage cyber-risk management fundamentals by having a large multi-domain community and plenty of expertise. E-MAF refers to the analysis of challenges and opportunities derived from sector-specific use cases, transversal cybersecurity needs analysis and development of inter-sector technology roadmaps involving horizontal cybersecurity disciplines. Since a risk management framework must include risk assessment, in the core of E-MAF is cyber risk assessment methodology. In risk assessment, three important steps take place: risk identification (the process of determining, document and communicating risks that could potentially prevent an organisation or a process from achieving the foreseen objectives), risk analysis (analysis of potential issues which could negatively impact processes or systems) and risk evaluation (a comparison of the results of the risk analysis with the risk evaluation criteria to determine whether the level of cyber-risks is acceptable).

Analysis of existing frameworks identified that the current risk assessment frameworks do not take into account relations between sectors and are not able to address multi-domain and transversal issues effectively and transparently. This is the added value of E-MAF. In order to fully define the new risk management methodology, the following three processes must also be implemented.

- Risk Treatment – all actions aimed at selecting and implementing options for addressing risk. This process modifies risk through actions like: avoiding the risk by desisting to perform the activity rising the risk, taking risk to pursue different goals or opportunities, removing the risk source, changing the likelihood.
- Monitoring and Review, by working to assure and improve the level of the quality and effectiveness of design, implementation and outcomes of risk management as a periodic process.
- Context Analysis, by establishing the scope, the context (both internal and external), and all necessary criteria to tune the risk management process and, within this, validating and refining risk assessment and risk treatment policies.
  E-MAF should not definitely be an updated version of currently existing cybersecurity frameworks but should refer to them to take inspiration in defining a new approach based on a multi-sector, transversal reference to cybersecurity risk management. It should be voluntary guidance easy to customize by different sectors and individual organisations to best suit their needs and requirements.
  Organisations and sectors will still have unique risks (different threats, vulnerabilities, risk tolerances) and implementation of practices to achieve positive outcomes. Therefore, the E-MAF will not be implemented as a non-customised checklist or a one-size-fits-all approach for all critical infrastructure organisations but as the overlap of the three different complex subsystems. For this reason, the architectural design of E-MAF deploys a three-tier architecture comprising:
- **ECHO MAF Transversal Foundation Tier (E-MAF TFT)**, guiding every organisations in managing and reducing their cybersecurity risks in a way that complements an organisation's existing cybersecurity and risk management processes;
- **ECHO MAF Multi-sector Implementation Tier (E-MAF MIT)**, where all the multi-sector and inter-sector specific aspects are managed – this tier will support organisations by providing context on how they view cybersecurity risk management (risks, priorities, budgeting); and
- **ECHO MAF Security Alignment Tier (E-MAF SAT)** where security controls will be defined and implemented, also specific organisation's alignment to ECHO MIT and TFT will take place by identifying and prioritising opportunities for improving cybersecurity in general and in a use cases-driven manner.
  Fig. 1 depicts all the elements of the E-MAF and highlights the dependencies between them, as well as inputs and output it provides to other actors and processes.
  The **ECHO MAF Transversal Foundation Tier** can identify three layers:
- The *ECHO Risk Assessment Framework layer* implementing solutions for Risk Identification, Risk Analysis, and Risk Evaluation.

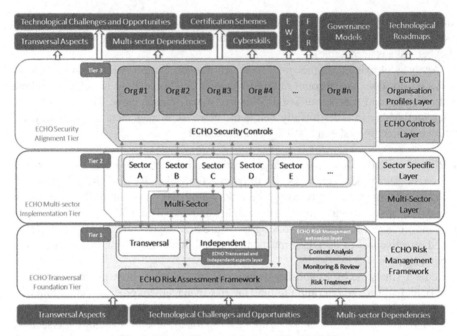

Fig. 1. The architectural design of the E-MAF.

- The *ECHO Transversal and Independent aspects layer* where two different modules take place: (a) the Transversal aspects module enabling focus on horizontal technologies and cybersecurity in critical sectors, addressing inter-sector cybersecurity disciplines and transversal security aspects that are independent of sector or discipline; transversal cybersecurity factors include those which are present regardless of the industrial sector, while inter-sector factors are those which may be sector related, but span more than one sector; and (b) the Independent aspects module focusing on technical and technological factors which are independent from the industrial section and commonly present.
- The *ECHO Risk Management extension layer*, complementing the Risk Assessment layer toward the implementation of a full Risk Management Framework. It comprises the implementation of processes for Risk Treatment, Monitoring and Review feature, Context Analysis capabilities.

  All these layers together build the ECHO Risk Management Framework, which is fed by the definition of Transversal Aspects, the identification of Technological Challenges and Opportunities, the list of multi-sector dependencies.

  The **ECHO MAF Multi-sector Implementation Tier** deploys two layers.

- The *ECHO Multi-sector layer*, identifying and isolating multi-sector aspects (not independent ones) which are common to two or more domains (consequently not to all); the goal is providing instruments to fulfil corresponding technology requirements by identifying a common foundation for multi-sector needs.
- The *ECHO Sector Specific layer* where the multi-sector approach will be complemented by the set of additional implementation features needed in order to fulfil the

specific needs for a given sector. The sector-specific implementation must face all specific needs of the possible sectors deploying the E-MAF.

The **ECHO MAF Security Alignment Tier** comprises the final two layers.

- The *ECHO Controls layer*, implementing many controls that adequately mitigate information risks that the organisation finds unacceptable and unavoidable (ISO/IEC 27008: 2019). Information security controls should be "fit-for-purpose". The controls will make reference to the whole Risk Management process and obviously implement all the actions referred to transversal, independent, multi-sector factor and sector-specific issues.
- The *ECHO Organisation Profiles layer* where Organisations will implement governance of their specific risks related to threats and vulnerabilities, and proper risk tolerance levels, which are different from ones related to other organisation as well as practices to achieve positive outcomes.

The overlapping of these three main components, the tight cooperation between their layers as well as the longitudinal and transversal interaction among the components are aimed at defining and implementing a full cybersecurity risk governance at hosting organisations by providing a huge added value through adoption of a multi-sector approach, definition of curricula and skills, binding with technology roadmaps.

E-MAF requires input information: transversal aspects, technological challenges and opportunities as well as multi-sector dependencies. In the top section of Fig. 1 the output or the processes benefitting of outcomes produced by the adoption of E-MAF are depicted. First of all, in the top right end side, four entities are shown:

- The Governance Model definition, and in particular the information sharing model definition activities since the services will produce the unavoidable review of information sharing and trust models from within the cyber domain and the other domains involved (e.g., healthcare information sharing models);
- The Inter-sector Technology Roadmaps design and development activities, where the E-MAF outputs will act as input in the further analysis of transversal technical cybersecurity towards the identification and categorisation of the most pressing security concerns leading to a shared vision on the emerging technical cybersecurity challenges for multiple horizontal cybersecurity disciplines;
- The Early Warning System (EWS) and the Federated Cyber Range (FCR) whose system architectures, reference models and the corresponding research, development and implementation activities will be fed by results of E-MAF adoption.

Additionally, the remaining elements in the top section describe that the outputs produced by E-MAF application will represent the input for other project activities in order to improve whole project outcomes in terms of: (a) transversal aspects by fostering the transversal cybersecurity challenges and opportunities definition through the enhancement of detailed analysis process applied to prevalent transversal cybersecurity challenges; (b) technology challenges and opportunities to enhance activities ensuring inter-sector cybersecurity methodologies and improve outcomes of its application; and (c) multi-sector dependencies by feeding and enhancing analysis of inter-sector cybersecurity challenges prevalent and touch on multiple sectors; (d) cyberskills by providing key information to the develop learning-outcome based competence framework for professionals; and (e) cybersecurity certification scheme by fostering the matching of the diverse needs of sector-specific and inter-sector issues.

5 Summary

This paper presented a conceptual model of the E-MAF architecture, which evaluates and prioritizes cybersecurity risks in trans-sectoral and inter-sectoral contexts, and, thus, enables a relevant risk management process. Therefore, the paper assessed and analysed initially existing risk assessment frameworks in order to analyse, whether they cover by design technological, transversal, and inter-sectoral risk assessment requirements. The analysis of existing frameworks identified that current risk assessment frameworks do not take into consideration relations between sectors and are not able to address multi-sector and transversal issues.

Consequently, the architecture proposed is a result of this analysis. The E-MAF is not an upgrade of an existing cybersecurity risk assessment framework. It exploits valuable approaches and ideas from several analysed frameworks and defines a new approach based on a multi-sector, transversal reference to cybersecurity risk assessment and management.

The E-MAF is based on a comprehensive study of cybersecurity technological, transversal, and inter-sectoral challenges and opportunities. The respective technological challenges and opportunities identified as well as multi-sector dependencies and transversal aspects listed now define the input data for the new framework. The E-MAF provides a structured method for a multi-dimensional analysis. Its architectural design deploys a three-tier architecture, encompassing: transversal foundation tier which identifies the transversal and independent cybersecurity challenges and opportunities; multi-sector implementation tier supports organisations by providing context on how they view cybersecurity risk management (risks, priorities, budgeting); and a security alignment tier, where ECHO security controls are implemented and a specific organisation's alignment to the previous two layers is taken place by identifying and prioritising opportunities for improving cybersecurity.

The next steps of the E-MAF development process will be focused on the definition of specific metrics and scoring of risk levels, development of checklists and operational plans, recommendations for the risk financing strategies, and study of certification and assurance procedures.

Acknowledgements. This work has been funded by the European Union's Horizon 2020 Research and Innovation Programme, under Grant Agreement no. 830943, the ECHO project and partially by the European Union's Horizon 2020 Research and Innovation Program under Grant Agreement no. 830927, the CONCORDIA project.

The authors would like to thank all partners involved in ECHO project who contributed to WP2 deliverables D2.1, D2.2, D2.3, D2.4, and D2.5.

References

1. Tselkov, V.: A glance at the general personal data protection regulation. In: Proceedings of the International Scientific Conference on European Union policy on the protection of information and personal data, Shumen, pp. 209–214 (2018)
2. Iliev, R., Genchev, A.: Information security and cybersecurity of corporate information systems. In: Proceedings of the HEMUS International Scientific Conference, Plovdiv (2018)

3. Nikolov, A., Hristozov, I.: Issues and challenges for the development of a national system for cybersecurity. Mil. J. **3**, 7–13 (2015)
4. Cybersecurity in Europe: stronger rules and better protection. https://www.consilium.europa.eu/en/policies/cybersecurity/. Accessed 26 Feb 2020
5. ECHO Project Website. https://echonetwork.eu. Accessed 02 Feb 2020
6. Niemiec, M., Jaglarz, P., Jekot, M., Chołda, P., Boryło, P.: Risk assessment approach to secure northbound interface of SDN networks. In: 2019 International Conference on Computing, Networking and Communications (ICNC), Honolulu (2019)
7. D2.2 ECHO Multi-Sector Assessment Framework. ECHO project consortium (2019)
8. ISO 31000:2018 Risk management—Guidelines. https://www.iso.org/standard/65694.html. Accessed 28 Feb 2020
9. The TOGAF Standard. https://publications.opengroup.org/c182. Accessed 28 Feb 2020
10. NIST Special Publication 800-30 Guide for Conducting Risk Assessments. https://nvlpubs.nist.gov/nistpubs/Legacy/SP/nistspecialpublication800-30r1.pdf. Accessed 28 Feb 2020
11. MEHARI Overview. http://meharipedia.x10host.com/wp/wp-content/uploads/2019/05/MEHARI-Overview-2019.pdf. Accessed 28 Feb 2020
12. MAGERIT v.3: Metodología de Análisis y Gestión de Riesgos de los Sistemas de Información. https://administracionelectronica.gob.es/pae_Home/pae_Documentacion/pae_Metodolog/pae_Magerit.html?idioma=en#.Xl1XC0pCdPY. Accessed 28 Feb 2020
13. D2.4 Inter-Sector Technology Challenges And Opportunities. ECHO project consortium (2020)
14. Nai-Fovino, I., et al.: A Proposal for a European Cybersecurity Taxonomy. Publications Office of the European Union (2019)
15. Mikolic-Torreira, I., et al.: Cybersecurity policy options, RAND Corporation (2016)
16. Moulinos, K., Drougkas, A., Dellios, K., Kasse, P.: Good practices on interdependencies between OES and DSPs, ENISA (2018)
17. Global research shows AI will shape 2020 tech but pose potential risks. https://www.contracts.mod.uk/do-uk-and-international-news/global-research-shows-ai-will-shape-2020-tech-but-pose-potential-risks/. Accessed 15 Feb 2020
18. Mattioli, R., Moulinos, K.: Communication network interdependencies in smart grids, ENISA (2015)
19. Egozcue, E., Herreras Rodríguez, D., Ortiz, J., Fidalgo Villar, V., Tarrafeta, L.: Smart Grid Security Recommendations, ENISA (2012)
20. D2.5 Multi-sector Requirements Definition and Demonstration Cases, ECHO project consortium (2020)
21. D2.1 Sector Scenarios and Use Case Analysis. ECHO project consortium (2019)
22. D2.3 Transversal Cybersecurity Challenges and Opportunities. ECHO project consortium (2019)

New Approach of Solving Congruence Equation System

Andrey G. Ivanov and Nikolai T. Stoianov[✉]

Bulgarian Defence Institute, Sofia, Bulgaria
andry.g.ivanov@gmail.com, n.stoianov@di.mod.bg

Abstract. Nowadays in public key cryptography, some special basic algorithms are used. Extended Euclidian Algorithm and Chinese Remainder Theorem are the most spread basic algorithms with major contribution. Along the century's mathematicians made a lot to improve these algorithm's execution speed. In the paper, new approach of solving congruence equation system is presented.

Keywords: Chinese Remainder Theorem · Congruence system equation · New approach

1 Introduction

In a person's work there are a set of different tasks that he/she is forced to solve. Some of them come down to solving systems of congruence equations. Such tasks are: resolve multiple range ambiguities in many radar systems, to speed up RSA algorithm, to construct a Gödel numbering for sequences, Cryptanalysis tasks and etc. [1–4].

The method allowing the solution of such systems of equations is an algorithm created based on a theorem created and proved by Sun Tzu in ancient China (2nd century B.C.) [4]. The importance of this method and the speed of its execution have influenced many mathematicians and algorithmists and are the reason for the search for new approaches and solutions.

Algorithms for solving systems of congruence equations find a wide field of use in cryptography. Based on the Chinese theorem, both encryption algorithms and those for cryptanalysis and attack of cryptographic systems are made. It is used in both main sections of cryptography: public key cryptography and cryptography based on symmetric keys.

Some of the cybersecurity and cryptography problems we had to solve forced us to look for an algorithm for solving systems of congruence equations in which modular numbers do not have to be mutually prime and the algorithm does not need to decompose numbers to factors to find the solution of such a system.

In this article, we present the classical method for solving such systems using the Chinese Remainder Theorem (CRT) described in the second part and our new approach, which is presented in the third part of this article.

© Springer Nature Switzerland AG 2020
A. Dziech et al. (Eds.): MCSS 2020, CCIS 1284, pp. 16–24, 2020.
https://doi.org/10.1007/978-3-030-59000-0_2

2 Classical Way of Solving System of Congruence Equations

If simultaneous congruence system is

$$x \equiv a_1 \bmod m_1$$
$$x \equiv a_2 \bmod m_2$$
$$x \equiv a_3 \bmod m_3 \qquad (2.1)$$
$$x \equiv a_4 \bmod m_4$$

We can get solution by using CRT: If m_1, m_2, m_3, ..., m_k are pairwise relatively prime positive integers, and if a_1, a_2, a_3, ..., a_k are any integers, then the simultaneous congruences of all equations $x \equiv a_i \bmod m_i$ have a solution, and the solution is unique modulo m, where $m = \prod \sum_{k=0}^{i} m_k$ [5, 6].

Proof That a Solution Exists: To keep the notation simpler, we will assume $k = 4$. Note the proof is constructive, i.e., it shows us how to actually construct a solution [7].

Our goal is to find integers w_1, w_2, w_3, w_4 such that:

Table 1. Equation composition dependency for minimal value x.

	Value mod m_1	Value mod m_2	Value mod m_3	Value mod m_4
w_1	1	0	0	0
w_2	0	1	0	0
w_3	0	0	1	0
w_4	0	0	0	1

Once we have found w_1, w_2, w_3, w_4 it is easy to construct x:

$$x = a_1.w_1 + a_2.w_2 + a_3.w_3 + a_4.w_4 \qquad (2.2)$$

If the all moduli numbers m_i remains the same we can use the same w_i. To continue we have to define numbers z_i such: $z_i = m/m_i$. Note that:

i. $z_i \equiv 0 \bmod m_j$, where $j \in 1..4$ and $j \neq i$
ii. $GCD(z_i, m_i) = 1$, if arbitrary prime p divides z_i then will divides some of m_j, where $j \in 1..4$ and $j \neq i$

Calculate y_i, where $i \in 1..4$ and $y_i = z_i^{-1} \bmod m_i$. The inverses exist by (ii) above, and we can find them by Euclid's extended algorithm. Note that:

i. $y_i.z_i \equiv 1 \bmod m_i$
ii. $y_i.z_i \equiv 0 \bmod m_j$, where $j \in 1..4$ and $j \neq i$.

Lastly define $w_i \equiv y_i.z_i \bmod m$. Then every $w_i i \in 1..4$ have the properties in the Table 1.

3   New Approach of Solution

In this part of the paper, new algorithm to solve system of congruence equations is presented. Our motivation to do this research is related to two things: to make it possible to compute systems of congruence equations in cases where modular numbers are not coprime, and to enable their application in systems for parallel computations of large numbers. This algorithm we will future use in a method for evaluating the process of studying the resilience of one of the most common algorithms in public cryptography, RSA and algorithms based on Discrete Logarithm Problem (DLP).

To explain the idea of this approach we will derive a mathematical equation, which will be the base of that algorithm. We start from the congruence system:

$$
\begin{aligned}
x &\equiv r_1 \bmod u_1 \\
x &\equiv r_2 \bmod u_2 \\
x &\equiv r_3 \bmod u_3 \\
&\quad . \\
&\quad . \\
&\quad . \\
x &\equiv r_i \bmod u_i
\end{aligned}
\tag{3.1}
$$

If we just represent fist two equations as: $x_0 = r_1 + k_1.u_1$ and $x_0 = r_2 + k_2.u_2$ we will have a solution of minimal x_0 if we have values of k_1 and k_2 where: $1 \le k_1 < u_2$ and $1 \le k_2 < u_1$. That value of x_0 will be solution of the first two equation from the system.

If we multiply both sides of the equations, we will get:

$$
x_0^2 = (r_1 + k_1.u_1)(r_2 + k_2.u_2)
\tag{3.2}
$$

$$
x_0^2 = u_1.u_2.k_1.k_2 + k_1.u_1.r_2 + k_2.u_2.r_1 + r_1.r_2
\tag{3.3}
$$

If we calculated by modulo A the both sides of (3.3), where $A = u_1.u_2$, we will get next congruence equation:

$$
x_0^2 \equiv (u_1.u_2.k_1.k_2 + k_1.u_1.r_2 + k_2.u_2.r_1 + r_1.r_2) \bmod A
\tag{3.4}
$$

The value of $u_1.u_2.k_1.k_2 \bmod A$ is equal to zero, hence:

$$
x_0^2 \equiv (k_1.u_1.r_2 + k_2.u_2.r_1 + r_1.r_2) \bmod A
\tag{3.5}
$$

Due to definition $r_1 + k_1.u_1 = r_2 + k_2.u_2$ we can represent $k_1 = \frac{k_2.u_2 + r_2 - r_1}{u_1}$ and substitute in (3.5). Hence:

$$
x_0^2 \equiv \left(\frac{k_2.u_2 + r_2 - r_1}{u_1}.u_1.r_2 + k_2.u_2.r_1 + r_1.r_2 \right) \bmod A
\tag{3.6}
$$

$$
x_0^2 \equiv \left(k_2.u_2.r_2 + r_2^2 - r_1.r_2 + k_2.u_2.r_1 + r_1.r_2 \right) \bmod A
\tag{3.7}
$$

$$x^2 \equiv \left[k_2.u_2.(r_2 + r_1) + r_2^2\right] mod\ A \tag{3.8}$$

From congruence Eq. (3.8) we can get next congruence:

$$x^2 \equiv \left[k_2.u_2.(r_2 + r_1) + r_2^2\right] mod\ u_1 \tag{3.9}$$

Because of $x_0 \equiv r_1\ mod\ u_1$, hence $x_0^2 \equiv r_1^2\ mod\ u_1$ we substitute $z = x^2 = r_1^2\ mod\ u_1$ in (3.9) and get:

$$z \equiv \left[k_2.u_2.(r_2 + r_1) + r_2^2\right] mod\ u_1 \tag{3.10}$$

Hence to get value of k_2 we have to calculate next Diophantine equation:

$$b.k_2 - u_1.y = z - r_2^2 \tag{3.11}$$

where $b = u_2.(r_2 + r_1)$

We use the minimal positive obtained value of k_2 in $x_0 = r_2 + k_2.u_2$ to calculate x_0 which is a solution of the first two equations of the system. The advantage of Eq. (3.11) is that always has a solution, because $z - r_2^2$ is always divisible by $GCD(b, u_1)$.

Using the Eq. (3.11) into the next algorithm we can solve the whole congruence system (3.1) and to obtain value of x.

Algorithm 1

INPUT:

   Reminders $[r_0, r_1, r_2, \ldots, r_n]$
   modNumbers $[u_0, u_1, u_2, \ldots, u_n]$

OUTPUT:

   x_0 - minimal value of unknown x

STEPS:

   $uniqLCM = u_0$
   $bValue = r_0$
   $loop\ i \in 1..n$
        $m_1 = uniqLCM$
        $uniqLCM = (uniqLCM . u_i)$
        $z = (bValue^2\ mod\ m_1) - r_i^2$
        $b = (bValue + r_i) . u_i$
        $solve: b . k_2 - m_1 . y = z$
        $bValue = m_2 . minpositive(k_2) + a_2$
   $x_0 = bValue$

That algorithm can be applied without following the rule that each pair of modular numbers u_i, u_j $(i \neq j)$ have to be mutually prime. Due to that, we have no need to decompose every number u_i to solve the system. Loop iterations of the suggested algorithm is equal to the count of the equations into the system minus one. In that suggested algorithm, values of the numbers increase by every iteration. Into the classical algorithm, all mathematical operations have to be done with binary size of numbers close to the product of all modulo numbers. The only one disadvantage of the described algorithm above is that if some pair u_i and u_j is not coprime then x will not be the minimal value, which is satisfying the solution of the system. To overcome this disadvantage next algorithm could be used which is extension of Algorithm 1.

Algorithm 2

INPUT:
  $Reminders\ [r_0, r_1, r_2, \dots, r_n]$
  $modNumbers\ [u_0, u_1, u_2, \dots, u_n]$

OUTPUT:
  x_0 - minimal value of unknown x

STEPS:
  $uniqLCM = u_0$
  $bValue = r_0$
  $loop\ i \in 1..n$
      $m_1 = uniqLCM$
      $g = GCD(uniqLCM, u_i)$
      $uniqLCM = (uniqLCM . u_i)\ div\ g$
      $if\ (u_i > m_1)$
          $m_2 = m_1$
          $a_2 = bValue$
          $m_1 = u_i$
          $a_1 = r_i$
      $else$
          $a_1 = bValue$
          $m_2 = u_i$
          $a_2 = r_i$
      $z = (a_1{}^2\ mod\ m_1) - a_2{}^2$
      $b = [(a_1 + a_2) . m_2]$
      $solve: b . k_2 - m_1 . y = z$
      $bValue = m_2 . minpositive(k_2) + a_2$
      $if(bValue\ mod\ m_1\ <>\ a_1)$
          $t = a_1 - bValue$
          $w = m_2 . minpositive(k_2)$
          $solve: w . n - m_1 . y = t$
          $bValue = bValue + w . minpositive(n)$
  $x_0 = bValue$

Next, we will give an example of the proposal new approach algorithm. Into the example modulo numbers will not be pairwise coprime.

$uniqLCM = 43757$ $bValue = 3061$	

loop 1 *to* 3 :	

Step 1	$m_1 = uniqLCM = 43757$ $g = GCD(uniqLCM, u_i) = 19$ $uniqLCM = (uniqLCM \cdot u_i) \, div \, g = 77318619$ $(u_i < m_1)$ $\quad a_1 = 3061$ $\quad m_2 = 33573$ $\quad a_2 = 32264$ $z = (a_1{}^2 \, mod \, m_1) - a_2{}^2 = -1040959973$ $b = [(a_1 + a_2) \cdot m_2] \, mod \, m1 = 20254$ $solve: 20254 \cdot k_2 - 43757 \cdot y = -1040959973$ $bValue = m_2 \cdot minpositive(k_2) + a_2 = 24506981$ $if \, bValue \, mod \, m_1 = a_1$ $bValue = 24506981$
Step 2	$m_1 = uniqLCM = 77318619$ $g = GCD(uniqLCM, u_i) = 133$ $uniqLCM = (uniqLCM \cdot u_i) \, div \, g = 169869005943$ $(u_i < m_1)$ $\quad a_1 = 24506981$ $\quad m_2 = 292201$ $\quad a_2 = 173700$ $z = (a_1{}^2 \, mod \, m_1) - a_2{}^2 = -30143285984$ $b = [(a_1 + a_2) \cdot m_2] \, mod \, m1 = 57437513$ $solve: 57437513 \cdot k_2 - 77318619 \cdot y = -30143285984$ $bValue = m_2 \cdot minpositive(k_2) + a_2 = 1540949573$ $if \, bValue \, mod \, m_1 <> a_1$ $\quad t = -1516442592$ $\quad w = 5479645353$ $\quad solve: 5479645353 \cdot n - 77318619 \cdot y = -1516442592$ $\quad bValue = bValue + w \cdot minpositive(n) = 154971019457$
Step 3	$m_1 = uniqLCM = 169869005943$ $g = GCD(uniqLCM, u_i) = 1183$ $uniqLCM = (uniqLCM \cdot u_i) \, div \, g = 679476023772$ $(u_i < m_1)$ $\quad a_1 = 154971019457$ $\quad m_2 = 4732$ $\quad a_2 = 4531$ $z = (a_1{}^2 \, mod \, m_1) - a_2{}^2 = 42687751743$ $b = [(a_1 + a_2) \cdot m_2] \, mod \, m1 = 168255861228$ $solve: 168255861228 \cdot k_2 - 169869005943 \cdot y = 42687751743$ $bValue = m_2 \cdot minpositive(k_2) + a_2 = 41725015495$

> $if\ bValue\ mod\ m_1 <> a_1$
> $t = 113246003962$
> $w = 226492007924$
> $solve: 226492007924.n - 169869005943.y = 113246003962$
> $bValue = bValue + w\ .\ minpositive(n) = 494709031343$

result $X = \mathbf{494709031343}$

Check:
$$494709031343 \equiv 3061\ mod\ 43757$$
$$494709031343 \equiv 32264\ mod\ 33573$$
$$494709031343 \equiv 173700\ mod\ 292201$$
$$494709031343 \equiv 4531\ mod\ 4732$$

The result is correct

Input Congruence:

$$x \equiv 3061 (mod\ 43757)$$
$$x \equiv 32264 (mod\ 33573)$$
$$x \equiv 173700 (mod\ 292201)$$
$$x \equiv 4531 (mod\ 4732)$$

Where: $u_0 = 43757, u_1 = 33573, u_2 = 292201, u_3 = 4732$ are modulo numbers and $r_0 = 3061, r_1 = 32264, r_2 = 173700, r_3 = 4531$ are the corresponding residues. If we calculate greatest common divisor of all pairs we will see: $GCD(u_0, u_1) = 19$, $GCD(u_0, u_2) = 133, GCD(u_0, u_3) = 7$, $GCD(u_1, u_2) = 19$, $GCD(u_1, u_3) = 1$, $GCD(u_2, u_3) = 1183$

If we use "Algorithm 2" we will solve that congruence system by next steps.

If someone has to use classical approach (CRT for example) to solve congruence system above, he/she have to factorize modulo numbers values. That belongs to rule to eliminate the pairs that are not coprime to ensure we do not get a contradiction. Therefore, we have to do next decomposition:

$$u_0 = 43757 = 7^2.19.47$$
$$u_1 = 33573 = 3.19^2.31$$
$$u_2 = 292201 = 7.13^3.19$$
$$u_3 = 4732 = 2^2.7.13^2$$

Next, we have to form new congruence system of equations where modulo numbers have to form coprime pairs:

$$x \equiv 1\left(mod\ 7^2\right)$$

$$x \equiv 21 (mod\ 47)$$

$$x \equiv 1 (mod\ 3)$$

$$x \equiv 286 \left(mod\ 19^2 \right)$$

$$x \equiv 29 (mod\ 31)$$

$$x \equiv 1153 \left(mod\ 13^3 \right)$$

$$x \equiv 3 \left(mod\ 2^2 \right)$$

As we known, factorization process has non–polynomial time complexity. In opposite in our new approach we have to use onetime extended Euclidian algorithm (polynomial time complexity) and in some steps extra one calculation of extended Euclidian algorithm when calculation needs to be equal between temporary value of x and current value of the remainder ($bValue\ mod\ m_1 <> a_1$). In other words, both methods use extended Euclidian algorithm once in each step but in situation when modulo numbers are not coprime, classical algorithm have to be applied after number factorization which add more complexity than to apply one time more extended Euclidian algorithm in each step. Especially when modulo number are big number with hundreds digits this new approach is more suitable to be use.

4 Conclusion

In conclusion, we can say that the proposed new approach is an opportunity to solve complex problems related to congruence systems of equations. This would make it possible to more quickly and easily find the desired result in linear approximation processes in quantum mechanics for example or lead to the ability to solve problems faster in cryptanalysis in public key cryptosystems, which are based on Discrete Logarithm Problem. The reason for this will be the possibility to use all possible values of modular numbers without them being selected to be coprime or to be multiplied by factors.

References

1. Childs, L.N.: Applications of the chinese remainder theorem. In: Childs, L.N. (ed.) A Concrete Introduction to Higher Algebra. UTM, pp. 310–322. Springer, New York (1995). https://doi. org/10.1007/978-1-4419-8702-0_21
2. van Tilborg, H.: Chinese remainder theorem. In: van Tilborg, H.C.A. (ed.) Encyclopedia of Cryptography and Security. Springer, Boston (2005). https://doi.org/10.1007/0-387-23483-7_58
3. Tilborg, H.C.A.: Chinese remainder theorem. In: van Tilborg, H.C.A., Jajodia, S. (eds.) Encyclopedia of Cryptography and Security. Springer, Boston (2011). https://doi.org/10.1007/978-1-4419-5906-5
4. Kangsheng, S.: Historical development of the Chinese remainder theorem. Arch. Hist. Exact Sci. **38**, 285–305 (1988). https://doi.org/10.1007/BF00357063
5. Childs, L.: Chinese remainder theorem. In: Childs, L. (ed.) A Concrete Introduction to Higher Algebra. UTM. Springer, New York (2011). https://doi.org/10.1007/978-1-4684-0065-6_14

6. Childs, L.N.: Chinese remainder theorem. In: Childs, L.N. (ed.) A Concrete Introduction to Higher Algebra. UTM. Springer, New York (2009). https://doi.org/10.1007/978-0-387-74725-5_12
7. http://homepages.math.uic.edu/~leon/mcs425-s08/handouts/chinese_remainder.pdf
8. Rivest, R.L., Shamir, A., Adleman, L.: A method for obtaining digital signatures and public-key cryptosystems. Commun. ACM **21**(2), 120–126 (1978)

A Machine Learning Approach to Dataset Imputation for Software Vulnerabilities

Shahin Rostami[1,2]([✉]), Agnieszka Kleszcz[3], Daniel Dimanov[1], and Vasilios Katos[1]

[1] Bournemouth University, Poole, UK
{srostami,vkatos}@bournemouth.ac.uk
[2] Data Science Lab, Polyra Limited, Bournemouth, UK
shahin@polyra.com
[3] AGH University of Science and Technology, Cracow, Lesser Poland District, Poland
akleszcz@agh.edu.pl

Abstract. This paper proposes a supervised machine learning approach for the imputation of missing categorical values in a dataset where the majority of samples are incomplete. Twelve models have been designed that can predict nine of the twelve Adversarial Tactics, Techniques, and Common Knowledge (ATT&CK) tactic categories using only the Common Attack Pattern Enumeration and Classification (CAPEC). The proposed method has been evaluated on a test dataset consisting of 867 unseen samples, with the classification accuracy ranging from 99.88% to 100%. These models were employed to generate a more complete dataset with no missing ATT&CK tactic features.

Keywords: Cyber security · Vulnerability · Mitre ATT&CK · Machine learning · Dataset · Imputation

1 Introduction

Software vulnerabilities are a representative cause of security policy violations in computer systems. The omnipresent nature of vulnerabilities as evidenced by the constantly increasing number of discovered vulnerabilities per year has triggered significant efforts in their study. The importance and impact of vulnerabilities on practical computer security have led to the development of vulnerability management frameworks and analysis approaches, see for example the vulnerability lifecycle [1]. At the same time, the progress in the field of machine learning and its applications in several domains has sparked a body of research on analytics for cybersecurity-related problems.

Unsurprisingly, datasets are a key ingredient to such thread of research and in cybersecurity, there are many readily available datasets published by the research and academic community as well as by the cybersecurity industry. In cybersecurity we can distinguish two types of dataset based on the way they are generated; one type consists of datasets that are synthesised from emulated or simulated

© Springer Nature Switzerland AG 2020
A. Dziech et al. (Eds.): MCSS 2020, CCIS 1284, pp. 25–36, 2020.
https://doi.org/10.1007/978-3-030-59000-0_3

data in order to enable the research community to study a particular computing environment. The other type consists of datasets that are generated from actual security incidents, i.e. real-world data. Honeynet and honeypot data are also included in this category as they capture events from real attackers, but their actions do not have an actual impact on the target infrastructure and business. Interestingly, vulnerability related data fall under the second category. This makes the collection of the relevant data challenging, as it requires one to invest on a systematic effort to triage, evaluate, consolidate and catalogue the vulnerability data from different sources in order to develop a meaningful dataset. Acknowledging the limitations and challenges the development of a complete vulnerability dataset entails, this research proposes an approach to bridge the gap between the two dataset types by enriching a vulnerability dataset with synthetic data in a way that it will enable further study of vulnerabilities.

1.1   Motivation

Obtaining and maintaining complete and high-quality datasets is not a trivial task. Despite the wealth and availability of disparate datasets in many domains, information sharing of cybersecurity-related data displays certain nuances; researchers may have a financial motivation not to share vulnerability information and particularly any associated with zero-day vulnerabilities. This is mitigated to some extent by bug bounty programmes and responsible disclosure policies. Organisations who deploy and use the software to deliver their business models, on the other hand, may not be forthcoming in disclosing attack and vulnerability information as this may result in a higher risk of exposure. Finally, third parties who have developed business models on the commercialisation of threat information sharing are understandably reluctant to support the wider community with freely available data and prefer to make these available to their premium customers.

   All the above contribute to a tessellated landscape of cybersecurity datasets that can be of varying reliability and trustworthiness as well as being incomplete. Furthermore, despite the ongoing attempts to standardise the expression of threat data through several taxonomies, the actual datasets end up having conflicting or contradictory values.

Contribution. This paper focusses on the incompleteness aspect of a vulnerabilities dataset by proposing a supervised machine learning approach for the imputation of missing categorical values from the majority of samples. The feature selected for the imputation is the Adversarial Tactics, Techniques, and Common Knowledge (ATT&CK) tactic, which is typically used to communicate the high-level modus operandi of an attacker. Twelve models have been designed that are able to predict nine of the twelve ATT&CK tactic categories using only one feature, namely the Common Attack Pattern Enumeration and Classification (CAPEC). This has been evaluated on an 867 sample test set with classification accuracy in the range of 99.88%–100%. Using these models, a more complete dataset has been generated with no missing values for the ATT&CK tactic feature.

2   The Emerging Ecosystem of Software Vulnerabilities

Vulnerabilities constitute a key element of ICT systems security as they enable both threat actors and defenders to realise their respective and competing agendas; an attacker would exploit the vulnerability in order to succeed in system compromise, whereas a defender would use the knowledge to conduct, inform, and eventually establish an effective and practical risk management plan. As vulnerabilities contribute to actionable cyber threat intelligence, they also inherit the properties and quality requirements of such type of information, such as relevance, timeliness, accuracy, completeness, and ingestibility [2]. Moreover, the description of vulnerabilities has been fairly standardised, with the Common Vulnerabilities and Exposures (CVE) [3] programme being the most popular convention for cataloguing and classifying vulnerabilities. The CVE catalogue has been enriched with further initiatives such as the Common Vulnerability Scoring System (CVSS) which attaches a quantitative measure of the severity of a particular vulnerability, the Common Attack Pattern Enumeration and Classification (CAPEC) [5] programme that associates vulnerabilities with attacks, and the more generic Common Weakness Enumeration (CWE) [4] that attempts to represent the software weaknesses through a standardisation language. A vulnerability that enters the aforementioned ecosystem has a minimum requirement of a CVE identification (CVE-id), whereas any other information could be optional. Although there is in principle an "authoritative" database with the CVE-ids, ensuring that these ids are unique and refer to vulnerabilities in a non-arbitrary manner, all other descriptors are not necessarily complete or correct. In fact, it was found in [6] that CVSS scores for the same CVE-id can differ significantly between different versions or databases.

Apart from the generic quality criteria that vulnerabilities inherit from being actionable cyber threat intelligence items, they also have their own, esoteric ones. The authors in [7] list two main categories that a vulnerabilities database (or dataset) should cover, namely *information coverage* and *capabilities*. In terms of the former, the evaluation criteria cover the *scope, impact & risk, resolution, vendor, products, exploit, categorisation*, and *relations*. Regarding the capabilities of the database, the authors highlight the supported *standards*, the existence and prevalence of a *community* adopting and supporting the data, the *interfacing* capabilities, and *freshness* of the contained data.

Vulnerabilities are also observed through their so-called vulnerability lifecycle [8]. The lifecycle introduces a chronological contextualisation to the vulnerability by identifying significant milestones and events that define risk-transitioning boundaries. More specifically, upon the discovery of a vulnerability, the associated risk follows an upward trend which spikes when a practical exploit is created; if this happens prior to the notification of the software vendor the risk reaches the highest peak, as the exploit will be considered a *zero-day*. The researcher who discovered the vulnerability may choose to notify the vendor following a responsible disclosure practice, or publicise its details. Bug bounty programmes attempt to regulate and streamline the vulnerability discovery and reporting process through financial incentive schemes. It should be evident that for each of the aforementioned events the risk will be affected. As such, timing - and timeliness - are significant and influencing factors.

The vulnerabilities may also be studied through an organisational and geopolitical perspective. In [9] the authors examine whether there are differences between different China-based organisations in respect of their status or sector (established, public sector, education, or startup), revealing that startups experienced the greatest challenges. Such a study was possible by employing publicly available vulnerability data.

The efforts to increase both the understanding and effective sharing of vulnerabilities are also reflected through the emergence of frameworks and tools such as the Structured Threat Information eXpression (STIX) and the ATT&CK framework. In STIX, the specification language for structured cyber threat intelligence sharing, vulnerabilities are expressed through a dedicated and specific object type. The ATT&CK framework is a curated knowledge-base of adversarial *techniques* and *tactics*. As these have recently gained popularity, not all published vulnerabilities have been mapped or assigned to the above schemes. Enriching the datasets with these dimensions is expected to generate considerable added value.

3   The ENISA Vulnerabilities Dataset

When constructing a dataset from multiple sources it is anticipated that this would inevitably lead to having empty values, as the different data sources do not necessarily overlap horizontally. The vulnerability dataset contains missing values due to the missing data from the source database but also due to the operation of joining the different sources. In December 2019, the European Union Agency for Cybersecurity (ENISA) published a report entitled "State of Vulnerabilities 2018/2019: Analysis of Events in the life of Vulnerabilities" [6]. This dataset covers the period of vulnerabilities published between January 1st 2018 to August 31st (Q1 - Q3) 2019. The vulnerabilities were collected and hosted in the compiled dataset until the cut-off date of September the 30th. The data is organised into a two-dimensional tabular structure in the shape of (27471 rows × 59 columns). Out of the 59 columns, those containing the vulnerability id, CVSS scores (both versions), Common Weakness Enumeration (CWE), and the number of exploits had filled values, although the number of exploits had the value of 0 on over 90% of the vulnerabilities. The noteworthy columns of missing values are CAPEC (77% completed), ATT&CK techniques and tactics (approx. 29% complete), and price information (approx 12% complete). In terms of the Common Platform Enumeration (CPE), the vendor and product information was complete at 84%, but the platform information had low completion, with only 8.6% of the values being populated. The smallest measure of completeness was observed in the sector information with only 0.5% completion. In terms of absolute numbers, this amounted to 137 vulnerabilities annotated with sector information. Although this allowed the execution of some rudimentary statistical tests, it was not considered adequate for more advanced research techniques using machine learning.

The dataset combines different open sources such as the National Vulnerability Database (NVD), Common Weakness Scoring System (CWSS), Common Vulnerabilities and Exposures (CVE), Shodan, Zerodium, and so forth. Table 1 presents data sources. The dataset was made publicly available[1] together with the associated Jupyter Notebooks in order to allow the research community to scrutinise the findings contained in the report, but also to enable further research.

4 Dataset Imputation Through Machine Learning

Since the influential publications of Rubin many decades ago, e.g. [11–14], there has been increasing awareness of the drawbacks associated with analyses conducted on datasets with missing values. This is prevalent in many fields of study, particularly medical (clinical) datasets which can often be missing values for over half of the samples available [15].

Classical imputation methods often relied on the use of measures of central tendency of available data to populate the missing values, e.g. the arithmetic mean, mode, and median. However, these methods are now considered to be ineffective for computing candidates for the population of missing data and are more likely to reduce the accuracy and integrity of a dataset [10], e.g. in the case of heteroskedasticity. Hot-deck imputation, an approach which uses randomly selected *similar* records to impute missing values, performs poorly when the majority of samples contain missing values and are outperformed by other approaches [18].

More recent studies suggest that artificial neural networks, particularly multilayer perceptrons [16] and autoencoders [17], can outperform these classical methods, including regression and hot-deck, for the imputation of categorical variables. Artificial neural network methods have also been shown to outperform Expectation-Maximisation techniques in the presence of non-linear relationships between sample variables [19].

4.1 Experiment Design

Following the suggestions in the literature a machine learning approach, i.e. artificial neural networks, will be used for the imputation of missing categorical values. This experiment aims to estimate categorical variables where there are missing values in the *tactics* feature of the ENISA vulnerabilities dataset. This will be achieved by detecting patterns in the sub-components of the CAPEC and their mappings to one or many tactic categorical values. This will be treated as multiple sub-problems, whereby each tactic can be considered a flag on a binary string where the binary value is determined by a binary classifier. The dataset consists of 27471 samples, where 19404 of these samples have no value for the tactic feature. Each sample can be labelled with multiple unique tactic categories from the following list:

---

[1] https://github.com/enisaeu/vuln-report.

Table 1. Data sources characteristic [6]

Source type	Data type	Description
NVD database	CVE data	The NVD is the U.S. government repository of standards-based vulnerability management data. The NVD includes databases of security checklist references, security-related software flaws, misconfigurations, product names, and impact metrics[a]
ATT&CK	Attacker's patterns (techniques & tactics)	MITRE ATT&CK^{TM} is a globally-accessible knowledge base of adversary tactics and techniques based on real-world observations[b]
Shodan	Number of exploits	Database of internet-connected devices (e.g. webcams, routers, servers, etc.) acquiring data from various HTTP/HTTPS - port 80, 8080, 443, 8443)[c]
Exploit database	Non-CVE data	Contains information on public exploits and corresponding vulnerable software. The collection of exploits is acquired from direct submissions, mailing lists and other public sources[d]
CVE details	CVE data	The database containing details of individual publicly known cybersecurity vulnerabilities including an identification number, a description, and at least one public reference[e]
Zero-Day Initiative	CVE and non-CVE	Encourages reporting of zero-day vulnerabilities privately to affected vendors by financially rewarding researchers (a vendor-agnostic bug bounty program). No technical details on individual vulnerabilities are made public until after vendor released patches. ZDI do not resell or redistribute the vulnerabilities[f]
ThreatConnect	Number of incidents related to CVE	Automated threat intelligence for Intel systems[g]
VulDB	Exploit prices and software categories	Vulnerability database documenting and explaining security vulnerabilities and exploits[h]
US CERT	Industry sector	The US Department for Homeland Security's Cybersecurity and Infrastructure Security Agency (CISA) aims to enhance the security, resiliency, and reliability of the USA's cybersecurity and communications infrastructure [i]
Zerodium	Bug bounty exploit prices	A zero-day acquisition platform. Founded by cybersecurity experts with experience in advanced vulnerability research [j]

[a] bibitemnvdhttps://nvd.nist.gov
[b] https://attack.mitre.org
[c] https://www.shodan.io
[d] https://www.exploit-db.com/about-exploit-db
[e] https://cve.mitre.org
[f] https://www.zerodayinitiative.com
[g] https://threatconnect.com
[h] https://vuldb.com
[i] https://www.us-cert.gov
[j] https://zerodium.com

- Initial Access
- Execution
- Persistence
- Privilege Escalation
- Defense Evasion
- Credential Access
- Discovery
- Lateral Movement
- Collection
- Command and Control
- Exfiltration
- Impact

Figure 1 illustrates the distribution of tactic category assignments where it can be seen that three of these twelve categories are not represented at all. Without examples for all twelve categories, it is expected that a dataset populated through imputation will also not represent these entirely missing categories.

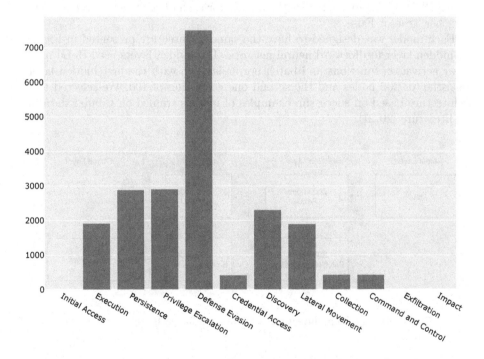

Fig. 1. The distribution of ATT&CK tactic labels within the original dataset.

The CAPEC cannot be used directly and therefore it must first be preprocessed and encoded. For reproducibility, this consisted of the following steps:

1. All CAPEC IDs were obtained using the Domains of Attack resource from Mitre (https://capec.mitre.org/data/definitions/3000.html).
2. The CAPEC IDs are then used to create a truth table with all elements initialised to false.
3. Using the CAPEC feature in the ENISA Vulnerabilities dataset, the corresponding CAPEC ID in the truth table is changed to true.

The tactic feature required similar encoding as it exists as a comma-separated variable in the ENISA vulnerabilities dataset:

1. The tactics were obtained using the ATT&CK Matrix resource from Mitre (https://attack.mitre.org/).
2. The tactics are then used to create a truth table with all elements initialised to false.
3. Using the tactic feature in the ENISA Vulnerabilities dataset, the corresponding tactic in the truth table is changed to true.

These two truth tables were used to design individual models per tactic using supervised machine learning. The inputs for all the models were to be the same, the CAPEC truth table, whereas the output for each of the twelve models could be either True or False.

Each model was designed to have the same architecture presented in Fig. 2, a 2 hidden layer feedforward neural network. The hidden layers used ReLu non-linear activation functions and batch normalisation, with the first hidden layer consisting of 200 nodes and the second one consisting of 100. We selected this architecture based on successful examples of models trained on tabular data in the literature [20,21].

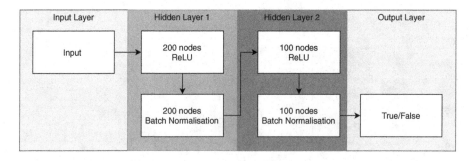

Fig. 2. The model architecture configuration for each tactic category.

The optimiser employed during the supervised learning process was the Adam algorithm configured with 0.9 and 0.99 respectively as the beta coefficients used for computing running averages of gradient and its square, a weight decay rate of $1e-2$, and a learning rate of $1e-3$. Adam was selected because of its performance and memory advantage over other optimisation algorithms, especially for multivariate data [22].

All twelve models were trained on a 6500 sample subset of the 8067 samples for which the tactic categorisations were present. A further 700 of these samples were used for validation, with the final 867 samples reserved for testing.

4.2   Results

Each model was trained for 5 epochs before achieving at least 99.88% accuracy, indicating the likelihood of a prominent pattern in the mappings of CAPECs to tactics.

On the unseen data reserved for the test set the models predicting Persistence, Privilege Escalation, Defence Evasion, Credential Access, and Collection achieved 99.88% accuracy, with the remaining classifiers achieving 100%.

The models were then used to collectively predict the tactics for the entire dataset, including those 19404 samples which had missing values. Figure 3 illustrates the distribution of tactic category assignments in the dataset with imputation, where it can be seen that as expected the same three categories are still not represented at all.

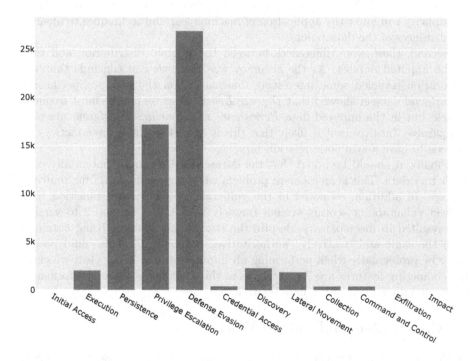

Fig. 3. The distribution of ATT&CK tactic labels within the imputed dataset.

5   Discussion

Whilst from a machine learning perspective the results are completely satisfactory, several limitations need to be acknowledged.

First, the ATT&CK tactics which are closely coupled to the concept of the Cyber Kill Chain (CKC) [23], inherit the limitations and disadvantages of such taxonomy. Specifically, the CKC phases were mainly intended to help communicate the main stages of a cyber attack as a sequence of events, similar to the description of an attack vector. Mapping a particular attack action to the respective kill chain phase carries a degree of subjectivity. This can be easily evidenced by studying the structure and approach of the ATT&CK framework, where the techniques do not have an exclusive membership under the tactics. In fact, some techniques can appear in as many as four different tactics. As such, when investigating a particular cyber incident, the placement of an identified technique is a task for the security analyst. Therefore, the proposed machine learning method has not taken into account such implicit knowledge. This is a much more complex problem and certainly deserves a separate and dedicated research thread. A way forward for future research is to include more features and particularly the techniques which can appear having multiple values per vulnerability. This multiplicity will allow the application of machine learning techniques to identify the distances of the data points.

Second, there were differences between the original distribution and that of the imputed dataset. As the accuracy was high, we can conclude that the imputation revealed some interesting information on the tactics. Specifically, the original dataset showed that *Defence Evasion* was by far the most frequent attack, but in the imputed data *Persistence* and *Privilege Escalation* are now comparable. Intuitively it is likely that this is correct as these three tactics can be seen to have a symbiotic relationship.

Finally, it should be noted that the dataset itself contains potentially contradictory data. This is an inherent problem when ingressing data from multiple sources. In addition, as noted in the vulnerability study, the transition to a revised vulnerability scoring system (namely from CVSS version 2 to version 3.x) resulted in discrepancies, despite the two scoring systems being obtained from the same and relatively "authoritative" database [6]. This could potentially be problematic when performing an imputation if it is not clear which of the competing features are "correct", as in this case the accuracy performance of the imputation algorithm may be irrelevant.

6   Conclusions and Future Work

In this paper we attempted to enrich a real-world dataset using supervised machine learning. We demonstrated that it is possible to completely fill a sparse column of the dataset and we selected the ATT&CK tactic feature to showcase this approach.

The significance of the results is two-fold. First, the high accuracy achieved showed the performance and feasibility of the proposed approach. Second, we demonstrated that it is possible to escape from the inherent limitation where only real-world data are available due to the nature of the problem, e.g. the study of vulnerabilities which cannot be created by completely synthesised data.

As a future direction, we will investigate the imputation of other features, including those that describe financial aspects of the vulnerabilities.

Acknowledgement. This work has received funding from the European Union's Horizon 2020 research and innovation program under the grant agreement no. 830943 (ECHO).

References

1. Joh, H., Malaiya, Y.K.: A framework for software security risk evaluation using the vulnerability lifecycle and CVSS metrics. In: Proceedings of the International Workshop on Risk and Trust in Extended Enterprises, pp. 430–434, November 2010
2. ENISA: Actionable Information for Security Incident Response. Heraklion, Greece (2015). https://doi.org/10.2824/38111
3. MITRE, Common Vulnerabilities and Exposures. https://cve.mitre.org/. Accessed 16 Feb 2020
4. MITRE, Common Weakness Enumeration. https://cwe.mitre.org/. Accessed 16 Feb 2020
5. MITRE, Common Attack Pattern Enumeration and Classification. https://capec. mitre.org/. Accessed 16 Feb 2020
6. ENISA: State of Vulnerabilities 2018/2019 - Analysis of Events in the life of Vulnerabilities, Heraklion, Greece (2019). https://www.enisa.europa.eu/ publications/technical-reports-on-cybersecurity-situation-the-state-of-cyber-security-vulnerabilities/at_download/fullReport
7. Kritikos, K., Magoutis, K., Papoutsakis, M., Ioannidis, S.: A survey on vulnerability assessment tools and databases for cloud-based web applications. Array **3**, 100011 (2019)
8. Arbaugh, W.A., Fithen, W.L., McHugh, J.: Windows of vulnerability: a case study analysis. Computer **33**(12), 52–59 (2000)
9. Huang, C., Liu, J., Fang, Y., Zuo, Z.: A study on Web security incidents in China by analyzing vulnerability disclosure platforms. Comput. Secur. **58**, 47–62 (2016)
10. Royston, P.: Multiple imputation of missing values. Stata J. **4**(3), 227–241 (2004)
11. Rubin, D.B.: Multiple Imputation for Nonresponse in Surveys, vol. 81. Wiley, Hoboken (2004)
12. Rubin, D.B.: Inference and missing data. Biometrika **63**(3), 581–592 (1976)
13. Rubin, D.B.: Multiple imputation after 18+ years. J. Am. Stat. Assoc. **91**(434), 473–489 (1996)
14. Rubin, D.B., Schenker, N.: Multiple imputation in health-are databases: an overview and some applications. Stat. Med. **10**(4), 585–598 (1991)
15. Clark, T.G., Altman, D.G.: Developing a prognostic model in the presence of missing data: an ovarian cancer case study. J. Clin. Epidemiol. **56**(1), 28–37 (2003)
16. Silva-Ramírez, E.L., Pino-Mejías, R., López-Coello, M., Cubiles-de-la-Vega, M.D.: Missing value imputation on missing completely at random data using multilayer perceptrons. Neural Netw. **24**(1), 121–129 (2011)

17. Choudhury, S.J., Pal, N.R.: Imputation of missing data with neural networks for classification. Knowl.-Based Syst. **182**, 104838 (2019)
18. Wilmot, C.G., Shivananjappa, S.: Comparison of hot-deck and neural-network imputation. Transp. Surv. Qual. Innov. 543–554 (2003)
19. Nelwamondo, F.V., Mohamed, S., Marwala, T.: Missing data: a comparison of neural network and expectation maximization techniques. Curr. Sci. 1514–1521 (2007)
20. Guo, C., Berkhahn, F.: Entity embeddings of categorical variables. arXiv preprint arXiv:1604.06737 (2016)
21. De Brébisson, A., Simon, É., Auvolat, A., Vincent, P., Bengio, Y.: Artificial neural networks applied to taxi destination prediction. arXiv preprint arXiv:1508.00021 (2015)
22. Kingma, D.P., Ba, J.: Adam: A method for stochastic optimization. arXiv preprint arXiv:1412.6980 (2014)
23. Hutchins, E.M., Cloppert, M.J., Amin, R.M.: Intelligence-driven computer network defense informed by analysis of adversary campaigns and intrusion kill chains. Leading Issues Inf. Warfare Secur. Res. **1**(1), 80 (2011)

Towards the Design of a Cybersecurity Competence Network: Findings from the Analysis of Existing Network Organisations

Todor Tagarev[1]([✉]) [iD] and Bríd Á. Davis[2] [iD]

[1] Institute of Information and Communication Technologies, Bulgarian Academy of Sciences,
"Acad. G. Bonchev" Str., Bl. 2, 1113 Sofia, Bulgaria
tagarev@bas.bg
[2] Department of Psychology, National University of Ireland Maynooth, Maynooth W23 F2H6,
County Kildare, Ireland
Brid.Davis@mu.ie

Abstract. The increasing reliance of economy, society and state on cyberspace and proliferating cyber risks require not only technologies and qualified workforce, but also innovative organisational solutions. The European Union sees one such solution in the establishment of a network of cybersecurity competence centres. In the past two decades, the creation of collaborative networked organisations in other fields has proven its utility in sharing knowledge, resources and risk to exploit quickly emerging market opportunities. The major challenge in creating networked organisations is to provide long-term, effective collaboration through adequate governance and management.

To support the elaboration of a solid governance model of a cybersecurity competence network in a Horizon 2020 research project, this paper presents the results of a study of 92 existing network organisations active in cybersecurity and closely related fields. It outlines the implemented methodological approach, the identification of two main types of business models depending on funding streams and degree of coordination among partners, a prioritised list of governance requirements, and prevailing governance models depending on member representation on senior governance bodies and decision-making principles.

Keywords: Cybersecurity · Collaborative networked organisation · Business model · Governance requirements · Governance model · ECHO project

1 Introduction

The provision of cybersecurity requires a variety of competences both to respond to new types of attack and to prepare for future risks in a timely manner [1]. Very few organisations and, in fact, only a few countries can afford to invest in people and technologies to an extent that would allow them to deal effectively with current and future cybersecurity challenges on their own [2, 3].

© Springer Nature Switzerland AG 2020
A. Dziech et al. (Eds.): MCSS 2020, CCIS 1284, pp. 37–50, 2020.
https://doi.org/10.1007/978-3-030-59000-0_4

Individual EU member states [4] and the European Union have approached this challenge by embarking on the creation of an EU-wide reliable, safe, and open cyber ecosystem. Thus, in 2018 the European Parliament and the Council issued a proposal for a Regulation on establishing a European cybersecurity industrial, technology and research competence centre and a network of national coordination centres [5]. A call for proposals SU-ICT-03-2018 in the Horizon 2020 programme was issued in parallel, aiming to overcome the fragmentation of EU research capacities and ensure that "the EU retains and develops essential capacities to secure its digital economy, infrastructures, society, and democracy". One of the objectives of the call was to establish and operate a pilot for a "Cybersecurity Competence Network". The ECHO project is one of the four pilots, performed by 30 organisations from 14 European countries – public and private, for-profit and non-for-profit, civilian and defence organisations, as well as one consortium, with representatives of the energy, transport, health, defence, and the space sectors [6]. Compared with the other three pilot projects, ECHO puts a particular emphasis on elaborating, implementing and enhancing a governance model of a future networked organisation based on the ECHO project consortium.

Towards that goal, the research team conducted a comprehensive study of needs and objectives of the governance of networked organisations, their business and governance models. The study included interviews with representatives of two main groups of stakeholders – funding organisations and potential major customers, analysis of norms and regulations, academic sources, and existing networks.

This paper presents the results of the latter. Accounting for the limited volume of the paper, the focus is on the results from the quantitative analysis of the description of 92 existing networks. Section 2 outlines the methodological foundation of the study. Section 3 presents statistical results on business models, allowing to identify two clusters, corresponding to models most often implemented in practice. Section 4 provides the ranking of 34 governance objectives and requirements, while Sect. 5 presents the findings on governance models, i.e. the main considerations or 'dimensions' for presenting the governance model of a networked organisation and identified clusters. The final section concludes the paper and outlines the main directions of follow-on use of the study results.

2 Methodological Approach

This study was organised in four phases: (1) Preparation; (2) Preliminary analysis; (3) Secondary analysis; and (4) Aggregation.

In the *Preparation* phase, based on analysis of the project documents, own experience and desktop research, the team prepared a preliminary list of governance issues and issues related to business and governance models of networked organisations and a list of existing networked organisation of possible interest to this study. The lists were amended during a brainstorming session in a project meeting. A final draft list of governance issues and a respective template in Excel format to present the analysis of networked organisations were created as a result of these crowd sourcing activities. The template was piloted by six ECHO partner organisations, analysing 12 networks in total. The feedback received from piloting the template and the overall analysis process was used to prepare the final template and detailed instructions for analysing network organisations. The template included fields for administrative information, 17 governance issues and main parameters of the business and governance models.

In the second phase of *Preliminary analysis* researchers from 12 ECHO partners, using the template, analysed 92 existing network organisations in four types:

- networks dedicated to information/cybersecurity research and services;
- cybersecurity incubators/ accelerators/ tech parks/ ecosystems;
- other research-intensive networks;
- networked organisations providing (among others) information services related to cybersecurity.

To ensure that the scope of the analysis was inclusive and robust, networks which operated worldwide were also selected, not just those which originate from European Union countries. When the publicly available information on a certain network was not sufficient to analyse it properly, the respective partner could either select from networks unassigned at the time (the full list contained more than 100 networks) or propose to the study leader another network. Such proposals were approved as long as they addressed a Collaborative Networked Organisation (CNO), i.e. "a network consisting of a variety of entities (e.g. organisations and people) that are largely autonomous, geographically distributed, and heterogeneous in terms of their operating environment, culture, social capital and goals, but that collaborate to better achieve common or compatible goals, thus jointly generating value" [7]. Networks consisting of geographically distributed entities which may bring specific competences in the field of cybersecurity, and all part of a larger hierarchical organisation, were not included in the analysis.

This paper presents the results of the *Secondary analysis*, conducted by the authors. In the fourth phase these results will be aggregated with the analyses of normative documents and the academic literature and the results of the interviews.

3   Business Models and Patterns

3.1   Business Models: Dimension 1 - Degree of Coordination

This section outlines the various values under the remit of 'Degree of coordination'. The provision of services and sales of products (including information exchange with customers, contracting, contract management, etc.) can potentially be realised in a spectrum from a single centralised point to fully decentralised arrangements:

- a single centralised point for provision of services and sales of products;
- a designated point of contact (POC; responsible organisation) for each main service or product;
- several points of contact (lead organisations) for each of the main services/products;
- each CNO member can contract the delivery of network products and services.

Network development decisions (including on adding new members, establishing partnerships, investing in R&D or new capabilities, etc.) can be made in a spectrum of potential arrangements, e.g. from a single decision-making process for the CNO to fully independent decisions by each organisation (i.e. without coordination):

- Decisions are made in a single process for the CNO as a whole;
- Decisions on main 'issues' (e.g. capabilities to be developed) are coordinated within the CNO;
- Decisions are coordinated among some CNO member organisations (variable configurations; possibly ad-hoc);
- No coordination, i.e. each CNO member decides independently.

All qualitative data collated with respect to the degree of coordination (i.e. network development decisions and the provision of goods and services) were assessed in accordance with the respective categorical labels.

Complete data with respect to the degree of coordination was not available for 45 CNOs; these CNOs were excluded from further analysis. A pie graph (Fig. 1) was generated to detail the distribution of provision of products and services interrelated with network development decisions for the remaining 47 CNOs.

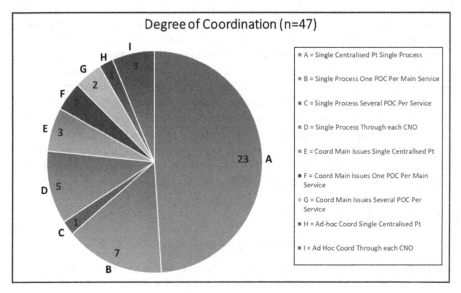

Fig. 1. Degree of coordination among CNOs.

The majority of CNOs coordinate network development decisions on a single process basis and provide products and services also through a single centralised point; this subset accounted for 49% of the sample (n = 23). This essentially means that for a majority of the surveyed CNOs, all decisions which impacted the operation and development of the network in addition to the provision of goods and services were coordinated at network level.

Similarly, but to a lesser extent, 15% of the analysed CNOs utilised one designated point of contact for each main service/product (n = 7), while 11% of the sample positioned each CNO member to contract network products and services (n = 5); both types coordinated development decisions on a single process basis.

3.2 Business Models: Dimension 2 - Profit Orientation and Funding Streams

Profit orientation and funding streams was also considered in relation to CNOs' business models. An arbitrary numerical scale was devised in an effort to visualise these characteristics of the business model in two dimensions (outlined in Table 1).

Table 1. Existing networks: profit and funding streams, scale from −5 to 5.

Profit orientation funding streams	Non-for-profit	For profit
Exclusively/entirely/public funding	5	Not applicable
Primarily public funding	3	1 (unlikely)
Balanced funding streams	1	−1
Primarily commercial funding	−1 (unlikely)	−3
Exclusively commercial funding	Not applicable	−5

'Commercial' in this context refers to funding from sales of products and services. Additionally, while the labels used in the assessment of this dimension include 'exclusively', 'primarily', 'balanced', which are decidedly subjective, such values are useful at denoting such criteria as these parameters are not regulated by law or statutory documents.

All qualitative data from the primary analysis was collated with respect to profit orientation and funding streams and assessed in accordance with the categorical anchors outlined above.

Complete data with respect to the profit orientation and funding streams was not available for 32 CNOs; these CNOs were excluded from further analysis. Of the 60 remaining CNOs, a total of 53 were deemed to be not-for-profit, with 7 denoted as for-profit networks.

The majority of *not-for-profit CNOs* operated utilizing "balanced funding streams" – essentially the combination of public and commercial funding; this subset accounted for 41% (n = 22) of the sample. In the current context this is typically manifested when CNOs received public funding (e.g. from the national government, EU, etc.) and commercial funding (including sponsorship or donations from the private sector). Exclusive utilisation of public funding represented the second largest funding model on which not-for-profits relied; this subset accounted for 36% of the sample (n = 19).

The majority of for-profit CNOs operated under the exclusive utilisation of commercial funding; this subset accounted for 71% of the sample (n = 5). Notwithstanding, 29% for-profit CNOs (n = 2) relied upon a balanced funding stream – the relative equal combination of public and commercial funding.

3.3 Visualisation of CNO Business Models

A contingency table analysis was conducted in IBM SPSS™ 25 to investigate the association between Dimension 1: Degree of coordination and Dimension 2: Profit and funding streams.

It was established that with regards to the 'degree of coordination' classification, a majority of existing networks were not-for-profit, utilising exclusively public funding (n = 9; 23%) or a balanced funding stream (n = 6; 16%) operationalised within the constraints of a single process-single centralised point.

These results indicate that of the 92 networks which were critiqued, the provision of services and sales of products is coordinated through a single centralised point, whether this pertains to information exchange with customers, or contracting, or indeed contract management. Moreover, these organisations rely on either public funding exclusively (i.e. government grants, etc.) or a balanced combination of commercial and public funding. A graphical representation of these findings, in the form of a scatterplot is illustrated in Fig. 2. This graph shows that a significant majority (clusters) of the surveyed CNO's were not-for-profit networks which utilised exclusively public funding (n = 9; 23%) or networks which employed a balanced funding stream (n = 6; 16%) operationalised within the constraints of a single process-single centralised point.

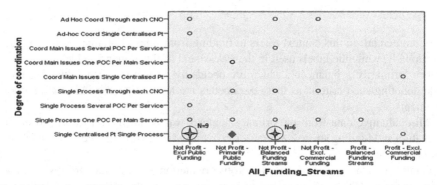

Fig. 2. Clustering CNO's business models – Profit and funding stream vs Degree of coordination.

4   Requirements to the Governance of Networked Organisations

All key information on governance requirements, sourced from the primary analysis of 92 existing networks, was collated and is summarised in this section, starting with qualitative analysis of statutory documents vis-à-vis the 17 governance issues in the template for primary analysis and then ranking all identified governance objectives and requirements.

4.1   Governance Requirements in Existing Networks

As expected, *geographical representation or exclusion zone* appear to be an important issue in statutory documents of existing networks, as it is a crucial parameter by which the reach of the network with respect to provision of services and products can be measured. Crucially, the jurisdictions which networks endeavour to operate within can have implications on how effectively a CNO performs across country borders; likewise operating within the confines of larger governing territories – i.e. EU, USA, Asia-Pacific, etc. – can also impact CNO performance. A majority of networks have scope within the EU, USA and, to a slightly less extent, Asian Pacific countries; this is particularly evident when CNOs are based in these jurisdictions. Notably, however, a vast majority of networks aim to represent members on a worldwide scale and are not just limited by geographic location. This is especially notable for CNOs which represent a specific profession in the cyber-security industry (i.e. auditors, researchers, finance personnel, etc.), which endeavour to provide a base from which professionals can network and upskill (internationally). Typically, the major, more established organisations had the largest quantity of members, especially when compared to grassroot organisations. Findings from this analysis, however, did highlight that while the coverage of many organisations was at an international level – continental Africa, Russia and Middle Eastern countries were majorly underrepresented, with few or no organisations in place.

One of the key ways of progressing a CNO centres on the *involvement of external stakeholders*; hence this parameter was also recorded in the primary analysis. The main ways in which external stakeholders connected with CNOs included involvement in advisory boards or coordination/ strategic/ management/ steering/ industry expertise committees; academic collaboration; engagement with training, education and skills. Such involvement facilitates up-skilling, provision of professional accreditation; information of funding schemes for cybersecurity projects, or communication with EU and national level funding authorities; coordinating networks of practitioners and researchers; and hosting cybersecurity conferences and networking events.

The reviewed CNOs are highly heterogenous given that they are scattered across the globe, have a diverse range of objectives and represent a myriad of professional organisations, industries, researchers and individuals. It was therefore crucial to record the various *standards or methodologies* utilised in the operation of these networks. Findings from the qualitative analysis highlighted that the most commonly used standards were Control Objectives for Information and Related Technologies (COBIT) and Information Technology Infrastructure Library (ITIL), and to a lesser extent project management tools such as Microsoft Project and PRINCE II.

With respect to the *representation on senior governance bodies*, the majority of CNOs host the following directing officers: a President, a Secretary and a Treasurer, each of whom are elected by the Board of Directors. A Chair of the Board, Vice Chairs and/or Vice Presidents, and such other officers and assistant officers and agents as may be deemed necessary may also be elected or appointed by the Board of Directors. Likewise, the business affairs of the CNOs were typically managed by or under the direction of the Board of Directors. The number of personnel assigned to the board depended on the size of the CNO (i.e. what types and how many members are represented and what products/ services are offered), the funding stream of the CNO, remuneration status (voluntary or salaried positions), and the geographical scope of the CNO.

While various officers can oversee the management of the CNO, the *decision-making* principles on which the CNO relies upon are indispensable for the successful operation of the network. In a majority of cases, steering committees or steering boards typically have the authority with regards to decision making for the CNO. Steering committees typically act within the framework of the guidelines and guidance of the Council (i.e. administrative board). Consensus, when a board has reached quorum – individually determined depending on the size of the panel and the number of senior officers present, a qualified majority vote—2/3rds of the panel or above—were the most common frameworks on which motions were passed. In some instances, senior representatives may be required to be present in order for a motion to be voted on in the first instance; a board also has the power to adjourn a vote until such a condition is met.

Regular *internal and/or external auditing* ensures the effective operation of a CNO. A majority of the reviewed CNOs had procedures in place with respect to auditing practice. A majority of the CNOs ensured that internal audits were conducted by an independent party (outsourced) to ensure transparency and no bias. Steering boards or board of directors usually appoint the auditor (either an individual or a corporation), wherein the outcome of the audit (report) and recommendations for the future are usually made available to steering committee officers and/or senior officers on the board (i.e. Chief Executive). It is therefore the responsibility of the respective officer(s) to ensure the regular monitoring of the implementation of audit recommendations. An annual report containing a summary of the number and type of internal audits carried out, the recommendations made and the action taken on those recommendations is compiled and forwarded to senior executives and/or committee members (where relevant). The respective parties then examine the information and assess whether the recommendations have been implemented fully and in a timely manner. The reports and findings of the internal auditor shall be made accessible by the public only after validation by the internal auditor of the action taken for their implementation.

To a lesser extent, internal audits were found to be conducted by voting members of the CNO (not board executives) or an Internal Audit Committee—composed of the Treasurer and at least two other Members who are not Officers of the Board While this practice was less common, it can confound findings. Yet, this measure may have been due to financial necessity (as the CNO may have limited funds to support the contracting of an outside auditor).

Primary analysis of the CNOs indicated that many networks had arrangements in place with regards to *dispute/ conflict management*. Members are required to be transparent in the first instance if they were in a position to improperly gain from the products/ services under the auspices of the CNO. A typical procedure for when a conflict of interest is discovered first involves the respective party ceasing all activities in the matter. Senior executive personnel then determine if appropriate actions need to be taken, wherein a board of directors meets quorum and a decision is led by consensus. The following processes could then be actioned depending on the outcome: 1) written reprimand, 2) a one-year probation or 3) termination of membership. A number of CNOs allow for an arbitration tribunal to ensure due process.

Confidentiality practices across the CNOs vary; however, all CNOs based in the EU were General Data Protection Regulation (GDPR) compliant. Indeed, a majority of CNOs had a declaration of confidentiality in place – detailing how data was managed, processed and stored. This information was readily available to stakeholders, members and consumers alike. Binding confidentiality policies and statutes were continually up-dated across the lifespan of the organisation. Some CNOs were compliant with additional EU security policy regulations (i.e. Decision 2013/488/EU for protecting EU classified information) depending on their remit. The CNOs which were surveyed stated in principle that no confidential information would be exchanged, and that the appropriate confidentiality of proprietary or otherwise sensitive information encountered in the course of professional activities would be maintained. Moreover, members (individuals, academics, corporate, etc.) are required to adhere to a code of conduct with respect to confidentiality; if this is breached, a disciplinary process is initiated.

Protecting *intellectual property* (IP) is integral to the effective operation of an organisation. It is therefore understandable that many CNOs have stipulations in place with respect to how their IP is managed (legally binding Intellectual property rights). Additionally, Intellectual property rights, including patent rights, copyrights, proprietary technical information and other sensitive commercial or industrial matters pertaining to the CNO are handled according to the CNO's policies and directives.

While CNOs most likely are ethically run, establishing and enforcing an *ethics code* promotes transparency, can be a positive step for building trust, retaining members, gaining future members and, overall, ensuring the successful management of a network in long term. The most common ways in which ethical codes and standards were prescribed in the surveyed CNOs were by devising a transparent declaration or a binding statute with respect to code of conduct/ ethics code/ framework of principles; establishing an Ethics committee; providing transparency with regards to the ethics complaint process; and prohibiting personnel, during the 12 months after leaving the service, from engaging in lobbying or advocacy vis-à-vis staff of their former institution for their business, clients or employers on matters for which they were responsible during service.

Specific ethical issues (e.g. policy in regard to *slavery* or use of *labour of minors* in the supply chain), *'green' policies, transparency and anti-corruption/ integrity policy* (e.g. whistle-blowers protection) across all networks were rarely noted during the primary analysis. This outcome could indicate that such issues were not specifically highlighted by CNOs in the first instance (i.e. not explicitly outlined on organisations' website, social media streams or governance documentation). Some CNOs made positive steps towards ensuring *gender balance* by establishing initiatives and charters to encourage and retain female personnel in the cybersecurity domain. However, the primary analysis phase of these CNOs highlighted that the vast majority of networks did not make any significant contributions towards addressing gender balance.

4.2 Ranking of Governance Objectives and Requirements

The results of the primary analysis were also processed quantitatively. Each of the 17 governance issues listed in the template for primary analysis is addressed by statutory documents of at least one of the analysed networked organisations. The number of networked organisations that address a specific governance issue in their bylaws or other statutory documents is given in Fig. 3.

In addition to the template, another 17 governance issues were identified in the interviews with stakeholders and the analysis of the academic literature [8]. Each one is addressed by statutory documents of one or more of the 92 networks subject to analysis (see Fig. 4).

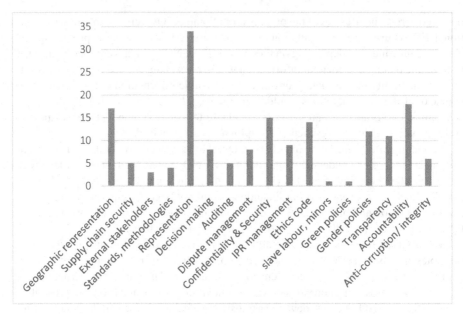

Fig. 3. Ranking of initial governance issues based on the analysis of existing networks.

The *representation* of member organisations on the senior governance bodies of the CNO and *knowledge management* have been addressed most often – each in the documents of 34 of the analysed networks. This maximum of 34 was used to construct four quartiles and place the governance issues in four respective tiers:

- In addition to *representation* and *knowledge management*, Tier 1 includes the *long-term perspective* on collaboration;
- Tier 2 includes *geographic representation, accountability, innovation, adaptiveness, cohesion, trust,* and *leadership*;
- *Confidentiality and security, IPR management, ethics code, gender policies, transparency, sustainability, communication and engagement, organisational culture,* and *risk management* fit into Tier 3;
- The remaining governance issues have a score less than 25% of the maximum and, respectively, are placed in Tier 4.

5 Prevailing Governance Models

Key indicators concerning the governance models of CNOs were assessed. Two dimensions were evaluated and compared – *Dimension 1*: Representation on the senior governance body/ies vs *Dimension 2*: Decision making principles.

The following two-dimensional scale was devised in an effort to classify the two dimensions. Step two involved plotting this data and identifying prevailing models.

Scale for Dimension 1. Representation on the senior governance body/ies:

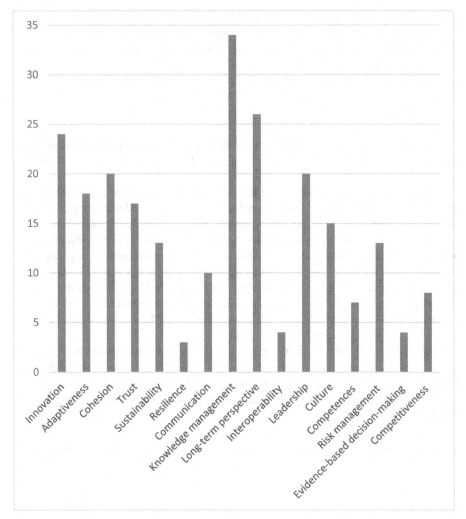

Fig. 4. Ranking of additionally identified governance issues based on the analysis of existing networks.

1. Only few core members are represented;
2. Selective representation, e.g. of founding members or members above a certain 'size' or with certain roles (an example here would be a Horizon 2020 "Project Management Team");
3. Broad representation, e.g. a representative of any organisation may be elected through a vote open to all CNO member organisations;
4. All CNO member organisations are represented (e.g. a General Assembly of a Horizon 2020 Consortium).

Scale for Dimension 2. Decision of CNO bodies are taken by:

1. Simple majority, i.e. over 1/2 of the weighted votes of CNO members;
2. Qualified majority, e.g. over 2/3 of the weighted votes of CNO members;
3. Simple majority (i.e. over 1/2 of the votes), with equal weight of the vote of each CNO member;
4. Qualified majority (e.g. 2/3 of the votes), with equal weight of the vote of each CNO member;
5. Consensus.

Note: votes can be weighted for example depending on the 'size' (e.g. annual turnover or personnel size) of CNO members or their financial contribution to some of the CNO expenditures.

A (crosstabs) contingency table analysis was conducted in IBM SPSS™ 25 to investigate the association between Dimension 1: Representation on the senior governance body/ies and Dimension 2: Decision making principles for all analysed networked organisations. Combining and critiquing the findings for both types of profit orientation (i.e. for-profit and not-for-profit) indicates that *universal CNO representation* appears to be the most common form of representation on senior governance bodies, accounting for 43% of the sample (n = 26). Likewise, the most predominant means of making decisions which were adopted by all CNOs (irrespective of profit orientation) was by *simple majority (decision-making with over 1/2 of the votes)* at 30% (n = 18), whereby votes from each CNO member carried equal weight.

Furthermore, 15% of the sample operated under the system that *All CNO member organisations were represented, with equal vote for each CNO member* (n = 9), followed in turn by CNOs adopting a *Broad representation* at 10% (n = 6). Both operationalised a *simple majority (with over 1/2 of the votes)* voting system. These results are illustrated visually in Fig. 5.

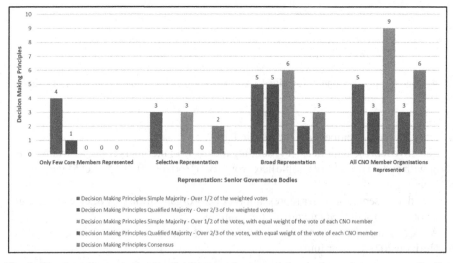

Fig. 5. Bar chart demonstrating the distribution of representation on the senior governance bodies vs decision-making principles (irrespective of profit orientation).

6   Conclusions and Way Ahead

Existing networks, with the governance objectives and requirements they publicly declare, and their business and governance models, demonstrate what is the current practice. Their analysis provides valuable information on governance needs and priorities, and serves as the main source of insight into actual—vis-à-vis prescribed or theoretical—business and governance models of collaborative networked organisations.

This study allowed to identify representation on senior governance bodies, knowledge management, and long-term perspective on collaboration (usually based on some sort of strategy) as governance issues of key concern, followed by geographic representation or exclusion in CNO membership, accountability, innovation, adaptiveness, CNO cohesion, trust among members and to the CNO as a whole, and leadership.

With regards to business models, findings in the current study indicate that a majority of cybersecurity CNOs coordinate their development decisions on a single process basis while providing products and services through a single centralised point. This result highlights that for a majority of the surveyed CNOs, all decisions which impacted the operation and development of the network in addition to the provision of goods and services were all coordinated by the network itself. While operating through a single centralised point was deemed the most common means of coordination, other modalities exist, and future networks would need to determine which arrangement suits best the CNO's objectives and priorities.

Likewise, with regards to governance models, the current study identified *universal CNO representation* as the most prevalent form of representation on senior governance bodies overall (irrespective of profit orientation or funding stream). Moreover, the most predominant model adopted by CNOs in regard to decisions making practices was by *simple majority model, with over 1/2 of the votes cast, whereby votes from each CNO member carried equal weight*. Nonetheless, other models are also used widely. In line with these results, establishing how members are represented on the senior governance body/ies in the first instance and determining which decision-making principles should be adopted could potentially give networks a strong foundation upon which to build an effective collaboration.

In a follow-on study, the findings from existing networks are aggregated with those from the analysis of norms and regulations and 60 selected books, articles, and papers, and analysis of interviews with major stakeholders. Such inclusiveness and complementarity of the primary sources allows to treat the subject of governance comprehensively; to identify and describe good practices in the elaboration and implementation of business and governance models of collaborative networked organisations; to cluster examples of business and governance models of existing networks and thus indicate possible alternative models in the consequent ECHO research; and to prioritise governance needs and objectives.

The results in terms of identified best practice, clusters of business and governance models and the prioritised list of governance needs and objectives are expected to *inform* and *orient* the development of alternative governance models and their evaluation, and thus to develop a sound governance model of the future ECHO network.

Acknowledgements. This work was supported by the ECHO project which has received funding from the European Union's Horizon 2020 research and innovation programme under the grant agreement no. 830943. The authors gratefully acknowledge the contribution to the primary analysis of existing networks by fellow researchers from RHEA Group, the Bulgarian Defence Institute, Tallinn University of Technology, the European Software Institute – Centre Eastern Europe (Sofia), the Institute of ICT of the Bulgarian Academy of Sciences, the Centre for Research and Technology Hellas (Thessaloniki), Telefonica Moviles Espana SA, Semmelweis University (Budapest), Vitrociset Belgium, Zanasi & Partners (Modena), Link Campus University (Rome).

References

1. Radunović, V., Rüfenacht, D.: Cybersecurity Competence Building Trends. Research Report. DiploFoundation, Msida, Malta (2016). https://www.diplomacy.edu/sites/default/files/Cyb ersecurity%20Competence%20Building%20Trends%20in%20OECD.pdf. Accessed 05 Mar 2020
2. Talton, E., Tonar, R.: A lack of cybersecurity funding and expertise threatens US infrastructure. Forbes Magazine, 23 April 2018. https://www.forbes.com/sites/ellistalton/2018/04/23/the-u-s-governments-lack-of-cybersecurity-expertise-threatens-our-infrastructure/. Accessed 06 Mar 2020
3. Dynes, S., Goetz, E., Freeman, M.: Cyber security: are economic incentives adequate? In: Goetz, E., Shenoi, S. (eds.) ICCIP 2007. IIFIP, vol. 253, pp. 15–27. Springer, Boston, MA (2008). https://doi.org/10.1007/978-0-387-75462-8_2
4. Sharkov, G.: From cybersecurity to collaborative resiliency. In: Proceedings of the 2016 ACM Workshop on Automated Decision Making for Active Cyber Defense, pp. 3–9 (2016)
5. Proposal for a Regulation of the European Parliament and of the Council establishing the European Cybersecurity Industrial, Technology and Research Competence Centre and the Network of National Coordination Centres. A contribution from the European Commission to the Leaders' meeting in Salzburg on 19–20 September 2018, COM/2018/630 final. https://eur-lex.europa.eu/legal-content/en/TXT/?uri=CELEX%3A52018PC0630
6. European Network of Cybersecurity Centres and Competence Hub for Innovation and Operations (ECHO). https://echonetwork.eu/
7. Camarinha-Matos, L.M., Afsarmanesh, H., Galeano, N., Molina, A.: Collaborative networked organizations – concepts and practice in manufacturing enterprises. Comput. Ind. Eng. **57**(1), 46–60 (2009)
8. Tagarev, T.: Towards the design of a collaborative cybersecurity networked organisation: identification and prioritisation of governance needs and objectives. Future Internet **12**(4), 62 (2020). https://doi.org/10.3390/fi12040062

On the Assessment of Completeness and Timeliness of Actionable Cyber Threat Intelligence Artefacts

Cagatay Yucel(✉), Ioannis Chalkias, Dimitrios Mallis, Evangelos Karagiannis, Deniz Cetinkaya, and Vasilios Katos

Bournemouth University, Fern Barrow, Wallisdown, Poole BH12 5BB, UK
{cyucel,ichalkias,dmallis,ekaragiannis,dcetinkaya,
vkatos}@bournemouth.ac.uk

Abstract. In this paper we propose an approach for hunting adversarial tactics, techniques and procedures by leveraging information described in structured cyber threat intelligence models. We focused on the properties of timeliness and completeness of cyber threat intelligence indicators to drive the discovery of tactics, techniques and procedures placed highly on the so-called Pyramid of Pain.

We used the unit 42 playbooks dataset to evaluate the proposed approach and illustrate the limitations and opportunities of a systematic intelligence sharing process for high pain tactics, techniques and procedures discovery. We applied the Levenshtein Distance in order to present a metric between the attack vectors constructed from the kill chain phases for completeness and timeliness.

Keywords: ATT&CK framework · Cyber threat intelligence · Unified cyber kill chain · Pyramid of pain · Data quality dimensions

1 Introduction

The continuous evolution and adaptability of cyber threat actors reflected in their fluid modus operandi is mandating radical changes in the cybersecurity sector. At the same time, the constantly increasing number of cyber-physical and IoT devices, the use of new tools with extended capabilities and devices with limited consideration to security bring forth new attack vectors that are reshaping the threat landscape [1], introducing new or advanced threat actors. Advanced Persistent Threat (APT) groups with enhanced means and recourses to cause significant damage to operations both in private and public sector cannot be confronted by the standard incident management mechanisms [2] and require new approaches in organizing cybersecurity in the technical, tactical, operational and strategic level [3].

Information sharing offers the potential of building a trusted network of partners with the purpose of circulating cyber threat related information in order to raise awareness for newly discovered cyber threats and provide with solutions to already known security issues. This action of information sharing is encumbered with mitigating factors that

© Springer Nature Switzerland AG 2020
A. Dziech et al. (Eds.): MCSS 2020, CCIS 1284, pp. 51–66, 2020.
https://doi.org/10.1007/978-3-030-59000-0_5

constitute the process challenging. It requires a coordinated approach from partners that could enable a common culture in terms of the sharing practice. The amount of data produced and consumed by organizations is constantly increasing, forcing them to adopt automation in order to analyze and evaluate threat information over a number of properties such as its value, relativity, context, timeliness and ingestibility [4]. By overcoming those challenges, the organizations that participate in the information sharing constituencies manage to gain information about threats and attacks on their information systems.

In this research, we contextualized our approach around Pyramid of Pain (PoP) in order to evaluate quality in threat intelligence sharing [5]. To elaborate on the mapping of CTI documents to the PoP, the following articulation can be considered: A cyber threat intelligence (CTI) that contains information about a hash or an IP might be mapped low in the PoP but it will serve critical purpose in order to address an urgent incident in a time that can be considered acceptable in terms of incident response. As long as the levels of completeness of the CTI increase (i.e. the CTI contains information about the payload, the attack patterns and the actor) the CTI is mapped higher to the PoP and the information shared offers a more complete description of the attack which has higher value.

The mapping to the PoP allows us to gain a better understanding regarding the level of the CTI (technical, tactical, operational, and strategic). CTIs with information that hangs low in the PoP belong to the technical level, where information is provided with the forms of Indicators of Compromise (IoCs), Indicators of Attack (IoAs), forensic evidence and technical description. The tactical level contains information related to the upper levels of the PoP which are harder to obtain; tools and Tactics, Techniques and Procedures (TTPs) offer context to the analysis of the attack and provide information regarding the actors, thus increasing the completeness of the report, with time being the trade-off of that case. For the operational and strategic levels of threat intelligence a higher-level analysis of data is required. The information derived from such analysis has the potential to offer not only incident managing solutions for post-mortem or live isolated artefacts but also to predict impending attacks or analyze attack behaviors in enterprise level.

The relationship between PoP and the levels of CTI can be defined by timeliness and completeness. The two dimensions have an inversely proportional relationship that can be illustrated with the use of a kill chain. The discovery of an incident at the early stages of a kill chain provides with a timely incident detection; the indicators lie in the low levels of the PoP and threat intelligence levels addressed are the technical and operational level. On the other hand, when an incident is detected at one of the later stages of a kill chain, the event is mapped on the higher level of the pyramid of pain, since its detection is more onerous. The dimension of completeness is reflected by the number of mapped stages in the kill chain.

The increased number of the identified stages in the kill chain provides with adequate information of the organizational and strategic levels of threat intelligence and possibly, an understanding of the timeline of the investigated attack. For this reason, we propose a novel approach of constructing a timeline using low pain indicators in order to reach to TTP level of the PoP.

The paper is organized as follows. Section 2 discusses the landscape of challenges that complicate the process of sharing threat intelligence. Section 3 introduces the proposed approach and methodology. Evaluation is discussed in Sect. 4. Finally, conclusions are drawn, and future work is suggested in Sect. 5.

2 Challenges of Cyber Threat Intelligence

Cyber threat intelligence (CTI) sharing has been highly acknowledged in the last decade as a promising answer to the ever-increasing complexity of cyberattacks [1, 6, 7]. Despite the possible benefits, CTI producers and consumers are facing several issues and challenges [8].

At the top of this list is the Threat Data Overload; the first and most common struggle for those who try to acclaim the benefits of the CTI sharing process and are actively involved in it. The aim of the Threat Intelligence Sharing Platforms (TISPs) is to manage CTI data and feed consumers and threat management teams with actionable information. However, there are still lots of limitations and obstacles to achieve that goal. A recent survey among 1200 IT and IT security practitioners, showed that most respondents are partially or not satisfied at all regarding the CTI feeds they receive [9]. For example, high percentages (from 30% up to 70%) reflect the significant inadequacy of CTI information in terms of relevance, timeliness, accuracy, completeness, and ingestibility; which, according to the European Union Agency for Network and Information Security (ENISA), are the five criteria an information should meet to be actionable and support decisionmakers [10].

The Data Quality (DQ) of the shared feeds is also among those challenges, with implications in the decision-making processes which mainly derive from the fact that data quality is inherently subjective and directly related to the actionability of information [10]. These criteria are used to measure the quality of data and further evaluate the available threat intelligent feeds (i.e. mainly public blacklists) in the literature [11]. The same approach was followed by M. Faiella et al. [12] to define the "weighting criteria" and use them as part of the proposed Threat Score (TS) function; a function used to evaluate IoCs collected from various sources in order to support Security Operations Center (SOC) analysts to prioritize the incidents' analysis. However, this was only a part of their overall contribution towards enriching threat intelligent platforms capabilities. Also, the study in [4] investigates the qualities (i.e. timeliness, completeness, robustness) of IoCs collected by several open sources in order to understand how effective these sources are.

The challenges of data quality in threat intelligence sharing platforms were also investigated by Sillaber et al. [13]. Aiming to address the factors affecting data quality of CTI at each of the following levels (i.e. gathering, storing, processing, and sharing data), the authors conducted studies, starting from interviewing several security-related stakeholders operating within international organizations. Their analysis was based on five traditional data quality dimensions which include accuracy, completeness, consistency, timeliness, and relevance respectively. As a result of that research they presented various findings and recommendations regarding threat intelligence data quality. The authors of [14], focused on the topic of quality of data generated by incident response teams during investigations. Their methodology was based on a case study within a financial organization to empirically evaluate data quality. During the second phase of data gathering they conducted analysis in terms of the accuracy, timeliness, completeness, and consistency of the collected data. According to this analysis, there is still a lot of future work to be done towards enhancing the quality of data generated by incident response teams in order to facilitate and support CTI. The same metrics were suggested by S. Sadiq in his handbook [15] under the category of data values which is one of the three main categories defining the dimensions of data quality.

3   Proposed Approach

3.1   Justification of the Methodology

As mentioned, CTI data can be incomplete, unreliable or subjective. At the same time, a significant amount of work has been invested into standardizing and harmonizing the description and sharing of CTI data. In this section, we propose an approach to assess the quality aspects of CTI data via mining and exploring the captured information, and to evaluate the quality of the underlying information sharing scheme while identifying areas for improvement. As such, in order to assess the quality aspects of CTI data, we propose an approach that builds upon a widely accepted threat intelligence sharing standard and show how though mining and exploring the captured information we can evaluate the quality of the underlying information sharing scheme as well as identify areas for improving it.

Our proposed approach builds upon a widely accepted threat intelligence sharing standard, more specifically, we sample a number of incidents and campaigns that have been studied and expressed in a STIX notation. Although a STIX diagram may effectively reveal relationships between the different objects (such as threat actors, victims, campaigns, IoCs and so forth), it does not show the sequence of the underlying attack vector, although timeline information may be included as a field in the object properties. We conjecture that timing information is critical when extracting TTP descriptions, as this is inferred and assumed in other threat modelling approaches such as the cyber kill chain. For instance, since APT type of attacks involve more than one stages and are prescribed through a sequence of actions, we explore how timeline information can trigger the understanding and extraction of the TTP descriptors. Moreover, this information will be used not only to show the sequence of an attack, but also to use attack tree views to express the TTP. This will also allow the identification of bottlenecks in the attack sequence and the establishment of highly disruptive security controls and remedies, yielding the highest "pain" to the threat actor.

The overall approach is described in Fig. 1. Starting with a given case study, it is assumed that a group of expert security analysts have extensively studied the case and developed a narrative describing the incidents in the most accurate manner. As such, the narrative constitutes the ground truth. Following the free text description, a number of modus operandi are extracted and enriched with IoCs in order to construct the STIX model.

In this work, we use the STIX model and respected narrative as input to the proposed process. More specifically, we first consider the STIX model and use this to generate two models, a timeline of events and an attack tree. The timeline is constructed from the available timestamp information contained in the STIX objects. In addition, we leverage the standardized description of the threat actors' tactics by referencing the incidents using the ATT&CK framework. This also helps to map the events to the Cyber Kill Chain. In order to be as inclusive as possible, we adopt the unified kill chain [16] that can in principle cover for any foreseeable permutation of the dataset.

The kill chain also helps to evaluate the quality of the STIX model as well as the correctness of the examined data captured in the STIX object properties. As the kill chain suggests a loosely coupled – yet in some cases strict – sequence of events and attack patterns, we can evaluate the correctness of the captured data. Formally, given an alphabet S representing elements of an attack set (that is, standardized attack techniques or tactics), we define the range of all possible *valid* words that compose the attack space A_s, that is, all actions that can be potentially observed as an attack vector. The attack space is a subset of the free monoid S^*, under the word concatenation operation. By following such convention, A_s would be constructed following a number of rules using formal expressions that leverage the field of combinatorics on words. In essence, the informal description of the rules will still be provided by the expertise and knowledge found in the cybersecurity domain, but the modelling will be formally constructed leveraging the aforementioned field of theoretical computer science.

An example of such an arrangement is as follows. Let S contain elements of a cyber kill chain phases. The number of phases would be $|S|$. Let u be a word describing a sequence of phases that need to proceed an attack pattern described by the phases of word v. Then, a valid attack w containing v, is the one where u is the prefix of v, that is $u = vw^{-1}$.

Let w_R be the actual attack and w_T the attack pattern specified by the generated timeline. w_R is a member of A_S, but for w_T the following can hold:

- $w_R = w_T$. In this case the timeline describes the attack accurately, and the quality of the CTI can be considered as high;
- $w_R \neq w_T$ and $w_T \in A_S$. In this case the timeline describes a valid attack, but not the actual one. The CTI can be considered to be of a medium quality;
- $w_R \neq w_T$, and $w_T \notin A_S$. In this case the timeline describes an invalid, unrealistic type of attack and the CTI can be considered to be of a low quality.

Moreover, in the case where $w_R \neq w_S$, a distance metric can be applied in order to establish the proximity of the timeline CTI to the actual attack, as described by the narrative.

This research also leverages attack trees in order to enrich the description of an attack and identify potential TTPs. In a general setting, attack trees have significant drawbacks mainly due to the complexity of attacks, making them an uninviting tool for security assessment and management exercises. Attack trees can be effective when the complexity is relatively low, or when we study a particular attack subset. As such, whilst attack trees are not suitable for security assessments, they can be employed in post-mortem analysis of security incidents, following the investigation and to contribute to the "lessons learned" phase of the incident response process [17]. By doing this, we argue that TTPs will be evident in the generated attack trees, as they will describe the actual attack rather than some instance of a likely attack.

3.2 Methodology

The followed methodology for this research starts with importing the STIX documents given in the dataset section. As explained in the challenges section, the indicators given in the CTI file are considered as low-pain intelligence data. It is relatively easy for an attacker to evade the security measurements generated for these indicators comparing to the case where the TTP and modus operandi of the adversary is known. In this study, the processed STIX documents are converted to an attack tree on the time axis and an attack vector formed from unified kill chain phases of attack patterns ordered by the timestamps of indicators. The methodology is given in Fig. 1.

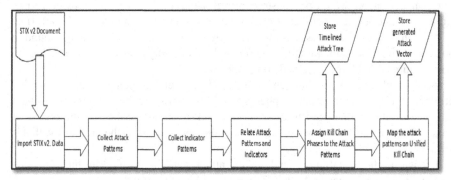

Fig. 1. The general methodology of generation of the timelines attack trees and kill-chain attack vectors

3.3 Construction of Timeline of Attack Trees and Kill Chain Attack Vectors

For the demonstration of our methodology, this section contains the construction of the attack trees and the kill chain vectors for a simple STIX file provided within the dataset by the UNIT42 group [19]. This STIX file is a fictional one created to demonstrate their playbook viewer given in the references. The attack patterns from MITRE's ATT&CK Framework provided in this scenario is given in Table 1. This CTI document describes an attack campaign where a spearfishing (hyper)link is sent and through scripting on commonly used ports more than one communication is established to the targeted system. Indicators in this event shows that at least one screenshot is captured from the targeted system as an objective.

In the first step of the methodology, the attack patterns and indicators are filtered from the CTI document and merged. There are eight indicators given for the above five attack patterns. The indicators are as follows in Table 2. As can be seen from the table, there are three dates provided for each indicator. 'Created' date represents the timestamp

Table 1. Attack patterns provided for the simple-playbook

Attack technique code	Description
T1192	Spearphishing link
T1043	Commonly used port
T1064	Scripting
T1108	Redundant access
T1113	Screen capture

Table 2. Indicators for the simple-playbook scenario

Name	Created	Modified	Valid from
<SHA1 value placeholder>	2019-06-25 18:13:55.619	2019-06-25 18:24:15.157	2019-06-25 18:13:55.619
https://verysuspicious.com:443	2019-06-25 18:10:03.432	2019-06-25 18:24:15.157	2019-06-25 18:10:03.432
https://notsuspicious.com/givecreds	2019-06-25 18:07:17.633	2019-06-25 18:24:15.157	2019-06-25 18:07:17.633
https://dailymemes.net	2019-06-25 18:15:42.452	2019-06-25 18:24:15.157	2019-06-25 18:15:42.452
<SHA1 value placeholder>	2019-06-25 18:17:50.493	2019-06-25 18:24:15.157	2019-06-25 18:17:50.493
<SHA1 value placeholder>	2019-06-25 18:21:42.106	2019-06-25 18:24:15.157	2019-06-25 18:21:42.106
https://canhazcreds.xyz/kthanks	2019-06-25 18:23:00.359	2019-06-25 18:24:15.157	2019-06-25 18:23:00.359

when the indicator is created, 'modified' is the last modified date and the date 'valid from' represents the date that this indicator is started to be observed.

As can be seen from the indicators, the attack campaign ends within approximately 20 min and the attack patterns containing indicators are given in the timeline. The number of indicators shows the count of the indicators grouped by the timestamps. If there are more than one type of attack pattern for a given timestamp, they are separated with a comma as can be seen from Fig. 2.

In order to further map this information onto vector space, the attack patterns are vectorized using unified kill chain. The unified kill chain is a merge of kill chain standards that show some degree of recognition and adoption by the security community. As it will be explained in the next section on dataset details, the data that this proof of concept work has been implemented on is using ATT&CK and Lockheed kill chain definitions. Thus, how these two definitions are merged in this research is shown on the following Table 3. This merging implementation is adapted from the work of [16].

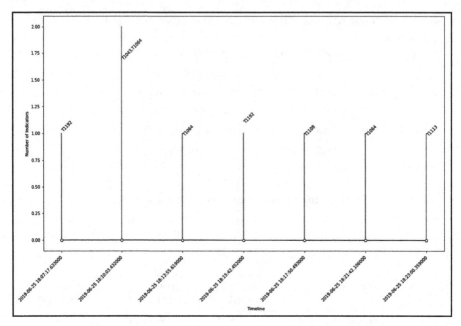

Fig. 2. Resulting timeline of the simple-playbook file.

Hence, following this vectorization scheme, the attack vector of the simple-playbook document maps onto the following vector:

$$v_{simpleplaybook} = (2, 14, 7, 5, 7, 5, 2, 7, 9, 7, \ 5, 13)$$

3.4   Utilization of Levenshtein Metric

As given in the introduction, a good level of maturity is reached among the cyber threat intelligence sharing platforms on which format to share the intelligence data. However, to measure the quality of the intelligence data and analyzing its merits is still an open question. By providing an approach to mapping onto vector space and a metric integration, this study aims to extend the literature further on this ramification. For this aim, the Levenshtein Metric on vectors is chosen to be similarity metric. The pseudocode of the straightforward calculation of this metric is given as follows:

Table 3. Unified Kill Chain Mapping

ATT&CK	Lockheed-martin	Unified kill chain	Vectorization
Initial access	Reconnaissance	Reconnaissance	0
Execution	Weaponization	Weaponization	1
Persistence	Delivery	Initial access	2
Privilege escalation	Exploitation	Delivery	3
Defense evasion	Installation	Exploitation	4
Credential access	Command and control	Execution	5
Discovery	Actions on objectives	Privilege escalation	6
Lateral movement		Defense evasion	7
Collection		Installation	8
Exfiltration		Persistence	9
Command and control		Credential access	10
Impact		Discovery	11
		Lateral movement	12
		Collection	13
		Command and control	14
		Exfiltration	15
		Impact	16
		Actions on objectives	17

Input: $w_R, w_S \in A_S$, two attack vectors with length $|r|$ and $|s|$ respectively,
Output: Levenshtein distance of these two vectors

```
Procedure levenshtein(w_R,w_S):
    |r| = len(w_R) + 1, |s| = len(w_S) + 1
    matrix = Zero matrix with dimensions (|r|, |s|).
    for x in range(0, |r|):
        matrix [x, 0] = x
    for y in range(0, |s|):
        matrix [0, y] = y
    for x in range(1, |r|):
        for y in range(1, |s|):
            if w_R[x-1] == w_S[y-1]:
                matrix [x,y] = min(matrix[x-1, y] + 1,
                                    matrix[x-1, y-1],
                                    matrix[x, y-1] + 1)
            else:
                matrix [x,y] = min(matrix[x-1,y] + 1,
                                    matrix[x-1,y-1] + 1,
                                    matrix[x,y-1] + 1)
    return (matrix[|r| - 1, |s| - 1])
```

In an ideal analysis, where all the evidence and indicators are extracted in the right chronological order, we expect the order of the attack vector to have a small distance from the order of the kill chain. However, in a real-world scenario, it is rarely the case; the timelines of the indicators are not aligned in most cases. This can be witnessed not only in the CTI dataset of the Unit 42 [19] but also in other datasets as well. To converge the ideal chronological order from the kill chain phases, application of machine or deep learning algorithms over huge datasets which is out of the scope of this paper is required. Despite the limiting factors of our metric, to show our methodology, we used the order of the unified kill chain phases described in Sect. 3b.

The timeline of the kill chain might not be aligned for several reasons. For example, in the attack patterns of muddy water CTI document, see Fig. 3, the indicators begin with the identification of a communication channel between the targeted system and the malicious adversary. This is the point where the forensics investigation starts. After the point of the discovery, other indicators and evidence are collected and mapped on the timeline. In an ideal and successful incident identification and response, it is expected to trace an attack event from the beginning of the kill chain (i.e. the reconnaissance stage) or at least at the delivery stage of the kill chain and continue tracing the stages of the kill chain in the order that derives from the theoretical analysis of kill chains.

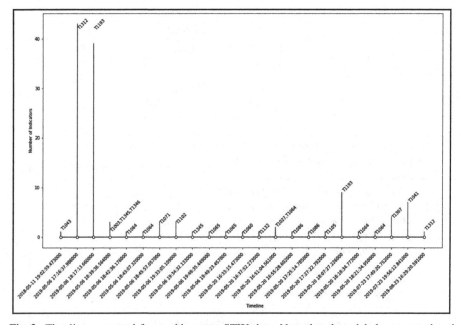

Fig. 3. Timeline generated for muddy water STIX data. Note that the x labels are not placed proportionally for the sake of readability. The indicators timeline starts with the discovery of an attack pattern T1043 – commonly used port.

The analysis utilized in this research also reflects on the data quality dimensions directly. The quality dimensions of completeness and accuracy can be considered of "higher" quality by having at least one indicator on every possible kill chain; timeliness-having started recording attackers' actions and sharing accordingly through indicators from the delivery phase; relevance and consistency – presenting only the related indicators in a CTI document and not inserting unrelated events.

4 Evaluation

4.1 Dataset

The dataset used in this research is gathered from the STIX documents created from the Palo Alto Unit 42 cyber security reports. These reports and the STIX data can be found in [19]. STIX v2 [18] documents are composed of entries from the types of indicators, observables, attack patterns, incidents, threat actors, reports, campaigns, exploit targets, packages, course of actions, TTPs (tactics, techniques and procedures).

There are 23 CTI document provided in STIX v0.2 format constructed from campaigns of advanced persistence threats (APTs); regarding the intelligence data, these files contain indicators formed of the malicious executables, payloads, malicious websites and IP addresses. These indicators are connected to the attack patterns from MITRE's ATT&CK framework through relationships within the CTI data [20].

4.2 Findings

In this section, two examples from the dataset are inspected and interpreted. The first one is adversary group named "Scarlet Mimic" and the attack timeline is given in Fig. 4.

By extraction of the TTP (can be seen in Table 3), we understand from the generated timeline that the analysis starts from the discovery of persistence phase of the attack pattern "T1060 – Registry Run Keys/Start-up Folder". This leads to the revealing of custom payloads which is given by the attack pattern T1345. Next step is the utilization of obfuscation in the payloads and malicious files. Their attack pattern includes usage of defense evasion techniques by leveraging the standard communication and cryptographic protocols through the uncommonly used ports (Fig. 5).

By analyzing the chronological order of the events, we can deduce the timeline from the attack pattern. This analysis gives us an overview of Sofacy's deployment. As can be seen, the adversary initiates the attack by sending an email which contains a malicious code (T1367, T1193). Additionally, the tactic id, T1319, identifies the fact that the script in the malicious attachment is obfuscated. This is a common technique to avoid AV detection. The malicious code affects the.dll Rundll32 (tactic id T1805). The purpose of the Rundll32 is to load and run 32-bit dynamic-link libraries (DLLs). From this attack pattern code, we can understand that some piece of malicious code is being installed in the infected computers. From the attack ID T1071 we conclude that the malware uses the application layer protocol (OSI layer 7 applications, such as HTTP, HTTPS, SMTP, or DNS) to communicate with the adversaries' command and control servers (T1094). Finally, with the information given from the attack pattern codes T1346 and T1112, we can observe that the malware code has features that render it persistent. The above information can offer to the analyst a quick overview of the Sofacy's malware features

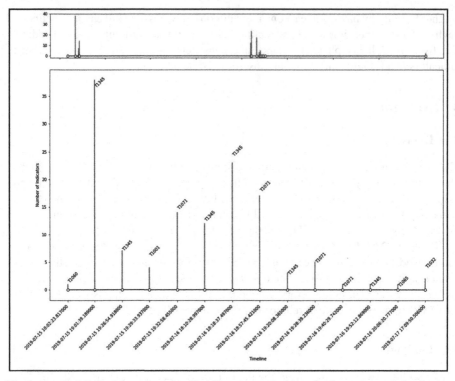

Fig. 4. Scarlet Mimic Adversary - timeline. The top graph shows the frequency and distribution of the attack patterns generated with the methodology described in Sect. 3. The timeline is then reformatted to the graph in the lower part of the image in order to improve the readability.

Table 4. Extracted TTP from the timeline of "Scarlet Mimic"

T1060	Registry run keys/startup folder.
T1345	Create custom payloads
T1001	Data obfuscation
T1071	Standard application layer protocol
T1065	Uncommonly used port
T1032	Standard cryptographic protocol

and operations in order to respond in a more organized and accurate manner, in case of an incident.

By utilizing the knowledge of the list of techniques (Table 4 and Table 5), the timeline and any constraint rules, we can obtain the following representations of TTPs in the form of an attack tree. The root of the tree is the goal which is set as the "deepest" observed phase of the kill chain (in this case Command and Control), whereas the leaves are the

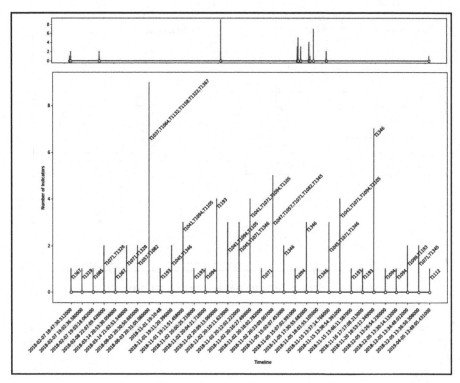

Fig. 5. Sofacy's timeline

Table 5. Extracted TTP from the timeline of "Sofacy"

T1367	Spearphishing messages with malicious attachments
T1319	Obfuscate or encrypt code
T1085	Rundll32
T1193	Spearphishing attachment
T1094	Custom command and control protocol
T1071	Standard application layer protocol
T1346	Obtain/re-use payloads
T1112	Modify registry

observed techniques prioritized through valid kill chain sequences (or words). Figure 6 illustrates the attack trees for both playbooks, Scarlet-Mimic and Sofacy.

Finally, we apply the Levenshtein algorithm on each attack in order to calculate the distance between the attack vector constructed from the kill chain phases and the order of the unified kill chain (Fig. 7). The bigger the distance of the attack vector from the unified kill chain, the more distorted the timeline could be from the actual chronology

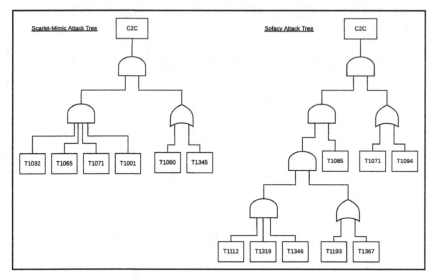

Fig. 6. Attack trees for Scarlet-Mimic and Sofacy playbooks.

of the attack. As can be seen in Fig. 7, the distance of 14 (observed in th3bug, chafer, darkhydrus) is recorded as the minimum distance. 51 is the highest distance observed in Sofacy.

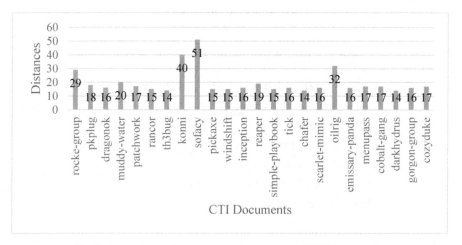

Fig. 7. Levenshtein distances for attack vectors of CTI documents.

5   Conclusion

In this paper, we presented an approach to represent and visualize CTI data for further analysis in a timely manner. The proposed method constructs a timeline and a unified kill chain using indicators of varying "pain" level, in order to reach to the highest level at the PoP (i.e. capturing the modus operandi by identifying the TTP patterns). The unified kill chain can be very useful in the hands of a security operations analyst. An analyst can use this more practical approach of the unified kill chain as guide to perform various of tasks in his day to day activities. An analyst can use the proposed methodology for prevention. Given a CTI document such as the "muddy waters" from Fig. 3 one can analyze and investigate the patterns. Having a timeline and the attack pattern codes in a single graph as shown in the Fig. 2, the analyst has a quick reference guide on how the cyberattack has been deployed and which attack patterns codes have been deployed in each stage. Then the analyst can extract valuable information related to the attack pattern and use this information to create alerts, in a Security Information and Event Management (SIEM) in order to identify or even to prevent future attacks that follow similar patterns.

The proposed method may also be of use in incident response. The analyst can compare his incident flags and attack patterns, with the pre-analyzed datasets form the previous analyses and observe if any of the previous attack patterns match the current attack pattern. Consequently, the necessary counter measures and mitigation strategies can be decided.

As a future work, mathematical basis for this research is going to be extended with possible directions of combinatorics on words, graph theoretical applications and hidden markov models for kill chain phased attack trees.

Acknowledgements. This work has received funding from the European Union's Horizon 2020 research and innovation program under the grant agreement no. 830943 (ECHO).

References

1. ENISA: ENISA threat landscape report 2018. (2019). https://doi.org/10.2824/622757
2. Hutchins, E., Cloppert, M., Amin, R.: Intelligence-driven computer network defense informed by analysis of adversary campaigns and intrusion kill chains. Lead Issues Inf. Warf. Secur. Res. 1(1), 80–106 (2011)
3. Qiang, L., Zhengwei, J., Zeming, Y., Baoxu, L., Xin, W., Yunan, Z.: A quality evaluation method of cyber threat intelligence in user perspective. In: Proceedings of 17th IEEE International Conference on Trust, Security and Privacy in Computing and Communications/12th IEEE International Conference on Big Data Science and Engineering Trust, pp. 269–276 (2018). https://doi.org/10.1109/TrustCom/BigDataSE.2018.00049
4. Liao, X., Yuan, K., Wang, X., Li, Z., Xing, L., Beyah, R.: Acing the IOC game : toward automatic discovery and analysis of open-source cyber threat intelligence, pp. 755–766 (2016)
5. Bianco, D.: Pyramid of Pain. http://detect-respond.blogspot.gr/2013/03/the-pyramid-of-pain.html. Accessed 02 March 2020
6. ENISA: Detect, SHARE, protect solutions for improving threat data exchange among CERTs (2013)
7. ENISA: Exploring the opportunities and limitations of current Threat Intelligence Platforms, p. 42 (2017)
8. Rahayu, S.S., Robiah, Y.: Cyber threat intelligence – issue and challenges cyber threat intelligence – issue and challenges, pp. 371–379 (2018). https://doi.org/10.11591/ijeecs.v10.i1

9. Ponemon Institute: Third annual study on exchanging cyber threat intelligence: there has to be a better way (2018)
10. ENISA: Actionable information for security incident response (2014)
11. Kompanek, A.: Evaluating threat intelligence feeds. FIRST technical colloquium for threat intelligence (2016)
12. Faiella, M., Gonzalez-granadillo, G.: Enriching threat intelligence platforms capabilities (2016)
13. Sillaber, C., Sauerwein, C., Mussmann, A., Breu, R.: Data quality challenges and future research directions in threat intelligence sharing practice, pp. 65–70 (2016)
14. Grispos, G., Glisson, W.B., Storer, T.: How good is your data? Investigating the quality of data generated during security incident response investigations (2019)
15. Sadiq, S.: Handbook of Data Quality. Springer, Heidelberg (2013)
16. Pols, P.: The unified kill chain. Cyber Security Academy (2017)
17. Cichonski, P.: Computer security incident handling guide: recommendations of the national institute of standards and technology. NIST Spec. Publ. **800–61**, 79 (2012). https://doi.org/10.6028/NIST.SP.800-61r2
18. MITRE: A structured language for cyber threat intelligence. https://oasis-open.github.io/cti-documentation/. Accessed 2 March 2020
19. Unit 42: Unit 42 playbook viewer. https://pan-unit42.github.io/playbook_viewer/. Accessed 2 March 2020
20. MITRE: ATT&CK framework. https://attack.mitre.org/. Accessed 02 March 2020

A Novel Watermark Method for Image Protection Based on Periodic Haar Piecewise-Linear Transform

Andrzej Dziech⬤, Piotr Bogacki$^{(\boxtimes)}$⬤, and Jan Derkacz⬤

The Faculty of Computer Science, Electronics and Telecommunications,
The Department of Telecommunications,
AGH University of Science and Technology, Krakow, Poland
{dziech,derkacz}@kt.agh.edu.pl, pbogacki@agh.edu.pl

Abstract. In this paper, a novel watermark method based on Periodic Haar Piecewise-Linear (PHL) transform is proposed. This solution provides high embedding capacity with negligible degradation of image quality. The PHL transform is based on integration and differentiation of periodic Haar functions. Its major advantage is the fact that it is notably fast and easy to implement and beyond that it provides good reconstruction quality. The procedure for constructing two-dimensional PHL functions and transform is introduced.

Furthermore, the analysis of embedding capacity and imperceptibility of the proposed algorithm is performed. PSNR (Peak Signal to Noise Ratio) is taken as a measure of perceptual quality. The method is compared with DCT approach in certain aspects of watermarking algorithms.

Keywords: Watermarking · Data embedding · Multimedia systems · PHL transform · Image processing

1 Introduction

Digital watermarking is a technique of embedding secret information into multimedia objects, such as images, videos, voice recordings or other audio files. Nowadays, there is a high pressure put on the security and privacy aspects in the cyber world. Watermarking technology provides protection of the digital content against undesired manipulations, infringement of copyrights or disclosure of private information. Watermarking solutions may be also applied for steganography purposes or for private and sensitive data anonymization and protection.

An effective watermarking algorithm should satisfy the imperceptibility and robustness requirements. This means that the inserted information should not degrade the visual perception of an original image, Moreover, it should be difficult to remove the watermark from any multimedia object by an unauthorized person or group.

Embedding a watermark into an image can be realized in spatial or transform domain. Usually, spatial domain techniques result in direct changes of

© Springer Nature Switzerland AG 2020
A. Dziech et al. (Eds.): MCSS 2020, CCIS 1284, pp. 67–77, 2020.
https://doi.org/10.1007/978-3-030-59000-0_6

image data, such as its brightness, color bands or a combination of both. Typical method for inserting a watermark in the spatial domain is the Least Significant Bit (LSB) method where the hidden information is embedded into least significant bits of pixels from the host image. Transform domain methods are based on the changes of spectral coefficients in the given transform domain. The image with inserted watermark is obtained by performing the corresponding inverse transform. The watermarks inserted in the transform domains are usually more robust than the watermarks embedded in the spatial domain [1,2].

The most common transform domains used for watermark embedding are discrete cosine transform (DCT) [3–6], discrete wavelet transform (DWT) [7,8] and discrete Fourier transform (DFT) [9,10]. Hybrid approaches might be also used, e.g. a combination of the DCT and DWT transforms [11–13]. Sometimes, they are also combined with other techniques, e.g. discrete fractional random transform (DFRNT) [2] or singular value decomposition (SVD) [14].

In [15] Yang et al. proposed a method for reversible data hiding in images by symmetrical histogram expansion in the domain of Piecewise-Linear Haar transform. Yan et al. in [16] also used this transform for data hiding algorithm which embeds the secret information into the least significant bits of the transform coefficients for audio signals.

Periodic Haar Piecewise-Linear (PHL) transform in the literature is only mentioned in case of image compression schemes [17].

The paper is organized as follows. The following section is devoted to Periodic Haar Piecewise-Linear Transform. Section 3 describes a new proposed method for data embedding. Section 4 contains the experimental results and comparisons of the proposed solution with the DCT approach. Finally, Sect. 5 presents the conclusions and future work.

2 Periodic Haar Piecewise-Linear PHL Transform

In this section the proposed Periodic Haar Piecewise-Linear (PHL) functions and transform will be introduced. The set of PHL functions is obtained by integrating the well known set of Haar functions. The set of N Haar functions is defined by:

$$har(0, t) = 1 \qquad \text{for } t \in (-\infty, \infty), \quad \text{usually } T = 1 \tag{1a}$$

$$har(i, t) = \begin{cases} 2^{\frac{k-1}{2}} & \text{for } [\frac{i}{2^{k-1}} - 1] \le t < [\frac{i+\frac{1}{2}}{2^k - 1}] \\ -2^{\frac{k-1}{2}} & \text{for } [\frac{i+\frac{1}{2}}{2^{k-1}} - 1] \le t < [\frac{i+1}{2^{k-1}} - 1] \\ 0 & \text{otherwise} \end{cases} \tag{1b}$$

where $\quad 0 < k < \log_2 N, \quad 1 \le i \le 2^k$

The set of periodic Haar Piecewise-Linear functions is determined by:

$$PHL(0,t) = 1 \quad t \in (-\infty, \infty) \tag{2a}$$

$$PHL(1,t) = [\frac{2}{T} \int\limits_{mT}^{t+mT} har(1,\tau)d\tau] + \frac{1}{2} \tag{2b}$$

$$PHL(i+1,t) = \frac{2^{k+1}}{T} \int\limits_{mT}^{t+mT} har(i+1,\tau)d\tau \tag{2c}$$

where $i = 1, 2, ..., N-2$; $k = 1, 2, ..., \log_2 N - 1$; $m = 0, 1, 2, ...$
       k - index of group of PHL functions
       m - number of period

The normalization factor (2^{k+1}) is applied to normalize the maximum amplitude of the PHL functions. The derivatives (in distributive sense) of Haar functions are represented by a set of delta impulses with proper coefficients. The set of PHL functions is linearly independent but not orthogonal.

2.1   Two-Dimensional PHL Functions and Transform

The set of 2D PHL functions is obtained by integrating 2D Haar functions as follows:

$$PHL(0,0,x,y) = 1 \qquad x \in (-\infty, \infty), \quad y \in (-\infty, \infty) \tag{3a}$$

$$PHL(1,1,x,y) = \frac{2}{T_x} \cdot \frac{2}{T_y} \int\limits_{mT_x}^{x+mT_x} \int\limits_{mT_y}^{y+mT_y} har(1,1,\tau_x,\tau_y)d\tau_x d\tau_y + \frac{1}{2} \tag{3b}$$

$$PHL(i+1,j+1,x,y) = \frac{2^{k_x+1}}{T_x} \cdot \frac{2^{k_y+1}}{T_y} \int\limits_{mT_x}^{x+mT_x} \int\limits_{mT_y}^{y+mT_y} har(i+1,j+1,\tau_x,\tau_y)d\tau_x d\tau_y \tag{3c}$$

where $k_x = 1, 2, ..., \log_2 N_x - 1,$ $k_x = 1, 2, ..., \log_2 N_y - 1$
       $i = 1, 2, ..., N_x - 2,$ $j = 1, 2, ..., N_y - 2$
       $har(i+1, j+1, \tau_x, \tau_y)$ - 2D Haar functions
       $har(i+1, \tau_x), har(j+1, \tau_y)$ - 1D Haar functions
       k_x, k_y - indices of groups of 2D PHL functions
       T_x, T_y - periods of PHL functions
       m - number of period

The set of 2D PHL functions is linearly independent but not orthogonal within the periods T_x, T_y. Expansion of a continuous 2D signal $f(x,y)$ into 2D PHL series is given by:

$$f(x,y) = \sum_{i=0}^{\infty} \sum_{j=0}^{\infty} c_{i,j} \cdot PHL(i,j,x,y) \tag{4}$$

where the 2D PHL functions can be treated as a product of 1D PHL functions.

$$PHL(i, j, x, y) = PHL(i, x) \cdot PHL(j, y) \tag{5}$$

The set of coefficients $c_{i,j}$ representing the PHL spectrum may be determined as follows:

$$c_{0,0} = f(0,0) \tag{6a}$$

$$c_{i,j} = \frac{1}{2^{k_x+1}} \frac{1}{2^{k_y+1}} \int_0^{T_x} \int_0^{T_y} f(x,y) \cdot har'(i,j,x,y) dx dy \tag{6b}$$

$$c_{i,0} = -\frac{1}{2^{k_x+1}} \int_0^{T_x} f(x,y) \cdot har'(i,x) dx \tag{6c}$$

$$c_{0,j} = -\frac{1}{2^{k_y+1}} \int_0^{T_y} f(x,y) \cdot har'(j,y) dy \tag{6d}$$

where $har'(i, j, x, y)$ - derivatives (in distributive sense) of 2D Haar functions.

Since the derivatives of Haar functions are treated in distributive sense, Eqs. 6(a-d) can be rewritten as:

$$c_{0,0} = f(0,0) \tag{7a}$$

$$c_{i,j} = \frac{1}{2^{k_x+1}} \frac{1}{2^{k_y+1}} \sum_{n=0}^{N_x-1} \sum_{m=0}^{N_y-1} f(n,m) \cdot har'(i,j,n,m) \tag{7b}$$

$$c_{i,0} = -\frac{1}{2^{k_x+1}} \sum_{n=0}^{N_x-1} f(n,m) \cdot har'(i,n) \tag{7c}$$

$$c_{0,j} = -\frac{1}{2^{k_y+1}} \sum_{m=0}^{N_y-1} f(n,m) \cdot har'(j,m) \tag{7d}$$

where $i = 1, 2, ..., N_x - 1,$ $j = 1, 2, ..., N_y - 1$
$k_x = 1, 2, ..., \log_2 N_x - 1,$ $k_x = 1, 2, ..., \log_2 N_y - 1$
$f(n, m)$ - discrete 2D signal obtained by sampling $f(x, y)$

Now we write the matrix equation of the 2D PHL transform in the following form:

a. Forward transform

$$[C(N_x, N_y)] = [-\frac{1}{2^{k_y+1}}][PHL(N_y)][F(N_x, N_y)][PHL(N_x)]^T [-\frac{1}{2^{k_x+1}}]^T \tag{8}$$

b. Inverse transform

$$[F(N_x, N_y)] = [IPHL(N_y)][C(N_x, N_y)][IPHL(N_x)]^T \tag{9}$$

where $[F(N_x, N_y)]$ - matrix of 2D signal
            $[C(N_x, N_y)]$ - matrix of coefficients (2D PHL spectrum)
            $[PHL(N_y)], [PHL(N_x)]$ - matrices of 1D PHL forward transform
            $[IPHL(N_y)], [IPHL(N_x)]$ - matrices of 1D PHL inverse transform
            $[-\frac{1}{2^{k_y+1}}], [-\frac{1}{2^{k_x+1}}]$ - diagonal matrices of normalization

The matrix of the forward transform is constructed in such a way that, except for the first row in which the first element is equal to one and the other elements are zeros, all other rows of the matrix are represented by derivatives (in distributive sense) of periodic Haar functions. The inverse transform matrix $[IPHL(N)]$, is obtained in such a way that the rows of the matrix are represented by means of PHL functions for the same samples. For illustration, the $[PHL(N)]$ and $[IPHL(N)]$ matrices, for $N = 8$, are shown below:

$$[PHL(8)] = \begin{bmatrix} 1 & 0 & 0 & 0 & 0 & 0 & 0 & 0 \\ 2 & 0 & 0 & 0 & -2 & 0 & 0 & 0 \\ \sqrt{2} & 0 & -2\sqrt{2} & 0 & \sqrt{2} & 0 & 0 & 0 \\ \sqrt{2} & 0 & 0 & 0 & \sqrt{2} & 0 & -2\sqrt{2} & 0 \\ 2 & -4 & 2 & 0 & 0 & 0 & 0 & 0 \\ 0 & 0 & 2 & -4 & 2 & 0 & 0 & 0 \\ 0 & 0 & 0 & 0 & 2 & -4 & 2 & 0 \\ 2 & 0 & 0 & 0 & 0 & 0 & 2 & -4 \end{bmatrix} \tag{10}$$

$$[IPHL(8)] = \begin{bmatrix} 1 & 0 & 0 & 0 & 0 & 0 & 0 & 0 \\ 1 & \frac{1}{4} & \frac{\sqrt{2}}{2} & 0 & 2 & 0 & 0 & 0 \\ 1 & \frac{1}{2} & \sqrt{2} & 0 & 0 & 0 & 0 & 0 \\ 1 & \frac{3}{4} & \frac{\sqrt{2}}{2} & 0 & 0 & 2 & 0 & 0 \\ 1 & 1 & 0 & 0 & 0 & 0 & 0 & 0 \\ 1 & \frac{3}{4} & 0 & \frac{\sqrt{2}}{2} & 0 & 0 & 2 & 0 \\ 1 & \frac{1}{2} & 0 & \sqrt{2} & 0 & 0 & 0 & 0 \\ 1 & \frac{1}{4} & 0 & \frac{\sqrt{2}}{2} & 0 & 0 & 0 & 2 \end{bmatrix} \tag{11}$$

$$\left[-\frac{1}{2^{k+1}}\right] = \begin{bmatrix} 1 & 0 & 0 & 0 & 0 & 0 & 0 & 0 \\ 0 & -\frac{1}{2} & 0 & 0 & 0 & 0 & 0 & 0 \\ 0 & 0 & -\frac{1}{4} & 0 & 0 & 0 & 0 & 0 \\ 0 & 0 & 0 & -\frac{1}{4} & 0 & 0 & 0 & 0 \\ 0 & 0 & 0 & 0 & -\frac{1}{8} & 0 & 0 & 0 \\ 0 & 0 & 0 & 0 & 0 & -\frac{1}{8} & 0 & 0 \\ 0 & 0 & 0 & 0 & 0 & 0 & -\frac{1}{8} & 0 \\ 0 & 0 & 0 & 0 & 0 & 0 & 0 & -\frac{1}{8} \end{bmatrix} \tag{12}$$

It can be seen that:

$$[-\frac{1}{2^{k+1}}][PHL(8)][IPHL(8)] = [I(N)] \tag{13}$$

where [I(N)] is the identity matrix.

The periodic piecewise-linear transforms are shown to have an order (N) while the non-periodic piecewise-linear transforms have an order $(N + 1)$. This ensures that periodic piecewise-linear transforms will be more suitable for applications in digital signal and image processing where the dimension of data is usually an integer power of 2.

3   Data Embedding in PHL Spectrum

The watermarking method, proposed in this paper, is based on embedding a secret information in the Periodic Haar Piecewise-Linear Transform domain. It is assumed that only the luminance channel of the input image, representing a grayscale image, is processed. In order to get PHL spectrum of the given image, the input image needs to be firstly divided into smaller blocks with the size: 8 × 8 pixels. Each block is then processed by calculating the forward PHL transform, using Eq. 8 and the matrices 10 and 11.

As a result, after applying the above operation to the analyzed signal, we obtain its spectral representation in the PHL transform domain. Typical signal spectra usually show the ability to cumulate the signal energy in a limited number of spectral coefficients [19, 20].

In [18] the PHL transform is used for image compression purposes. In this case, the spectral coefficients above a concrete threshold are retained while all others are set to zero. Based on that approach, in our method we embed the watermark by modifying the coefficients with relatively low values. In order to perform this step, the coefficients of the PHL spectrum matrix are grouped into channels. Each channel contains all the spectral coefficients taken from the same position of each block processed in the forward transform step. This results in obtaining 64 PHL transform channels. The analysis of a set of diverse images shows that the top-left channel contains most of the signal energy. It is well depicted in Fig. 2 which presents the PHL spectrum coefficients grouped into 64 channels. They were calculated for the image shown in Fig. 1. Furthermore, the tests indicate that the blocks: 37–39, 45–47 and 53–55, highlighted in Fig. 3, are usually in the area of our interest. This was deduced based on analyzing the spectra of various images with different content and characteristics. In order to find the best channel for inserting the secret information, the mean of all absolute values inside each block is calculated. The channel with the lowest mean is selected for the following data embedding process.

The coefficients of the selected channel are substituted by the consecutive bit values of the information that is to be hidden in the image. Afterwards, the channel coefficients are relocated to their original positions. Then the inverse PHL transform is performed resulting in the image with an embedded watermark.

Fig. 1. Sample image: landscape.

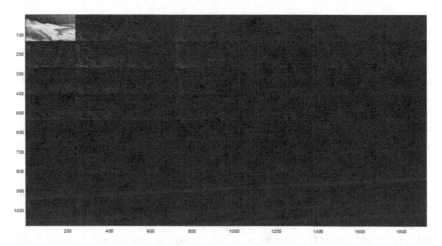

Fig. 2. PHL spectrum coefficients grouped into channels.

In order to recover the embedded information, one needs to perform the same steps as previously - performing the forward transform, grouping the PHL coefficients into channels and finally extracting information from the given channel.

The channel in which the data is inserted can be adaptively selected by analyzing the values of the coefficients, as described earlier, or can be selected as one of the possible nine blocks and can be treated as an extra key at the watermark extraction phase.

1	9	17	25	33	41	49	57
2	10	18	26	34	42	50	58
3	11	19	27	35	43	51	59
4	12	20	28	36	44	52	60
5	13	21	29	37	45	53	61
6	14	22	30	38	46	54	62
7	15	23	31	39	47	55	63
8	16	24	32	40	48	56	64

Fig. 3. Blocks selected for data embedding.

4   Experimental Results

The verification of the proposed solution is based on the measurement of the visual quality of an image with a watermark in relation with the total size of the inserted information. Additionally, bit error rate is also considered for different sizes of a watermark. Both measurements were performed for a watermark inserted in DCT and PHL transform domains in order to compare the performance of these two data embedding techniques. For tests purposes, the embedded data is just a random bit stream. The tests were performed in MATLAB environment. The referenced DCT method is the one inspired by [3].

The relation between PSNR ratio and the size of a watermark is presented in Fig. 4. It can be observed that an image with a watermark inserted in PHL spectrum has much better perceptual quality than the one embedded in DCT domain. However, both techniques provide satisfying results as far as the imperceptibility of a watermark is concerned.

The relation between BER ratio and the length of a hidden bit stream is shown in Fig. 5. It can be seen that both methods enable relatively high capacity of the inserted information while, simultaneously, guarantee low bit error rate. In case of PHL approach, BER does not exceed 0.1% in all cases with total length of the watermark bit stream ranging from 10000 to 30000 bits. Although, a watermark embedded in PHL domain seems to be more reliable, both approaches are useful when the high amount of information needs to be hidden in an image.

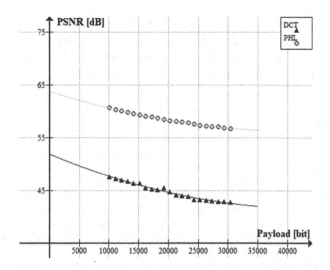

Fig. 4. Relation between PSNR ratio and the watermark capacity (PHL vs DCT).

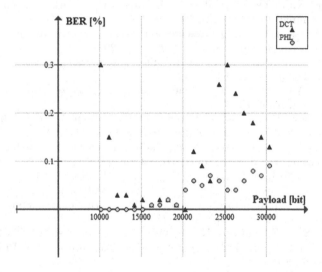

Fig. 5. Relation between BER ratio and the watermark capacity (PHL vs DCT).

5   Conclusions and Future Work

We have presented a novel watermarking algorithm which is based on embedding secret information in the PHL transform domain. The method provides high capacity of the embedded information and at the same time fulfills the initially defined requirements of low BER and high perceptual quality. Therefore, it is a promising technique that could be used in a wide range of multimedia systems and services.

Further steps will include increasing embedding capacity by better distribution of inserted data in the PHL spectrum. Furthermore, potential improvements in order to assure robustness against various attacks will be analyzed. Finally, we expect to apply our method to many watermarking applications in the near future.

References

1. Sharma, P.K., Sau, P.C., Sharma, D.: Digital image watermarking: an approach by different transforms using level indicator. In: 2015 Communication, Control and Intelligent Systems (CCIS), pp. 259–263, Mathura (2015)
2. Zhou, N.R., Hou, W.M.X., Wen, R.H., Zou, W.P.: Imperceptible digital watermarking scheme in multiple transform domains. Multimed. Tools Appl. **77**(23), 30251–30267 (2018). https://doi.org/10.1007/s11042-018-6128-9
3. Lan, T.-H., Tewfik, A.H.: A novel high-capacity data-embedding system. IEEE Trans. Image Process. **15**(8), 2431–2440 (2006)
4. Suhail, M.A., Obaidat, M.S.: Digital watermarking-based DCT and JPEG model. IEEE Trans. Instrum. Meas. **52**(5), 1640–1647 (2003)
5. Li, H., Guo, X.: Embedding and extracting digital watermark based on DCT algorithm. J. Comput. Commun. **06**, 287–298 (2018)
6. Xu, Z.J., Wang, Z.Z., Lu, Q.: Research on image watermarking algorithm based on DCT. Procedia Environ. Sci. **10**, 1129–1135 (2011)
7. Candik, M., Matus, E., Levicky, D.: Digital watermarking in wavelet transform domain. Radioengineering **10**, 1–4 (2001)
8. Narang, M., Vashisth, S.: Digital watermarking using discrete wavelet transform. Int. J. Comput. Appl. **74**, 34–38 (2013)
9. Pun, C.: A novel DFT-based digital watermarking system for images. In: 2006 8th International Conference On Signal Processing, Beijing (2006)
10. Liao, X., Li, K., Yin, J.: Separable data hiding in encrypted image based on compressive sensing and discrete fourier transform. Multimed. Tools Appl. **76**(20), 20739–20753 (2016). https://doi.org/10.1007/s11042-016-3971-4
11. Jiansheng, M., Sukang, L., Xiaomei, T. A digital watermarking algorithm based on DCT and DWT. In: Proceedings of the 2009 International Symposium on Web Information Systems and Applications (WISA 2009) (2009)
12. Hazim, N., Saeb, Z., Hameed, K.: Digital watermarking based on DWT (Discrete Wavelet Transform) and DCT (Discrete Cosine Transform). Int. J. Eng. Technol. **7**, 4825–4829 (2019)
13. Akter, A., Nur-E-Tajnina, Ullah, M.: Digital image watermarking based on DWT-DCT: Evaluate for a new embedding algorithm. In: 2014 International Conference on Informatics, Electronics & Vision (ICIEV) (2014)
14. He, Y., Hu, Y.: A proposed digital image watermarking based on DWT-DCT-SVD. In: 2018 2nd IEEE Advanced Information Management, Communicates, Electronic and Automation Control Conference (IMCEC), Xi'an, pp. 1214–1218 (2018)
15. Yang, L., Hao, P., Zhang, C.: Progressive reversible data hiding by symmetrical histogram expansion with piecewise-linear Haar transform. In: 2007 IEEE International Conference on Acoustics, Speech and Signal Processing - ICASSP 2007, Honolulu, HI, pp. II-265–II-268 (2007)
16. Yan, D., Wang, R.: Data hiding for audio based on piecewise linear haar transform. In: 2008 Congress on Image and Signal Processing, Sanya, Hainan, pp. 688–691 (2008)

17. Dziech, A., Tibken, B., Slusarczyk, P.: Image compression using periodic Haar piecewise-linear PHL transform. In: 2002 14th International Conference on Digital Signal Processing Proceedings. DSP 2002 (Cat. No. 02TH8628), Santorini, Greece, vol. 2, pp. 1333–1336 (2002)
18. Dziech, A., Ślusarczyk, P., Tibken, B.: Methods of image compression by PHL transform. J. Intell. Robot. System. **39**, 447–458 (2004)
19. Dziech, A., Belgassem, F., Nern, H.J.: Image data compression using zonal sampling and piecewise-linear transforms. J. Intell. Robot. Syst. **28**, 61–68 (2000)
20. Baran, R., Wiraszka, D.: Application of piecewise-linear transforms in threshold compression of contours. Logistyka **4**, 2341–2348 (2015)

Criticality Assessment of Critical Information Infrastructure Objects: A Category Based Methodology and Ukrainian Experience

Oleksandr Potii[1], Yurii Tsyplinskyi[2], Oleg Illiashenko[3]([✉]),
and Vyacheslav Kharchenko[3]

[1] JSC Institute of Information Technology, 12 Bakulina Street, Kharkiv 61066, Ukraine
potav@ua.fm
[2] State Special Communications Service of Ukraine, 13 Solomianska Street,
Kiev 03110, Ukraine
ts_yuri@meta.ua
[3] Department of Computer Systems, Networks and Cybersecurity, National Aerospace
University "KhAI", 17 Chkalova Street, Kharkiv 61070, Ukraine
{o.illiashenko,v.kharchenko}@csn.khai.edu

Abstract. The paper outlines the basic principles and assumptions used to assess the criticality of critical infrastructure object (CIO) and critical information infrastructure objects (CIIO). Methods for assigning critical information infrastructure objects to the criticality levels are described. The sequence of carrying out the criticality assessment of CIOs is provided. The recommendations concerning evolving regulation in the field of critical information infrastructure objects protection are given. According to the results of the research, several drafts of the Ukrainian state-level normative documents were developed such as "Classification of critical information infrastructure objects by severity (criticality)" and "Criteria and procedure for assigning critical information infrastructure objects to one of the significance (criticality)". The implementation of the developed documents is an important step in the construction of the Ukrainian state system of protection of critical information infrastructure.

Keywords: Critical information infrastructure · Critical infrastructure object · Categorization · Assessment techniques · Cybersecurity

1 Introduction

Assessing the criticality of critical infrastructure is an important task in the complex of tasks for ensuring the protection of the critical infrastructure of the state in EU [1–3], USA [4], Canada [5] and other countries [6]. It is important to understand the difference in methodological approaches to criticality assessment and risk assessment. When assessing the criticality of an infrastructure object, it shall be first taken into account the assessment of the negative impact of the object on the population, society, environment, state economy, national security, etc. That is, it is important to evaluate the damage that

A. Dziech et al. (Eds.): MCSS 2020, CCIS 1284, pp. 78–97, 2020.
https://doi.org/10.1007/978-3-030-59000-0_7

would be caused if the object ceased to function or its destruction. The probability of an incident is considered to be equal to one. When analyzing risks, threat to the objects is analyzed firstly and the damage that will be caused to the object itself is evaluated. This is a fundamental difference between approaches to criticality and risk assessment.

The main criteria used when to assess criticality according to [7, 8] are the following:

- impact on society (number of affected population, casualties, evacuation volumes, panic levels, etc.);
- economic effect – impact on GDP, losses of budgets on different levels, economic losses directly of the critical infrastructure object);
- environmental impact – losses from environmental incidents, costs of restoring safe living conditions;
- political influence – public confidence in state institutions, protest moods, influence on the international state of the state;
- impact on national security and defense; interdependence assessment – the impact on the functioning of other critical infrastructures.

The assessment also takes into account:

- scale of impact (cascading effects, geographical scale, etc.);
- temporal characteristics – the rate of manifestation of negative impact, duration of exposure, time to restore safe status.

Objectives of the paper are the following: to analyse the basic principles and assumptions used to assess the criticality of critical infrastructure object (CIO) and critical information infrastructure objects (CIIO), to suggest category based methodology of criticality CIO and CIIO assessment and to describe the recommendations concerning evolving regulation in the field of CIIO protection basing on Ukrainian experience.

2 Critical Information Infrastructure Object Approach General Characteristics

The best practices of the leading countries in the world (USA, Canada, EU countries, etc.), as well as the methodological recommendations of ENISA, say that an important step in the assessment is to identify a national list of critical infrastructure sectors and critical functions (services). This is also in line with the views of the Ukrainian expert community at this time [9]. Thus, the draft Law of Ukraine "On Critical Infrastructure and its Protection" (Article 32) establishes the organizational principles of critical infrastructure protection, including the following elements:

- critical infrastructure sectors identification, responsible individuals for critical infrastructure protection identification for specific sectors;
- categorization of critical infrastructure objects to determine the level of critical infrastructure security requirements, authorities and responsibilities of individuals;
- compiling and maintaining a national inventory of critical infrastructure objects;

- certification of critical infrastructure objects;
- introduction of criteria and methodology for assigning infrastructure objects to critical infrastructure.

This confirms the relevance of the research that is conducted on the development of a methodological apparatus for assessing the critical infrastructure objects criticality.

The Draft Law establishes the methodological and legal bases for assessing the criticality of the CIO. Figure 1 provides an ontological diagram of the subject area of the Critical Infrastructure according to the Law.

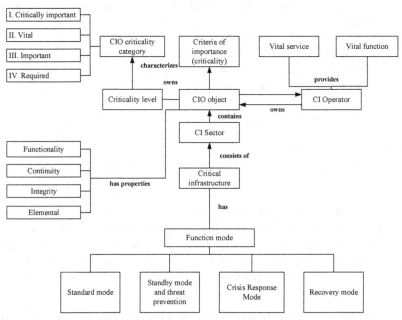

Fig. 1. Ontological model of the subject area of the draft Law «On critical infrastructure and its protection»

Critical infrastructure is a set of objects that are strategically important to the economy and national security of a state, the disruption of which can damage vital national interests. This definition integrates an objective and functional approach to interpreting critical infrastructure. Also, the definition does not contradict the definition given in EU regulations (EC Directive 2008/114). Namely, the critical infrastructure is the objects (material resources, fixed assets), systems or their parts, located in the EU Member States, which are essential for the maintenance of vital functions of society, health, safety, security, economic and social well-being of people. Disruption of their functioning will have a significant impact on the country and will lead to the inability to provide these functions.

Critical infrastructure consists of sectors which, in turn, contain critical infrastructure objects. Critical Infrastructure Sector is a set of critical infrastructure assets that belong to one sector of the economy and/or have a common functional orientation. In turn, critical infrastructure object is an integral part of critical infrastructure. Features such as functionality, continuity, integrity, and sustainability ensure the realization of vital national interests. These properties can be achieved in case of continuous and secure operation of critical infrastructure. *Critical infrastructure objects* are owned by *critical infrastructure operators* (owned or leased).

The Draft Law (Article 8) also specifies that CIO may include enterprises, institutions, organizations that carry out activities and provide services in the fields of energy, chemical industry, transport, information and telecommunication technologies, electronic communications, banking and financial sectors, providing services in the areas of centralized water supply and sewerage, supply of heat, hot water, electricity and gas, food production and health, have a strategic value for state economy and security.

Critical Information Infrastructure means a set of automated control systems for production and technological processes of critical infrastructure of Ukraine, and those that provide the interconnection of information and telecommunication networks, IT systems and communication networks intended for public administration solutions, defense and law enforcement (including national electronic information resources, state registries, databases, etc.). Critical Information Infrastructure is composed of information infrastructure objects used at critical infrastructure objects in their respective sectors.

The operator of the CI may be a state body, an enterprise, an institution, an organization, a legal individual and/or an individual responsible for the current functioning of the CIO. Operators provide vital services, disruptions and interruptions of which lead to rapid adverse effects on national security, and perform vital functions which violations lead to rapid adverse effects on national security.

In turn, the *CII operator* may be government bodies and institutions, businesses, legal or physical persons who own, lease, or otherwise own a CII object or who provide a CIIO interaction.

Thus, in Ukraine, the usage basics of the methodological principle of loss characterization due to the violation of the provision of vital services and functions are being formed, which also corresponds to the methodological approach in the EU countries. Based on the Draft Law and the opinion of domestic experts, it is an urgent task to formulate a list of sub-sectors and basic vital services and functions that need to be legally enshrined. This is the first step in implementing a common methodology for assessing the criticality of CIOs and CIIOs.

National lists of critical infrastructure sectors analysis has shown that the most common approach to defining them is the administrative approach (i.e. top-down). For example, EU countries use the indicative list of critical infrastructure sectors provided in the ENISA recommendations and agreed with the European Commission [10–12]. This approach allows:

- Not to spend resources to identify a national list of critical infrastructure sectors through a large body of peer review and approval;
- ensure harmonization of national lists of EU Member States;
- ensure that the methodological approach is critical to the pan-European approach and ensure that the structure of the national critical infrastructure is consistent with European Critical Infrastructure.

Table 1. List of critical infrastructure sectors of Ukraine and relevant vital services (functions)

№	Sector	Subsector	Vital service (function) type
1	Fuel and energy sector	Electricity	Electricity production
			Electricity sale
			Transmission systems and power supply management
			Electricity distribution system services
		Oil and petroleum products	Oil production
			Transmission of oil and petroleum products
			Oil purification, refining and treatment
			Oil pipelines operation
			Storage and supply of oil and petroleum products
		Gas	Gas production
			Gas treatment and purification
			Transmission (transit) of gas
			Gas distribution
			Gas transmission system operation
			Storage of natural gas
			Operation of natural gas liquefaction systems
			Selling gas to consumers
		Nuclear power	Production of electricity at nuclear power plants
			Nuclear power plant operation
2	Information sector	Information Technologies	Data processing services in data centers (DCs) and/or cloud storage
			Web services
			Electronic trust services

(continued)

Table 1. (*continued*)

№	Sector	Subsector	Vital service (function) type
		Telecommunications	Distribution of television (including digital) and radio signals
			Internet connection
			Internet Domain Name System (DNS) support
		Communication	Transmission of data through fixed, mobile and special communications and telecommunication networks
3	Life support networks	Drinking water	Production, transportation, and/or supply of drinking water
			Operation of district water supply systems
		Sewage	Wastewater collection and treatment
			Centralized drainage systems operation
		Heat supply	Heat production
			Operation of district heating systems
4	Food industry and agro-industrial complex		Production and processing of agricultural and/or food products
			Operation of large irrigation systems, canals
			Provision of food security of the state (storage of strategic state stocks and reserves)
			Food quality and safety assurance
5	Health care		Emergency medical care provision
			Hospital and outpatient treatment and other medical services provision

(*continued*)

Table 1. (*continued*)

№	Sector	Subsector	Vital service (function) type
			Production, procurement and supply of medicines, vaccines, blood and other medicines and medical equipment.
			eHealth Services provision
			Control of infectious diseases and/or epidemics
6	The financial sector		Banking services
			Insurance services
			Stock exchange services and stock market
7	Transportation and mail	Air transport	Air traffic control
			Air transportation (air transport work)
			Airports and ancillary facilities operating at airports
		Road transport	Bus transportation services (long distance, international and tourist transportation)
			City transportation services (buses, trams, trolleybuses, subway)
			Maintenance of transport infrastructure (roads, bridges, tunnels, overpasses)
			Traffic control services
			Functioning of intelligent transport systems (traffic management, mobility, interaction with other means of transport)
		Railway transport	Passenger rail transportation services
			Freight rail transportation

(*continued*)

Table 1. (*continued*)

№	Sector	Subsector	Vital service (function) type
			Operation and maintenance of the railway
			Station work
		Sea and river transport	Control and management of shipping
			Inland, sea or coastal passenger and freight operations
			Functioning of managing bodies of ports or operators of port facilities
			Operation and maintenance of infrastructure (channels, dams, fairways, etc.)
		Mail	Mail services
8	Public security and the rule of law		Ensuring public order and security
			Judicial and criminal systems functioning
9	Industry	Chemical and nuclear industry	Production of industrial gas
			Manufacture of fertilizers or nitrogen compounds
			Production of pesticides or other agrochemical products
			Production of explosives
			Processing and storage of nuclear fuel
			Manufacture of basic pharmaceutical products
			Manufacture of pharmaceuticals
			Manufacture of other basic inorganic substances
			Manufacture of other basic organic chemicals

(*continued*)

Table 1. (*continued*)

№	Sector	Subsector	Vital service (function) type
		The military industry	Manufacture and supply of weapons and military equipment (military-industrial complex)
			Supply (sale) and purchase of arms and military equipment under international contracts
		Space rocket and aviation industry	Manufacturing and supply of rocket and aerospace industry products
10	Governance		Functioning of public authorities
			E-government system functioning
11	Civil protection of the population and territories		Emergency telephone service
			Emergency notification of the population, liquidation and disaster recovery, organization and coordination of rescue of residents and property
12	Ecological safety		Air pollution monitoring and early warning
			Meteorological observation and early warning
			Surface water monitoring (rivers, lakes) and early warning
			Monitoring and control of marine pollution
13	National security and defense		State defense
			National security
			Cybersecurity
14	Foreign and security policy		Implementation of foreign and security policy

The administrative approach as a methodological approach is used to developing the list, as recommended by ENISA. Refinement of the national list by structure and form has been made taking into account the indicative list of the EU and national lists of the EU Member States. Table 1 provides a National List of Critical Infrastructure Sectors that is proposed for approval as a regulatory document.

Considering the subject area of critical infrastructure, it can be said that one of the top properties of the CIO *is criticality*. *Criticality* is a relative measure of the importance of the CIO, which takes into account the impact of the sudden cessation of functioning or functional failure on the continuous and secure supply, the provision of vital goods and services to society. Criticality has several categories. An analysis of the regulatory documents of those countries where the division of CIOs into criticality categories is normatively established, showed the most widespread adoption of 3–5 criticality categories (Table 2).

Table 2. Examples of widespread adoption of criticality categories

Country or economic and political union	Number of critical categories
EU Recommendations	4
Russian Federation	3
Lithuania	4
Canada	6
USA	3

This number of categories is due to system-wide properties and principles of classification. Because criticality assessment relies, for the most part, on informal methods of systematic analysis, and also taking into account the Miller Law, which states that short-term human memory can operate 7 ± 2 elements.

In domestic works [9] and [13] and in the draft Law it is proposed to introduce 4 categories of criticality:

1. *Criticality Category I.* Critical Objects – Objects of nationwide importance, with extensive connections and significant impact on other infrastructure. These objects are included in the National List of Critical Infrastructure Objects, requirements for their protection are being formulated;
2. *Criticality Category II.* Vital Objects – whose malfunctioning will cause a crisis of regional importance. These objects are included in the National List of Critical Infrastructure Objects, requirements are created for the separation of tasks and powers of state authorities and operators of critical infrastructure aimed at ensuring their protection and restoration of functioning;
3. *Criticality Category III.* Important Objects – the priority of protecting such assets is to ensure rapid restoration of functions through diversification and reserves. Operators are responsible for the stability of the functioning of the facilities in compliance with the legal requirements for interaction with public authorities;

4. *Criticality Category IV*. Required Objects – Infrastructure objects, the immediate protection of which is the responsibility of the operator, who must have a crisis response plan.

It should be noted that the established practice of criticality classification for critical information infrastructure objects is the principle that the CIIO criticality category is assigned by the CIOs criticality category, in the interests of which the appropriate automated systems, networks and information technologies are used. This approach is used, for example, in the Russian Federation, Lithuania, the Czech Republic, etc. It is only necessary to establish at the stage of the assessment that the object of the information infrastructure really influences the provision of vital services and functions of the CIO. Exclusions are only for critical IT infrastructures that are in the IT, telecommunications and communications sectors (such as data centers, cloud repositories, key certification centers, government registers, etc.). It is proposed to use four categories for such CIOs, as well as for CIOs from other critical infrastructure sectors. This approach will simplify the task of compiling a list of critical information infrastructure objects.

3   Methods for Assigning Critical Information Infrastructure Objects to One of the Criticality Levels

3.1   CIIO Categorization Method General Characteristics

The methodology is developed based on the following principles and assumptions.

1   The identification of critical information infrastructure objects is carried out within the critical infrastructure sectors (sub-sectors) and taking into account the identification of critical infrastructure objects and the corresponding types of vital services and functions.
2   CIO is seen as an asset of critical infrastructure, as an organizational and technical system that directly delivers vital services or implements vital functions for citizens, society and the state
3   The identification and categorization of CIOs and CIIOs is carried out within the critical infrastructure sub-sector.
4   The CIO is categorized according to two sets of criteria. The first group is the sectoral criteria, the second group is the cross-sectoral criteria. Sectoral criteria are developed individually for each sector and are applied exclusively to the CIO of that sector of CI. Cross-sectoral criteria are applied to all CIOs, regardless of their relevance to a specific sector. The use of two sets of criteria is a common practice in EU Member States.
5   The assignment of an CIO to a particular criticality category is based on the received CIO scores for each criticality criterion. The determination of the criticality category is based on the analysis of the sum of points obtained and the use of the Harrington universal scale.
6   Criticality assessment of the critical information infrastructure object is based on the criteria of assessing the impact of the CIIOs (information, telecommunication

systems, automated systems, etc.) on the functionality and integrity of the CIOs, the ability to operate continuously and sustainably and to provide vital services and functions. In the case of determining the influence of the CIIO on the functioning of the CIO, the criticality category of the CIIO is equal to the criticality of the CIO.

7   The order of attribution to one of the degrees of criticality (hereinafter – *the Order*) consists of three stages:

- *Stage 1* – Identification and categorization (criticality assessment) of a critical infrastructure object.
- *Stage 2* – Identification and categorization (criticality assessment) of the critical information infrastructure object.
- *Stage 3* – Formation of the list of objects of criticality of information infrastructure.

3.2   Critical Infrastructure Identification and Categorization

The identification and categorization of the CIOs is performed by the following procedure:

1. Critical infrastructure sector (sub-sector) objects are identified by the critical infrastructure operator (see Table 1). The responsible institution will identify (list) all critical infrastructure entities operating within its activity that provide the provision of critical services/functions and operations of which is based on the use of the IT infrastructure.
2. The criticality of an infrastructure object is assessed by the critical infrastructure operator together with the enterprise (organization, institution) or its structural unit using a two parts questionnaire. The first part is sectoral criteria for criticality. The second part is the intersectoral criteria of criticality. Criticality criteria were developed on the basis of an analysis of similar criteria systems, which are set out in the Czech Republic, the Russian Federation and Lithuania.
3. The importance of an infrastructure object must be determined by analyzing the potential damage to society, the environment, the economy, and the national security of the state as a result of the disruption or termination of the infrastructure. The importance of infrastructure objects is assessed using the following sets of criteria:

- Social importance of the infrastructure object (causing harm to human life and health, level of panic of the population, causing harm to the environment);
- Political importance of the infrastructure object (termination or disruption of functioning of state authorities; negative impact on people's trust in state institutions; damage to interests of other partner states of Ukraine; level of protest mood);
- Economic significance of the infrastructure object (causing damage to the critical infrastructure object; causing damage to the state budget of Ukraine, causing damage to local budgets);
- Interconnection between critical infrastructure objects (negative impact on the continuous and sustainable operation of another infrastructure object, which provides the same vital service (function); negative impact on the security-interrupted

and sustainable operation of another infrastructure object providing other vital services (functions);

- Significance for ensuring the defense of the country and the security of the state (termination or violation (failure to meet established indicators) of the operation of the control point (situational center), reduction of indicators of the state defense order.

4. The analysis of the draft Law of Ukraine "On Critical Infrastructure and its Protection" allowed to build an ontological scheme of possible criteria for assessing the importance of critical infrastructure objects. Figure 2 provides an ontological diagram of the evaluation criteria. These provisions of the draft Law were also taken into account when developing a proposal on the criteria and indicators for criticality assessment of critical infrastructure objects. The recommendations of domestic experts cited in [9, 13] were also taken into account.

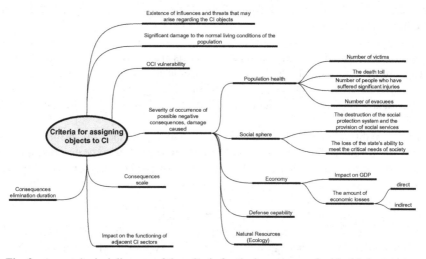

Fig. 2. An ontological diagram of the criteria for the importance of critical infrastructure

5. Thus, it is proposed to introduce sectoral criteria for assessing the criticality of critical infrastructure objects (Table 3) and intersectoral criteria for evaluating critical infrastructure objects (Table 4). Official statistics and other information were used to determine specific numerical indicators of the criteria.

Each criterion has corresponding indicators that accord to one of four categories of criticality. For categorization, a group is formed that evaluates the object by each criteria. In this case, it is recommended to organize brainstorming.

Each answer is scored in points: *Category I* – 4 points, *Category II* – 3 points, *Category III* – 2 points, *Category IV* – 1 point. *A non-critical answer is given* – 0 points.

The generalized criticality category is determined by the generalized index and Harrington's universal scale [19].

Table 3. Example of industry criteria: characterization of a negative impact on the provision of a critical service in the event of destruction, damage or disruption of the functioning of the critical infrastructure object

№	Sector/Subsector	Sector/sub-sector negative impact factor	Level of negative impact: catastrophic consequences (4 points)	Level of negative impact: critical consequences (3 points)	Level of negative impact: significant consequences (2 points)	Level of negative impact: minor consequences (1 point)	Score PK_i
1	Services provided by the electricity and nuclear sub-sectors	In case of destruction, damage or malfunction of the critical infrastructure object, the power supply will be stopped	For more than 145,000 residents OR for consumers of the first category in the territory of more than one region OR in the territory of not less than 3 cities of regional importance	For more than 30 000 residents OR for consumers of the second category in the territory of one region OR in the territory of more than one district of the city of the regional center OR the whole territory of one city of regional importance	For more than 2000 residents	For less than 2000 residents	
			Recovery time in standard mode may not exceed 6 h	Recovery time in standard mode can be from 6 to 24 h	Recovery time in standard mode may be from 1 to 3 days	Recovery time in standard mode may be more than 3 days	
2	Services provided by the oil and petroleum products sub-sector	in case of destruction, damage or disruption of critical infrastructure, supply of oil and petroleum products for consumption in the domestic market of Ukraine will decrease	more than 25% relatively to the same period of the calendar year or the previous calendar month within the limit determined by the Central Executive Body that implements the State Material Reserve Policy	from 12 to 25% relatively to the same period of the calendar year or the previous calendar month within the limit of specified by CEBMR	from 7 to 12% relatively to the same period of the calendar year or the previous calendar month within the limit of specified by CEBMR	Less than 7% relatively to the same period of the calendar year or the previous calendar month within the limit of specified by CEBMR	
Total score: $\Sigma\, PK_i$							...

Let it be m metrics by which the object criticality level is assessed $[PK]_i$. Object can get maximal number of points $[PK]_{max}$, if it is rated as critical in the first category. Then a generalized indicator of the level of criticality can be calculated by the formula:

$$PK_{OCI} = \Sigma_{i=1}^{m} PK_i / PK_{max} \qquad (1)$$

The decision to classify the CIO as one of the levels of criticality proposes to use the Harrington universal scale. It is a multi-interval discrete verbal-numerical scale consisting of five intervals of a single segment that characterize the degree of approximation to an ideal. The numerical values of scale graduation are obtained from the analysis and processing of a large mass of static expert data. The scale translates the qualitative estimates into quantitative ones in the range from 0 to 1 on the basis of statistical processing of psychological features of the person. Thus, the classification of criticality is as a rule:

- *Criticality category I – if $0.8 < PK_{OCI} \leq 1$;*
- *Criticality category II – if $0.63 < PK_{OCI} \leq 0.8$;*
- *Criticality category III – if $0.37 < PK_{OCI} \leq 0.63$;*
- *Criticality category IV – if $0.2 < PK_{OCI} \leq 0.37$;*
- *the object is not critical –if $PK_{OCI} \leq 0.2$.*

Table 4. Cross-sectoral criteria for infrastructure criticality assessment (example)

№	Negative impact	Level of negative impact: catastrophic consequences (4 points)	Level of negative impact: critical consequences (3 points)	Level of negative impact: significant consequences (2 points)	Level of negative impact: minor consequences (1 point)	Level of negative impact: minor consequences Negligible (0 points)	Score PK_i
I. The social significance of the infrastructure object							
1	Causing harm to human life and health	The number of people who may be affected					
		Risk to life or health of 75,000 people	More than 5000 people are at risk for life and health	More than 50 people are at risk for life or health	Less than 50 people are at risk for life or health	Not critical	PK_1
		Geographic scale					
		Danger to life and health of residents in one or more than one region OR in a territory of 3 and more cities of regional importance	Danger to the life and health of residents in the same region OR urban area of the city of the regional center OR throughout the territory of one city of the regional significance	Danger to the life and health for people on site and for residents living in close proximity to the location of the property	Danger to life and health of people on site	Not critical	PK_2
2	The level of panic in the population	Very high level of panic moods: panic moods spread in more than one region OR not less than 3 cities of regional importance	High level of panic moods: panic moods spread in one region OR one city of regional importance	Panic moods spread over part of the territory of the city of regional significance	Panic moods spread throughout the site	Not critical	PK_3
Total score $\Sigma\ PK_{1-3}$							

3.3 Identification and Categorization (Criticality Assessment) of a Critical Information Infrastructure Object

After determining the criticality category of the infrastructure object, the information infrastructure objects are determined. For this purpose, the operator (individual) of the critical infrastructure facility shall compile a complete list of information and telecommunication systems and networks used at the critical infrastructure facility and evaluate the impact of those systems on the continuity and sustainability of the provision of vital services (functions) the CIO provides.

The operator of a critical infrastructure facility identifies and evaluates the criticality (categorization) of information infrastructure objects that support the functioning of the CIO and the provision of vital services (functions) together with the owner (manager) of the information infrastructure object.

The process of identifying information infrastructure objects is carried out in this order:

- The CIO operator identifies all information infrastructure objects operated by the CIO and populates the information infrastructure identification table.
- When identifying objects of information infrastructure, the operator determines which systems are required to ensure continuous and stable functioning of the CIO. Special attention should be paid to automated process control systems (ACS), access control systems, alert systems, information and telecommunication systems that process information with restricted access, information systems that process personal data.
- If collaboration with a system and communications network operator takes place, an Internet service provider, an electronic trust service provider is required during categorization, the CIO operator must involve third party representatives in the categorization process.

Criticality assessment is carried out only for those objects of information infrastructure that are necessary for the continuous and stable functioning of the CIO.

Three criteria of importance are used to evaluate the criticality of an information infrastructure object:

- The provision of vital services (functions) is critically dependent on the proper functioning of the information infrastructure object (yes/no);
- An information security incident (cyber incident) on an information infrastructure object can have a significant impact on the continuity and sustainability of a vital service (function) (yes/no);
- In case of failure of the information infrastructure object, there are no other alternatives to ensure the continuous and sustainable provision of the vital service (function) (yes/no).

Objects of information infrastructure that meet all the criteria are defined as objects of critical information infrastructure (CIIO). The CIIO criticality category is established by the CIO criticality category.

After identifying and determining the criticality of the critical information infrastructure object, information about the CIIO is submitted to the authorized body for critical information protection of the information infrastructure for the formation of the CIIO list.

4   Conclusions

An analysis of existing methodological approaches and recommendations showed that the methodology for assessing the criticality of information infrastructure objects consists of three stages:

- identification and regulation of critical infrastructure sectors (and sub-sectors) and typical vital services provided in the relevant sector;
- evaluation of the criticality of the infrastructure. The assessment is carried out according to the normative criteria of criticality assessment. The assessment is carried out by informal analysis methods – expert survey methods, brainstorming methods, etc.;
- Third step: criticality assessment of information infrastructure objects. The criticality of information infrastructure objects is usually assessed on the basis of an analysis of the need for information and telecommunication systems for the continuous functioning of the CIO and an assessment of the impact of the information and telecommunication systems on the continuity and sustainability of the provision of vital services and functions.

Identification of sectors of critical infrastructure is carried out by administrative means (i.e., top to bottom). Experience analysis allows to recommend to Ukraine to determine the list of infrastructure sectors on the basis of the indicative list recommended by the EU. Most of the EU countries in this way determine the list of sectors of critical infrastructure. The comparative analysis also shows that almost similar sector defined in the United States, Canada and Russia. I.e. the use of the indicative list is more or less objective.

Analysis of existing fixed regulatory methods to assess the criticality of the CIO showed that there are two main approaches to the classification of categories of criticality of the infrastructure object. The first approach is the threshold, and binary. That is, an infrastructure object, basing on an analysis of its impact and determining the level of impact, refers to either critical or non-critical objects. The threshold is determined either on the basis of qualitative assessment or on the basis of accumulated point evaluation on several criteria (Czech Republic, Lithuania). Another approach is that infrastructure objects are classified by criticality classes (categories). Usually it is used from three to five categories of criticality. The criticality category is determined by each criterion individually, and then decisions are made based on an analysis of all the estimations obtained. In the Russian Federation, for example, the overall criticality category is determined by the maximum rating among all criticality ratings. This approach is not optimal because it can lead to overestimation of infrastructure criticality categories and excessive security costs.

It is suggested to use a mixed approach. Infrastructure criticality criteria is determined by the object's criticality level by each criterion, and the criticality level is scored in points. The overall level of criticality is estimated on the basis of an analysis of the generalized regulatory assessment (the sum of all points), followed by the Harrington universal scale. This will allow to apply a more flexible approach to the definition of critical objects of different categories, to optimize the cost of ensuring the objects protection. In the long run, adjusting weights for the criteria can be used to obtain more accurate estimations. But this requires additional research with the involvement of a wide range of experts (yes, a similar task in Lithuania was solved with the involvement of more than 120 experts from different fields.) This is the first perspective of the development of the proposed approach.

The criticality category of an information infrastructure object is assigned to the criticality category of an CIO, for which the information systems are used for continuous functioning. This is a recognized practice that avoids the dual classification of critical infrastructure and critical information infrastructure objects.

Criteria for assessing criticality are proposed to use the criteria for the following groups:

- *I. Social significance of the infrastructure object* (causing harm to human life and health, level of panic of the population, harming the environment).
- *II. The political significance of the infrastructure object* (termination or disruption of the functioning of public authorities, negative impact on people's trust in state institutions, damage to interests of other partner states of Ukraine, level of protest and anti-state sentiment).
- *III. Economic significance of the infrastructure object* (causing damage to the critical infrastructure object, causing damage to the state budget of Ukraine, causing damage to local budgets.
- *IV. Relationship between critical infrastructure objects* (adverse impact on continuous and sustainable functioning of another infrastructure object that provides the same vital service (function), negative impact on security continuous and sustainable operation of another infrastructure object that provides other vital services (functions).
- *V. The importance of ensuring the defense of the country and the security of the state* (termination or disruption of the operation of the control point (situational center), reduction of indicators of the state defense order).

According to the results of the research the drafts of the Ukrainian state-level normative documents "Classification of critical information infrastructure objects by severity (criticality)" and "Criteria and procedure for assigning critical information infrastructure objects to one of the significance (criticality)" were developed. The implementation of the developed documents is an important step in the construction of the Ukrainian state system of protection of critical information infrastructure.

Further development of the regulatory framework in this area can be undertaken in the following directions:

- improvement of the methods of assessment of criticality of critical infrastructure objects and critical information infrastructure objects. On the basic generalization of the practice of applying the proposed documents, it is necessary to improve the method of assessing the criticality of the CIO by introducing the weighting coefficients of the

criticality criteria, which will allow to provide the flexibility and objectivity of the criticality assessment of the CIO, as well as to introduce more detailed CIIO criticality assessment methodology (e.g., using the experience of South Korea);
- developing common cybersecurity requirements that enable critical infrastructure operators to build an CIIO security system or an CIO information security management system;
- developing of case-based techniques [14–17] and specification of CIIO considering green IT engineering issue [18].

Acknowledgements. This work was supported by the ECHO project which has received funding from the European Union's Horizon 2020 research and innovation programme under the grant agreement no 830943. The authors very appreciated to scientific society of consortium and in particular the staff of Department of Computer Systems, Networks and Cybersecurity of National aerospace university «Kharkiv Aviation Institute» for invaluable inspiration, hardworking and creative analysis during the preparation of this paper.

References

1. European Commission: Communication from the Commission of 12 December 2006 on a European Programme for Critical Infrastructure Protection, COM (2006) 786 Final, Brussels, Belgium (2006)
2. European Commission: Proposal for a Directive of the Council on the Identification and Designation of European Critical Infrastructure and the Assessment of the Need to Improve Their Protection, COM (2006) 787 Final, Brussels, Belgium (2006)
3. Ministry of the Interior and Kingdom Relations: National Risk Assessment Method Guide 2008, The Hague, The Netherlands (2008)
4. U.S. Department of Homeland Security: National Infrastructure Protection Plan 2009, Washington, DC (2009)
5. Public Safety and Emergency Preparedness Canada: Selection Criteria to Identify and Rank Critical Infrastructure Assets, Ottawa, Canada (2004)
6. Kroger, W.: Critical infrastructures at risk: a need for a new conceptual approach and extended analytical tools. Reliabil. Eng. Syst. Saf. **93**(12), 1781–1787 (2008)
7. Brunner, E., Suter, M.: International CIIP Handbook 2008/2009: An Inventory of 25 National and 7 International Critical Infrastructure Protection Policies, Center for Security Studies, ETH Zurich, Zurich, Switzerland (2008)
8. Gritzalis, D., Stergiopoulos, G., Kotzanikolaou, P., Magkos, E., Lykou, G.: Critical infrastructure protection: a holistic methodology for Greece. In: Cuppens-Boulahia, N., Lambrinoudakis, C., Cuppens, F., Katsikas, S. (eds.) CyberICPS 2016. LNCS, vol. 10166, pp. 19–34. Springer, Cham (2017). https://doi.org/10.1007/978-3-319-61437-3_2
9. Green paper on critical infrastructure protection in Ukraine. In: Proceedings of International Expert Meetings. National Institute for Strategic Studies, Kyiv, p. 176
10. Council Directive 2008/114/EC. (2008, 12 23): Official Journal of the European Union, vol. 51, p. 75 (2008)
11. EU Commission (2012, 6 22): Review of the European Programme for Critical Infrastructure Protection (EPCIP)

12. Rossella, M., Cedric, L.-B.: Methodologies for the identification of Critical Information Infrastructure assets and services. In: European Union Agency for Network and Information Security (ENISA), ENISA, Brussels (2015)
13. Bobro, D.G., Methodology of estimation of infrastructure objects criticality level, 3(40), 77–85 (2016)
14. Potii, O., Illiashenko, O., Komin, D.: Advanced security assurance case based on ISO/IEC 15408. In: Zamojski, W., Mazurkiewicz, J., Sugier, J., Walkowiak, T., Kacprzyk, J. (eds.) Theory and Engineering of Complex Systems and Dependability. AISC, vol. 365, pp. 391–401. Springer, Cham (2015). https://doi.org/10.1007/978-3-319-19216-1_37
15. Strielkina, A., Illiashenko, O., Zhydenko, M., Uzun, D.: Cybersecurity of healthcare IoT-based systems: regulation and case-oriented assessment. In: 2018 IEEE 9th International Conference on Dependable Systems, Services and Technologies (DESSERT), Kiev, pp. 67–73 (2018)
16. Kharchenko, V., Illiashenko, O.: Diversity for security: case assessment for FPGA-based safety-critical systems. In: MATEC Web Conference, vol. 76, p. 02051 (2016)
17. Illiashenko, O., Kharchenko, V., Brezhniev, E., Boyarchuk, A., Golovanevskiy, V.: Security informed safety assessment of industrial FPGA-based systems. In: Proceedings of Probabilistic Safety Assessment and Management Conference PSAM, 24–27 June 2014, Hololulu, Hawaii, USA, vol. 12, p. 11 (2014)
18. Kharchenko, V., Illiashenko, O.: Concepts of green IT engineering: taxonomy, principles and implementation. In: Kharchenko, V., Kondratenko, Y., Kacprzyk, J. (eds.) Green IT Engineering: Concepts, Models, Complex Systems Architectures. SSDC, vol. 74, pp. 3–19. Springer, Cham (2017). https://doi.org/10.1007/978-3-319-44162-7_1
19. Harrington, E.C.: The desirability function. Ind. Qual. Control 21, 494–498 (1965)

Evaluating Calibration and Robustness of Pedestrian Detectors

Sebastian Cygert$^{(\boxtimes)}$ and Andrzej Czyżewski

Faculty of Electronics, Telecommunication and Informatics Multimedia Systems
Department, Gdansk University of Technology, Gdańsk, Poland
sebcyg@multimed.org

Abstract. In this work the robustness and calibration of modern pedestrian detectors are evaluated. Pedestrian detection is a crucial perception component in autonomous driving and in this article its performance under different image distortions is studied. Furthermore, we provide an analysis of classification calibration of pedestrian detectors and a positive effect of using the style-transfer augmentation technique is presented. Our analysis is aimed as a step towards understanding and improving current safety-critical detection systems.

Keywords: AI safety · Robustness · Uncertainty estimation · Pedestrian detection · Object detection

1 Introduction

Recent methods based on Convolutional Neural Networks achieved significant progress in the past decade. Results on many benchmarks have increased by order of the magnitude including classification (ImageNet [5]) and object detection (MS COCO [17]). Yet, despite that, successful applications of modern statistical approaches to medicine and robotics have been very limited. Despite great progress in deep learning, still this type of algorithms might not be robust in many cases, and even small changes in the testing conditions (compared to the training dataset) can cause the erroneous output of the network [1,23]. What is more current model often return miscalibrated confidence score, e.g. they produce wrong prediction with high confidence score [10]. Obtaining meaningful uncertainty estimates is an important step in safety-critical applications which would also allow to build trust for such systems. For example in the case of a multimodal perception system (e.g. LiDAR sensors and RGB camera), each component should be able to estimate its reliability [7].

A task of special importance for safe AI is pedestrian detection, which is a crucial component of perception systems in autonomous driving. Self-driving

This work has been partially supported by Statutory Funds of Electronics, Telecommunications and Informatics Faculty, Gdansk University of Technology, and partially by the Polish National Centre for Research and Development (NCBR) from the European Regional Development Fund No. POIR.04.01.04-00-0089/16.

vehicles need to be accurate in varying outdoor conditions such as fog, snow, changes in illumination. However, evaluating the robustness and calibration of such algorithms were not well studied yet. In this work we evaluate a state-of-the-art algorithm Faster R-CNN [21] for detecting pedestrians in different lighting conditions (day and night) and under different image corruptions (different types of noise, changes in contrast etc.) as proposed by Hendrycks et al. [12]. The model is evaluated in terms of its accuracy but also in terms of its uncertainty calibration.

For evaluation two big pedestrian datasets are used: Citypersons [24] and EuroCity [2] recorded from a camera placed inside a car, in various cities in Europe. The evaluation is performed under a realistic scenario when the model is trained on one dataset and tested on the other. The contribution of this paper is as follows:

– the robustness of the pedestrian detector to common perturbations as well as to dataset shift is evaluated
– we evaluate the classification calibration error of the returned detections and show that using style-transfer data augmentation can improve the calibration.

The outline of this paper is as follows. In Sect. 2 related work is presented. Section 3 presents all the necessary background: datasets, relevant metrics and object detection model. In Sect. 4 relevant experiments are performed, testing accuracy and uncertainty calibration of the models in different settings, as well as measuring the effect of using style-transfer data augmentation on different metrics. Last Section presents the conclusions and future work.

2 Related Work

Pedestrian Detection. Pedestrian detection is a topic that grabs a lot of attention, especially in the context of autonomous vehicles and is greatly influenced by object detection methods. Currently, object detector methods are dominated by two-stage detectors, i.e Faster R-CNN [21]. In the first stage bounding boxes that may contain any objects are proposed. In the second stage, a classifier assigns each bounding box into a class. Specialized algorithms exists for pedestrian detection [18], however Faster R-CNN still provides a very strong baseline [11]. For that reason Faster R-CNN is utilized in our work, as it is a general purpose object-detection neural network that can be used in broader context (for example detecting also another objects on the road).

To benchmark existing algorithms large-scale datasets have been annotated, e.g. Citypersons [24], or recently presented Euro-City dataset [2] which includes a large set of annotations from night-time driving. In this work we are interested in detection from RGB camera, however pedestrian detection from LiDAR data is also an active research area [7].

Uncertainty Estimation. Various techniques exist for computing predictive uncertainty. Sampling-based methods approximate an output probability distribution by predicting multiple outputs from one image, e.g. using test-time

Dropout [8] or ensemble of models [16]. Simpler methods employ post-hoc calibration by using a held-out validation set, i.e. temperature scaling [20].

Robustness. Deep learning-based approaches are known to fail to generalize outside of the training domain or training data distribution. Most spectacular failure includes adversarial examples [18], where minor, invisible to human eye changes in the intensity of the pixels, cause the wrong prediction of the network. Evaluating the robustness of neural networks to distributional shift in test-time distributions, that are shifted from the training distribution is recently gaining attention. Hendrycks et al., studies robustness to common corruptions and perturbations such as Gaussian Noise, Motion Blur or changes in brightness [12]. Ovadia et al. [22] studies uncertainty calibration under dataset shift but only for the task of classification. Different data augmentation techniques were used to increase the robustness of neural networks [9,13].

Our work is mostly related to Michaelis's et al. [19] where the robustness of modern object detectors is studied, but without measuring uncertainty calibration. Additionally, the cross-dataset evaluation is performed.

3 Datasets and Metrics

3.1 Datasets

CityPersons [24] is a pedestrian detection dataset on top of the semantic segmentation dataset CityScapes [4] for autonomous driving. The dataset includes 5000 images (2975 for training, 500 for validation, and 1525 for testing) captured in 27 cities in Germany with around 35000 manually annotated persons and 13000 ignored annotations. On average there are 7 pedestrians per image, which is significantly more than in another popular Caltech dataset [6], posing a significant challenge for the detectors. Ignore regions are areas where the annotator cannot tell if a person is present or absent, and person groups where individuals cannot be told apart or other situations like people's reflection in the mirror or window. Additionally, for each person, an occlusion level is provided.

EuroCity Persons [2] is one of the most comprehensive publicly available datasets for pedestrian detection. The images for this dataset were collected onboard a moving vehicle in 31 cities of 12 European countries. There are around 238200 person instances manually labeled in over 47300 images collected during all seasons, in both dry and weather conditions. What is very important around 7000 annotated images were recorded during the night-time. As a result, ECP provides great diversity and is a great choice for training and or testing pedestrian detection algorithms.

Common Corruptions. As it was stated in the introduction, convolutional networks are vulnerable to small distortions in the image. To test the robustness of pedestrian detection models we use 15 corruptions as provided by Hendrycks et al. [12]. The corruption list is divided into 4 categories: noise (Gaussian noise, Shot noise, Impulse noise, salt-and-pepper noise), blur (defocus blur, frosted glass blur, motion blur, zoom blur), digital (elastic transformations, pixelation, JPEG lossy compression) and weather corruptions (snow, fog, brightness, contrast). The ideal perception system for autonomous vehicles would be robust to all those types of corruption. Each corruption type is synthetically generated and has five levels of severity. In the experiments section those corruptions are used only during the test, to evaluate the robustness of algorithms which is a common practice in the computer vision community [19,22]. Example corruptions are presented in the Fig. 1.

Fig. 1. Different corruption types from Hendrycks et al. Top left original image, top right - jpeg compression artifacts, bottom left - shot noise, bottom right - fog effect.

Style-Transfer [14] is a popular technique that combines the content of one image and the style of another image. It was shown in the literature that using style-transfer as additional data augmentation provides an improvement of the robustness of trained models [9]. Here, the same setting as in Michaelis et al. [19] is followed. First, a stylized version of each image from the training set is created, using a style from randomly chosen texture information of Kaggle's Painter by Numbers[1] (Fig. 2). Then during training, images from both datasets are used: the original one and its stylized version.

3.2 Preliminaries

Object Detection. Object detectors for each image return a set bounding box coordinates, together with predicted class and the corresponding score. Currently, the best results are obtained by so-called two-stage object detectors, of which a prominent example is Faster R-CNN [21]. In the first bounding box

---

[1] https://www.kaggle.com/c/painter-by-numbers/.

Fig. 2. Original images from Cityscapes dataset and corresponding stylized versions (right column).

regression stage, a list of candidates' windows is returned which are the most likely to contain some object. Afterward, each proposal window is being classified as belonging to one of the predefined classes (including background). At that stage, the neural network for each bounding box proposal returns a logit vector $z \in R_k$, where K is the number of classes (in case of pedestrian detection there are two classes: pedestrian and background). To get a probability a sigmoid function is used, $p = softmax(z)$, which results in a distribution of predicted class probabilities. Probability value for the most probable class is the being used as the confidence value. Given detection is considered true positive when its overlap with ground truth is bigger than the selected threshold, in pedestrian detection the threshold of 0.5 is commonly used. Intersection over union is computed as:

$$IOU(a,b) = \frac{Area(a) \cap Area(b)}{Area(a) \cup Area(b)} \tag{1}$$

Detections with the highest confidence are matched with ground-truth first, in the case of multiple matches the detection with the largest score is selected, whereas all other matching detections are considered false positives. All not matching ground-truth annotations and detections are counted as false negatives and false positives, respectively.

LAMR A standard metric used to estimate detector accuracy is the log-average miss rate (LAMR). Firstly the miss-rate *(mr)* and false positives per image *(fppi)* are computed as follows:

$$mr(c) = \frac{fn(c)}{tp(c) + fp(c)} \tag{2}$$

$$fppi(c) = \frac{fp(c)}{\#img} \tag{3}$$

where *fn* stands for false negatives, *tp* is the number of true positives, *fp* is the number of false positives for given confidence value *c*, such that all detections with a score lower than *c* are ignored. Decreasing *c* means that more detections are taken into account (which may increase *fp* and *tp* value, and decrease *fp* value). The final LAMR metric is computed by averaging at nine *fppi* rates equally spaced in the log-space in the range 10^{-2} to 10^{0} as it is commonly done in the literature [2,6,24]:

$$LAMR(c) = exp(\frac{1}{9}\sum_{f} log(mr(\underset{fppi(c)<=f}{arg\,max}\ fppi(c)))) \tag{4}$$

Expected Calibration Error (ECE) is used to measure the correspondence between predicted probabilities and empirical accuracy [24]. Intuitively when a well-calibrated algorithm returns a bounding box with a pedestrian class with 90% confidence it should be accurate in 90% cases. To compute ECE score predictions are partitioned into M bins of the same size based on its confidence, and then the weighted average of the bins' difference between confidence and accuracy is computed:

$$ECE(c) = \sum_{m=1}^{M} \frac{|B_m|}{n}|acc(B_m) - conf(B_m)| \tag{5}$$

where B_m **is the set** of indices of samples whose prediction confidence falls into the mth interval. ECE value of 0 means perfect calibration. In our case ECE measures the classification calibration of the pedestrian detector. It is possible also to obtain miscalibration measures for the localization part of the detector using sampling-based methods [7], but we leave it for future work.

Negative log likelihood is a standard measure of a probabilistic model's quality. Given n pedestrian detections returned by the detector, the negative log-likelihood can be computed as:

$$\mathcal{L} = \sum_{i=1}^{n} log(p(y_i|x_i)) \tag{6}$$

where x_i is the object being classified, $p(y_i|x_i)$ is the probability returned by the model for the ground truth class of that object (in our case background or pedestrian).

Temperature scaling is a popular method of neural network calibration. Given the logit vector z_i, the scaled logit vector is:

$$\hat{z}_i = softmax(z_i/T) \tag{7}$$

where T is responsible for scaling the output probability. If $T > 1$, then the output distribution becomes sharper, whereas when $T < 1$ the distribution becomes broader (more uncertain). With $T = 1$ original output probability remains unchanged. The optimal T can be found by maximizing the Negative Log-Likelihood (NLL) on the validation set [10].

4   Experiments

In the experiments section, firstly a pedestrian detection model is trained on Citypersons dataset and evaluate its robustness to different perturbations in terms of pedestrian detection accuracy as well as its uncertainty calibration. In Sect. 4.2 the same metrics are evaluated but the model is tested on another dataset (EuroCity), in particular, differences between day and night-time prediction are studied. In Sect. 4.3 we quantify how data augmentation (Style Transfer) affects the measured metrics.

Implementation Details. Firstly a pedestrian detector model is trained on the Cityscapes dataset. Similarly to [15] data recorded from 3 cities from the training set is used as our validation set and results on the original validation set are reported. Faster RCNN with standard Resnet-50 backbone is used from the mmdetection library [3]. For testing the model with the best accuracy on the validation set is used. Consistently with [24] only the reasonable subset of pedestrians is used for training (and testing): i.e. cyclists, ignore regions and heavily occluded people are ignored during training. Neural networks are pre-trained on ImageNet dataset as it is a standard practice in the community. The initial learning rate for stochastic gradient descent is set to 0.01, with 0.9 momentum and weight decay of 0.0001. The model is trained for 30 epochs on single Tesla V100 card on DGX station with batch size of 2. Each epoch lasts for around 10 mins.

4.1   Evaluating Robustness to Perturbations

Firstly, the model trained on Citypersons is tested on the validation set and the distorted version of it. Figure 3 shows the results. For standard dataset (without distortions) the LAMR score of 16.18% is reported. With increased corruption magnitude the network performance is drastically reduced, even for a small level of corruption. For level 1 of corruption, LAMR already raises from 16.18% to 29.77% (averaged over all types of corruption). Also, it can be noticed that there is a big difference between different types of distortions. The obtained model was the most affected by Gaussian, shot and impulse noise, zoom blur and snow effect - for those distortions the LAMR raises to over 69% for corruption level of one. Changes in brightness and elastic transform causes the smallest decrease in performance.

Similar observations can be made for the calibration of the neural network output. The ECE metric increases with the corruption level, and the corruption types that cause the biggest drop in accuracy also worsens calibration the most. However, on average, the ECE value does not change as much as the LAMR metric. A standard way to visualize a calibration error are the so-called reliability

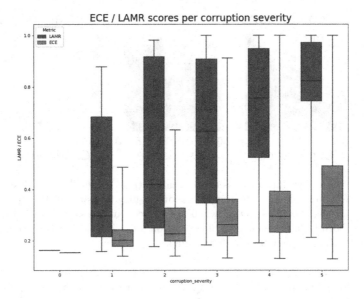

Fig. 3. ECE (blue bar) and LAMR (orange bar) metrics under the distributional shift on each intensity level of corruption. Each box shows the quartiles summarizing the results across all types of corruption, and the error bars indicate the minimum and maximum value. The lower value is better for both metrics. (Color figure online)

diagrams which are presented in Fig. 4. Firstly, it can be noticed that neural networks' output is under-confident. For example for the case with no disruptions, when the predicted probability is in the range [0.3, 0.4) the actual accuracy reaches 62% (when expected accuracy is 35%). This is a dangerous situation because it means that low confidence predictions are actually very important. Note that even when the neural network predicts confidence in the range [0.0-0.1) it is correct in 40% of cases. The effect is magnified when distortions are added, i.e. for the gaussian noise the network outputs only very low confidence predictions, but when it does it is almost always correct.

Temperature scaling algorithm was also used for improving the calibration, however there was only minor improvement, i.e. the ECE is reduced by 0.012 when no distortions are applied. This is because temperature scaling shifts the output distribution towards the more confident or more uncertain region which might significantly improve the calibration when the output distribution is over-confident in some confidence interval and under-confident in another, which is not the case in our setting (Fig. 4). We leave the evaluation of other calibration methods as future work.

4.2   Cross-Dataset Evaluation for Pedestrian Detection

In this section, a cross-dataset evaluation is performed, i.e. the model trained on Citypersons is evaluated on the EuroCity dataset for both daytime and night-

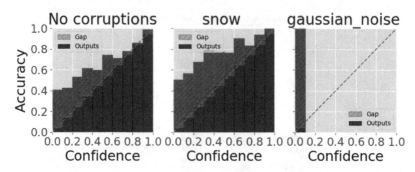

Fig. 4. Reliability diagrams for classification calibration. Values that are close to diagonal are well-calibrated. The left diagram shows calibration on CityPersons and the following diagrams show calibration when snow effect and gaussian noise distortions were added (both for a medium level of corruption intensity). The corresponding ECE values are 0.1537, 0.3216, 0.9106 (left to right).

time recordings. Such a setting is important for real-world applications. Even though both datasets were recorded from the dash camera inside, there might occur different performances of the detector between both datasets because of the different camera sensors, position of the dash camera and different geographical locations which cause changes in the background, the density of pedestrians etc. Additionally, we study here the performance gap on night-time detection (when the model was trained only using day-time images).

Table 1 shows the obtained results. Ideally, there should be no significant drop in performance when evaluating the other dataset, and here the LAMR raises from 16.18% to 21.91% for ECP day time images. Interestingly the ECE value is slightly smaller for the ECP dataset. For night-time images, there is a significant loss in accuracy (which is expected as the networks were trained only on day-time images) and the ECE increases as well.

Table 1. LAMR and ECE metrics for corresponding datasets.

Dataset	LAMR	ECE
CityPersons	16.18	15.53
ECP day	21.91	14.49
ECP night	38.35	19.39

4.3 Style Transfer

In this section, the effect of style-transfer data augmentation on the performance of the network is measured. Style-transfer was previously reported to increase the detection robustness however its effect on the uncertainty calibration was not

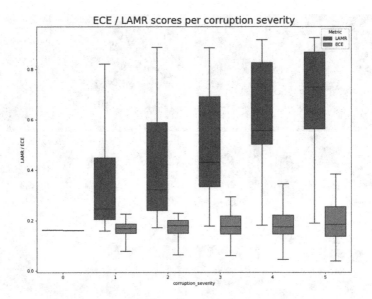

Fig. 5. ECE and LAMR metrics under distributional shift on each intensity level of corruption after when using Style Transfer data augmentation.

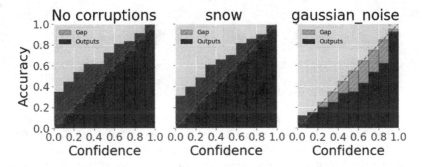

Fig. 6. Reliability diagrams for classification calibration. Values that are close to diagonal are well-calibrated. The left diagram shows calibration on CityPersons and the following diagrams show calibration when motion blur and shot noise distortions were added. The corresponding ECE values are 0.1601, 0.1913, 0.0591 (left to right).

evaluated before. A new pedestrian detection is trained with additional style-transfer data augmentation (rest of the settings remainted unchanged. Subsequently, the model robustness is tested in the same way as in Sect. 4.1. Figure 5 confirms previous findings, namely the style-transfer increases detection robustness, but here it is further showed that it has a positive effect on the detection model classification calibration. Comparing to Fig. 3 the LAMR is improved on average, however the distortions still greatly worsen the performance. It can

Fig. 7. Examples of detection for the baseline model and the "stylized" model (right column). The first row shows night-time detections on the ECP dataset, and the following rows show detections on the Cityscapes dataset under following corruption types (from top to the bottom): gaussian noise, motion blur, snow effect. The confidence score for each predicted bounding box is presented.

be also observed that ECE metric has significantly improved and Fig. 6 sheds some light on the source of the improvement. Comparing to Fig. 4 the calibration without any distortions didn't improve, whereas it has improved for the distorted images. For the snow effect the output distribution is better calibrated and for the Gaussian noise the output distribution is now almost perfectly calibrated. This is linked to the fact that the style transfer improves the robustness of a different type of distortions.

The effect of style transfer is also evaluated on the setting from experiment 4.2. The detection accuracy has improved: decrease of LAMR from 21.91 to 19.03 for day-time images, and from 38.35 to 30.69 for night-time images. However, there no major differences in the ECE metric.

Qualitative Analysis. Figure 7 shows compared detections of the original model (Sect. 4.1) and the model which used style transfer data augmentation. First of all, it can be noticed that the "stylized" model predicts many more boxes. Even though many false positives occur they usually have a low confidence score (biggest false-positive box in the third row has a confidence score of 0.07). Further the new model performs quite well in noise conditions (second row), whereas the baseline model does not make any predictions. Predictions under different illumination and weather conditions are also improved (first and fourth row).

5   Conclusions

In this work, an evaluation in terms of accuracy and classification calibration error of modern pedestrian detector under common perturbations and dataset shift is performed. It was shown that a trained pedestrian detector returns under-confident detections and that for the perturbations case (including night-time images) the calibration error increases rapidly, together with loss in the accuracy. However, when style-transfer data augmentation is used during training, the calibration error increases only slightly. Interestingly we found that dataset shift (CityPersons to EuroCity) does not affect classification calibration, however there is still a gap in detection accuracy.

Future work may include some more advanced calibration techniques, such as Monte Carlo dropout [8] and different object detection methods applied to be more confident that the presented results are not specific to the choice of object detector. Also, we should measure the full detection calibration (including localization).

References

1. Amodei, D., Olah, C., Steinhardt, J., Christiano, P., Schulman, J., Mané, D.: Concrete problems in ai safety. arXiv preprint arXiv:1606.06565 (2016)
2. Braun, M., Krebs, S., Flohr, F., Gavrila, D.M.: Eurocity persons: a novel benchmark for person detection in traffic scenes. IEEE Trans. Pattern Anal. Mach. Intell. **41**(8), 1844–1861 (2019)
3. Chen, K., et al.: Mmdetection: Open mmlab detection toolbox and benchmark. arXiv preprint arXiv:1906.07155 (2019)
4. Cordts, M., et al.: The cityscapes dataset for semantic urban scene understanding. In: Proceedings of the IEEE Conference on Computer Vision and Pattern Recognition, pp. 3213–3223 (2016)
5. Deng, J., Dong, W., Socher, R., Li, L.J., Li, K., Fei-Fei, L.: ImageNet: a large-scale hierarchical image database. In: 2009 IEEE Conference on Computer Vision and Pattern Recognition, pp. 248–255 (2009)

6. Dollár, P., Wojek, C., Schiele, B., Perona, P.: Pedestrian detection: a benchmark. In: 2009 IEEE Conference on Computer Vision and Pattern Recognition, pp. 304–311 (2009)
7. Feng, D., Rosenbaum, L., Glaeser, C., Timm, F., Dietmayer, K.: Can we trust you? On calibration of a probabilistic object detector for autonomous driving. arXiv preprint arXiv:1909.12358 (2019)
8. Gal, Y., Ghahramani, Z.: Dropout as a Bayesian approximation: representing model uncertainty in deep learning. In: Proceedings of the 33nd International Conference on Machine Learning. ICML 2016, New York City, NY, USA, 19–24 June 2016, vol. 48, pp. 1050–1059 (2016)
9. Geirhos, R., Rubisch, P., Michaelis, C., Bethge, M., Wichmann, F.A., Brendel, W.: ImageNet-trained CNNs are biased towards texture; increasing shape bias improves accuracy and robustness. In: 7th International Conference on Learning Representations. ICLR 2019, New Orleans, LA, USA, 6–9 May 2019 (2019)
10. Guo, C., Pleiss, G., Sun, Y., Weinberger, K.Q.: On calibration of modern neural networks. In: Proceedings of the 34th International Conference on Machine Learning, vol. 70, pp. 1321–1330 (2017)
11. Hasan, I., Liao, S., Li, J., Akram, S.U., Shao, L.: Pedestrian detection: the elephant in the room. CoRR (2020). https://arxiv.org/abs/2003.08799
12. Hendrycks, D., Dietterich, T.G.: Benchmarking neural network robustness to common corruptions and perturbations. In: 7th International Conference on Learning Representations. ICLR 2019, New Orleans, LA, USA, 6–9 May 2019 (2019)
13. Hendrycks, D., Mu, N., Cubuk, E.D., Zoph, B., Gilmer, J., Lakshminarayanan, B.: Augmix: a simple data processing method to improve robustness and uncertainty. In: 8th International Conference on Learning Representations. ICLR 2020, Addis Ababa, Ethiopia, 26–30 April 2020 (2020)
14. Huang, X., Belongie, S.: Arbitrary style transfer in real-time with adaptive instance normalization. In: Proceedings of the IEEE International Conference on Computer Vision, pp. 1501–1510 (2017)
15. Kohl, S., et al.: A probabilistic U-net for segmentation of ambiguous images. In: Advances in Neural Information Processing Systems, pp. 6965–6975 (2018)
16. Lakshminarayanan, B., Pritzel, A., Blundell, C.: Simple and scalable predictive uncertainty estimation using deep ensembles. In: Advances in Neural Information Processing Systems, pp. 6402–6413 (2017)
17. Lin, T.-Y., et al.: Microsoft COCO: common objects in context. In: Fleet, D., Pajdla, T., Schiele, B., Tuytelaars, T. (eds.) ECCV 2014. LNCS, vol. 8693, pp. 740–755. Springer, Cham (2014). https://doi.org/10.1007/978-3-319-10602-1_48
18. Liu, W., Liao, S., Ren, W., Hu, W., Yu, Y.: High-level semantic feature detection: a new perspective for pedestrian detection. In: Proceedings of the IEEE Conference on Computer Vision and Pattern Recognition, pp. 5187–5196 (2019)
19. Michaelis, C., et al.: Benchmarking robustness in object detection: autonomous driving when winter is coming. arXiv preprint arXiv:1907.07484 (2019)
20. Platt, J., et al.: Probabilistic outputs for support vector machines and comparisons to regularized likelihood methods. Adv. Large Margin Classif. **10**(3), 61–74 (1999)
21. Ren, S., He, K., Girshick, R., Sun, J.: Faster R-CNN: towards real-time object detection with region proposal networks. In: Advances in Neural Information Processing Systems, pp. 91–99 (2015)
22. Snoek, J., et al.: Can you trust your model's uncertainty? Evaluating predictive uncertainty under dataset shift. In: Advances in Neural Information Processing Systems, pp. 13969–13980 (2019)

23. Szegedy, C., et al.: Intriguing properties of neural networks. In: 2nd International Conference on Learning Representations. ICLR 2014, Banff, AB, Canada, 14–16 April 2014, Conference Track Proceedings (2014)
24. Zhang, S., Benenson, R., Schiele, B.: CityPersons: a diverse dataset for pedestrian detection. In: Proceedings of the IEEE Conference on Computer Vision and Pattern Recognition, pp. 3213–3221 (2017)

A Smart Algorithm for CO_2 Emissions Reduction on Realistic Traffic Scenarios Exploiting VANET Architecture

Cesare Sottile[1], Nicola Cordeschi[1(✉)], and Danilo Amendola[2]

[1] University of Calabria, P. Bucci 39/C, Rende, CS, Italy
c.sottile@dimes.unical.it, nicola.cordeschi@unical.it
[2] University of Trieste, Piazzale Europa, 1, 34127 Trieste, FVG, Italy
damendola@units.it

Abstract. In this paper, a smart vehicular traffic management through Vehicular Ad-hoc NETworks (VANETs) infrastructure and communications (V2I and V2V) is propose. A distributed algorithm called SeaWave with the aim to build less congested path for the vehicles in a urban scenario has been developed. It is also considered the problem regarding to enhance air quality around the cities reducing the vehicles CO_2 emissions. There are different causes related to the CO_2 emissions such as the average travelled time spent by vehicles inside the city and their average speed. Hence, with a better traffic management the average time spent by the vehicles in the city will be considerably reduced as well as CO_2 emissions. These results are demonstrated in a discrete events simulator by using real traffic data. In particular, we used a congested scenario related a morning peak hour for the Bologna's City.

Keywords: VANET · CO_2 emission · Smart algorithm

1 Introduction

Nowadays, the problems of the CO_2 emissions and the high traffic situations in the cities, are very faced by the research communities. The main aim is to exploit the ICT infrastructures to increase air quality in the cities and also to reduce the vehicular traffic. In this work, we focused mainly to VANETs architecture [1], by exploiting the vehicle-to-vehicle communication (V2V) and vehicle-to-infrastructure communication (V2I), in order to know in real-time manner, the traffic condition of the city [2]. The advantages that we can attribute to vehicular networks are related to the nature of the 802.11p standard, because it was developed to ensure reliable communications in vehicular mobility scenarios where the channel plays an important role [3, 4]. V2V communication consists of a wireless network that enables vehicles to exchange message, that in case of electrical devices have to consider energy consumption [5, 6]. The data being exchanged include speed, location, direction of travel, braking and loss of stability. The vehicular communication can also take advantage from new technologies such as opportunistic

© Springer Nature Switzerland AG 2020
A. Dziech et al. (Eds.): MCSS 2020, CCIS 1284, pp. 112–124, 2020.
https://doi.org/10.1007/978-3-030-59000-0_9

approach or delay tolerant network [7, 8]. V2V technology uses dedicated short-range communication (DSRC) [9]. The range is approximate up to 450 m and the supported topology is a mesh network. Thus, every node could send, capture and retransmit signal and the emergency vehicle sends a message to all other vehicles and warns them to make a way [10]. V2I communication enables data transmission between vehicles and road infrastructure using wireless technology [11]. Data from vehicles contain speed of the vehicles, position of the vehicle etc. data from infrastructure contains congestion, surrounding road condition, controller status and routing information. The speed of vehicles is obtained from speedometer and the position is obtained from GPS [12]. In this paper, we demonstrated that by using a smart algorithm for vehicles traffic management, it is possible to reduce CO_2 emissions in urban scenario and the average time spent in the city by the vehicles.

This paper is composed by follows: Sect. 2 presents some previous work related to the realistic traffic modeling, smart sensing through VANET and smart traffic management; the proposed traffic management with its implementation is presented in Sect. 3; simulator and traffic modeling, simulation results are presented in Sect. 4 and conclusions are summarized in the last section.

2 Related Work

Proving that the issues of CO_2 emissions and the traffic conditions in the cities are very important topics for the research communities, it is easy to found many works in literature about these problems.

2.1 Realistic Traffic Scenarios

A reason to increase attention to use realistic traffic data is today commonly agreed that the high-speed, strongly-correlated and constrained movements of vehicles can dramatically affect the network performance. In [13], the authors described the process used to build the Luxembourg SUMO Traffic (LuST) Scenario. They started from a real mid-size city and with a typical European road topology and its mobility patterns. All road intersections with traffic lights and all highway ramps are equipped with inductive loops. To generate the traffic demand, they used realistic traffic information provided by various data sources. In this scenario, the traffic light systems use a static scheduler. Another realistic scenario for vehicular mobility is presented in [14]. This realistic synthetic dataset of the car traffic is referred to 24 h in a region around the city of Koln, in Germany. The authors also explained the original Koln dataset and it improvements and they proved the realistic nature by comparing with other well-known vehicular mobility traces. In [15], the authors developed a scenario for the city of Bologna (Italy), in which there are traffic demands and representations about the traffic infrastructure to simulate a real-world scenario in SUMO. These traffic data are collected and elaborated during the development of the European Project called "I-Tetris", an integrated wireless and traffic platform for real-time road traffic management solutions. The approach used by the authors to build real vehicular traffic data, it has been to place several detectors of vehicles for each road intersection, present in the considered map.

We decided to use this realistic traffic scenario because is referred to a peak hour of the day and consequently, it provides a very dense scenario of vehicles for re-routing mechanism. During this hour, all schools, offices and commercial activities are opening.

2.2 Smart Sensing by Exploiting VANET Architecture

In literature, there are some work related the different smart sensing architectures by exploiting VANETs. In [16], authors proposed to form a smart vehicular ad hoc network with a limited number of sensors and road side sinks. They integrated the VANET infrastructure with inexpensive wireless sensors. They designed a scheme for effective and efficient vehicle-to-sensor and sensor-to-sensor interactions.

In order to improve the performance in terms of data delivery ratio and data transmission reliability, they used a leader selection mechanism among vehicles. Thus, different types of data, such as video, audio and text, can be transmitted to passengers with other vehicles based on their interest. In [17], the authors developed a sensor-based model for reliable and efficient communication in vehicular ad hoc networks. In particular, they designed and prototyped the complete process of data transmission and aggregation. Normally, in the VANET environment there are network partitioning due to the absence of vehicles, these road side sensors can help to forward the packets to cellular base station, which is already exist in network. They obtained better performance in terms of packet loss and end-to-end delay in network. In [18] it is described a comprehensive framework of Internet of Vehicles (IoV). The two major objectives of IoV include automation of various security and efficiency features in vehicles and commercialization of vehicular networks. The benefits would be in terms of understanding the layered architecture, network model and challenges of IoV. Furthermore, is presented a five-layered architecture of IoV, considering functionalities and representations of each layer. A protocol stack for the layered architecture is structured considering management, operational, and security planes. The benefits of the design and development of IoV are highlighted by performing a qualitative comparison between IoV and VANETs. In [19], the authors designed an architecture called Sensor-Cloud, to prevent the vehicular traffic congestion by using VANET system and sensor nodes.

In this system, congestion can be identified only by non-moving nodes (10 or 15 vehicles) with same point.

However, they have integrated the existing sensors with cloud that will enable an open, extensible, scalable, interoperable, and easy to use network of sensors for several monitoring and controlling applications.

2.3 Routing Scheme for Smart Traffic Management in Vehicular Environment

In our previous work [20, 21], we designed a novel protocol able to gather important data about environment such as accidents, blocks, emission levels and so on. These data are collected by the City Traffic Manager (CTM) exploiting dedicated messages sent by the vehicle and infrastructure devices called RSU. After this exchange of messages between vehicles - RSU, the CTM, knowing the whole status of the road network, can avoid traffic blocks making some high-level decisions. Also, a smart traffic management system is addressed in the proposed framework in order to reduce vehicles' CO_2 emissions in the urban area increasing, where possible, air quality. In this previous work, the first effective limit is involved, to the use of the fictitious vehicle traffic, modeled according to the Poisson distribution. A better manner to evaluate the accuracy and the robustness of the proposed smart algorithm is to use realistic traffic data into the simulator, because when using statistical traffic flow to inject a map, the obtained results are limited to statistical approaches and not to real world traffic. Therefore, the mechanism of vehicles' re-routing is performed not considering the realistic traffic also in a neighborhood of roads, where the vehicular traffic Poisson flows are not present.

3   Congestion Management and Road Cost Computation

Sometimes, roads present several blocks that can influence the normal flow of the vehicles in the city areas. These blocks, commonly, are the main cause of congestion as well as accidents. They cannot be predicted due to the dynamics events directly connected with external factors. One of the goals is to spread information about rising congestion events, this can be made sending info messages along the network. Once these messages are received, other vehicles can change or rearrange their paths allowing network system to avoid critical traffic levels in the involved areas and closer areas as well. Of course, the higher is the traffic loads the higher is the probability to generate a certain level of congestion. To minimize traffic loads around the involved areas we have to use a smart routine in updating road cost in order to spread traffic along several exit gates avoiding to use the same exit gates for all vehicles. Moreover, if we concentrate several vehicles in the same areas, the probability to generate another critical point in terms of congestion is higher. This is a big issue to correctly address, a smarter weighting cost function has to be found in order to estimate the real impact of the accident on the urban mobility area. Therefore, it is important to establish when a generic lane is going to face congestion. the term $n_{j,i}$ is the number of the vehicles that are recognized on the $j-th$ lane of the $i-th$ road, where $C_{j,i}$ is the set of vehicles that are currently present on the lane (j) of the road (i). Therefore $n_{j,i}$ is defined as:

$$n_{j,i} = \left| C_{j,i} \right| \tag{1}$$

Since we have a model that the CTM can use to establish if a lane (j) is going towards congestion we can try to find a relation among several parameters such as travelling time and number of vehicles that are present on the lane to identify which is he upper-bound, in vehicles number, that the considered lane can serve avoiding congestion. Let us to define the *Average Travelling Time* (att) along the lane (j) as

$$att_{j,i} = \frac{n_{j,i} \cdot l_j}{\sum_{k=1}^{k=|n_j|} S_{k,j,i}} : j \in R_i \tag{2}$$

where $S_{k,j}$ is the current speed of the $k-th$ vehicle on the $j-th$ lane of the $i-th$ road; how it is commonly known the safety distance is directly related with the speed of the vehicle, therefore safety distance for a generic vehicle is given by:

$$sd_{k,j,i} = \frac{S_{k,j,i}}{k_{speed}}, \forall k \in C_{j,i} \tag{3}$$

In order to know the total spatial occupancy of a vehicle (k) with a certain speed $(Sd_{k,j,i})$ we can use the following equation:

$$O_{j,i} = E[lv_{k,j,i}] + E[sd_{k,j,i}] : k \in C_{j,i} \tag{4}$$

where in (4) the term $lv_{k,j,i}$ is the length of the $k-$th vehicle on the $j-$th lane of the $i-$th road. In order to find the upper-bound we have to know which is the outgoing rate $\eta_{j,i}$ of the lane (j) of the road (i). Moreover, another important parameter is the $MaxSpeed_{j,i}$ that is the maximum speed that a vehicle $(k \in C_{j,i})$ can reach on the given lane (j).

$$I_{j,i} = \frac{l_{j,i}}{MaxSpeed_{j,i}} \tag{5}$$

The term $I_{j,i}$ represents the lower-bound in terms of travelling time that a vehicle can spend passing through the lane (j) of the $i-$th road. As first step, we consider a lane without any kind of blocks on the end of the lane; this means, for example, that no traffic control devices are installed on it. In this case, the complete time to spend on the line is composed of travelling time plus the time spent by the car to leave the lane when it reaches a junction point (this time is called Lane Leave Time (llt)). This time is given by the following equation:

$$llt_{j,i} = \frac{2 * lw_{j,i}}{llSp} \tag{6}$$

Therefore, the Total Time Spent on Lane (TTSL) is given by:

$$TTSL_{j,i} = att_{j,i} + llt_{j,i} \tag{7}$$

Since the average spatial car occupancy and the average lane length are known, it is possible to find an upper bound $VN_{j,i}$ that represents the maximum number of vehicles that a lane can manage avoiding traffic blocks. The basic idea is to consider that when a lane is congested several vehicles take place in an Indian row. This queue length can be used as an index in order to reveal if the congested lane can cause traffic blocks involving closer roads that are located around it. Taking into consideration a factor k_{cong} we can model the queue length as shown in Eq. (8). In order to reach this length also the ingoing rate and the residual outgoing rate play an important role, in fact the higher is the difference among outgoing and ingoing rate the faster will be the queue saturation. The k_{cong} has been chosen to be 2/3 of lane length.

We are currently investigating on a variable value of k_{cong} because if several congestion events can be found on the same lanes this could mean that reducing the ingoing rate it will possible to reduce the impact of the congestion on the closer areas. This can be made reducing the queue length and therefore the value of $VN_{j,i}$. In this case the ingoing rate is reduced by the *CTM* that can change the associated weight on traffic map on the vehicles sending a *CongUpdate* message before the limit value is reached.

$$VN_{j,i} < \frac{k_{cong} \cdot l_{j,i}}{O_{j,i}} \tag{8}$$

As above stated considering the Vehicle Number upper bound (VN), which is evaluated by CTM, it is possible to reduce the ingoing rate in order to break down congestion levels along the city. Exploiting Eq. (8) it is possible to know the probability to have VN value on a particular lane. This can be used to make a forecast on the congestion levels, our attempt to face this issue is to minimize this probability acting on the best path finding process in a real-time way. This can be done triggering a routine for cost computation, made by the vehicles to reach their destinations as addressed in [28–30]. In order to reduce the probability that a lane block can happen, we can act on the ingoing rate of the lane sending a *CongUpdate* message to the RSU and OBU systems changing the weight of the related lane. In this way, the vehicles can change their path because a higher cost is found on the interested lane.

In order to perform the road cost computation and to better recognize when a lane is congested, it is possible to refer to the time spent along the lane monitoring the average travelling time, that we have already defined in Eq. (7). In this work, we consider the lower bound represented by Eq. (6) to associate a weight on the lane:

$$w_{j,i} = I_{j,i} + \left(n_{j,i} - VN_{j,i}\right) * TTSL_{j,i} \tag{9}$$

$$Cost_{j,i} = \begin{cases} TTSL_{j,i} & \text{if } n_{j,i} \le VN_{j,i} \\ w_{j,i} & \text{otherwise} \end{cases} \tag{10}$$

4 Advanced Simulation by Using Realistic Traffic Data

In this section, other simulation campaigns will be shown, in order to test in a better way, the previous proposed protocol, using the real traffic data relating to the city of Bologna [15]. This traffic data is collected and elaborated during the development of the European Project called "I-Tetris" [22], an integrated wireless and traffic platform for real-time road traffic management solutions. This project was co-funded by the European Commission between 2008 and 2011 and was concerned in developing a simulation system for evaluations of large-scale traffic management solutions that work via vehicular communications. The considered scenario included the demand for Bologna's peak hour (8:00 am 9:00 am). Additional data sets supported by the municipality of Bologna including positions of traffic lights, traffic light plans, inductive loop positions and measures. In order to realize the real traffic data, the passenger vehicles in the network are described in an aggregated manner: the numbers of vehicles to insert are given for certain roads located at the networks border. Following their initial route, the vehicles pass certain routing decision points at which they get a new route assigned randomly, according to a given distribution. This method is used for reproducing the turn percentages at intersections measured in reality using by 636 detection sites distributed in the map area, close to road junctions. Unfortunately, the detectors are measuring only the number of vehicles which are passing the detectors within five minutes and there are no other values like speed or vehicle type available. The provided network, traffic demand and additional infrastructure data is broad and a lot of work was done on improve the simulation quality.

4.1 Environmental Setting of the Considered Scenario

As network simulator, we used OMNET++ [23] with VEINS [24] framework for 802.11p Standard and the Simulator of Urban Mobility (SUMO) [25] to manage the mobility of the vehicles. SUMO and VEINS can communicate through TRACI class [26]. In the first step of this simulation campaign, we have deployed four RSU in order to cover all area of the map (see Fig. 1). The aim of the RSU is to receive road information from the vehicles and processing its and after send this information to the CTM. In this way, the CTM Server has the updated global status of all streets, in order to make soundness the costs calculation.

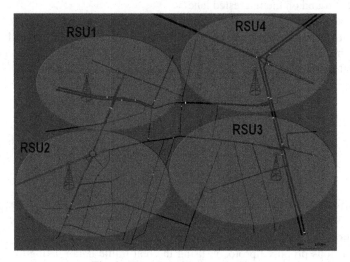

Fig. 1. The Map of Bologna's City.

After this, the second step was to reduce the protocol overhead due to high vehicles number that are travelling in the map. In order to avoid this issue, the vehicles that periodically send information (*PosUpdate* messages) to RSU, it was reduced by 50% avoiding the flooding mechanism, because the neighbor node of a specific vehicle, sends redundant information and its can be deleted and discarded. Another motivation is linked to the duration and the fluidity of the simulation in Omnet++ environment. In Fig. 2 is shown an example as the vehicles send *PosUpdate* messages to the RSU, by reducing the number of signaling packet.

The goal of this simulation campaign is to verify if the protocol for smart traffic management described previously is still working or not, by using realistic vehicular traffic data. The next step is to import these data regarding the city of Bologna into SUMO simulator.

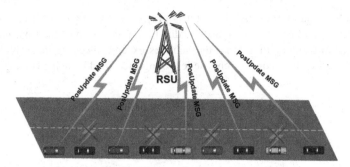

Fig. 2. Overhead and redundant information reduction

4.2 Vehicular Traffic Information

As written previously, we employed 4 RSU to cover all map area. In this sub-section, we describe in details how the vehicular traffic is distributed during the simulation. The Table 1 is used to better understand the performance evaluation that are shown in the next section. For example, it is normal to consider that the value of average CO_2 emission, or the average time spent of vehicles in the city, is higher in RSUs where pass-through a high number of vehicles. At the end of the simulation, the four RSUs detect 22703 vehicles (see the Table 1). During the one hour of observation, all vehicles are monitored in the real scenario trough the detectors fixed in the city of Bologna.

Table 1. Vehicular traffic data in the simulation

Fixed infrastructures	Total vehicles number
RSU 1	5406
RSU 2	6003
RSU 3	5324
RSU 4	5970

For each vehicle, a complete route or journey is set in SUMO, in order to simulate the real traffic scenario. In the following simulations, we compared the real traffic condition monitored by VANET Infrastructure, with the *SeaWave* Protocol in order to verify if by using a policy for traffic management, the road conditions are improved or not. During the *SeaWave* protocol performance, the routes of the vehicles may be changed, if it is detected a congestion state for a considered road, by acting the re-route mechanism.

4.3 CO_2 Emissions Evaluation

The first investigated parameter is CO_2 emissions of the vehicles. It is calculated in Veins framework following the assumptions described in [25] by Cappiello et al. Figure 3 shows that the *SeaWave* protocol by using a re-routing mechanism achieves better result than the real traffic situation detected by i-Tetris project, because the vehicles take roads less congested. Another possible reason is due to the reduction of the total number of accelerations and decelerations that the vehicles execute, because the vehicles pass-through less traffic blocks or they choose less congested road by using our algorithm.

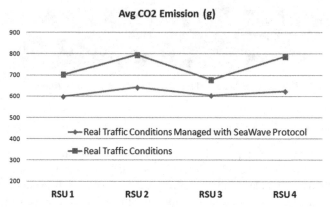

Fig. 3. The comparison between real traffic scenario and the Seawave protocol in term of CO_2 Emissions

4.4   Monitoring the Number of the Congested Roads

In this subsection is shown how by using the *SeaWave* protocol, the number of congested roads detected by the RSUs is reduced then the real traffic situation monitored only by *i*-Tetris project without the re-routing mechanism. This considered parameter represents the sum of the Congested Roads detected by the 4 RSU, every interval of 20 s. In the following figure, it is represented the total number of detected congested roads during the peak hour of observation in Bologna's City. The advantage to have a lower number of congested roads, as demonstrated by the Fig. 4, it can be translated in advantages in term of reduction of CO_2 emissions and time spent in the city by the vehicles, because the traffic is more fluent by using the *SeaWave* Protocol and the re-routing mechanism for the vehicles toward road less congested.

4.5   Total Average Time Spent in the City by the Vehicles

When the congestion check with re-routing mechanism is active through *SeaWave* protocol, it is possible to observe that the vehicles could find the roads status less congested then the case without the use of the re-routing mechanism. Thus, they can save the time to arrive at destination. Even if they take other path that is maybe little longer than the previous path, as demonstrated in Fig. 5, the time spent by vehicles is still lower than the realistic traffic condition without re-routing mechanism, because the vehicular traffic is more fluent on the new paths calculated by the smart protocol.

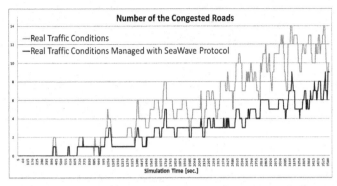

Fig. 4. The comparison of the number of congested roads between the real traffic scenario and the SeaWave Protocol

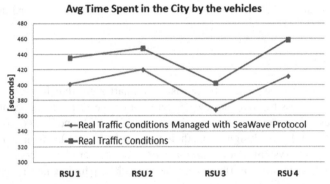

Fig. 5. The comparison of the average time spent of the vehicles in the city between the real traffic scenario and the SeaWave Protocol

4.6 The Trend of the Cumulative Vehicles' Number on a Congested Road

Another parameter that is important to show is the cumulative vehicles number on a congested road, during the entire simulation. In the case relating of the *SeaWave* Protocol, it is important to notice that this parameter when it reaches the congestion threshold, it tends to remain constant for a few seconds, and after it increases again but less rapidly, how it is possible to notice in Fig. 6.

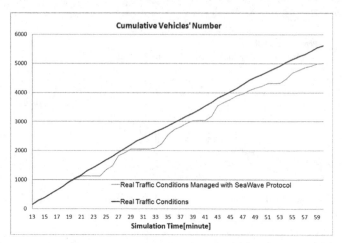

Fig. 6. The Cumulative Vehicles Number trend for the real traffic scenario and the SeaWave Protocol

5   Conclusions

In this paper, we demonstrated that by using a smart algorithm for vehicular traffic management, it is possible to reduce the CO_2 emissions, the average time spent in the city by the vehicles and to improve the traffic jams. Using the V2V and V2I communications provided by VANETs, we designed an efficient algorithm for traffic management allows us to enhance safety systems that may reduce the total number of accidents on the roads. Moreover, spreading traffic information on the network help finding new routes reducing time for travelling.

References

1. Mohammad, S.A., Rasheed, A., Qayyum, A.: VANET architectures and protocol stacks: a survey. In: Strang, T., Festag, A., Vinel, A., Mehmood, R., Rico Garcia, C., Röckl, M. (eds.) Nets4Cars/Nets4Trains 2011. LNCS, vol. 6596, pp. 95–105. Springer, Heidelberg (2011). https://doi.org/10.1007/978-3-642-19786-4_9
2. Kurmis, M., Andziulis, A., Dzemydiene, D., Jakovlev, S., Voznak, M., Gricius, G.: Cooperative context data acquisition and dissemination for situation identification in vehicular communication networks. Wirel. Pers. Commun. **85**(1), 49–62 (2015). https://doi.org/10.1007/s11277-015-2727-1
3. Nguyen, H.-S., Do, D.-T., Nguyen, T.-S., Voznak, M.: Exploiting hybrid time switching-based and power splitting-based relaying protocol in wireless powered communication networks with outdated channel state information. Automatika **58**(1), 111–118 (2017)
4. Nguyen, T.N., Minh, T.H.Q., Tran, P.T., Voznak, M.: Adaptive energy harvesting relaying protocol for two-way half-duplex system network over Rician fading channels. Wirel. Commun. Mob. Comput. **2018** (2018). Article no. 7693016
5. Fotino, M., et al.: Evaluating Energy consumption of proactive and reactive routing protocols in a MANET. In: Orozco-Barbosa, L., Olivares, T., Casado, R., Bermúdez, A. (eds.) WSAN 2007. IIFIP, vol. 248, pp. 119–130. Springer, Boston, MA (2007). https://doi.org/10.1007/978-0-387-74899-3_11

6. De Rango, F., Tropea, M.: Swarm intelligence based energy saving and load balancing in wireless ad hoc networks. In: Proceedings of the 2009 Workshop on Bio-Inspired Algorithms for Distributed Systems, pp. 77–84, June 2009

7. Socievole, A., De Rango, F., Coscarella, C.: Routing approaches and performance evaluation in delay tolerant networks. In: 2011 Wireless Telecommunications Symposium (WTS), pp. 1–6. IEEE, April 2011

8. Socievole, A., Yoneki, E., De Rango, F., Crowcroft, J.: Opportunistic message routing using multi-layer social networks. In: Proceedings of the 2nd ACM Workshop on High Performance Mobile Opportunistic Systems, pp. 39–46, November 2013

9. Ryu, M.-W., Cha, S.-H., Cho, K.-H.: DSRC-based channel allocation algorithm for emergency message dissemination in VANETs. In: Lee, G., Howard, D., Ślęzak, D. (eds.) ICHIT 2011. LNCS, vol. 6935, pp. 105–112. Springer, Heidelberg (2011). https://doi.org/10.1007/978-3-642-24082-9_13

10. Santamaria, A.F., Tropea, M., Fazio, P., De Rango, F.: Managing emergency situations in VANET through heterogeneous technologies cooperation. Sensors 18(5), 1461 (2018)

11. Nwizege, K.S., Bottero, M., Mmeah, S., Nwiwure, E.D.: Vehicles–to-infrastructure communication safety messaging in DSRC. In: International Workshop on the Design and Performance of Networks on Chip (DPNoC 2014), Procedia Computer Science, vol. 34, pp. 559–564 (2014)

12. Lee, E.-K., Yang, S., Oh, S.Y., Gerla, M.: RF-GPS: RFID assisted localization in VANETs. In: IEEE 6th International Conference on Mobile Adhoc and Sensor Systems (2009)

13. Codeca, L., Frank, R., Engel, T.: Luxembourg SUMO Traffic (LuST) scenario: 24 hours of mobility for vehicular networking research. In: IEEE Vehicular Networking Conference (VNC), Kyoto, Japan, 16–18 December 2015 (2015)

14. Uppoor, S., Trullols-Cruces, O., Fiore, M., Barcelo-Ordinas, J.M.: Generation and analysis of a large-scale urban vehicular mobility dataset. IEEE Trans. Mob. Comput. 13(5) (2014)

15. Bieker, L., Krajzewicz, D., Morra, A., Michelacci, C., Cartolano, F.: Traffic simulation for all: a real world traffic scenario from the city of Bologna. In: Behrisch, M., Weber, M. (eds.) Modeling Mobility with Open Data. LNM, pp. 47–60. Springer, Cham (2015). https://doi.org/10.1007/978-3-319-15024-6_4

16. Sahoo, P.K., Chiang, M.-J., Wu, S.-L.: SVANET: a smart vehicular ad hoc network for efficient data transmission with wireless sensors. Sensors 14, 22230–22260 (2014)

17. Qureshi, K.N., Abdullah, A.H., Bukhari, M., Anwar, R.W.: SSNM-smart sensor network model for vehicular ad hoc networks. In: International Conference on Smart Sensors and Application (ICSSA), Kuala Lumpur, Malaysia (2015)

18. Kaiwartya, O., et al.: Internet of vehicles: motivation, layered architecture, network model, challenges, and future aspects. Spec. Sect. IEEE Access: Future Netw.: Archit. Protoc. Appl. 4, 5356–5373 (2016)

19. Suresh, K., Preethi, R.A., Sarada Kiranmayee, T.: VANET based traffic analysis using cloud server. IIOABJ J. Emerg. Technol. Netw. Secur. (ETNS) 7, 144–149 (2016)

20. Santamaria, A.F., Sottile, C., De Rango, F., Marano, S.: Safety enhancement and Carbon Dioxide (CO₂) reduction in VANETs. Mob. Netw. Appl. 20(2), 220–238 (2015). https://doi.org/10.1007/s11036-015-0580-9

21. Santamaria, A.F., Fazio, P., Raimondo, P., Tropea, M., De Rango, F.: A new distributed predictive congestion aware re-routing algorithm for CO2 emissions reduction. IEEE Trans. Veh. Technol. 68(5), 4419–4433 (2019)

22. Rondinone, M.: iTETRIS: the integrated wireless and traffic simulation platform for real-time road traffic management solutions. COMeSafety Newsl. (8) (2010)

23. Varga, A.: OMNeT++. In: Wehrle, K., Güneş, M., Gross, J. (eds.) Modeling and Tools for Network Simulation, pp. 35–59. Springer, Heidelberg (2010). https://doi.org/10.1007/978-3-642-12331-3_3

24. Sommer, C., German, R., Dressler, F.: Bidirectionally coupled network and road traffic simulation for improved IVC analysis. IEEE Trans. Mob. Comput. **10**(1), 3–15 (2011)
25. Behrisch, M., Bieker, L., Erdmann, J., Krajzewicz, D.: Sumo - simulation of urban mobility: an overview. In: Proceedings of the 3rd International Conference on Advances in System Simulation (SIMUL 2011), Barcelona, Spain, pp. 63–68 (2011)
26. Wegener, A., Piorkowski, M., Raya, M., Hellbruck, H., Fischer, S., Hubaux, J.P.: Traci: an interface for coupling road traffic and network simulators. In: Proceedings of the 11th Communications and Networking Simulation Symposium, pp. 155–163. ACM (2008)
27. Cappiello, A., Chabini, I., Nam, E.K., Lue, A., AbouZeid, M.: A statistical model of vehicle emissions and fuel consumption. In: IEEE 5th International Conference on Intelligent Transportation Systems (IEEE ITSC), pp. 801–809 (2002)
28. Fazio, P., De Rango, F., Sottile, C.: A predictive cross-layered interference management in a multichannel MAC with reactive routing in VANET. IEEE Trans. Mob. Comput. **15**(8), 1850–1862 (2015)
29. Fazio, P., Sottile, C., Santamaria, A.F., Tropea, M.: Vehicular networking enhancement and multi-channel routing optimization, based on multi-objective metric and minimum spanning tree. Adv. Electr. Electron. Eng. **11**(5), 349–356 (2013)
30. Fazio, P., Tropea, M., De Rango, F., Voznak, M.: Pattern prediction and passive bandwidth management for hand-over optimization in QoS cellular networks with vehicular mobility. IEEE Trans. Mob. Comput. **15**(11), 2809–2824 (2016)

Ensemble Malware Classification Using Neural Networks

Piotr Wyrwinski$^{(\boxtimes)}$ ⓘ, Jakub Dutkiewicz$^{(\boxtimes)}$ ⓘ, and Czeslaw Jedrzejek$^{(\boxtimes)}$ ⓘ

Faculty of Computing, Poznan University of Technology, Poznań, Poland
czeslaw.jedrzejek@put.poznan.pl

Abstract. This work presents an experimental study of malware classification using the Microsoft Malware Classification Challenge 2015 dataset. We combine the approach of the winning solution to the Microsoft Malware Classification Challenge with the neural network approach. Using a combination of n-grams features for both assembly (asm) and byte code enables us to significantly improve the result. By mixing multiple approaches, we are able to get the best log-loss result of 0.0025, so far. This comes mostly from the classical XGBoost method with n-gram contributions from the binary and assembly code. However, understanding this result is still incomplete. The standard neural network approaches (even with LSTM) alone give poorer results compared to the XGBoost, based on mostly n-gram. It is not clear why adding 6-grams to the binary code analysis does not improve results. There are many more options to be tested in the future, in particular networks.

Keywords: Malware detection · Microsoft Malware Classification Challenge · Malware neural networks

1 Introduction

Machine learning has a clear advantage over signature methods still used in malware detection. Constantly changing malware signatures and the use of obfuscation methods require effective and fast detection and classification methods.

1.1 Machine Learning-Based Malware Detection

Different studies have demonstrated the proficiency of machine learning for the detection and classification of malware files. Further, the accuracy of these machine learning models can be improved by using feature selection algorithms to select the most essential features and by reducing the size of the dataset, which leads to decreased computational overhead. In general, there are two major approaches to malware classification. The first is the classical method based on

Supported by PUT statutory funds. One of the authors (CJ) acknowledges the NVIDIA GPU Grant of Quadro P6000 card.

A. Dziech et al. (Eds.): MCSS 2020, CCIS 1284, pp. 125–138, 2020.
https://doi.org/10.1007/978-3-030-59000-0_10

hand-crafted feature selection. The other is a neural network approach. The customary thinking is that the neural approach, where the progress in recent years has been tremendous, gives better results for very large systems independent of a domain. For example, for Question Answering on SQuAD2.0[1], the F-measure increased from 70.3% in 2017 to 93.011% in 2020. One would expect that using attention neural networks [16], or BERT [5] CNN+LSTM based networks, would give better results.

The objective of this work is to test many neural network approaches and the use of an ensemble method to verify whether richer neural architectures would lead to improvement. Also, we would like to establish the relative importance of binary vs assembly language (asm) data. Initially, our work followed the convolutional neural network (CNN) approach to bytecode, originated in the Gilbert's thesis [6] and the black-box approach of [11]. We make comparisons to other neural networks approaches in the literature and the winning Microsoft Malware Classification Challenge solution [17]. This work starts with a thorough comparison of existing lines of research and concentrates on analysis of the importance of various types of metadata, n-grams correlations in binary and asm code vs sequence capture in CNN and LTSM networks, as well as optimizing parameters and hyperparameters.

1.2   Microsoft Malware Classification Challenge 2015

The malware research area needs benchmarks to better calibrate results. The Microsoft Malware Classification Challenge was announced in 2015 along with the publication of a dataset consisting of disassembly and bytecode of more than 20K malware samples. Apart from serving in the Kaggle competition, the dataset (though rather small) has become a standard benchmark for research on modeling malware behavior. There are works using much larger and newer sets that are not reproducible because the data is not in the public domain.

Prior to February 2018, the dataset was cited in more than 50 research papers [13], and recently this value has surpassed 70 (June 2020). Almost all scientific papers employ neural networks but their results are weak, some having F-measure as low as 90%. The notable exception is the use of the ensemble method based on deep neural networks [18]. Our approach can be viewed as an extension of this work.

Surprisingly, the original first three best results, all obtained with XGBoost, were not improved till now. Despite a high-level comparison of the publications citing the dataset [13], there is little understanding as to the detailed characteristics of models.

2   Microsoft Malware Classification Challenge Benchmark

The data provided by Microsoft contained 10,868 samples for the training set and 10,873 for the test set, which was not publicly annotated. The training set

---

[1] https://paperswithcode.com/sota/question-answering-on-squad20.

is used to adjust parameters in the learning process of the model, for example classifier or neural networks, while the test set is independent of the training set and is intended for testing the learned parameters of the model. The total size of the files provided was over 400 GB after unpacking. Each sample was in one of nine malware families and was in two formats, asm and byte (Table 1).

Table 1. Malware families in the dataset

Family name	# Train samples	Type
Ramnit	1541	Worm
Lollipop	2478	Adware
Kelihos_ver3	2942	Backdoor
Vundo	475	Trojan
Simda	42	Backdoor
Tracur	751	TrojanDownloader
Kelihos_ver1	398	Backdoor
Obfuscator.ACY	1228	Any kind of obfuscated malware
Gatak	1013	Backdoor

2.1 Byte Files

The byte file represents the machine code as a sequence of hexadecimal numbers grouped into 1-byte words. Each line in the file starts with the start address of the machine code in the memory, followed by bytes which correspond to a code instruction or data.

2.2 Asm Files

One of the most popular recursive traversal disassemblers, the Interactive Disassembler (IDA), was used to create asm files. It performs automatic analysis of binary file code using cross-references. Figure 1 shows how the IDA interprets byte sequences. The lines belong to types such as a predefined section, a memory cell address, a sequence of bytes, an opcode and an operand. As a result of malware obfuscation techniques like packing, the default sections can be modified or reordered or new sections can be created.

2.3 The First Place Approach

Feature engineering and K-Fold cross-validation played a key role in the winners' approach [17], helping to prevent overfitting during feature and model evaluations. They created three XGBoost models with different parameters and using

```
.text:004159CC 66 8B 06        mov     ax, [esi]
.text:004159CF 66 3B 01        cmp     ax, [ecx]
.text:004159D2 74 35           jz      short loc_415A09
.text:004159D4 0F B6 11        movzx   edx, byte ptr [ecx]
.text:004159D7 0F B6 C0        movzx   eax, al
.text:004159DA 2B C2           sub     eax, edx
.text:004159DC 74 11           jz      short loc_4159EF
.text:004159DE 33 D2           xor     edx, edx
.text:004159E0 85 C0           test    eax, eax
.text:004159E2 0F 9F C2        setnle  dl
.text:004159E5 8D 54 12 FF     lea     edx, [edx+edx-1]
.text:004159E9 8B C2           mov     eax, edx
.text:004159EB 85 C0           test    eax, eax
.text:004159ED 75 1C           jnz     short locret 415A0B
```

Fig. 1. A fragment of the asm file from a training set.

different features. They then combined these models using a weighted geometric mean to improve the accuracy of the final model.

This measure, which is often used in imbalance dataset evaluation studies [14], is a metric that combines both the sensitivity and specificity by calculating their geometric mean. They found that from now on it is virtually impossible to improve accuracy, so taking advantage of the fact that the resulting model has such a high accuracy they decided to use a semi-supervised learning to improve the Logloss score. They created pseudo labels for the test set to use the best model to create a dataset containing a train and test set. Using K-Fold cross-validation, they then trained the new model on an enlarged dataset and generated new labels for the test set. This improved the Logloss score.

3   Information Extraction

At the beginning both byte code and asm files need preprocessing. Also n-gram processing is given here. N-grams are a basis of the XGBoost training for a classical classification method.

3.1   Asm File Preprocessing

Since the asm file contains a lot of additional information beyond the opcode instructions, it was necessary to perform filtering rules to extract the opcode sequences and obtain opcode statistics. Then, using the Gini feature importance from the Random Forest model trained on the resulting unigrams, the opcode set was reduced to 185 elements.

3.2   Byte File Preprocessing

The bytes in the byte file were saved in text format and converted to an integer between 0 and 255. Then, in order to limit the memory usage, the special characters '??' were saved as a number 0, which allowed us to limit the number range and thus save the data in int8 format. In addition, in order to preserve the information about special characters, a file with a .meta extension was created, which stores the sparse matrix of indexes of places where special characters '??' are located.

3.3 N-Grams

Language models for natural language processing often use n-gram statistics. As n increases, the need for a larger dataset increases, because longer sequences are more unique, so the number of occurrences will be very low. Then, by normalization, probabilities are obtained. N-gram models are often criticized because they lack any explicit representation of long-range dependency. For this reason, n-gram models have not made much impact on the linguistic theory. On the other hand, all winning solutions (particularly, the 1st place solution) to the Microsoft Malware Classification Challenge used n-grams as dominant features. The situation occurs despite the need for larger values of n due to the nature of content encoded in executable file formats. For example, if we consider byte n-grams for Microsoft Windows Portable Executable (PE) files, one x86 assembly code instruction could be up to 15 bytes long.

In the area of natural language processing, there is little comparison between neural networks vs an n-gram approach. For the third edition of the Discriminating between Similar Languages (DSL) shared task, which was organized as part of the VarDial'2016 workshop at COLING'2016, results showed [4] that the standard approach was much more accurate than the complex neural network (Convolution Neural Network with a Bidirectional Long Short Term Memory layer (CLSTM)). In the language modeling (LM) domain, the work [2] built n-grams into neural networks. LSTM n-gram matches the LSTM LM performance for $n = 9$ and slightly outperforms it for $n = 13$ [3]. These values of n are much larger than used in practical malware detection computations.

The leading contributions to the Microsoft Malware Classification Challenge owed their success to using the n-gram feature. Hence, the Analysis of correlations between n-grams in binary and asm code is justified. In [17] they used an elaborated way to select n-grams bigrams, trigrams, and 4-grams from the asm code. The standard procedure for creating and selecting n-grams was mentioned in [12]. A feature ranking scheme to reduce the number of n-grams is applied. Then based on this n-grams, evaluation with one or more classifiers is done.

For creating opcode n-grams from asm files, [17] modified that approach. The first change was to take into account only unigrams that appeared at least 200 times in one file. They also addressed the problem of infinite loops in files. If a particular unigram was present in an infinite loop defined by an unconditional jump, the number of occurrences of that unigram was multiplied by 10 to map in some way the real frequency of operating code execution in such a loop. In this way, 165 instructions were found and based on them, 27,225 bigrams were selected. When creating trigrams and 4 - grams, the infinite loop were not taken into account, but the required number of occurrences of a given n-gram in a given file was changed to 200.

In our approach 750 n - grams per malware family for each 2 - gram and 4 - gram using information gain criteria is selected, effectively reducing the sparsity of a feature set. This feature selection method allows us to decrease the training time of the model and reduce the noise in data which improves a model performance.

4   Architectures

In this Section, we analyze neural network methods used so far and are the basis for our extensions. The results in Sect. 4.1 (no word embedding, no one-hot encoding), 4.4, and 4.5 (only one-hot encoding) were recalculated with options as in the original papers. Our original results use word embedding (as in Sect. 4.2 and 4.3 and in part of 4.5).

4.1   CNN+LSTM

We adopted the architecture [7] and unlike others, such as [18], where the approach was to convert a malware binary file to a 2D image, we interpret the bytecode as a one-dimensional image and scaled it to a fixed size. This way of converting a binary file to a stream of bytes keeps the order as in the binary code of the original file. The dataset was divided in a 5-fold cross-validation manner [18].

4.2   MalConvLSTM

The concept of using the LSTM layer to build a model capable of learning long time dependencies is adopted from [7]. After preprocessing, the binary code is converted into sequences of the 1MB length. In order to appropriately encode the input sequence bytes, following [11], we use the Embedding layer. We map the character values in the sequence to the 8-dimensional space in order to prevent the model from, for example, considering the value of 32 as twice as big as 16. Two Gated Convolutionlayers with 512 filter size followed by Batch Normalization layers are used to create a stacked Gated CNN which greatly reduces the length of the sequence and allows use of the Bidirectional LSTM layer with 256 hidden units. The size of the filters is 500 and 50 respectively, with the same stride. The weights of the model are optimized by the Nadam optimizer with the learning rate of 1e−4.

4.3   CNN+LSTM+BN

In order to increase efficiency and improve the ability to generalize, we reduce the number of model parameters. Utilizing the same method of training as [7], we are able to train a model which is much lighter than [11] and achivies significantly better performance than [7]. The model consists of 25-dim Embedding and convolution layers followed by the batch normalization and max pooling.

The first convolution layers apply 64 2-dim filters of size 3 × 25 with the stride of size 1 × 25 and zero padding. The second convolution layers apply 128 1-dim filters of size 3 with the stride of size 1 and zero padding. The size of the max pooling window is 10. We utilize Bidirectional LSTM with 128 hidden units. The weights of the model are optimized by Adam optimizer with the learning rate of 1e−3.

4.4   LSTM

This method was used by [18] for dividing the long sequence into multiple subsequences with a fixed length and performing the classification task on only those subsequences. We use the maximum likelihood probability of the model's output in order to separate out subsequences containing malicious code. A Data Augmentation strategy that addresses the problem of imbalanced class was proposed in [18]. They created subsequences using a Sliding Window, with variable sliding window steps depending on classes.

The LSTM model consists of 185-dim One-Hot Encoding and LSTM layers with 185 hidden nodes followed by dropout with a rate of 0.5.

The training set for this model has been processed as follows. The length of the subsequences is set to 120. Using the Data Augmentation strategy, a variable sliding window step is selected for each class. Using the LSTM model, the above subsequence selection strategy is applied. The threshold is set to 0.975. The subsequences that remained are considered to be malicious and for them, the subsequence fusion is done.

4.5   Gated CNN

Next we check whether a model with stacked convolutions that is more efficient than RNN because it allows parallelization can be used for appropriately short sequences extracted by the previous method. The model consists of a 185-dim One-Hot Encoding layer, two Residual Blocks with 256 and 512 filters respectively and Global Max Pooling followed by a Fully Connected layer. It consists of a gated convolutional layer with linear and sigmoid activation function, followed by 3 gated convolutional layers. The output of the last gated layer is concatenated with output of the first gated layer by elementwise sum, followed by the Batch Normalization layer and ReLU activation function. The reduction factor of filters used in Residual Blocks was 4. The Fully Connected layer has 512 hidden nodes.

4.6   Metadata Features

Similar to [18], we collected simple metadata features containing global information about malware. Because earlier models were able to capture only local features, we explore how much information about a malware type contains global metadata. We use features that were easy to extract such as sizes and lengths

Table 2. List of Metadata features.

Name	Description
asm_size	Size of malware ASM file
binary_size	Size of malware Binary file
starting_address	Starting address of machine code in first line of binary file
asm_length	The total number of lines in ASM file
binary_length	The total number of lines in Binary file
.edata	The total number of lines in .edata section
.gnu_deb	The total number of lines in .gnu_deb section
.tls	The total number of lines in .tls section
.rsrc	The total number of lines in .rsrc section
.idata	The total number of lines in .idata section
.data	The total number of lines in .data section
.reloc	The total number of lines in .reloc section
.rata	The total number of lines in .rata section
.bss	The total number of lines in .bss section
.text	The total number of lines in .test section
.code	The total number of lines in .code section
.Tls	The total number of lines in .Tls section
.rdata	The total number of lines in .rdata section

of binary and asm files, starting address and various PE segments. Then, using Random Forest, the number of features is reduced. After this step, we reduce the number of features from 331 to 18. This list of features is presented in Table 2. As seen in Fig. 2, visualizing data on the plane using T-distributed Stochastic Neighbor Embedding (T-SNE), the features are highly nonlinear; therefore, the linear model obtains poor results. Nevertheless, it was noted that even such simple features are very helpful to separate samples into classes. We then use these features to train a model. To address the problem of non-linearity of features, we use the eXtreme Gradient Boosting, XGBoost model.

4.7   Ensemble

We propose a stacking ensemble approach shown in Fig. 3 for combining models that extract a lot of useful features. Second level Ensemble methods (data fusion) often improve results quite significantly. Here, we call second level inputs (first level outputs) first-level learners, Fig. 3. The training dataset was split into two groups of 90% and 10%, with equally distributed classes for training first-level learners mentioned above and Ensemble classifier. This 10% of the training set was called the hold-out set. Using predictions on the Hold-out set, a training set for learners was created. This way each weak learner provides nine features. As

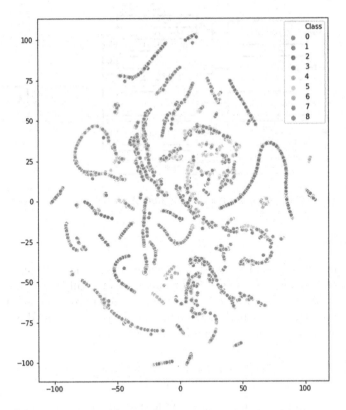

Fig. 2. Metadata features visualized on the plane.

a second-level learner, several models were tested to explain the advantages and disadvantages of this method and to show possible directions for improvement.

First, we combined all the Neural Network models with the Metadata XGBoost model using the Ensemble method. We use the obtained features and fed them into the Elastic-Net regularized Logistic Regression. Using a combination of n-grams features for asm and byte code, we were able to significantly improve the result; therefore, n-gram model trained for byte and asm n-grams was added to the solution. We verified whether adding the first place approach models using the ensemble of our approach could improve the results. We added three of their best models to our solution. We use the Hold-out set for evaluation. As a second-level learner, we use Logistic Regression with Elastic Net regularization and XGBoost. For the evaluation of these models, we use K-Fold cross-validation. We also study how the Ensemble model with weighted geometric mean [15] would behave. As weights, we use the normalized inverse of Logloss results obtained by each of the models.

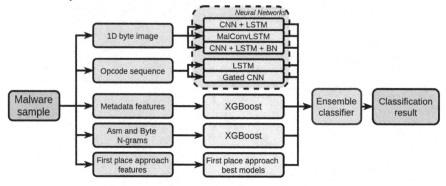

Fig. 3. Proposed Ensemble Architecture.

5   Results

We show that each Neural Network independently did not obtain satisfactory results. Moreover, the performance of the model is not highly correlated with the number of parameters of this model; the selection of appropriate architecture is much more important. The performance in classification is assessed by using two measures, the accuracy, and the logarithmic loss:

$$logloss = -\frac{1}{N} \sum_{i=1}^{N} \sum_{j=1}^{M} p_{ij} log p_{ij},$$

where N is the number of observations, M is the number of class labels. Logloss is the cross entropy between the distribution of the true labels and the predicted probabilities. This measure is more important than accuracy because it involves the concept of probabilistic confidence. For the test phase accuracy was not given by the Challenge organizers, contrary to logloss. The large difference between the Logloss validation and test results shown in Table 4 suggests the possible presence of overfitting. At this level, accuracy is fixed. Using such a small validation set with very accurate models results in overfitting. In such a situation, the geometric mean seems to be a better choice because it is not directly dependent on the validation set. It uses information only about how the model is performing. Although the validation Logloss is high, the validation accuracy is very good. The reason is the misclassification of several samples. Nevertheless, the model generalization is much better.

Recently, [10] proposed an ensemble method that combines assembly data preprocessed as sequences and compiled data preprocessed as images using SVM. Their accuracy is slightly worse than ours, and their confusion matrix is much worse than ours Fig. 4. In Table 3, we present the results for our implementation of various neural network methods. The are mostly better than the corresponding implementations in the literature. In Table 4, comparison of results obtained using three data fusion (ensemble) methods is shown. It is to be noted that the XGBoost used for ensemble learners is different than the XGBoost used in the first stage learning (Table 5).

Table 3. The number of parameters of the models and their evalution.

Configuration		No. params	Val			Test
Model	Data type		Accuracy	Logloss	Logloss	
CNN+LSTM	BYTE	268,949	**0.9872**	0.0561	0.0798	
MalConvLSTM	BYTE	31,900,185	0.9863	**0.0364**	**0.0461**	
CNN+LSTM+BN	BYTE	303,241	0.9826	0.0743	0.0478	
LSTM	ASM	552,234	0.9808	0.0901	0.0632	
Gated CNN	ASM	1,795,337	0.9808	0.1528	0.0706	

Table 4. Comparison of results obtained using three data fusion (ensemble) methods.

Configurations	Val		Test
	Accuracy	Logloss	Logloss
Logistic regression	**1.0000**	**0.0012**	0.0033
XGBoost	0.9936	0.0341	0.0277
Weighted geometric mean	0.9982	0.0646	**0.0025**

Table 5. Classification metrics on Hold-out set for weighted geometric mean Ensamble model.

Class	Precision	Recall	F_1-score	Support
Ramnit	1.0000	1.0000	1.0000	155
Lollipop	1.0000	1.0000	1.0000	248
Kelihos_ver3	1.0000	1.0000	1.0000	295
Vundo	0.9600	1.0000	0.9796	48
Simda	1.0000	1.0000	1.0000	5
Tracur	1.0000	0.9737	0.9867	76
Kelihos_ver1	1.0000	1.0000	1.0000	40
Obfuscator.ACY	1.0000	1.0000	1.0000	123
Gatak	1.0000	1.0000	1.0000	102
Accuracy			0.9982	1092
Macro avg	0.9956	0.9971	0.9963	1092
Weighted avg	0.9982	0.9982	0.9982	1092

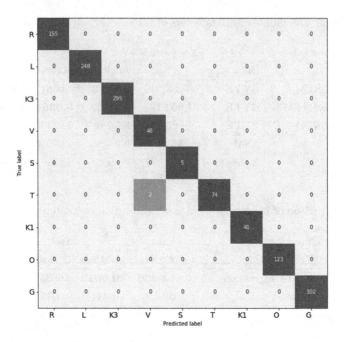

Fig. 4. Confusion matrix of weighted geometric mean Ensemble model.

6   Discussion

This work aims at surpassing the best results obtained by the first three solutions based on log-loss for the Microsoft Malware Classification Challenge (Big 2015). The task was to classify malware into families based on the input file content and characteristics. Currently these leading results have not been surpassed. Out of the over 70 subsequent papers, many were of low quality (achieving poor log-loss and accuracy values). The most informative was the documentation of the winners (the first three teams), who achieved values of log-loss of 0.00283, 0.00324, 0.00396, respectively; however, their methods were ad-hoc, guided by log-loss intermediate results on 30% of the testing set. Among recent work, one can point out [1] and [18]. Interestingly, systematic feature selection used by [1] was not able to beat a contribution by partially the same authors in the original challenge [9]. We combined the approach of the Microsoft Malware Classification Challenge with the neural network approach of [18]. Using a combination of n-grams features for both asm and byte code enables us to significantly improve the result. By mixing many approaches we are able to get the best log-loss result so far, 0.0025. This mostly comes from the XGBoost method with n-gram contribution from the binary and assembly code. However, understanding this result is still not adequate. A standard neural network approach (even with LSTM) alone gives poor results compared to the XGBoost based on mostly n-gram. It is not clear why adding 6-grams to the binary code analysis does not improve results. The complex scheme we use is responsible for only 10% of improvement over the winning Microsoft Malware Classification Challenge submission. We intend to verify statements in [12] and [19] (using private malware samples, unrelated to the Microsoft Malware Classification Challenge) related to the following claim: "While n-grams do have some merit as a feature for executable files, their results have been significantly over-estimated in the literature". In the future we intend to implement many options, such as NN with soft n-grams, the use of symbol frequency instead of infogain for a feature selection, more metadata. Recently, a novel interpretable malware detector using a hierarchical transformer method was proposed and classification performed on the malicious executables collected from MalShare and VirusShare in 2018 [8]. However, their accuracy of 98.5% is not overwhelming.

References

1. Ahmadi, M., Ulyanov, D., Semenov, S., Trofimov, M., Giacinto, G.: Novel feature extraction, selection and fusion for effective malware family classification. In: Proceedings of the Sixth ACM on Conference on Data and Application Security and Privacy, CODASPY 2016, pp. 183–194 (2016). https://doi.org/10.1145/2857705.2857713

2. Bengio, Y., Ducharme, R., Vincent, P., Janvin, C.: A neural probabilistic language model. J. Mach. Learn. Res. **3**, 1137–1155 (2003). http://jmlr.org/papers/v3/bengio03a.html

3. Chelba, C., Norouzi, M., Bengio, S.: N-gram language modeling using recurrent neural network estimation. CoRR abs/1703.10724 (2017)

4. Cianflone, A., Kosseim, L.: N-gram and neural language models for discriminating similar languages. CoRR abs/1708.03421 (2017)

5. Devlin, J., Chang, M., Lee, K., Toutanova, K.: BERT: pre-training of deep bidirectional transformers for language understanding. CoRR abs/1810.04805 (2018). http://arxiv.org/abs/1810.04805

6. Gibert, D., Mateu, C., Planes, J., Vicens, R.: Using convolutional neural networks for classification of malware represented as images. J. Comput. Virol. Hacking Tech. **15**(1), 15–28 (2018). https://doi.org/10.1007/s11416-018-0323-0

7. Le, Q., Boydell, O., Mac Namee, B., Scanlon, M.: Deep learning at the shallow end: malware classification for non-domain experts. Digit. Invest. **26**, S118–S126 (2018)

8. Li, M.Q., Fung, B.C.M., Charland, P., Ding, S.H.H.: I-MAD: a novel interpretable malware detector using hierarchical transformer. CoRR abs/1909.06865 (2019)

9. Trofimov, M., Dmitry Ulyanov, S.S.: Kaggle 'Microsoft malware classification challenge' 3rd place solution. https://github.com/geffy/kaggle-malware

10. Narayanan, B.N., Davuluru, V.S.P.: Ensemble malware classification system using deep neural networks. Electronics **9**, 721 (2020). https://doi.org/10.3390/electronics9050721

11. Pieczynski, D., Jedrzejek, C.: Malware detection using black-box neural method. In: Proceedings of MISSI - Multimedia and Network Information Systems 2018, pp. 180–189 (2018). https://doi.org/10.1007/978-3-319-98678-4_20

12. Raff, E., et al.: An investigation of byte n-gram features for malware classification. J. Comput. Virol. Hacking Tech. **14**(1), 1–20 (2016). https://doi.org/10.1007/s11416-016-0283-1
13. Ronen, R., Radu, M., Feuerstein, C., Yom-Tov, E., Ahmadi, M.: Microsoft malware classification challenge. CoRR abs/1802.10135 (2018)
14. Shabtai, A., Moskovitch, R., Feher, C., Dolev, S., Elovici, Y.: Detecting unknown malicious code by applying classification techniques on opcode patterns. Secur. Informat. **1**(1), 1 (2012). https://doi.org/10.1186/2190-8532-1-1
15. Simopoulos, C.M.A., Weretilnyk, E.A., Golding, G.B.: Prediction of plant lncRNA by ensemble machine learning classifiers. BMC Genom. **19**(1), 316 (2018). https://doi.org/10.1186/s12864-018-4665-2
16. Vaswani, A., et al.: Attention is all you need. In: Annual Conference on Neural Information Processing Systems 2017, pp. 5998–6008 (2017). http://papers.nips.cc/paper/7181-attention-is-all-you-need
17. Wang, X., Liu, J., Chen, Q.: Big 2015 Microsoft malware classification challenge, first place say no to overfitting. https://github.com/xiaozhouwang/kaggle_Microsoft_Malware
18. Yan, J., Qi, Y., Rao, Q.: Detecting malware with an ensemble method based on deep neural network. Sec. Commun. Netw. **2018** (2018). https://doi.org/10.1155/2018/7247095
19. Zak, R., Raff, E., Nicholas, C.: What can n-grams learn for malware detection? In: 12th International Conference on Malicious and Unwanted Software, MALWARE 2017, Fajardo, PR, USA, pp. 109–118 (2017). https://doi.org/10.1109/MALWARE.2017.8323963

A Resilient Distributed Measurement System for Smart Grid Application

Giovanni Artale[1] ⓘ, Christof Brandauer[2], Giuseppe Caravello[1] ⓘ,
Antonio Cataliotti[1] ⓘ, Valentina Cosentino[1] ⓘ, Dario Di Cara[3](✉) ⓘ,
Salvatore Guaiana[1] ⓘ, Nicola Panzavecchia[3] ⓘ, Stefano Salsano[4] ⓘ,
and Giovanni Tinè[3] ⓘ

[1] Department of Engineering, University of Palermo, Palermo, Italy
{giovanni.artale,giuseppe.caravello02,antonio.cataliotti,
valentina.cosentino,salvatore.guaiana}@unipa.it
[2] Salzburg Research Forschungsgesellschaft, Salzburg, Austria
christof.brandauer@salzburgresearch.at
[3] National Research Council, Institute of Marine Engineering, Palermo, Italy
{dario.dicara,nicola.panzavecchia,giovanni.tine}@cnr.it
[4] University of Rome Tor Vergata/CNIT, Rome, Italy
stefano.salsano@uniroma2.it

Abstract. Since the production of energy from renewable energy sources is strongly increasing, the migration from the classical electric grid toward the smart grid is becoming a reality. Distribution System Operators, along with the control of the entire network and its stability, need to address the security and the reliability of the communication channels and the data itself. In this paper a solution is proposed to address these issues. It is based on a distributed measurement system that relies on a wireless network as well as a redundant Power Line communication system in order to transfer the electrical measures to a centralized SCADA server. The collected data are used to run a power flow algorithm in order to give the operator the whole picture of the network energy flow and to suggest specific actions aimed to keep the electricity network stable. An external computational layer has the role to check and validate the data collected using different approaches, in order to avoid that a malicious alteration of data tricks the operator into performing an incorrect action on the electrical network.

Keywords: Smart grid · SCADA · Distributed measurement systems · Human-machine interfaces

1 Introduction

Historically, security of industrial control systems (ICS) was guaranteed by restrictions on physical access, isolation from public communication systems and employment of proprietary technologies. In recent years, the need of reducing implementation costs, increasing the number of controlled equipment and standardizing the communication protocols have caused a migration of traditional ICS toward modern ICT solutions widely

A. Dziech et al. (Eds.): MCSS 2020, CCIS 1284, pp. 139–153, 2020.
https://doi.org/10.1007/978-3-030-59000-0_11

adopted in ordinary networks and systems as well as the adoption of standard Internet protocols (e.g. TCP/IP, HTTP, etc.). This has caused a significant increase of ICS and SCADA system vulnerabilities from cyber-attacks. Some ICSs still don't have any cryptographic protection in their internal network and often even in their connection to the Internet [1, 2]. The number of vulnerability revelations has significantly increased in recent years: from 19 in 2010 to 189 in 2015 [3]. Moreover, these vulnerabilities are often detected only after many days sometimes months from SCADA software [4]. For example, the attacker of the Ukrainian Power Grid infrastructure [5] was discovered 6 months after the first access to the system. In this long time, the attacker could meticulously prepare the attack by performing network reconnaissance, harvesting credentials, escalating privileges, etc.

This paper wants to discuss and to propose solutions on these issues, with a particular focus on SCADA systems dedicated to electrical networks. Due to the large increase of energy production from renewable energy sources, in fact, the migration from the classical electric grid toward smart grid is becoming a reality. This is causing the Distribution System Operators needs to exchange sensitive monitoring data and control signals with users and prosumers to preserve network stability. Thus, new needs are arising to address security and reliability of the communication channels and the data itself. In this paper, a solution is proposed to address these issues specifically tailored for smart grid SCADA systems. The proposed solution combines the results of two research projects. The first project, named SCISSOR, has proposed and developed a complex platform for data security integrating both physical and virtual devices [6]. The second project, named I-SOLE, still under development, aims at improving data security by introducing redundancy on the communication and an additional layer of data validation. Thus, the final proposed solution entails three combined approaches to assess data security:

1. redundancy of the communication system used for data collection (studied in the project I-SOLE);
2. first data validation performed by the SCADA control center and based on the knowledge of the electrical network operation (I-SOLE);
3. second data validation performed remotely by a four layer external agent for industrial control systems security (SCISSOR).

The paper is organized as follows: Firstly, the proposed architectures for industrial control systems security and smart grid distributed measurement system are summarized. Secondly, the essential physical elements for its implementation are described for the case study of the electrical network of Favignana island. Then the SCADA Human Machine Interface and Server implementation as well as the data analysis methods are presented.

2   The Proposed Architecture for Industrial Control Systems Security

The proposed architecture for industrial control systems security assessment is shown in Fig. 1 [6]. It consists in four layers. The first one is the monitoring layer (ML).

Data collected from this layer can be of different types. Depending on the sources, the monitored data can be classified as: i) environmental data such as temperature, humidity and more generally all data obtained from ambient sensors; ii) alerts revealed by traffic analysis probes; iii) ICT logs gathered on the hardware and software components of the critical infrastructure and used for integrity checks; iv) events generated by object/pattern detection methods implemented on surveillance cameras; v) events natively produced by the SCADA system based on the analysis of the monitored quantities. The second layer is the Control and Coordination Layer (CCL), which decouples this heterogeneous multi-source, multi-technology, and multipurpose data from the overlying Decision and Analysis Layer (DAL). Extracting the peculiarities of the various monitored data, such as their formats, protocols, and configuration interfaces, this layer allows simplifying the event correlation and triggering of dynamic reactions in the DAL modules. These pre-processed data are sent from the CCL to the Messaging Infrastructure (MI), which provides a fault-tolerant, resilient, high-throughput and low-latency cloud computing messaging infrastructure. Advanced probabilistic and statistical models are then used for data correlation and event detection. Finally a Human-Machine Interface (HMI) was designed to present the operator the system behavior in real time.

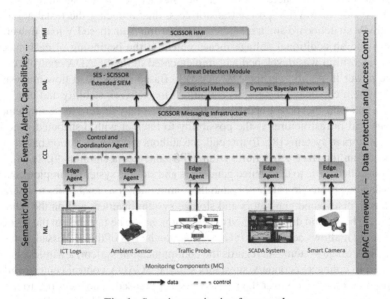

Fig. 1. Security monitoring framework.

3 The Proposed Architecture for Smart Grid Distributed Measurement System

Among the different monitoring components (MC), in this paper the attention will be focused on the SCADA system implemented for electrical network monitoring and control. These types of SCADA systems are today an urgent need for Distribution System

Operators because of the large increase of distributed generation connections both at medium (MV) and low voltage (LV) level. This increase is causing power flow inversions in different points of the network, which are not monitored and controlled because network are traditionally designed for unidirectional power flows from transmission lines to distribution networks. Moreover, the variability of distributed energy production, due to the aleatory nature of the renewable energy sources, in fact, can cause instability and malfunctioning of the network such as voltage and frequency variation, unwanted islanding operation and even blackout of the whole network. These issues can be faced only introducing a real time cooperation of distributed generators and energy storage systems in voltage and frequency regulation. Thus, traditional electrical networks should evolve into smart grids with the introduction of a real-time monitoring system, adequate communication systems and a supervisory center, which can take decisions and send commands to distributed generators, energy storage systems and energy users. Authors have investigated these topics in different previous researches and they have designed a new architecture tailored for MV and LV smart grid applications. The proposed architecture is shown in Fig. 2. The proposed solution is based on the use of low cost equipment to monitor the network and control distributed generator and energy storage systems. In detail, the active and reactive power drained in each secondary substation are measured at LV side of MV/LV power transformers, thus reducing the installation costs related to MV switchboard and transducers [7]. Starting from these LV load power measurements and an additional voltage measurement at the beginning of each feeder, a load flow algorithm was developed and implemented in the SCADA control center to calculate power flows all over the MV network. Based on the load flow analysis, the SCADA system can detect dangerous conditions for network stability and take proper actions to maintain its correct operation. To do this, a new feature to be implemented into smart grid infrastructures is the possibility to interact with distributed generators and energy storage systems [8]. To this end, the authors propose a solution based on two new devices: an interface protection system (IPS) and a concentrator [9]. The first one has to be installed close to distributed generators and storage system. It implements both an anti-islanding protection algorithm and the communication capabilities to interact on one side with distributed generators and storage system inverters and on the other side with DSOs. The second device, named concentrator, has to be installed in the secondary substation and it allows delivering DSO messages to the IPS of the addressed distributed generator or storage system. As regards the communication system, a wireless network is proposed to connect secondary substations to the SCADA control center, while the power line communication over the LV network is proposed to connect IPS to the concentrator. This solution is suggested as it is already widely implemented with success for automatic meter reading (AMR) purposes [10]. Furthermore, the proposed solution contemplates the presence of a MV coupler in each substation, in order to keep a double redundant communication system [11]. When a substation is not reachable via wireless network, data can be delivered by a nearby substation that receives them via MV network, which represents an always-on secure communication channel. Such a system can be also extended to be used not only in a disaster recovery situation, but as a parallel communication channel in order to double check the measures at the end point.

As mentioned, the SCADA system for this Smart Grid performs a load flow analysis of the whole medium voltage distribution network and based on the results it can take decisions and send control commands to distributed generators. As this is an active production system, direct access from external agents cannot be permitted. Consequently, SCADA log files have to be transferred to a remote server so that they can be accessed by the external agents. Figure 3 shows the process. The external log forwarder is a software component that inspects the current log files for changes and then takes care of sending SCADA log files to the security monitoring system. More details on this part of the architecture were analyzed in [6]. Thus, in the following section, the attention will be instead focused on the implementation of the rest the architecture for the real case study of Favignana.

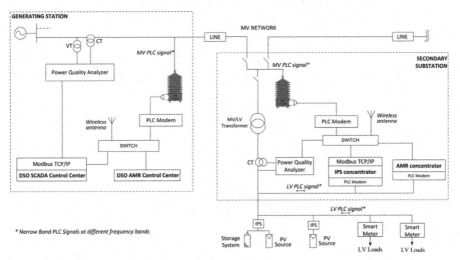

Fig. 2. System architecture for power flow monitoring and distributed generator and storage systems remote control with two communication channel: wireless and PLC on medium voltage network.

4 Favignana Smart Grid Test Bench

The above mentioned proposed solutions have been tested in the electrical power system of the island of Favignana. The system has 40 electrical substations, a 16 MVA power plant (with 7 generators), and a number of low-voltage photovoltaic generators distributed around the island (see Fig. 4).

The implementation of the proposed architecture is aimed at turning the classical electric network into a Smart Grid. In order to give the DSO the ability to be aware of how the network evolves in real-time, a distributed measurement system, a SCADA control center, concentrators, IPSs and a hybrid communication system were designed and installed. In the following, all these solutions will be described in detail. Thanks to the developed system, the DSO is able to collect, to process and to log the distributed

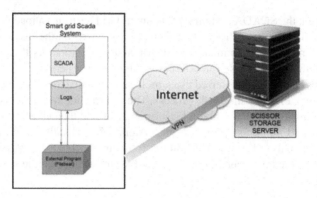

Fig. 3. Log forwarder for SEA SCADA.

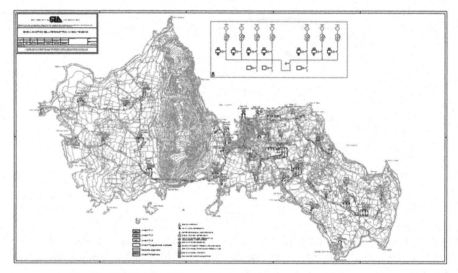

Fig. 4. MV distribution network and MV/LV secondary substations

measurements and to communicate with IPSs in order to send commands to distributed generators and storage system inverters, thus having a constant monitoring and control of the network to guarantee its stability and correct operation.

4.1 Distributed Measurement System

In each of the 40 MV/LV secondary substations, a Janitza UMG604 Power Quality Analyzer (PQA) has been installed on the LV side of the power transformer, by using current transformers installed as shown in Fig. 5. This measurement instrument can measure the active and reactive power required by the load flow algorithm. It can also perform other kinds of measures such as interruption, over-/under-voltage, swells, and harmonics, which can be used for power quality analysis [12]. All these measurements are made available via different types of protocols. For the sake of applications, the MODBUS over TCP protocol has been used. Moreover each PQA has its own internal memory that can log up years of measures. The internal database of measures can be dumped from specific software at the control center.

All the devices are part of the same LAN network, synced thanks to an NTP server.

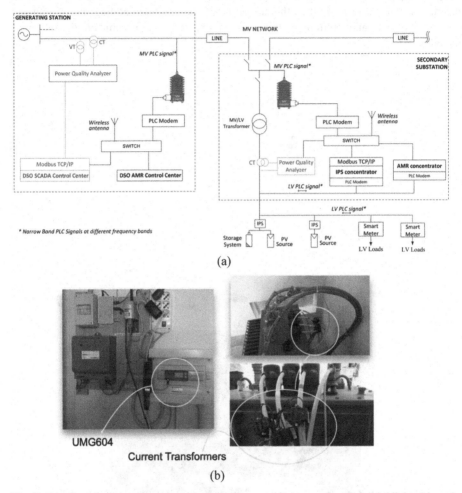

Fig. 5. Distributed measurement system: (a) system architecture where it is highlighted in red; (b) PQA (UMG 604) installed along with CT sensors. (Color figure online)

4.2 Redundant PLC/HiperLAN Communication System

The main and more sensitive part of the proposed solution is, for sure, the communication system. The data path and the crossed media affect data integrity, thus the security of the communication system is crucial for the health of the network. The local measures made by the IPS are aggregated at prosumer level and collected via PLC over the LV network by a concentrator that is installed in the secondary substation. Both the concentrator and PQA are connected through a switch to a wireless network. Favignana island has been equipped with a 5.4 GHz and 70 Mbps HiperLAN network, that connects point-to-point the 40 secondary substations to a supervisor by means of three point-multipoint backbones (developed in the research project named REIPERSEI) [13]. Under the more recent research project I-SOLE, this network will be extended adding more point-to-point connections and a redundant backbone, thanks to the orographic configuration of the island.

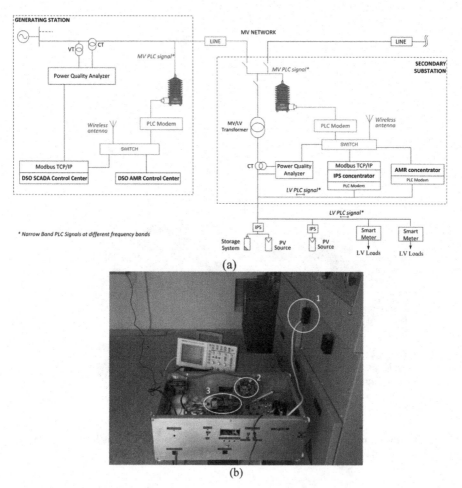

Fig. 6. PLC/HiperLAN communication system: (a) System architecture where it is highlighted in red; (b) MV-coupler. 1: VDS socket 2: PLC modem 3: Arduino network interface and bridge. (Color figure online)

In order to deal with the redundancy between the wireless and the PLC-MV channel, a special coupler has been developed. As showed in Fig. 6, the coupler consists of a custom electronic board that is connected to the MV line through the Voltage Detection System socket. The board adjusts its internal inductance network in order to set the best transmission configuration. An Arduino board is installed and configured as a bridge between the LAN and the PLC-MV modem and it acts like a data forwarder to the MV line. Details on the set-up and experimental results have been presented in [10].

4.3 Distributed Generation Remote Control System

In the peripheral nodes of the network, at prosumer level, an IPS is installed that acts as an interface to the DSO and as a local measurement system to match the anti-islanding requirements of the CEI 0-21 standard [14]. The IPS has been developed joining the same electronic platform of the concentrator with a measurement section that deals with voltage, current and phase measures (Fig. 7).

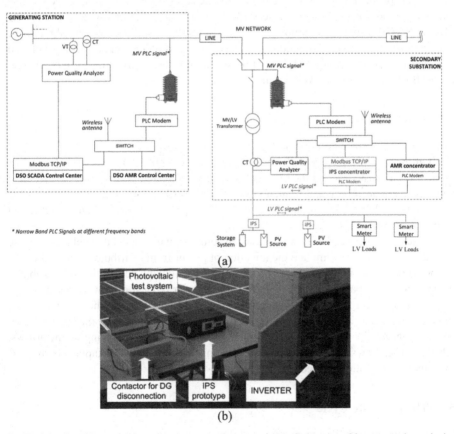

Fig. 7. Distributed generation remote control system: (a) System architecture where it is highlighted in red. (b) Picture of the experimental installation. (Color figure online)

It can communicate via RS232 with the inverter and it gives a DSO the ability to remotely control the distributed generation and storage system. Thus, exploiting the communication infrastructure, the DSO can control the power injection on LV lines from each generator and change the inverter functional mode, to let the network leafs participate in the voltage and frequency regulation of the whole network. These advanced functionalities, with respect to traditional network, can help the increase and integration of distributed generation in modern smart grids, thus guaranteeing the full exploitation of renewable energy sources without impacting on network stability and its correct operation. The details on IPS development, laboratory and on-field tests have been presented in [9].

5   Favignana SCADA HMI and Server

A SCADA server is installed in the DSO control center. It acts as a centralized controller for the distributed measurement system and, thanks to its own HMI, as a graphical real-time snapshot for the operator. The developed SCADA asynchronously collects active and reactive power measures from secondary substations in approximately 150 ms via ModBUS/TCP. It makes the proposed solution suitable for smart grids critical real-time applications. A backward/forward sweep class load flow algorithm has been developed [15] and it runs on top of the collected measures in order to give the operator the real power flow on the medium voltage lines.

5.1   SCADA Interface

The SCADA interface is shown in Fig. 8.

It allows exploring each feeder of the electrical network, giving the operator a clear view of each substation and the lines in terms of percentage of transformer load, active and reactive load power and branch power flows. Furthermore, a global status of the network is available and alarms are configured to show the operator when and where an inversion of power flow occurs.

For design purpose, the SCADA has been equipped with a special panel for each line where the operator can simulate the injection of power from distributed generation into the network. In this mode the distributor can forecast how the penetration of distributed generation can impact the network and match the user request of new plants at design stage. A graphical result of the simulation is shown in Fig. 9, where the inserted values of power in the left panel lead to a power flow inversion as indicated by the red arrows on some branches. The amount of the inversion can be checked by clicking on the arrows. All the power flows are logged into a file, along with the network input measures as explained in the following section.

5.2   The Data Life-Cycle

The data measures needed to run the load flow are generated by the PQA at secondary substation level. Their instant values are collected by the SCADA server every 2 s. The measures are used by the load flow algorithm and the power flow output data are

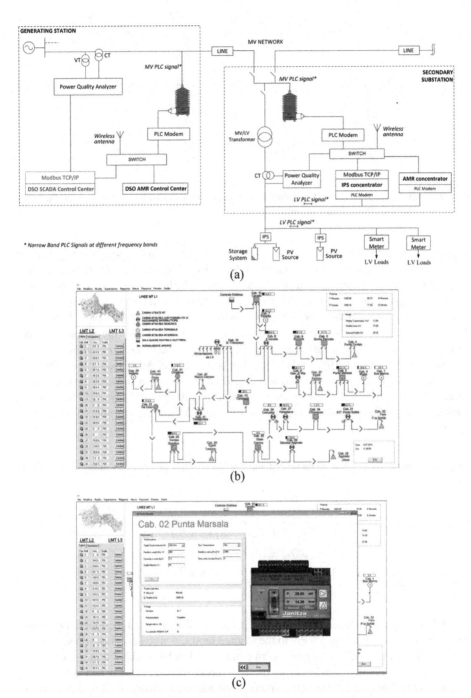

Fig. 8. SCADA HMI interface: (a) System architecture where it is highlighted in red. HMI interface of line 1 (b) main view and (c) Cab.02 substation detail. (Color figure online)

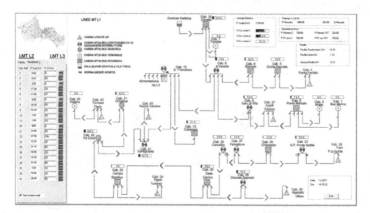

Fig. 9. A distributed generation simulation that deals with the inversions of power flows in different branches. (Color figure online)

logged, along with the measures, within files per day. Each file reports the log data of the SCADA load flow algorithm relative to the active (P) or reactive (Q) powers of one of the three feeders. More in detail, each file logs both the load powers measured in each secondary substation and the voltage measured at the beginning of the line, i.e. the input variables, and the calculated branch power flows, i.e. the output variables. Moreover, the active and reactive powers measured at the beginning of the line are also stored in the file, since a PQA is installed at the beginning of the feeder instead of a simple voltmeter. This allows verifying the algorithm performance. As an example in Table 1, the compatibility between estimated and measured active power flows at the beginning of each line is verified for the load condition measured the 31st of May, 2018 at 9 a.m. A further comparison is shown in Fig. 10 for a full day. Measurement points are reported for each 2 s.

Table 1. Compatibility between measured and estimated active power flows at beginning of the line.

Line	Measured [kW]	Estimated [kW]
1	811.7 ± 5.2	813.5 ± 5.3
2	547.5 ± 3.9	544.6 ± 4.2
3	560.7 ± 4.1	559.8 ± 4.3

All the logs are checked by an external program (filebeat[1]) and incrementally transferred each minute through a VPN to the storage server, where they stay at rest. During the activities of the SCISSOR project, an extra layer has been added that use dynamic Bayesian networks and Statistical methods in order to detect threat and data inconsistency [6]. However before being shipped outside the network, data are checked at

---

[1] https://www.elastic.co/beats/filebeat.

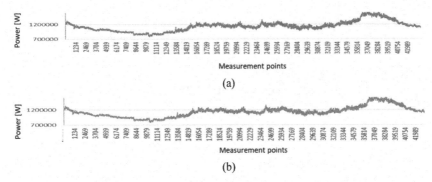

Fig. 10. Compatibility between measured (a) and estimated (b) active power flows.

SCADA level. The validation consists in giving data an electrical meaning using all the information acquired from the network and adding extra information owned by the distributor. The indicators used in the first layer of validation are summarized in Table 2.

Table 2. Indicators used in the first layer of validation.

Indicators	Type	Electrical meaning
IS_INV	Boolean	It reports a power inversion: it is 1 if at least one power flux is negative
LEV_INV	Integer	If there is a power inversion, it provides the severity of the inversion. 1 is the maximum severity (nearest to the central power generator)
IS_CENTRAL	Boolean	It indicates the reachability and the correct reading of the meters in the central power generator (value = 1). If the value is 0 the log row has no meaning
IS_MISMATCH	Boolean	It reports if the power measured at the beginning of the MV feeder is different from the correspondent value calculated by the load flow algorithm. This could testify a possible data inconsistency
ID_DG	Boolean	It indicates the presence of some distributed generators

5.3 Threat Simulation on Real Data

The above-mentioned first layer of validation is added to a second one, developed in the SCISSOR project, which relies only on numerical method. This second layer uses data stripped of their intrinsic meaning. In order to test this data analysis layer, a data alteration software has been developed in the LabVIEW platform. The virtual instrument (VI) uses as input the SCADA log files. It adds a specific set of alterations and it returns the logs file with perturbed data. The developed VI is shown in Fig. 11.

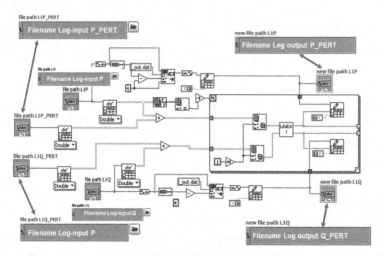

Fig. 11. LabVIEW VI for log alteration.

6 Conclusions

An architecture of a SCADA system for distributed measurements and remote control of MV and LV electrical networks was presented in this paper. The proposed solution is based on low-cost equipment, which ensures its scalability to widely extended distribution networks. Moreover, it includes the use of innovative intelligent electronic devices developed by the authors for the remote monitoring of distributed generation and storage systems. A load flow algorithm was implemented in the SCADA control center. It was shown that it allows the real time monitoring of the network and thus to take proper decisions on distributed power injection or storage in order to maintain network stability, reduce voltage and frequency variations and avoid critical situations, such as unwanted islanding or blackouts. The proposed SCADA system allows also simulating an increase of distributed generation energy production, thus evaluating the influence on correct network operation, highlighting inversions on power flows.

The resiliency of the proposed SCADA system to cyber-attacks was also considered. Three solutions were adopted. The first is the redundancy of the communication channel, based on a new coupler designed by the authors to couple PLC signals into MV networks. The second solution presented in the paper allows data validation in the SCADA control center and it is based on the knowledge of the electrical network operation. Indicators were defined for verifying data consistency in different network scenarios. The third solution is a second layer of validation based on numerical method and performed remotely by an external agent.

Acknowledgements. This research was supported by grant PO FESR Sicilia 2014–2020, Action 1.1.5, Project n. 08000PA90246, Project title: "Smart grids per le isole minori (Smart grids for small islands)", acronym: I-Sole, CUP: G99J18000540007.

References

1. Matherly, J.: Shodan search engine. http://www.shodan.io. Accessed 29 Sept 2017
2. Radvanosky, B., Brodsky, J.: Project shine (SHodan Intelligence Extraction) findings report (2014). https://de.slideshare.net/BobRadvanovsky/project-shine-findings-report-dated-1oct2014. Accessed 29 Sept 2017
3. Andreeva, O., et al.: Industrial control systems vulnerabilities statistics. Report. Kaspersky Lab (2016)
4. Secunia: Secunia vulnerability review (2015). https://secuniaresearch.flexerasoftware.com/?action=fetch&filename=secuniavulnerabilityreview2015pdf.pdf. Accessed 29 Sept 2017
5. E-ISAC Electricity Information Sharing and Analysis Center: Analysis of the cyber attack on the Ukrainian power grid (2016). https://ics.sans.org/media/E-ISACSANSUkraineDUC5.pdf. Accessed 29 Sept 2017
6. Brandauer, C., Dorfinger, P., Arbs Paiva, P.Y., Salsano, S.: An approach to scalable security monitoring. In: IEEE World Congress on Industrial Control System Security, WCICSS 2017, Cambridge, UK, 11–14 December 2017 (2017)
7. Cataliotti, A., et al.: An improved load flow method for MV networks based on LV load measurements and estimations. IEEE Trans. Instrum. Measur. **68**(2), 430–438 (2019)
8. Artale, G., et al.: Real time power flow monitoring and control system for microgrids integration in islanded scenarios. IEEE Trans. Ind. Appl. **55**(6), 7186–7197 (2019)
9. Cataliotti, A., Cosentino, V., Di Cara, D., Guaiana, S., Panzavecchia, N., Tine, G.: A new solution for low-voltage distributed generation interface protection system. IEEE Trans. Instrum. Measur. **64**(8), 2086–2095 (2015)
10. Artale, G., et al.: A new PLC-based smart metering architecture for medium/low voltage grids: feasibility and experimental characterization. Measurement **129**, 479–488 (2018)
11. Artale, G., et al.: A new low cost coupling system for power line communication on medium voltage smart grids. IEEE Trans. Smart Grid **9**(4), 3321–3329 (2018)
12. Gallo, D., Landi, C., Luiso, M.: Issues in the characterization of power quality instruments. Measurement **43**(8), 1069–1076 (2010)
13. Cataliotti, A., et al.: Experimental evaluation of an hybrid communication system architecture for smart grid applications. In: IEEE International Workshop on Applied Measurements for Power Systems, AMPS 2015, Aachen, Germany, 23–25 September 2015, pp. 96–101 (2015)
14. Regola tecnica di riferimento per la connessione di utenti attivi e passivi alle reti BT delle imprese distributrici di energia elettrica. (Reference technical rules for the connection of active and passive users to the LV electrical Utilities), CEI 0-21, September 2014. (in Italian)
15. Cataliotti, A., et al.: Measurement uncertainty impact on simplified load flow analysis in MV smart grids. In: 2018 IEEE International Instrumentation and Measurement Technology Conference (I2MTC), Houston, TX, USA, 14–17 May 2018, pp. 1354–1359 (2018)

Impact of Bloom Filters on Security and Efficiency of SecaaS Services

Maciej Mencner and Marcin Niemiec[✉]

AGH University of Science and Technology, Mickiewicza 30, 30-059 Krakow, Poland
niemiec@agh.edu.pl

Abstract. With a rapid growth of cybercrime, security services play a crucial role in protecting modern networks. In order to minimize the costs of deployment and management of the infrastructure, businesses have started outsourcing those services to cloud service providers. A privacy preserving solution becomes necessary to protect confidentiality of a security policy. Therefore, a certain level of false positive packets is introduced using a tree-based structure of security policy and Bloom Filters in a public cloud. This approach results in shading the decision made for each of packets. A conventional firewall placed in a private cloud is responsible for performing the ultimate filtering and dropping all unwanted traffic. Usage of this hybrid cloud model allows to anonymize the security policy itself and reduce the possibility of information gaining after traffic eavesdropping. However, the appropriate choice of Bloom Filters' parameters is crucial to distribute the load between potentially unlimited public cloud resources and finite private cloud resources. The results of research reveals that lowering the number of false positive packets that have to be filtered within the private cloud has an effect only to some point. Thus, a trade-off between a level of privacy of the security policy and utilization of private cloud can be found. It allows to meet security and performance requirements of the customers of SecaaS services.

Keywords: Security · Privacy · Bloom Filters · SecaaS services · Cloud

1 Introduction

Broadband access to the Internet can be considered critical in modern times, for both private users and business organizations. With the ever-growing amount of data traffic, network security plays a crucial role in protecting sensitive information and ensuring availability of the network-based services. According to the 2019 Official Annual Cybercrime Report by Cybersecurity Ventures, cybercrime annual damage cost will double from $3 trillion in 2015, to $6 trillion by 2021 [1]. One of the solutions, to solve the problem of unauthorized access to network resources, is to use a particular security appliance – such as firewall, which examines every packet entering or leaving the private network, and decides whether to accept, or discard it [2].

Following the global market trends in terms of cloud shift, companies have already started looking for cloud-based firewall solutions [3]. Outsourcing the service to the

© Springer Nature Switzerland AG 2020
A. Dziech et al. (Eds.): MCSS 2020, CCIS 1284, pp. 154–167, 2020.
https://doi.org/10.1007/978-3-030-59000-0_12

public cloud providers, can potentially save costs in deployment and management of the IT infrastructure. However, this forces businesses to disclose their hitherto confidential security policies to service providers. The price can no longer be analyzed only by the actual cash value, but has to also include the potential loss of privacy and its possible consequences.

In attempt to preserve the privacy of security appliance policies in cloud services, the first framework leveraging an anonymized firewall have been proposed by A. Khakpour and A. Liu [4]. The Ladon framework, as referred to by its authors, utilizes a firewall decision diagram and Bloom Filters to provide packet filtering based on anonymized policies. However, even though the service provider no longer has any insight into the original policy, the final decision for each packet is still known. By performing analysis of the eavesdropped traffic, the original policy can eventually be determined.

To further reduce the risk of losing security policy confidentiality, a Ladon Hybrid Cloud framework was introduced in [5]. It builds upon the Ladon framework, with significant improvements in terms of privacy preserving. By modifying Bloom Filters to intentionally introduce ambiguous packet decisions, the ability of information gaining by the cloud service provider is significantly reduced. However, because the novel framework requires performing additional packet filtering within a private cloud, to fully eliminate the unwanted network traffic, choosing appropriate parameters for Bloom Filters is essential to control the traffic rate at the private cloud entrance and, in effect, the cloud utilization.

The rest of this paper proceeds as follows. The basics of Bloom Filters are introduced in Sect. 2. In Sect. 3, a cloud computing approach, including different service models, such as SecaaS solutions is discussed. Three security policy representations – set or rules, tree-based structure and policy with Bloom Filters – are presented in Sect. 4. Experimental results concerning impact of Bloom Filters on security and efficiency of a SecaaS service follow in Sect. 5. Finally, Sect. 6 concludes the paper.

2 Bloom Filters

A Bloom Filter is a time- and space-efficient, probabilistic data structure that can be used to answer the question if an object is a set member. For each of the n elements constituting a set, k hash functions are calculated and its results, which are in the range of $\{0, 1, ..., m-1\}$, determine fields of the m-sized bit array that are set to 1. To perform a check whether an element x is included in the set, hash calculations are performed with x as an input, and results are compared with the Bloom Filter indexes. If any element is set to 0, x is definitely not a member of the original set. Otherwise, if all are set to 1, x may be a member of the set. This indicates that Bloom Filters may emerge in false positives, but they do not produce false negatives [6].

The probability of false positives in Bloom Filters can be adjusted according to the requirements of a specific use case. Formula 1 allows to approximate this probability:

$$p_{fp} \approx \left(1 - e^{-kn/m}\right)^k \tag{1}$$

With the usage of optimal number of hash functions that minimizes the probability of false positives (Formula 2), the number of bits per item can be calculated using Formula 3.

$$k = \frac{m}{n} \ln 2 \tag{2}$$

$$\frac{m}{n} = -\frac{\log_2 p}{\ln 2} \tag{3}$$

This proves that as a result of not storing the actual data items, Bloom Filters are very efficient in terms of space requirements, requiring only about 10 bits per element with a 1% false positive ratio. At a cost of small number of bogus results and impossibility of removing items, they provide a fixed time complexity of $O(k)$, for both adding elements and checking whether an element is included in the set, making them the only constant-space data structure with such property.

Example operation of adding elements to a Bloom Filter is shown in Fig. 1. First, hash functions are calculated for x_1. The results indicate that filter bits BF_0, BF_4 and BF_m need to be set to 1. The same procedure is then repeated for item x_2, with the hash calculations results of 2, 4 and 5. Since bit BF_4 has already been set before, only the value of bits BF_2 and BF_5 is changed to 1.

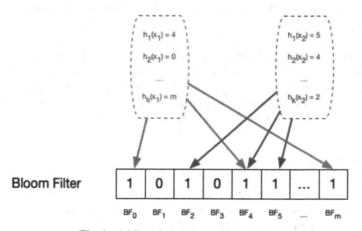

Fig. 1. Adding elements to a Bloom Filter.

The operation of checking whether a given element is included in the filter is shown in Fig. 2. Hash functions results for item x indicate that Bloom Filter bits BF_0, BF_1 and BF_5 has to be checked to confirm that element's presence in the set. Although both BF_0 and BF_5 are set to 1, the zeroed bit BF_1 clearly determines that x is not included in the analyzed filter. When the same check is performed for element y, all bits corresponding to the results of hash functions have the value of 1. This signifies that the item might be included in the evaluated Bloom Filter, with a probability of being a false positive, as the checked bits could have potentially been set while adding different items.

As a result of their advantages and design characteristics, Bloom Filters are widely used to reduce the number of disk lookups and improve the performance of database

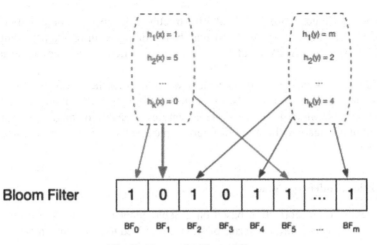

Fig. 2. Usage of a Bloom Filter.

systems [7]. They were also used for the purpose of identification of malicious URLs in a Chromium web browser and detecting articles that have already been viewed by users on a Medium publishing platform [8, 9]. Akamai Technologies utilizes Bloom Filters to prevent its caches from storing "one-hit-wonders" (objects requested by users just once) and, as an effect, reduce disks workload [10].

3   Cloud Computing

Term "cloud computing" was officially defined by the United States' National Institute of Standards and Technology (NIST) in 2011 in a Special Publication 800-145. It was defined as *"a new model for enabling ubiquitous, convenient, on-demand network access to a shared pool of configurable computing resources (e.g., networks, servers, storage, applications, and services) that can be rapidly provisioned and released with minimal management effort or service provider interaction"* [11]. NIST introduces also five essential characteristics of cloud computing: broad network access, measured service, on-demand self-service, rapid elasticity, and resource pooling.

Cloud computing can be classified by the usage restrictions, which address possible security vulnerabilities, and aim to satisfy strict compliance standards. Four cloud deployment models can be distinguished.

- Public Clouds – resources are provisioned for open use by the general public and exist on the premises of the service provider. While being the easiest model to deploy, it also poses some serious risks and challenges in terms of security. As a result of being exposed via the Internet, public cloud may suffer from insecure interfaces, account and traffic hijacking, as well as data breaches. With a limited control over the resources, it requires a full trust between the customer and the cloud service provider.
- Private Clouds – usually, but not always, implemented on premises for exclusive use by a single organization. Sacrifices elasticity and OPEX model for a superior security and full control over the resources.

- Community Clouds – provide cloud infrastructure for a specific community of organizations that share concerns. Used mainly to comply with regulatory compliance standards, such as HIPAA, PCI DSS, or SOX, and is often subject to periodic auditing reviews.
- Hybrid Clouds – enable cloud consumers to put together the best features of each of the previously described models, by bounding together two or more distinct cloud infrastructures, which remain individual entities. Capable of migrating workloads and entire applications between different deployments (e.g. during high utilization periods).

3.1 Service Models in Cloud

Independently to categorization based on a deployment model, there are three main service models, which differ in terms of service provided to cloud customers.

- Software as a Service (SaaS), where the cloud service provider takes over all the responsibilities from its users, enabling them to use fully functional applications, without the necessity to manage the underlying hardware or software infrastructure. Despite being a widely adopted model, SaaS is not suitable for critical, real-time applications and often does not allow portability between different cloud providers.
- Platform as a Service (PaaS) that provides developers and testers with a predefined environment that is ready for custom applications' deployment, allowing for quicker and cheaper software development. The main drawbacks include the possible incompatibility with the already existing infrastructure and possible vendor lock-in after choosing a single service provider.
- Infrastructure as a Service (IaaS), which offers fundamental computing resources (e.g., processing power, storage, networking) and is targeted at systems' administrators, as the closest model to the traditional on-premises deployments, allowing for an easy migration of legacy applications to the cloud. However, it offers a lower level of security, and due to the high level of flexibility may suffer from actions of other tenants that are utilizing the same physical infrastructure.

Figure 3 shows the distribution of duties between service providers and cloud consumers in each of the models. Choice of the appropriate model should be based on its limitations and business specific requirements, considering the benefits and drawbacks of each of the models.

Apart from the NIST-defined cloud service models, a myriad of models has been presented in form of "as a Service", or "aaS". In the literature it is often referred to as either Everything as a Service, or Anything as a Service (Xaas) [12, 13]. Examples include Backup as a Service, Database as a Service, IP Telephony as a Service, Networking as a Service or Security as a Service.

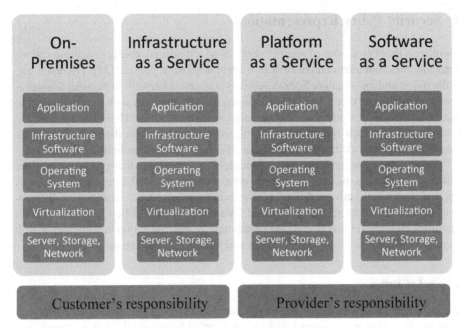

Fig. 3. Cloud computing service models.

3.2 Security as a Service

Security as a Service (often referred to as SecaaS or SECaaS) is an example of a cloud-based model that migrates security services into the cloud [14]. Solutions that are offered include, among others, intrusion detection systems, intrusion prevention systems, as well as firewalls.

Firewall as a Service is a new approach for providing network security that is directly related to the SecaaS model. It delivers firewall capabilities as a cloud-based service, allowing for a unified policy across different physical locations, improved scalability and management. Traffic from multiple sources can be aggregated into the cloud, for getting full visibility and control over the network, without the necessity to use dedicated physical appliances. Because the responsibility of software management is shifted towards the cloud service provider, the solution is expected to be always up to date, with all the vulnerabilities and known bugs fixed. It also solves the problem of security appliance being a bottleneck in the network, when the amount of filtered traffic increases.

While cutting costs is the obvious gain of incorporating the SecaaS model, it also increases attack surface for its users, because of the necessity to reveal the company's security policy (or its parts) to an unknown 3rd party vendor. The appropriate legal agreements are not sufficient, as cloud providers are subject to malicious and negligent insiders, who pose a serious risk for cloud customers. And even with an undisclosed policy in place, traffic flowing through the public network is prone to eavesdropping and further analysis. Hence, the confidentiality and privacy of security policy is a major concern with regards to the described model.

4 Security Policy Representations

There are a lot of cloud-based security services which primary role is to make decisions regarding the examined content of one or several network packets [15]. However, one of the oldest and most mature SecaaS services is stateless firewall. In general, firewall is a network appliance that controls the incoming and outgoing network traffic, in order to secure the trusted internal network from malicious activities. It acts based on a predefined security policy, which represents the confinements imposed on the traffic within an organization's network and limitations placed on inbound and outbound connections.

Security policy usually consists of multiple security rules that precisely indicate, which actions are permitted, and which do not comply with the company standards. Those schemes vary between different companies or organizations, as a result of different systems and networks that are protected. With the security policy in place, firewall examines each packet that is entering or leaving the internal network, compares it with security rules and decides to either accept and forward the packet, or discard it.

4.1 Set of Rules

The enforced security policy is commonly represented as an ordered set of rules, such as an example shown in Listing 1. Whenever a packet is passing through a firewall, it is compared against each of those rules sequentially, until a match is found. The packet is then either accepted or dropped, based on the action specified within the rule. However, such representation is prone to design errors that may include:

- Conflicting Rules – whenever the incoming packet satisfies more than one rule entry and actions specified within those rules differ;
- Redundant Rules – when removal of a given rule entry does not change the behavior of a firewall and actions taken with regards to the passing packets;
- Incomplete Set of Rules – whereas the packet does not match any of the specified rule entries [2].

```
# access-list permit ip 192.168.0.0 0.0.0.255 172.16.1.0 0.0.0.255
# access-list deny ip 172.16.1.0 0.0.0.255 192.168.0.0 0.0.0.255
# access-list permit tcp any 172.16.1.0 0.0.0.255
# access-list permit icmp 192.0.2.0 0.0.0.255 192.0.2.0 0.0.0.255
# access-list permit ip any host 192.168.1.10 eq 80
```

Listing 1. Example of a Security Policy Representation as an Ordered Set of Rules.

4.2 Tree-Based Structure

In order to address the concerns listed in Sect. 4.1, another approach to security policy representation has been presented. Instead of sequentially following the list of rules, a tree-based structure, often referred to as a policy tree, can be utilized for the purpose of packet matching. Each level of the tree is responsible for matching the value of only one tuple element, e.g. source IP address, destination IP address or used protocol. The matching operation is performed by comparing tree nodes at a given level, with the corresponding packet field. Once a condition is satisfied, the process is repeated for child nodes.

If the matching condition cannot be fulfilled, the search is rerun starting with parent nodes that have not been previously visited. Once all the rule tuples match, on each of the consecutive levels, the action associated with a given path is performed. Apart from dealing with the previously described drawbacks of a rule list representation, tree structures are proven to offer a significant improvement in terms of performance, especially when dealing with complex security policies [16]. An example of a tree-based firewall decision diagram is shown in Fig. 4.

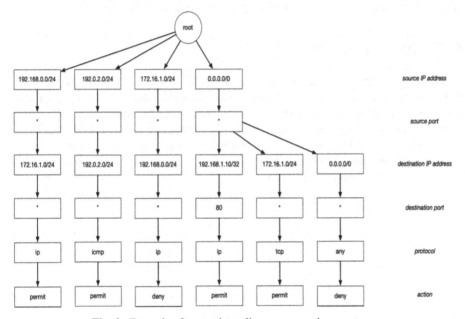

Fig. 4. Example of a security policy representation as a tree.

4.3 Security Policy with Bloom Filters

While the occurrence of false positives is usually considered a drawback in most Bloom Filter applications, it might be desirable in the network security area. By modifying the rule matching mechanisms in cloud-based firewall, the susceptibility to traffic eavesdropping and analysis can be largely reduced. A Bloom Filter Firewall Decision Diagram (BFFDD) provides the mechanism for introducing a certain amount of false positive decisions, which allows the transmission of packets that normally would be dropped. Any attempt to discover the applied security policy, based on the public traffic passing through the cloud, becomes highly complicated, if not impossible, thanks to a small, but very diverse group of false positive packets. Such design results in shadowing of the policy, thus increasing its privacy [5].

Another benefit is the anonymization of the firewall policy, which as a result of Bloom Filters usage, can be kept as a binary data structure preventing cloud service provider from having any insight into it. However, in order to not contradict the main principle of firewall applications, which is to filter all unwanted traffic and protect the network from any malicious activities, additional packet filtering is required. By adjusting the false positive rate, the load can be distributed between the Bloom Filter based firewall appliance placed in a public cloud (which performs the initial screening and discards majority of unwanted traffic) and the conventional solution that is responsible for dropping all the introduced false positives. The latter can be implemented as a physical appliance or be placed within the private cloud for constituting a hybrid cloud deployment. As a result, only packets allowed in the security policy are able to reach the secured network.

5   Practical Verification

Verification tests are crucial to thoroughly confirm the behavior of cloud-based firewall that is able to preserve the privacy of security policy using Bloom Filters. For this purpose, a fully virtualized topology comprising of an Internet traffic generator, public cloud and private cloud was brought up, within Oracle VM VirtualBox, as shown in Fig. 5. Both clouds were running *OpenStack Rocky* cloud operating system in a configuration with one compute and one controller node, while firewall instances utilized *Ubuntu 16.04.6 LTS* with *libnetfilter-queue-dev* library.

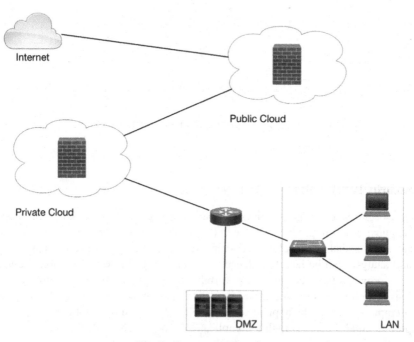

Fig. 5. Test network topology.

The deployed firewall uses a firewall decision diagram (FDD), which was first presented by Gouda and Liu in [2]. Converting security policy rules into a tree structure speeds up the processing time, while maintaining policy integrity, consistency and completeness. The process of tree generation starts with analyzing the provided security policy. Rules are then aggregated on each of the provided properties and constitute a complete firewall policy representation. Starting with the source network, source port, destination network, destination port and protocol are analyzed respectively. However, if a given packet does not match any of the tree elements on a given level, it is discarded, to fulfill the closed firewall requirement. In all cases, an unequivocal decision is determined for every packet.

For the purpose of security policy privacy preserving, FDD is further enhanced by the usage of Bloom Filters on network matching levels within the tree. This approach, called Bloom Filter Firewall Decision Diagram (BFFDD), was proposed by Kurek et al. [5]. As a result of introducing Bloom Filters into the decision tree, the decision for any packet can be uncertain, depending on the provided false positive ratio.

The test scenario was performed using the hybrid cloud architecture, with a Bloom Filter Firewall Decision Diagram used in the public cloud, and a conventional firewall placed in the private cloud. In order to simulate a network traffic, a packet generator script was used to send 100 000 packets with different source and destination IP addresses, as well as different protocols and transport layer port numbers.

Table 1 presents the number of packets and unique IP addresses matching three selected permit security policy rules for both FDD and BFFDD packages. Increased number of packets and unique source IP addresses are visible for all rules. Adding the rules' counters for BFFDD package totals in 19377 packets, with 3814 items missing when compared to the overall number of captured elements. Those packets are yet another occurrence of false positives, which cannot be however easily linked to the rules responsible for their presence (for example when the packet's destination IP address is outside the scope of any of the rules).

Table 1. Number of packets and unique IP addresses gathered in the public cloud.

Rule number	Filtering package	Number of packets	Number of unique source IP addresses
#1	FDD	2686	256
	BFFDD	3326	338
#2	FDD	3975	32
	BFFDD	7354	1122
#3	FDD	1290	256
	BFFDD	3313	767

In the described scenario, placement of the conventional firewall in private cloud is crucial to perform the ultimate filtering and drop all previously permitted false positive packets. Only such solution guarantees the proper enforcement of the desired security policy, while maintaining its confidentiality.

5.1   Impact of Bloom Filters on Security

Choosing the right parameters for Bloom Filters used within a cloud-based firewall is not a straightforward process. The more false positive packets are introduced, the better a privacy of security policy is preserved. On the other hand, more packet screening is required within a private cloud, whose resources are not unlimited. Finding a trade-off between those two is necessary to not overload the infrastructure, while maintaining a high level of policy confidentiality.

The objective of this analysis was to check if and how a change of Bloom Filter parameters affects the private cloud resources utilization. Adjustment of the false positive rate, which has a direct impact on the filter size (number of bits required for the storage of a single item) and the number of hash calculations performed when both creating the security policy and performing the matching operations, is expected to change the number of packets successfully transmitted through the public cloud. The percentage of false positive decisions issued by each of the filters, responsible for matching the source and destination IP addresses, is expected to not exceed the specified false positive rate.

Figure 6 shows the effective percentage of false positive packets, which is calculated as a percentage of the total number of transmitted packets, depending on a used Bloom Filters false positive rate. The selected rates varied between 0.5% and 50% and were referenced to the conventional firewall, represented by a rate of 0%.

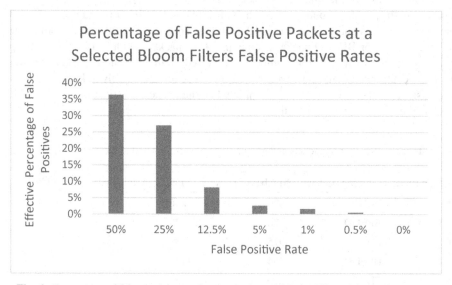

Fig. 6. Percentage of false positive packets at a selected Bloom Filters false positive rates.

The achieved results verify the proper behavior of the implemented solution, as the effective number of false positive packets follows the changes of specified false positive rate.

5.2 Impact of Bloom Filters on Efficiency

As the firewall instance within the private cloud has a very small requirements in terms of memory usage, which are constant regardless of the number of packets being processed, the utilization statistics focus only on the CPU usage, providing both the average and peak percentage, for selected Bloom Filter false positive rates, as shown in Fig. 7.

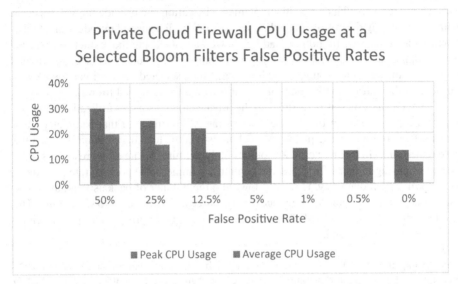

Fig. 7. Private cloud firewall CPU usage at a selected Bloom Filters false positive rates.

As expected, the results confirm that by allowing more false positive packets and, in effect, performing more packet filtering in the private cloud, the CPU utilization increases. However, on the lower range, the CPU load stabilizes and is no longer affected by any subsequent decreases of the false positive ratio. This allows to find parameters that will provide a trade-off between the achieved level of privacy and the resources required within a private cloud to provide the final filtering. Even the choice of a small Bloom Filter false positive rate, which puts a minimal load on the CPU, is enough to protect the confidentiality of the security policy.

6 Conclusions

Cloud computing is widely adopted by modern companies. Apart from allowing to avoid or minimize IT infrastructure costs, it provides a superior scalability, mobility and manageability of resources. While migration of most workloads to the cloud can be easily done, security services require a special treatment, as their configurations contain confidential data regarding the protected infrastructure. A privacy preserving solution must be implemented to prevent possible information gaining by the cloud service provider.

In this paper, a privacy preserving solution for cloud-based firewall services was presented and implemented in the OpenStack environment. By using tree-based structure and Bloom Filters for firewall policy representation, it allows to both anonymize the policy and prevent information gathering by traffic eavesdropping and its further analysis. The solution utilizes a hybrid cloud model, with a public cloud performing the initial packet screening allowing a configurable number of false positives, and a private cloud responsible for the final packet filtering and fully enforcing the security policy. Verification tests concluded that the implemented solution can provide firewall services without sacrificing the privacy of applied security policy. Purposeful introduction of false positives led to successful policy shading, as well as increasing the resilience to traffic eavesdropping and its analysis. With the privacy preserving solution in place, the attempt to discover the permitted source IP address range for a selected destination network was unsuccessful, contrary to the result of scenario with a conventional firewall.

The main analysis was performed on the private cloud resources utilization, depending on the chosen Bloom Filter false positive rate. Adjustment of that parameter has a direct effect not only on the privacy level, but also on the load distribution between the potentially unlimited public cloud resources and the finite private cloud resources. At a cost of imposing higher CPU load on the latter, the higher false positive rate provides a better policy confidentiality. However, lowering the number of packets that have to be filtered within the private cloud, reduces the resource utilization only to some point. The results indicate that a trade-off between the security policy privacy and private cloud performance can be found.

Acknowledgements. This work has been funded by the European Union's Horizon 2020 Research and Innovation Programme, under Grant Agreement no. 830943, project ECHO (*European network of Cybersecurity centres and competence Hub for innovation and Operations*).

References

1. Official Annual Cybercrime Report. https://www.herjavecgroup.com/wp-content/uploads/2018/12/CV-HG-2019-Official-Annual-Cybercrime-Report.pdf. Accessed 02 Feb 2020
2. Gouda, M.G., Liu, X.-Y.A.: Firewall design: consistency, completeness and compactness. In: 24th IEEE International Conference on Distributed Computing Systems (2004)
3. Cloud Shift Impacts All IT Markets. www.gartner.com/smarterwithgartner/cloud-shift-impacts-all-it-markets. Accessed 02 Feb 2020
4. Khakpour, A.R., Liu, A.X.: First step toward cloud-based firewalling. In: 31st IEEE International Symposium on Reliable Distributed Systems, pp. 41–50 (2012)
5. Kurek, T., Niemiec, M., Lason, A.: Taking back control of privacy: a novel framework for preserving cloud-based firewall policy confidentiality. Int. J. Inf. Secur. **15**(3), 235–250 (2015). https://doi.org/10.1007/s10207-015-0292-y
6. Bloom, B.H.: Space/time trade-offs in hash coding with allowable errors. Commun. ACM **13**(7), 422–426 (1970)
7. Bloom Indexes in PostgreSQL. https://www.percona.com/blog/2019/06/14/bloom-indexes-in-postgresql. Accessed 02 Feb 2020
8. Chromium Code Review: Transition Safe Browsing from Bloom Filter to Prefix Set. https://chromiumcodereview.appspot.com/10896048/. Accessed 02 Feb 2020

9. Medium: What are Bloom Filters?. https://blog.medium.com/what-are-bloom-filters-1ec2a5 0c68ff. Accessed 02 Feb 2020
10. Maggs, B.M., Sitaraman, R.K.: Algorithmic nuggets in content delivery. ACM SIGCOMM Comput. Commun. **45**(3), 52–66 (2015)
11. Mell, P., Grance, T.: The NIST Definition of Cloud Computing. National Institute of Standards and Technology Special Publication 800-145, Gaithersburg (2016)
12. Duan, Y., Fu, G., Zhou, N., Sun, X., Narendra, N.C., Hu, B.: Everything as a service (Xaas) on the cloud: origins, current and future trends. In: 8th IEEE International Conference on Cloud Computing, pp. 621–628 (2015)
13. Duan, Y., Cao, Y., Sun, X.: Various "aaS" of everything as a service. In: 16th IEEE/ACIS International Conference on Software Engineering, Artificial Intelligence, Networking and Parallel/Distributed Computing (2015)
14. Varadharajan, V., Tupakula, U.: Security as a service model for cloud environment. IEEE Trans. Netw. Serv. Manag. **11**, 60–75 (2015)
15. Kurek, T., Niemiec, M., Lason, A., Pach, A.R.: Universal privacy-preserving platform for SecaaS services. Int. J. Netw. Manag. **27**, e1994 (2017)
16. Fulp, E.W., Tarsa, S.J.: Trie-based policy representations for network firewalls. In: 10th IEEE International Symposium on Computers and Communications, pp. 434–441 (2005)

Analysis of Available Microcontroller Computing Resources for the Application of Some Cryptographic Hash Functions on Different Internet of Things Platforms

Kristian Dokic[1]([⊠]) (ID), Tomislav Mesic[2] (ID), and Mirko Cobovic[3] (ID)

[1] Polytechnic in Pozega, Vukovarska 17, 34000 Pozega, Croatia
kdjokic@vup.hr
[2] Faculty of Economics and Administration, University of Pardubice,
53210 Pardubice, Czech Republic
tomislav.mesic@upce.cz
[3] College of Slavonski Brod, Pozega, Croatia
Mirko.Cobovic@vusb.hr

Abstract. In the last few years, there have been more and more security vulnerabilities in IoT devices. Some authors suggest the use of security algorithms and methods used on computers for protection, but in this paper, we propose that some hash encryption algorithms can be used in IoT application to provide integrity and authenticity of a message. It can be used when the risk of data misuse and the need for strong protection are low.

Five different development boards are tested to prove that the proposed HMAC algorithm is not too computing-intensive. mbedTLS library has been used, and performance (speed) of boards have been measured with different secret key and payload size. We concluded that SHA256 and HMAC-SHA256 algorithms could be taken into account when deciding on the application of cryptography, primarily due to the ease of use and a low load of the microcontroller.

Keywords: HMAC · SHA256 · IoT · Arduino · mbedTLS

1 Introduction

New paradigm called "Internet of Things" becomes ubiquitous in this century. The term "Internet of Things" was coined by Kevin Ashton in 1999. but this original idea dealt with RFID implementation and connecting small devices using that technology [1]. Amount of IoT devices rises rapidly in the second decade of the twenty-first century. Still, in that race for profit, manufacturers are not careful enough considering the security of IoT devices. It is known that IoT devices have been used for DDOS attacks, and this attacks can be powerful with a traffic of 1.2 Tbps and with 100.000 malicious endpoints [2].

As the number of IoT devices rises, it becomes evident that in the future, lots of them will be connected via IPv6 protocol. With many new features, this approach also brings

© Springer Nature Switzerland AG 2020
A. Dziech et al. (Eds.): MCSS 2020, CCIS 1284, pp. 168–181, 2020.
https://doi.org/10.1007/978-3-030-59000-0_13

new dangers like a possibility of outside attack. To protect end devices encryption can be used. The lack of encryption algorithms that are often cited in the literature is the need for significant computing power, and it is time-consuming. This problem is highlighted in devices that are expected to consume little electricity and to have a fast response [3].

International Telecommunications Union proposed four dimensions' structure division of things: tagging things, feeling things, shrinking things and thinking things [4]. From the application perspective, some authors proposed four domains categorization: Logistics and Supply Chain Management, Transportation, Healthcare and finally Environment and Disaster [5, 6]. There are different levels of security required depending on the application category. Healthcare application IoT devices require a high level of reliability and privacy protection, but for Environment application, IoT devices requirements are lower.

In this paper, we suggest that some hash encryption algorithms can be used in IoT application to provide integrity and authenticity of a message when the risk of abuse is negligible. One example is temperature, humidity, and light monitoring in agriculture. There is an imperative need in agriculture to control these variables with a view to more efficient irrigation. On the other hand, the risk of misuse of this data and the need for strong protection is low.

There are several papers in the literature describing different cryptographic approaches in IoT development, but it is difficult to compare these solutions in the context of a hardware development platform. We decided to compare performance (speed) of simple hash cryptography algorithm application on the different platforms and to suggest what developers can expect from analyzed platforms. We chose the SHA256 hash algorithm and the HMAC algorithm with Arduino IDE and mbedTLS library [7, 8]. They were tested with five different hardware platforms, and the critical constraint set is that used microcontroller cost less than $10.

In Sect. 2, there is a literature review with a focus on cryptography on embedded platforms. In Sect. 3, analyzed embedded platforms are described and in the Sect. 4 software and applied testing methods are described. Section 5 is reserved for results, and in Sect. 6, you can find discussion and conclusion.

2   Cryptography on IoT Platforms

According to Forbes, the Internet of Things market will reach more than half-trillion by 2021 but in some newer analyze they also mentioned that some products would be targeted by ransomware attacks [9, 10].

Bastos et al. analyzed different aspects of IoT security and proposed four key concepts that developers must have in their minds:

a) Asset – anything that has some kind of value,
b) Threat – anything that can cause damage,
c) Vulnerability – weaknesses that can be exploited to compromise the asset,
d) Risk - the possibility of compromise, injury or loss [11, 12].

Authors also quoted and analyzed protocols used by IoT devices, and the leading protocols are MQTT, MQTT-SN, HTTP/REST, CoAP, AMQP and XMPP. They noted that

HTTP/REST is the most used that TLS library is a default tool for security improvement. They also stated that TLS increase microprocessor usage and adds overhead to communications. They conclude that TLS is too complicated to use, and some improved protocol based on MQTT or CoAP would be the best solution for IoT securing [12].

Ziimerli et al. proposed a set of key questions on which we have to know answers before select appropriate secure method. There are six of them:

a) cryptographic operations that are needed,
b) sensitive material that we have to protect,
c) which elliptic-curve cryptography to support,
d) which TLS cipher suite to use,
e) are cryptographic operations executed rarely or often,
f) the amount of energy we have at our disposal.

Answers on these questions help us to decide should we implement security in software or hardware. They also analyzed and tested five different security devices that provide a hardware solution for IoT security and cryptography [3].

El Jaouhari et al. are aware of the importance of security in medical data transmission between entities to prevent tampering personal data of patients, so they proposed security layer based on CoAP protocol secured with DTLS [13].

Pearson et al. tested and compared cryptographic software libraries and hardware crypto modules. They proved that cost and hardware are not the bottlenecks of IoT security applications. They used TI's CC3220, Espressif ESP32 and cryptographic device ATECC608A produced by Microchip. They tested various protocols and algorithms, but one of them was HMAC with SHA-256 on ESP32. With the key size of 15 bytes, they measured HMAC calculation time 154 μs [14].

Li analyzed open-source technologies that are available for IoT application development. He cited three open-source systems that implement TLS and DTLS mechanism. They are Eclipse TinyDTLS, mbedTLS and Eclipse Scandium. The first and the second are C-based, and the last one is Java-based. He also noted that a certain amount of computing resources are required by security mechanisms based on these systems/libraries [15].

Zhang et al. proposed outsourcing of cryptography and they developed a Java card that enables Arduino MEGA 2560 board to generate a digital signature using the RSA algorithm in 82.2 μs [16].

3 Analyzed IoT Platforms

When someone familiar with processors in the field of desktop computers tries to understand what is going on in the area of embedded or IoT platforms, he is probably quite confused. There are two dominant corporations in desktop processor production (Intel and AMD), but the situation is different in embedded platforms. We can say that a dominant corporation in that field is ARM, but they do not produce microcontrollers. They only develop RISC architecture and license it to other companies. Lots of companies produce SoC devices based on their architecture, but in the last few years, some new

manufacturers have emerged. That situation also had an impact on our choice of platforms, but we tried to choose different platforms to get a better overview of the market
situation.

In Fig. 1, there are five development board that we have elected. The sixth was
Arduino Duemilanova, but it has only two kB RAM and 32 kB FLASH memory, and it
was not enough for the first task – SHA256 hash algorithm implementation. Because of
that, this board and microcontroller were excluded from research and figure number 1.

In the top left corner of Fig. 1 is Arduino MEGA 2560 board and in the top right side
STM32 NUCLEO-L476RG board. In the centre of Fig. 1 is W600 TB-01. In the bottom
left corner of the figure is ESP32-Wroom and in the bottom right is Sipeed MAix BiT.
There is a pound coin next to Arduino MEGA 2560 board.

Fig. 1. Analyzed IoT platforms

3.1   Arduino MEGA 2560 with ATmega2560 (8-Bit)

The Arduino MEGA 2560 is a microcontroller board based on Atmel's ATmega2560
microcontroller. The ATmega2560 is 8-bit RISC microcontroller that has throughput
up to 16 MIPS at 16 MHz. It has eight kB SRAM and 248 kB FLASH memory. It
has four serial ports, sixteen analog inputs, ICSP header and generally fifty-four digital
input/output pins. The board can be bought on Aliexpress web site for about $9.00.

It is supported by Arduino IDE, and there is no need to install additional tools to
start programming.

3.2 W600 TB-01 with ARM Cortex-M3 Core (32-Bit)

A W600 TB-01 is based on the W600 WiFi module that is based on the ARM Cortex-M3 core. It has 288kB SRAM memory and 1 MB flash memory. It also has I2S, I2C, and UART implemented. On web page about this board, there is information that it has accelerator for SHA1/MD5/RC4/DES/3DES/AES/CRC, as well as pseudo-random number generator, but most of the documentation is in Chinese [17]. It can be bought on Aliexpress web site for only $2.50.

3.3 NUCLEO-L476RG with ARM Cortex-M4 Core (32-Bit)

A NUCLEO-L476RG is based on STM32L476 microcontroller which design is based in Cortex-M4 core. There are many NUCLEO boards, and letters and numbers in their names have different meanings. This one is based on STM32L4 microcontroller series, and it has 64 pins, 96 KB SRAM and 1 MB of flash memory. It is supported by many development toolchains like Arm Keil, IAR, Arm mbed and different GCC based IDE. The board can be bought on Aliexpress web site for about $20.00, but the only microcontroller can be purchased for $5 [18].

3.4 ESP32-Wroom with Tensilica Xtensa LX6 (32-Bit)

An ESP32-Wroom board is based on Tensilica Xtensa LX6 core based on 40 nm technology. It includes 802.11 b/g/n connectivity as well as Bluetooth v4.2 BR/EDR. It has throughput up to 600 MIPS at 240 MHz and 520 kB SRAM memory. This board has 8 MB flash memory, but up to 16 MB of external flash can be mapped. It also has UART, I2C and I2S interfaces. Interestingly, ESP32 is equipped with hardware accelerators for AES, SHA, RSA and ECC. It also has a random Number Generator [19]. The board can be bought on Aliexpress web site for about $4.50.

3.5 Sipeed MAix BiT with Kendryte K210 (64-Bit)

A Sipeed MAix BiT board is based on Kendryte K210 microprocessor that is based on RISC V architecture. It is 28 nm technology microprocessor, dual-core RISC-V 64bit that works on 400 MHz clock. It also can be overclocked to 800 MHz. It has hardware-accelerated AES, SHA256 and FFT. Like the other boards, it also includes UART, I2S and I2C. This microcontroller was released in September 2018, and it has Neural Network Processor implemented that support convolution kernels and any form of activation functions. It is based on open architecture, and manufacturers do not have to pay any licenses because its design is open source. The board can be bought on Seedstudio web site for about $13.00, but the only microcontroller can be purchased for $9 on Aliexpress web site [20].

In Table 1, the amount of SRAM and FLASH memory, as well as the clock speed of analyzed boards, can be seen.

Table 1. Characteristics of analyzed boards

BOARD	SRAM (kB)	FLASH (kB)	CLOCK
Arduino MEGA 2560	8	248	16 MHz
W600 TB-01	288	1024	48 MHz
NUCLEO-L476RG	96	1024	80 MHz
ESP32-Wroom	520	8192	240 MHz
Sipeed MAix BiT	8192	8192	400 MHz

4   Methods

Benchmarking is used in situations where the performance of a microcontroller needs to be compared. Some companies perform benchmark tests and advise designers in choosing a platform, such as the Embedded Microprocessor Benchmarking Consortium [21] and Berkeley Design Technology, Inc [22]. However, in actual applications, these results are sometimes not applicable [23].

To make different platforms and microcontrollers with different characteristics somewhat comparable, we decided to use Arduino IDE because it supports all described microcontrollers. Only Arduino MEGA 2560 is supported "out of the box" by Arduino IDE new installation. Still, the rest are supported by download toolchains, and most of them are automatically installed on the appropriate place on the Arduino IDE directory tree. This download and installation can be started by entering the Internet address of suitable JSON file in the field "Additional Boards Manager URLs" in Preferences.

In this paper, we suggest that some hash encryption algorithms can be used in IoT application when the risk of abuse is negligible. In some situation like data transfer from the agricultural weather station to a server, a hash function can be used for data integrity protection and the authenticity of a message. Data integrity can be protected with some hash algorithm like well-known SHA256, so it will be used in our research. On the other hand, hash functions do not protect data transfer from man-in-the-middle attacks. To protect it, some hash function with a secret cryptographic key can be used, and in this paper, HMAC-SHA256 is used. It is used to verify data integrity with SHA256 and authenticity of a message with a secret cryptographic key.

Many cryptography libraries have included these functions. Kumar et al. have analyzed seventeen general cryptography libraries and after that, five libraries that are applicable in the IoT field. General libraries are Borzoi, Crypto++, Libmcrypt, Botan, Libgcrypt, Bouncy Castle, Cryptlib, Catacomb, Cryptix, Flexiprovider, LibTomCrypt, MatrixSSL, MIRACL, Mozilla's NSS, OpenPGP, Nettle and OpenSSL. IoT cryptography libraries are: WolfSSL, AvrCryptoLib, WiseLib, TinyECC and RelicToolKit [24].

In this paper, the mbedTLS library has been used. mbedTLS library, previously known as PolarSSL, is an implementation of different cryptographic algorithms written in C [25]. It supports different ciphers algorithms like AES, DES, 3DES, Blowfish, as well as cryptographic hash functions like SHA-1, SHA-2, MD2, MD4, MD5. It also supports public-key cryptography like RSA, ECC, ECDH and ECDSA. It is available for most operating systems and also can be used without OS, on "bare metal". It has a dual license with GPLv2 and Apache license V2.

In the first part of the research, microcontrollers performances (speed) have been checked with SHA-256 hash algorithm implementation. This algorithm is the part of the set of cryptographic hash functions designed by NSA and published in 2002 [26, 27]. The SHA-2 family of algorithms are patented in US patent 6829355, but from 2007 it is available under a royalty-free license [28, 29].

In research, SHA-256 hash calculation time with different payloads has been measured on five various boards. The size of the smallest payload was 128 Bytes, and the size of the biggest was 2048 Bytes, as it can be seen in table number 2 in the results section. Hash calculation time has been measured with function *micros()* that return number of microseconds from microcontroller board reset. Execution time code block can be seen in Fig. 2. To make sure that the *micros()* function is accurate, we compared the measured values with the values obtained with an oscilloscope with a slightly adjusted program. The values were the same.

```
time_start = micros();
//some code
time_end = micros();
time = time_end - time_start;
```

Fig. 2. Execution time code block

In the second part of the research, microcontrollers performances (speed) have been checked with HMAC algorithm implementation. The abbreviation HMAC comes from a *hash-based message authentication code*. In addition to being used to preserve integrity, with a secret key, it enables the authenticity of a message. HMAC was presented in the paper by Bellare et al. in 1996, and it used within TLS, SSH and IPsec protocols [30]. The size of the used secret key determines the strength of the HMAC and a brute force is still the most common attack against HMAC. In RFC 6234, there is a recommendation to avoid HMAC with MD5 hash algorithm in the development of new cryptographic protocols, but in this paper HMAC with SHA256 is used [31].

In research HMAC based on SHA-256 hash calculation time with different payloads has been measured on five various boards. The size of the smallest payload was 128 Bytes, and the size of the biggest was 2048 Bytes, as it can be seen in table number 3 in the results section. In this part of the research, a key size has also been increased from 16 Bytes to 128 Bytes in 16-byte increments. The calculation time has been measured with function *micros()* that return number of microseconds from the microcontroller board reset. The source code can be found on Github repository: https://github.com/kristian1 971/MCSS2020.

5 Results

5.1 SHA256 Checksum

In Table 2, SHA256 checksum calculation times can be seen for different boards. In Fig. 3 in the bar chart, the SHA256 checksum calculation times can also be seen.

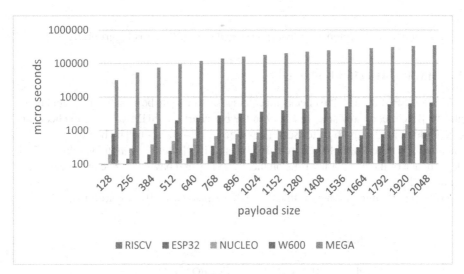

Fig. 3. SHA256 checksum calculation time

Table 2. SHA256 checksum calculation time

Payload size	RISCV	ESP32	NUCLEO	W600	MEGA
128 B	69 μs	91 μs	192 μs	788 μs	32044 μs
256 B	89 μs	141 μs	286 μs	1177 μs	53228 μs
384 B	108 μs	191 μs	379 μs	1566 μs	74412 μs
512 B	128 μs	241 μs	473 μs	1971 μs	95600 μs
640 B	149 μs	291 μs	567 μs	2368 μs	116788 μs
768 B	169 μs	341 μs	661 μs	2758 μs	137968 μs
896 B	188 μs	391 μs	754 μs	3148 μs	159156 μs
1024 B	208 μs	442 μs	848 μs	3536 μs	180340 μs
1152 B	228 μs	492 μs	942 μs	3936 μs	201524 μs
1280 B	248 μs	542 μs	1037 μs	4339 μs	222712 μs
1408 B	268 μs	592 μs	1130 μs	4728 μs	243896 μs
1536 B	288 μs	642 μs	1224 μs	5117 μs	265080 μs

(continued)

Table 2. (*continued*)

Payload size	RISCV	ESP32	NUCLEO	W600	MEGA
1664 B	308 μs	692 μs	1317 μs	5507 μs	286264 μs
1792 B	328 μs	743 μs	1411 μs	5906 μs	307452 μs
1920 B	348 μs	792 μs	1505 μs	6309 μs	328636 μs
2048 B	368 μs	842 μs	1599 μs	6698 μs	349824 μs

It is important to emphasize that the vertical axis in Fig. 3 is logarithmic.

5.2 HMAC-SHA256 Checksum

In Table 3, SHMAC-HA256 checksum calculation times can be seen for different boards and 16 Bytes secret key size. In Fig. 9 in the bar chart, the SHMAC-HA256 checksum calculation times with 16 Bytes secret key size can also be seen. The boards testing has included secret key size change from 16 Bytes to 128 Bytes in 16-byte increments. The dependence of the calculation time on the secret key and payload size can be seen in 3D graphs in Figs. 4, 5, 6, 7 and 8.

It is important to emphasize that the vertical axis in Fig. 9 is logarithmic.

Table 3. SHMAC-HA256 checksum calculation time

Payload size	RISCV	ESP32	NUCLEO	W600	MEGA
128 B	136 μs	184 μs	397 μs	1498 μs	64748 μs
256 B	156 μs	234 μs	491 μs	1895 μs	86084 μs
384 B	176 μs	284 μs	585 μs	2294 μs	107420 μs
512 B	196 μs	335 μs	679 μs	2682 μs	128752 μs
640 B	216 μs	385 μs	772 μs	3072 μs	150092 μs
768 B	236 μs	435 μs	867 μs	3461 μs	171428 μs
896 B	257 μs	485 μs	961 μs	3858 μs	192764 μs
1024 B	276 μs	535 μs	1055 μs	4249 μs	214100 μs
1152 B	297 μs	585 μs	1150 μs	4636 μs	235432 μs
1280 B	317 μs	635 μs	1243 μs	5034 μs	256768 μs
1408 B	337 μs	685 μs	1338 μs	5423 μs	278108 μs
1536 B	355 μs	735 μs	1432 μs	5821 μs	299444 μs
1664 B	375 μs	785 μs	1526 μs	6211 μs	320780 μs
1792 B	395 μs	835 μs	1620 μs	6602 μs	342120 μs
1920 B	415 μs	885 μs	1714 μs	6997 μs	363456 μs
2048 B	437 μs	936 μs	1808 μs	7387 μs	384788 μs

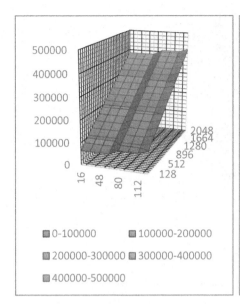

Fig. 4. MEGA – dependence of time on secret key size and payload size

Fig. 5. W600 – dependence of time on secret key size and payload size

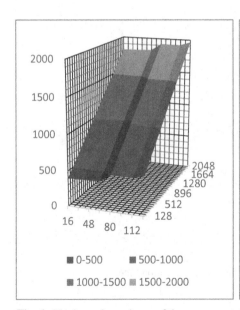

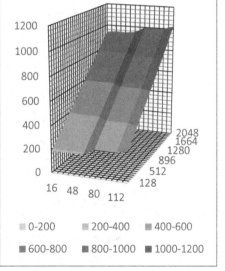

Fig. 6. Nucleo – dependence of time on secret key size and payload size

Fig. 7. ESP32 – dependence of time on secret key size and payload size

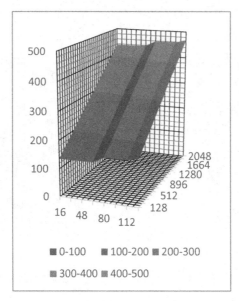

Fig. 8. RISCV – dependence of time on secret key size and payload size

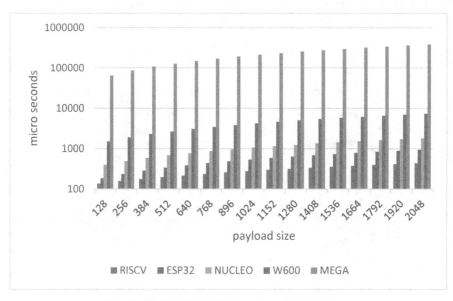

Fig. 9. HMAC-SHA256 checksum calculation time

6   Discussion and Conclusion

There are many ways to speed up cryptographic functions performance. Intel and AMD implemented some extensions for hardware acceleration of SHA family algorithms

[32, 33]. ARM also implemented hardware acceleration for some SHA functions in advanced processor designs [34]. Some manufacturers offer extern electronic components that are optimized for speed cryptographic function calculations, as well as designed to prevent extraction and cloning of stored secret keys [35, 14]. This makes sense in most situations, but if it is not about protecting sensitive data in communication and cryptographic operations are performed infrequently, then non-processor-intensive methods can be used. All calculations can be done locally on the microcontroller. These arguments are, in fact, two of six answers on the key questions proposed by Ziimerli et al. before deciding on the type of cryptography [3].

SHA256 checksum calculation times for 128 Bytes payload are less than one millisecond for four boards, and only for Arduino MEGA 2560, it is about 32 ms. With 2048 Bytes payload, checksum calculation times are longer five to ten times. In situations where response time is not critical, and when insensitive data is transmitted, the measured times are acceptable.

HMAC with SHA256 checksum calculation times for 128 Bytes payload and 16 Bytes secret key is less than 1.5 ms for four boards, and only for Arduino MEGA 2560, it is about 65 ms. With 2048 Bytes payload, checksum calculation times are longer four to six times. Again, in situations where response time is not critical and when insensitive data is transmitted, the measured times are acceptable.

Pearson et al. also analyzed different libraries and different boards and tested HMAC with SHA-256 on ESP32. With 15 Bytes key size, they measured 154 µs HMAC calculation time. This value is very similar to our 184 µs with 16 Bytes key size. Pearson et al. concluded that modern microcontrollers and modules can provide a satisfactory level of security through several precautions, but are generally powerful enough for essential cryptographic functions [14].

There is a generally accepted opinion that microcontrollers are too weak for cryptographic algorithms. Tested algorithms do not provide message encryption, but we point out that in some situations they can be taken into account when deciding on the application of cryptography, primarily due to the ease of use and a low load of the microcontroller.

References

1. Ashton, K., et al.: That 'internet of things' thing. RFID J. **22**, 97–114 (2009)
2. Woolf, N.: DDoS attack that disrupted internet was largest of its kind in history, experts say. The Guardian, 26 October 2016. https://www.theguardian.com/technology/2016/oct/26/ddos-attack-dyn-mirai-botnet. Accessed 16 May 2020
3. Zimmerli, L., Schläpfer, T., Rüst, A.: Securing the IoT: introducing an evaluation platform for secure elements. In: Konferenz Internet of Things-vom Sensor bis zur Cloud, Stuttgart, Deutschland, 20. November 2019 (2019)
4. Atzori, L., Iera, A., Morabito, G.: The internet of things: a survey. Comput. Netw. **54**, 2787–2805 (2010)
5. Vongsingthong, S., Smanchat, S.: Internet of things: a review of applications and technologies. Suranaree J. Sci. Technol. **21**, 359–374 (2014)
6. Yang, Q., Wang, Z., Yue, Y.: Summarize the technology of the things of Internet. In: 2012 2nd International Conference on Consumer Electronics, Communications and Networks (CECNet) (2012)

7. Arduino: Software, Arduino. https://www.arduino.cc/en/main/software. Accessed 22 May 2020

8. Trusted Firmware: https://www.trustedfirmware.org/. Accessed 23 May 2020

9. Columbus, L.: Iot market predicted to double by 2021, reaching $520b, Forbes, 16 August 2018. https://www.forbes.com/sites/louiscolumbus/2018/08/16/. Accessed 23 May 2020

10. Gillett, F.: Predictions 2020: IoT Expansion Brings Even More Change," Forrester, 1 November 2019. https://go.forrester.com/blogs/predictions-2020-iot/. Accessed 15 May 2020

11. Bastos, D.: Cloud for IoT-a Survey of Technologies and Security features of Public Cloud IoT solutions (2019)

12. Bastos, D., Shackleton, M., El-Moussa, F.: Internet of Things: a survey of technologies and security risks in smart home and city environments (2018)

13. El Jaouhari, S., Bouabdallah, A., Bonnin, J.-M., Lemlouma, T.: Securing the communications in a wot/webrtc-based smart healthcare architecture. In: 2017 14th International Symposium on Pervasive Systems, Algorithms and Networks & 2017 11th International Conference on Frontier of Computer Science and Technology & 2017 Third International Symposium of Creative Computing (ISPAN-FCST-ISCC) (2017)

14. Pearson, B., Luo, L., Zhang, Y., Dey, R., Ling, Z., Bassiouni, M., Fu, X.: On misconception of hardware and cost in IoT security and privacy. In: ICC 2019-2019 IEEE International Conference on Communications (ICC) (2019)

15. Li, Y.: An integrated platform for the internet of things based on an open source ecosystem. Fut. Internet **10**, 105 (2018)

16. Zhang, E.P., Fang, J., Li, D.C.C., Ching, M.W.H., Chim, T.W., Hui, L.C.K., Yiu, S.M.: A simple and efficient way to combine microcontrollers with RSA cryptography. Comput. Sci. (LNECS) **2207**, 7–11 (2013)

17. Thingsturn: Thingsturn.com, Thingsturn. https://www.thingsturn.com/. Accessed 21 May 2020

18. STMicroelectronics: NUCLEO-L476RG - STM32 Nucleo-64 development board with STM32L476RG MCU, supports Arduino and ST morpho connectivity, STMicroelectronics. https://www.st.com/en/evaluation-tools/nucleo-l476rg.html. Accessed 23 May 2020

19. Espressif: ESP32 Series Datasheet (2020). https://www.espressif.com/sites/default/files/doc umentation/esp32_datasheet_en.pdf. Accessed 14 May 2020

20. Seeed: Sipeed MAix BiT for RISC-V AI + IoT. https://www.seeedstudio.com/Sipeed-MAix-BiT-for-RISC-V-AI-IoT-p-2872.html. Accessed 12 May 2020

21. Embedded Microprocessor Benchmark Consortium: About EEMBC, Embedded Microprocessor Benchmark Consortium (2020). https://www.eembc.org/about/. Accessed 15 July 2020

22. Berkeley Design Technology, Inc.: Overview of BDTI Services, Berkeley Design Technology, Inc. (2020). https://www.bdti.com/company/overview-of-bdti-services. Accessed 15 July 2020

23. Nakutis, Ž.: Embedded microcontrollers benchmarking using sliding window algorithm. Elektronika ir Elektrotechnika **75**, 49–52 (2007)

24. Kumar, U., Borgohain, T., Sanyal, S.: Comparative analysis of cryptography library in IoT. CoRR, vol. abs/1504.04306, 2015

25. Bakker, P.: PolarSSL is now a part of ARM, arm mbed, 24 November 2014. https://tls.mbed. org/tech-updates/blog/polarssl-part-of-arm. Accessed 25 May 2020

26. Penard, W., van Werkhoven, T.: On the secure hash algorithm family. Cryptography in Context, pp. 1–18 (2008)

27. National Institute of Standards and Technology: Announcing Approval of Federal Informa-tion Processing Standard (FIPS) 180-2, Secure Hash Standard; a Revision of FIPS 180-1, 26 August 2002. https://www.federalregister.gov/documents/2002/08/26/02-21599/announ cing-approval-of-federal-information-processing-standard-fips-180-2-secure-hash-standa rd-a. Accessed 24 May 2020
28. IETF Secretariat: IPR Details, IETF Secretariat, 20 June 2007. https://datatracker.ietf.org/ipr/ 858/. Accessed 22 May 2020
29. Glenn, L.M.: Device for and method of one-way cryptographic hashing. United States of America Patent US6829355B2, 5 March 2001
30. Bellare, M., Canetti, R., Krawczyk, H.: Keying hash functions for message authentication (1996)
31. Turner, S., Chen, L.: Updated security considerations for the MD5 message-digest and the HMAC-MD5 algorithms (2011)
32. Gulley, S., Gopal, V., Yap, K., Feghali, W., Guilford, J., Wolrich, G.: Intel SHA Exten-sions, July 2013. https://software.intel.com/content/dam/develop/external/us/en/documents/ intel-sha-extensions-white-paper-402097.pdf. Accessed 12 June 2020
33. Larabel, M.: AMD starts linux enablement on next-gen "Zen" Architecture. Phoronix Media, 17 March 2015. https://www.phoronix.com/scan.php?page=news_item&px=AMD-Zen-CPU-Znver1. Accessed 1 June 2020
34. ARM: ARM Cortex-A53 MPCore Processor (2014). http://infocenter.arm.com/help/topic/ com.arm.doc.ddi0500e/DDI0500E_cortex_a53_r0p3_trm.pdf. Accessed 2 June 2020
35. Durand, A., Gremaud, P., Pasquier, J., Gerber, U.: Trusted lightweight communication for IoT systems using hardware security. In: Proceedings of the 9th International Conference on the Internet of Things, New York, NY, USA (2019)

Workflow Management System
with Automatic Correction

Wojciech Chmiel[1]([✉]) [iD], Jan Derkacz[1] [iD], Andrzej Dziech[1] [iD],
Stanisław Jędrusik[1] [iD], Piotr Kadłuczka[1], Bogusław Laskowski[2],
Zbigniew Mikrut[1] [iD], Dariusz Pałka[1] [iD], Piotr Rajchel[2], Iwona Skalna[1] [iD],
and Michał Turek[1] [iD]

[1] AGH University of Science and Technology, Krakow, Poland
wch@agh.edu.pl
[2] Doosan Babcock Energy Poland, Rybnik, Poland
http://www.agh.edu.pl
http://www.doosanbabcock.com/pl/

Abstract. This paper describes the implementation of the distributed
INRED system running in a real industrial environment, with a set of
intelligent tools and a workflow system. The INRED-Workflow system,
being the key components of the INRED system, provides the infrastructure for process automation. Participants of the (service) processes,
managed by INRED-Workflow, are controlled by the system and other
process participants, such as quality managers and technologists, at every
stage of the performed service procedures. All data gathered from the service processes is stored in the System Knowledge Repository (SKR) for
further processing by using advanced algorithms. The INRED-Workflow
system uses the so-called *Smart Procedures*, which allows easy implementation of newly defined algorithms based, among others, on machine
learning.

Keywords: INRED · Workflow · Smart Procedures · 3D device
models

1 Introduction

Maintaining highly technically advanced machinery and equipment in proper
condition requires the increasingly broader specialist knowledge in the field. Such
knowledge, which is indispensable to both satisfy the binding, rigorous technical
standards and to ensure the safety of employees performing their duties in a limited time, often in an environment dangerous to life and health, is incorporated
into the developed proprietary INRED system (see Sect. 1.1). The system integrates copyrighted and innovative solutions that use, among others, augmented

This work was supported by the European Regional Development Fund under the
Innovative Economy Operational Programme, POIR.01.01.01-00-0170/17.

reality to visualize renovation objects in 3D space and support employees during complex repairs and renovation procedures.

In this paper we describe the implementation of the sophisticated system to control highly complicated repair and service processes. The main objective of this system is to improve the quality of services by ensuring their proper execution, continuous surveillance and reporting their accomplishment. To this end, the systems allows each service procedure to be defined as a workflow process. The assistance of the system relies on delivering a detailed description of the tasks to be performed and technical documentation (pictures, technical drawings, 3D models with animation, movies, and parameter values). Moreover, the system automates some activities, such as measurements control and decision-making. Each serviceman is equipped with a mobile terminal or augmented reality (AR) glasses, camera and BlueTooth communication devices. These tools allows to automatically control the settings of devices from the procedure level, send the results of the measurements and validate them based on existing standards. The integration of the tools with the system is based on the Mobile Devices Communication Subsystem.

The system of the mobile and stationary cameras is used to document the tasks carried out, to provide the constant surveillance, and also to automatically correct services. The automatic correction is based on the advanced image recognition algorithms which detect several types of events (in the case of the considered in this paper repair and renovation services these could be the closing the valve or the order of tightening of the bolts). All the components of the system (repositories, databases, surveillance system, workflow engine, etc.) have been integrated by using the intelligent communication system.

The system presented in this paper has many elements of the concept of Industrial 4.0, Internet of Things (IoT) and Industrial Internet of Things (IIoT). The problem of implementing these concepts in industry has been discussed for many years. An interesting example of integration of IoT and blockchain was presented by Teslya et al. [15]. The authors developed an architecture that combines Smart-M3 information sharing platform and blockchain platform. The main features of their proposal was the use of smart contracts for processing and storing information related to the interaction between smart space components. Another interesting application of IoT is the proposal of Shrouf et al. [13] in the area of energy management. They present a reference architecture for IoT-based on smart factories with the focus on sustainability perspectives.

1.1 INRED System

The INRED system (Fig. 1) aims to control all phases of the repair and services processes. The main modules of the system include:

- *Platform Process Management Knowledge Base* – automates service process by managing the exchange of information between the Competence Center and service units.

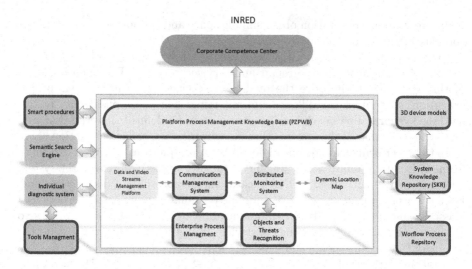

Fig. 1. General scheme of the INRED system.

- *Communication Management System* – self-organizing communication network.
- *Enterprise Process Management* – part of the INRED-Workflow system that manages service processes (workflows).
- *Tools Management* – manages the wireless tools.
- *3D device models* – includes 3D models of the services devices.
- *System Knowledge Repository* – advanced repository system based on ontology/ontologies responsible for storing and processing data from different sources; this data is used by other INRED modules such as *Objects and Threats Recognition*, *Platform Process Management Knowledge Base* and *Enterprise Process Management*. The module includes as well data from processes execution, used for reporting.
- *Objects and Threats Recognition* – intelligent system for objects recognition, thread detection and prediction using algorithms based on machine learning (neural network, deep learning, Bayes network, decision tree, rule system, soft computing, approximation optimization).
- *Individual Diagnostic System* – an advanced system for collecting the biometric data of employees.

In order to fully support the INRED system, additional modules will be implemented, such as:

- *Competence Center.*
- *Mobile Devices Communication Subsystem.*
- *Integrated Video and Data Streams Management Platform.*
- *Semantic Search Engine.*

An important element of the INRED system are *Smart Procedures* that merge services supplied by modules such as *Objects and Threats Recognition* (for instance using the image recognition and machine learning algorithms), *Tools Management* and *Mobile Devices Communication Subsystem*. *Smart Procedures* have standard programming interface which allows them to be easily integrated (already at the stage of their creation) with workflow procedures.

2 Related Works

Workflow Management (WfM) is an evolving technology which is increasingly often exploited in a variety of industries. Its primary characteristic is the automation of processes involving both human and machine-based activities. The first attempt to standardize workflow systems was made in 1993 by the Workflow Management Coallition (WfMC) [17]. WfMC created the workflow reference model which specifies a framework for workflow systems and interfaces between the workflow engine and cooperating applications and systems. Since then, workflow has been the subject of investigations in both industry and science. There are many papers discussing the limitations of existing workflow systems and outlining important research issues [1,5]. There exist several producers of the workflows system for different world markets, one can mention Appian, BP Logix, Creatio, Oracle Workflow and Nintex Workflow. However, there are no vendors that allow to integrate service processes with wireless tools, augmented reality technology and image recognition algorithms.

The methods based on image analysis consist of many successively implemented algorithms, broadly described in the literature. The most important algorithms are: camera calibration, preprocessing and image segmentation (object of interest extraction), and measurements. The detailed description of these algorithms together with a discussion of their advantages and limitations is presented in [18] and illustrated by an example of vertical displacement of the Humber Bridge.

The methods and results of measurements of flat, thin, rectangular objects with holes are presented, e.g., in [9] where the stationary camera was calibrated by using a standard gage.

Li [10], in turn, presents a measurement system for shaft parts that also uses a stationary camera mounted on the calibrated stand. Therein, the wavelet denoising algorithm was used at the preprocessing stage and then the edge of the object was detected by using a Canny operator. The measurement error of this method was less than 0.01 [mm].

There are a lot of publication concerning data acquisition based on Internet of Things (IoT). They generally refer to the implementation of systems that enable data flow from IoT devices to digital repositories. Data stored in a repository can be preprocessed whenever needed and used to improve the processes performed in various systems [16].

In [4] the authors presented an overview on the most important applications of Augmented Reality (AR) in the industrial practice.

Castano et al. [3] present wireless solution for industrial sensor monitoring. The proposed system can be applied in small to mid-size industrial environment.

Gore et al. [6] describe the solution based on Bluetooth Low Energy (BLE) technology to connect sensor nodes to Internet-based services and applications using gateway in an industrial plant. The authors also investigate the performance of BLE technology as a local communication for sensor device monitoring.

In [2] the authors discuss security threats and vulnerabilities of the IoT heterogeneous environment and propose possible solutions for improving the IoT security architecture.

Magliulo et al. [12] present the BlueTooth-Activity Tracker for workflow management and patients' performance monitoring in a Radiation Oncology Department. This solution is integrated with a novel electronic medical record archiving and retrieving system.

The concept of measurements presented in the present work differs from others concepts mainly in that the position of the camera is dynamic (relative to the measured object). The measurement is made by using an image obtained from the camera mounted on the tripod or installed on the helmet of an employee (this causes that the distance between the camera and the object is not fixed). Of course, the larger is the object in the image, the measurement will be more precise.

3 Process Management

The INRED-Workflow system is one of the key components of the INRED system. It provides the infrastructure for process automation. Each workflow process is a sequence of tasks and transitions between them. Tasks in a workflow may be performed in parallel or sequentially by a human or machine or both. INRED-Workflow stands out from other workflow systems in that it has, among others, the following unique features:

– Built-in media types to support images, movies and animations.
– The ability to annotate images.
– The ability to define and operate the so-called Smart Procedures.

Service procedures are carried out by a trained personnel which however often lacks adequate experience. In such cases, the system is ready to give hints on how to perform a specific task. A hint can take the form of a presentation of a technical drawing with selected elements that require action at a given moment. It can also take the form of an animation that enables the user to view the elements and activities from various perspectives and select the most interesting one. In addition, the system allows the user to watch movies showing previously completed service procedures. Additionally, each of the multimedia materials can be annotated. The INRED-Workflow system includes the following components:

– INRED-*ProcessDesigner*.
– INRED-*WorkflowEngine*.
– INRED-*WorkflowClient*.
– INRED-*AuditAndReportingTool*.

INRED-*ProcessDesigner* is a graphical editor of workflow processes. It allows to create a process definition according to the Business Process Model & Notation standard. INRED-*WorkflowEngine* is used to perform workflow processes. The engine interprets the process definition, creates tasks and supervises their execution. *WorkflowClient* is designed to support process participants. It provides workitems to all process participants, supervises the execution of tasks and supports process participants in the execution of certain tasks. INRED-*Workflow* has an advanced Audit Trial, designed for tracking and capturing all tasks and actions related to a particular workflow. It stores all data from the execution of processes for further analysis and reporting.

4   Repair and Service Procedures

Repair and service procedures supported by the process management system enable implementation of various (time-consuming, complicated and requiring many resources) industrial processes. One of such procedures is the procedure of the refurbishment of the steam rotor of the power generator at the power plant or valves repair. The repair and service procedures have to preserve a strongly defined order and should provide data which confirms the quality of the performed tasks. Therefore, the activity performer (participant of the process) is controlled at every stage of the procedure by the system and other process participants, such as quality managers and technologists. All data gathered from the process is stored in the System Knowledge Repository (SKR) for the future use. The SKR stores, among others (Fig. 2):

- current state of a process (if the process is currently performed),
- complete audit of a process (once the process is completed): performers, time of actions, positions, etc.,
- data gathered by the tools involved in the process execution (parameter values obtained during the measurement of the parts of repaired objects),
- multimedia data (photos and movies gathered during the service process).

The SKR includes the following input data for the service process:

- Employees – organizational chart.
- Parameters target values.
- Device part descriptions.
- Workflow procedures.
- 3D device models.
- Move and 3D animations.
- Repair manuals.
- Metadata.
- Smart procedures.

Below we present the model of the main flow of the valves repair process (cf. Fig. 3). As can be seen, this process involves several stages of repairing of different types of valves. Each stage (also called activity) of the main flow is implemented as a subprocess which returns data to the main process. We would like, however, to point out two activities:

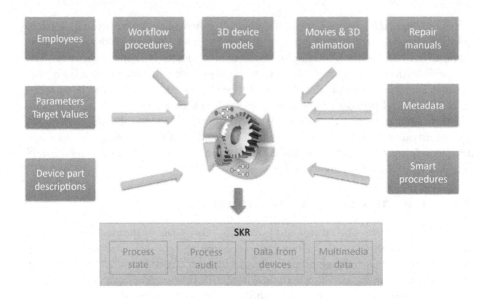

Fig. 2. Input and output data for/from process management.

- *Valve classification* in which the mobile communication subsystem automatically provides information about the parameters of the repaired valve parts. A participant in the process by using dedicated devices, such as a caliper equipped with the ability to transfer data (e.g., using BlueTooth), sends the obtained parameters directly to the workflow process. If the values of the parameters are correct then the process is continued. Otherwise, the process forces the repetition of incorrectly performed actions. The mobile devices communication subsystem is described in Sect. 5.
- *Check valve state* in which the quality of the performed activity is assessed by using intelligent image processing methods (one of such methods is described in Sect. 6. These methods allow, for example, to detect the incorrect valve state, i.e., the state which is different from the three acceptable positions: opened, partially opened or closed. If the detected state does not match any of the target positions, specified by the creator during the process definition, then the valve position should be corrected by repeating the adequate activity. This repetition can be implemented, as shown in Fig. 3, by the feedback between the activity *Check valve state* and activity *Set target valve state*.

The activity *Check valve state* is implemented by using so-called Smart Procedures. These procedures wrap the algorithm that evaluates the state of the valve by analyzing the video collected from a stationary or helmet-mounted camera.

More precisely, *Smart Procedures*, presented in Fig. 4, are a special software component which exposes the precisely defined interface. This approach allows newly defined algorithms to be easily implemented in the workflow, e.g., by using machine learning methods. All processes are created using the Workflow

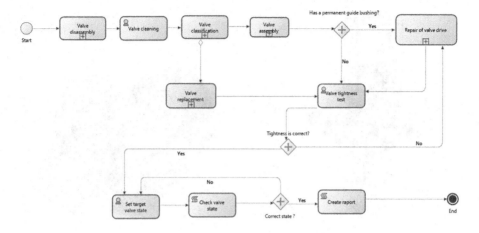

Fig. 3. Main flow of the process.

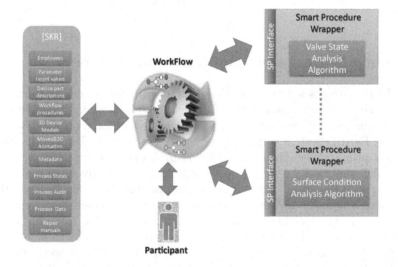

Fig. 4. Implementation of the external algorithms in the workflow process.

Editor. Apart from the process flow, process control parameters and the Smart Procedures, the Process Editor allows attaching to the process the animations with annotations in 2D and 3D space, permission to execution of the activity by the exactly specified employee or groups of employees and definition of the reports.

Fig. 5. An example of the 3D models - the valve.

Fig. 6. An example of the 3D models - the power generator.

5   Mobile Devices Communication Subsystem

The INRED system is also able to communicate with vast amount of Bluetooth-enabled, WiFi or other mobile devices - providing information for decision processes from industrial environment. Special signal-conversion units are developed within the INRED system to pass Bluetooth messages over IP networks (using WiFi as a primary medium in the system) by using TCP or UDP protocols. These mobile units will be spread by the system users over the industrial zone - connecting each Bluetooth device in range they can find (Fig. 7). They will then report these Bluetooth devices to the subsystem central server. Once reported, the devices will be available for users. Each user will be able to perform measurements or to steer the machinery during the repair process by using personal tools. The measurements taken, which will be automatically sent to the system, can affect the realization of the procedures that are managed by the workflow system, and thus can affect the tasks carried out by employees under its supervision.

In order to obtain the most flexible solution, an extraordinary dynamic integration system will be added to identify and integrate new types of Bluetooth-enabled devices. Because each mobile device can provide unknown set of features to be read over an unknown protocol – the integration mechanism must foresee unpredicted behavior of new devices. It is desired that each new types of devices are identified and accepted in real-time. These devices might not even yet exist during the system development – and still the integration should be possible in the future. To achieve that, a special device-driver format for Bluetooth devices will be prepared and drivers development process will be passed to outside vendors (driver developers). This special device format, coming together with driver API and a framework, will be used by developers to write translators of unknown Bluetooth protocols to a common system communication language (and vice versa). Thanks to this, each new Bluetooth device behavior will be able to be linked to a driver (translator) and to be recognized by a system after driver installation. Additionally, to gain scalability and system security, drivers (foreign codes) will not be hosted on a central server, but spread around to special auxiliary servers called bridge processors. Consequently, these processors will convert and pass data between central server and Bluetooth bridges. They can also be distributed near the industrial machinery providing direct links to communicate with Bluetooth terminals and other machinery terminal interfaces *via* Bluetooth bridges.

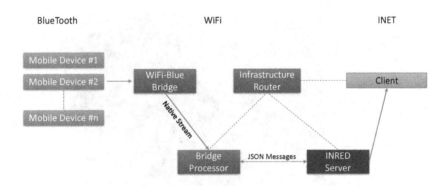

Fig. 7. Mobile devices subsystem architecture and dataflow.

To enforce extensibility of the system itself, all messages passed between servers and client components will be written in JSON. Hence, the development of future system components will be much easier. Mobile devices integration will achieve very good scalability – integrating high numbers of bridge processors, bridges and mobile devices. The system will provide device identification basing on MAC addresses, establishing relations between devices and users (each device can then send owned data, etc.). To improve user cooperation, devices can also be leased or shared between users.

Measurement data will be provided to endpoint users via client applications (specially designed for the system). Client software will be ported to standard desktop platforms and VR goggles. The software will render helper information (presented as 3D animations) as a standard 3D scene or VR hologram images in VR googles.

6   Service Activity Correction Example: Device State Detection Using Image Analysis

The final stage of the work – once the valve is properly assembled – is to set the valve to fully open position, which ensures the maximum fluid flow. This is referred to in paragraph III of the renovation instructions [8]: *"Valves are designed for two-position operation. This means that they should work in the fully open or fully closed position."* The fact that the valve is fully opened is very important, therefore it should be filmed during the renovation. It is also necessary to confirm this fact during renovation. Each valve has its own unique identifier, stored in the database. Additionally, the identifier in the form of a QR code is located on the valve rim (see Fig. 8). This way, one can easily access the technical description, which – among others – contains three important parameters: diameter and minimum and maximum length of the screw protruding beyond the handwheel (see Fig. 8).

Fig. 8. An example of valve.

These parameters are downloaded from the database by the workflow algorithm, which controls the renovation process using the commands, photos and video clips displayed on the monitor. The issuing of the "open valve" command is followed by checking whether the command has been carried out correctly.

Depending on the employee's equipment, the check is carried out in hardware or by using a vision method. The hardware check consists in measuring the length of the screw, protruding beyond the handwheel, using a special caliper (see Fig. 8). The caliper has a display and a BlueTooth communication module that transmits the measurement to the workflow algorithm. The algorithm compares the measurement with the data retrieved from the database and informs the employee whether the valve is fully opened.

If there is no a caliper or it is damaged, the measurement is carried out by using the vision method. In such case, an employee must properly set up one of two cameras: stationary or the one located on a helmet. The part of the screw protruding beyond the handwheel must be accordingly enlarged. In addition, the image of the screw should be placed parallel to the horizontal edges of the image and should stand out from the background. An employee obtains this information from the workflow algorithm, which shows as well the subsequent stages of image analysis. In the case of irregularities found in the operation of the algorithm, the employee can repeat the analysis by taking another photo.

The estimation of the screw length is implemented as follows (see Fig. 9):

- the image is converted to grayscale,
- the image is smoothed using median filtration,
- the image histogram is calculated,
- the background pixel range is determined (by comparing two red lines on the histogram graph),
- the image is binarized – pixel values outside the background range are set to 1,
- the binary image is projected onto the axes of the coordinate system,
- the pixel distances corresponding to the bolt diameter and length are calculated,
- the screw length is calculated according to formula (1).

The following results were obtained for the object shown in Fig. 9:

- $d_{pix} = 368 - 223$ (diameter of the screw in pixels, compare the red arrows on the projection chart)
- $d_{mm} = 16$ (diameter of the screw in millimeters, read from the database)
- $l_{pix} = 878 - 141$ (screw length in pixels, compare the blue arrows on the projection chart)

The screw length final calculation is:

$$l_{mm} = (l_{pix} * d_{mm})/d_{pix} = 81.3241[mm]. \tag{1}$$

The obtained value was compared with:

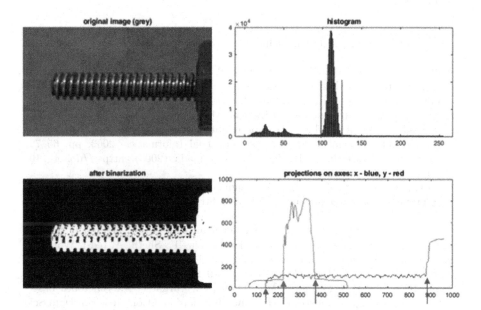

Fig. 9. Steps of image analysis - explanations in the text.

- $l_{mm}^{c} = 83[mm]$ (length measured with caliper),
- $l_{mm}^{d} = 80[mm]$ (length read from the database).

As can be seen, the estimated screw length is between the actual size, measured with a caliper, and the value read from the database.

7   Summary

The solutions implemented in the INRED system present an innovative approach to supporting the repair and renovation processes. One of the key innovative solutions was the employment of various tools equipped with BlueTooth connectivity. However, since there are no wide approved standards of BlueTooth communication, the Mobile Devices Communication Subsystem was implemented which allowed us to improve the measurement tasks (transferring the results into the system), eliminate errors of incorrect settings (e.g., torque wrenches), and simplify the configuration of the tools (what remained to be performed by employees was to register a tool in the system). The workflow engine, created for the purposes of our system, allows us to define repair and renovation procedures by using a dedicated workflow process editor. This editor enables not only editing the description and visualization of the procedure steps, but also the use of video stream analysis algorithms and cooperation with BT/WiFi tools. Thanks to these elements, an automatic correction of the detection and repair process has been implemented, and the reports have been partly automated.

References

1. Van der Aalst, W., Weske, M., Wirtz, G.: Advanced topics in workflow management: issues, requirements, and solutions. J. Integr. Des. Process Sci. **7**(3), 49–77 (2003)
2. Belli, L., Davoli, L., Medioli, A., Marchini, P. L., Ferrari, G.: Toward Industry 4.0 with IoT: optimizing business processes in an evolving manufacturing factory. In: Frontiers in ICT, vol. 6 (2019). https://doi.org/10.3389/fict.2019.00017
3. Castano, J.G., Andreasson, J., Ekstrom, M., Wrzesniewski, A., Ahlblom, H., Backlund, Y.: Wireless industrial sensor monitoring based on Bluetooth/spl trade/. In: IEEE International Conference on Industrial Informatics, 2003, pp. 65–72, INDIN 2003. Proceedings, Banff, Alberta, Canada (2003). https://doi.org/10.1109/INDIN.2003.1300205
4. De Pace, F., Manuri, F., Sanna, A.: Augmented reality in Industry 4.0. Am. J. Compt. Sci. Inform. Technol. **6**(1), 17 (2018). https://doi.org/10.21767/2349-3917.100017
5. Elmagarmid, A.; Di, W.: Workflow management: state of the art versus state of the products. In: Dogac, A., Kalinichenko, L., zsu, T., Sheth, A. (ed.). Workflow Management Systems and Interoperability, pp. 1–17. Springer, Heidelberg (2012). doi:https://doi.org/10.1007/978-3-642-58908-9_1
6. Gore, R. N., Kour, H., Gandhi, M., Tandur, D., Varghese, A., Bluetooth based Sensor Monitoring in Industrial IoT Plants, International Conference on Data Science and Communication (IconDSC), pp. 1–6, Bangalore, India (2019). https://doi.org/10.1109/IconDSC.2019.8816906

7. Harris, S.E., Katz, J.L.: Firm size and the information technology investment intensity of life insurers. MIS Quart. **15**, 333–352 (1991)

8. Kania, P., Szulcek, T., Chorebiewski, M., Wosko, R., Bedrunka, W., Reichel, P.: Remont zasuw srednio i wysokocisnieniowych z koncowkami do spawania. Instrukcja technologiczna IQ-04/2013/TA, Doosan Babcock Energy Polska (2016)

9. Leta, F.R., Feliciano, F. F., de Souza, I. L., Cataldo, E.: Discussing accuracy in an automatic measurement system using computer vision techniques. In: 18th International Congress of Mechanical Engineering, November 6–11, Ouro Preto, MG (2005)

10. Li, B.: Research on geometric dimension measurement system of shaft parts based on machine vision. EURASIP J. Image Video Process. **2018**(1), 1–9 (2018). https://doi.org/10.1186/s13640-018-0339-x

11. MATLAB release: The Math Works Inc, p. 2018. Massachusetts, Natick (2018)

12. Magliulo, M., Cella, L., Pacelli, R.: Bluetooth devices for the optimization of patients' workflow in a radiation oncology department. In: E-Health and Bioengineering Conference (EHB), Iasi, pp. 1–4 (2015). https://doi.org/10.1109/EHB.2015.7391515

13. Shrouf, F., Ordieres, J., Miragliotta, G.: Smart factories in Industry 4.0: a review of the concept and of energy management approached in production based on the Internet of Things paradigm. In: IEEE International Conference on Industrial Engineering and Engineering Management (IEEM) (Bandar Sunway: IEEE), pp. 697–701 (2014)

14. Swanson, E.B.: Information systems innovation among organizations. Manage. Sci. **40**, 1069–1092 (1994)

15. Teslya, N., Ryabchikov, I.: Blockchain-based platform architecture for industrial IoT. In: 21st Conference of Open Innovations Association (FRUCT), pp. 321–329, Helsinki (2017)

16. Ustundag, A., Cevikcan, E.: Industry 4.0: Managing The Digital Transformation. SSAM. Springer, Cham (2018). https://doi.org/10.1007/978-3-319-57870-5

17. Workflow Management Coalition: Workflow Reference Model. Workflow Management Coalition Standards, WfMC-TC-1003 (1994)

18. Xu, Y., Brownjohn, J.M.W.: Review of machine-vision based methodologies for displacement measurement in civil structures. J. Civ. Struct. Health Monit. **8**(1), 91–110 (2017). https://doi.org/10.1007/s13349-017-0261-4

19. Zimmermann, A., Schmidt, R., Jugel, D., Möhring, M.: Adaptive enterprise architecture for digital transformation. In: Celesti, A., Leitner, P. (eds.) ESOCC Workshops 2015. CCIS, vol. 567, pp. 308–319. Springer, Cham (2016). https://doi.org/10.1007/978-3-319-33313-7_24

Convolutional Neural Network Decoder for Enhanced Hadamard Error Correcting Code and Its Application in Video Watermarking

Jakob Wassermann$^{(\boxtimes)}$ and Michael Windisch

Department of Electronic and Telecommunications, University of Applied Sciences
Technikum-Wien, Vienna, Austria
{jakob.wassermann,windiscm}@technikum-wien.at

Abstract. Error Correcting Codes play an essential role in the digital communication. Especially a new digital technology like video watermarking demands sufficient error correcting capabilities, because of very high compression ratio (about 1:200). Normally the watermarks can barely survive such massive attacks, despite very sophisticated embedding strategies. In this paper, the authors introduce a new approach for Error Correcting Code based on 2D Hadamard Code and convolutional Neuronal Network (CNN). The main idea is that the 2D-Hadamard code words can be represented as 2D basis images. The errors cause a noise in these basis images. The decoding procedure of this 2D-Codewords is realized by a CNN, which was before trained with these basis images. With this approach, it is possible to overcome the theoretical limit of error correcting capability of $(d-1)/2$ bits, where d is a minimum Hamming distance. To prove the efficiency and practicability of this new 2D Hadamard Code, the method was applied to a video Watermarking Coding Scheme. The Video Watermarking Embedding procedure decomposes the initial video through Multi-Level Interframe Wavelet Transform. The low pass filtered part of the video stream is used for embedding the watermarks, which are protected respectively by CNN based 2D Hadamard Code.

Keywords: Hadamard Error Correcting Code · Basis images · CNN · Video Watermarking

1 Introduction

Many applications in telecommunication technologies are using Hadamard Error Correcting Code. Plotkin [1] was the first who discovered in 1960 error correcting capabilities of Hadamard matrices. Bose, Shrikhande [2] and Peterson [3] also have made important contributions. Levenshtein [4] was the first who introduced an algorithm for constructing a Hadamard Error Correcting Code. In the literature the Hadamard code is often mentioned as a special case of Reed-Muller code [5]. The most famous application of Hadamard Error Correcting Code was the NASA space mission in 1969 of Mariner

© Springer Nature Switzerland AG 2020
A. Dziech et al. (Eds.): MCSS 2020, CCIS 1284, pp. 196–208, 2020.
https://doi.org/10.1007/978-3-030-59000-0_15

and Voyager spacecrafts. Thanks to the powerful error correcting capability of this code it was possible to decode properly high-quality pictures of Mars, Jupiter, Saturn and Uranus [6].

In this paper, we introduced a new approach of Hadamard Code, in which its error correcting capability can be improved significantly by using Convolutional Neuronal Network. The application of this Code in Video Watermarking gives also a strong proof of its effectiveness. The reason for selecting Video Watermarking lies in strong compression ratio, normally factors greater than 1:200, which is applied to the video sequences. For example, an uncompressed HDTV video stream has a data rate of 1.2 Gbit/s and for distribution reason it must be compressed at least to 6 Mbit/s. For embedded watermarks, it is a big challenge to survive such a strong compression ratio. Error correcting code plays a decisive role in surviving of the embedded Watermarks. This paper has followed the structure: Section 2 contains the introduction into classical Hadamard Error Correcting Code, describes the 2D Hadamard Code and its error correcting capabilities as well as the implementation of CNN for the decoding process. In Sect. 3, the authors explain CNN approach for the decoding procedure. The Video Watermarking Scheme and the results are presented in Sect. 4 and 5, followed by a discussion.

2 Hadamard Code

The Hadamard Code of n-bit is a linear code, where the code word length n, can be calculated from $n = 2^m$, where m is a natural number $m \in N$. It can be generated by rows of a $n \times n$ Silvester-Hadamard Matrix H_n. The corresponding message word has the length of $k = m + 1$ bits. The Hamming distance between the code words is constant and is $d_{min} = 2^{m-1} = n/2$. The Hadamard Code can be denoted as a tuple $(2^m, m + 1, 2^{m-1})$, which components are: the code word length, message length and the Hamming distance, but in further consideration, we will use the abbreviation (n, k). The error correcting capability t can be calculated by

$$t = \left\lfloor \frac{n}{4} - 1 \right\rfloor \tag{1}$$

In case of $n = 8$ we can correct only one error.

2.1 Encoding Procedure

To obtain the n bit Hadamard Code at first we have to build a new composed matrix C_{2n}

$$C_{2n} = \begin{pmatrix} H_n \\ -H_n \end{pmatrix} \tag{2}$$

where H_n is the Hadamard Matrix. In case of $n = 8$ the Hadamard Matrix is

$$H_8 = \begin{pmatrix} 1 & 1 & 1 & 1 & 1 & 1 & 1 & 1 \\ 1 & -1 & 1 & -1 & 1 & -1 & 1 & -1 \\ 1 & 1 & -1 & -1 & 1 & 1 & -1 & -1 \\ 1 & -1 & -1 & 1 & 1 & -1 & -1 & 1 \\ 1 & 1 & 1 & 1 & -1 & 1 & -1 & -1 \\ 1 & -1 & - & -1 & -1 & -1 & -1 & 1 \\ 1 & 1 & -1 & -1 & -1 & 1 & 1 & 1 \\ 1 & -1 & -1 & 1 & -1 & -1 & 1 & -1 \end{pmatrix} \tag{3}$$

and the composed matrix C_{16} is

$$C_{16} = \begin{pmatrix} 1 & 1 & 1 & 1 & 1 & 1 & 1 & 1 \\ 1 & -1 & 1 & -1 & 1 & -1 & 1 & -1 \\ 1 & 1 & -1 & -1 & 1 & 1 & -1 & -1 \\ 1 & -1 & -1 & 1 & 1 & -1 & -1 & 1 \\ 1 & 1 & 1 & 1 & -1 & -1 & -1 & 1 \\ 1 & -1 & 1 & -1 & -1 & 1 & -1 & 1 \\ 1 & 1 & -1 & -1 & -1 & -1 & 1 & 1 \\ 1 & -1 & -1 & 1 & -1 & 1 & 1 & -1 \\ -1 & -1 & -1 & -1 & -1 & -1 & -1 & -1 \\ -1 & 1 & -1 & 1 & -1 & 1 & -1 & 1 \\ -1 & -1 & 1 & 1 & -1 & -1 & 1 & 1 \\ -1 & 1 & 1 & -1 & -1 & 1 & 1 & -1 \\ -1 & -1 & -1 & -1 & 1 & 1 & 1 & 1 \\ -1 & 1 & -1 & 1 & 1 & -1 & 1 & -1 \\ -1 & -1 & 1 & 1 & 1 & 1 & -1 & -1 \\ -1 & 1 & 1 & -1 & 1 & -1 & -1 & 1 \end{pmatrix} \tag{4}$$

The Hadamard Code is now defined by 16 rows of the matrix C_{16}, where each row is 8 bit long code word. In the Table 1 is shown the binary Hadamard Code (8,4,4), where -1 is substituted by 0.

2.2 Decoding Procedure

To understand the decoding procedure of Hadamard Code let's look upon its codewords. As mentioned before, the code words are the rows of the composite matrix C_{2n} and they are orthogonal to each other. Consider the i-th row, which is the n dimensional code word vector h_i, we can build a corresponding Hadamard spectrum represented by the n dimensional vector s_i

$$s_i = h_i \cdot H_n \tag{5}$$

All components of this vector s_i are zeros except the component i. This gives us the ability to decode the corresponding code word, simply by analyzing the Hadamard spectrum of

Table 1. Code Book of Hadamard Code (8,4,4)

Message word				Hadamard vector							
0	0	0	0	1	1	1	1	1	1	1	1
0	0	0	1	1	0	1	0	1	0	1	0
0	0	1	0	1	1	0	0	1	1	0	0
0	0	1	1	1	0	0	1	1	0	0	1
0	1	0	0	1	1	1	1	0	0	0	0
0	1	0	1	1	0	1	0	0	1	0	1
0	1	1	0	1	1	0	0	0	0	1	1
0	1	1	1	1	0	0	1	0	1	1	0
1	0	0	0	0	0	0	0	0	0	0	0
1	0	0	1	0	1	0	1	0	1	0	1
1	0	1	0	0	0	1	1	0	0	1	1
1	0	1	1	0	1	1	0	0	1	1	0
1	1	0	0	0	0	0	0	1	1	1	1
1	1	0	1	0	1	0	1	1	0	1	0
1	1	1	0	0	0	1	1	1	1	0	0
1	1	1	1	0	1	1	0	1	0	0	1

the received code words. The component of the spectrum vector with the highest value represents the code word.

Example:

We contemplate the third row (message word: 0010) of the Hadamard matrix C_{2n}

$$h_3 = \begin{bmatrix} 1 & 1 & -1 & -1 & 1 & 1 & -1 & -1 \end{bmatrix} \tag{7}$$

The decoded Hadamard spectrum vector is

$$s_3 = \begin{bmatrix} 1 & 1 & -1 & -1 & 1 & 1 & -1 & -1 \end{bmatrix} \cdot H_8 = \begin{bmatrix} 0 & 0 & 8 & 0 & 0 & 0 & 0 & 0 \end{bmatrix} \tag{8}$$

Only the third component of the spectrum vector s_3 is different from zero. It means that the position $i = 3$ determines the row in the Code Book (Table 2). The decoded code word belongs to the third row of the Hadamard matrix C_{2n} and has the message word [0 0 1 0] (see also the Table 2).

2.3 2D-Hadamard Error Correcting Code

The Hadamard Code can be extended by using so called basis images of Hadamard Transform. Instead of Hadamard vectors we will use the basis images as code words. The basis images functions are orthogonal to each other and can be generated from the

Hadamard matrix by multiplication of their columns and rows. Generally, the rule for generating a basis images is

$$A_{lm} = H_n(:, l) \cdot H_n(m, :) \tag{9}$$

For example, in case of 4×4 Hadamard matrix

$$H_4 = \begin{pmatrix} 1 & 1 & 1 & 1 \\ 1 & -1 & 1 & -1 \\ 1 & 1 & -1 & -1 \\ 1 & -1 & -1 & 1 \end{pmatrix} \tag{10}$$

A basis image A_{31} is

$$A_{31} = \begin{pmatrix} 1 \\ 1 \\ -1 \\ -1 \end{pmatrix} \cdot \begin{pmatrix} 1 & 1 & 1 & 1 \end{pmatrix} = \begin{pmatrix} 1 & 1 & 1 & 1 \\ 1 & 1 & 1 & 1 \\ -1 & -1 & -1 & -1 \\ -1 & -1 & -1 & -1 \end{pmatrix} \tag{11}$$

This basis image can be visualized if we substitute 1 by "black" and -1 by "white" (Fig. 1).

Fig. 1. Basis image A_{31}

For a Hadamard matrix H_4 there are 32 such basis images. They all can be easily calculated with Eq. (9) and they are depicted in Fig. 2.

Exactly as in case of one dimensional Hadamard Code, which is generated by positive and negative Hadamard matrices (see Eq. (2)), we have two sets of 16 basis images of a Hadamard transform, which are inverting version to each other. Totally, we have 32 basis images, that can be used as code words.

For the decoding procedure we need the 2D Hadamard spectrum of such basis images, which is denoted by S. It can be calculated according the equation

$$S = H_n \cdot A_{lm} \cdot H_n^T \tag{13}$$

where H_n is a $n \times n$ Hadamard matrix, H_n^T the transposed one, and A_{lm} are the basis images. The Hadamard matrices have the property, that the transpose and the original matrices are equal $H_n = H_n^T$, so there is no need for their calculation.

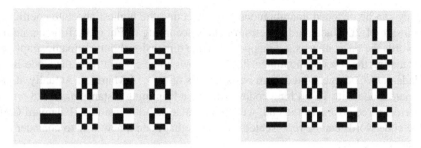

Fig. 2. Basis images of 2D Hadamard Transform (4 × 4)

The decoding procedure is the same as the one in one dimensional case. We consider the 2D-spectrum matrix, which is calculated according to Eq. (13). The spectrum has only one element which deviates from zero and it represents the corresponding basis image. The following example illustrates this procedure. In case of basis image A_{31} from Eq. (13) we can calculate the 2D Hadamard spectrum

$$S = H_4 \cdot A_{31} \cdot H_4 = \begin{pmatrix} 0 & 0 & 0 & 0 \\ 0 & 0 & 0 & 0 \\ 16 & 0 & 0 & 0 \\ 0 & 0 & 0 & 0 \end{pmatrix} \tag{14}$$

The coordinate of the greatest element in the matrix defines the encoded basis image. In our case is $S(3,1) = 16$, all other elements are zeros. It means the basis image A_{31} is our code word. The identification of the basis images through its spectral coefficients can be utilized to construct an error-correcting code. The code words are pattern of basis images,

Table 2. Excerpt from the Code Book of 2D Hadamard Code (16,5,8)

Message	Basis images	Matrix element	Code word
1 1 0 0 0		S(1,3)	1111111100000000
1 0 0 0 1		S(2,1)	1010101010101010
1 0 1 0 0		S(1,2)	1111000011110000
1 0 1 0 1		S(2,2)	1010010110100101

and they can be decoded unambiguously by detecting the highest absolute coefficient value inside of 2D Hadamard Spectrum matrix according to Eq. (13). To generate the code words the basis images are mapped into one dimensional pulse stream, simply by concatenating the rows of the image. Table 3 shows some excerpt from the Code Book for Hadamard Code generated from basis images of 4 × 4 Matrices. Actually, it is a Hadamard Code with 16-bit long codewords and a Hamming distance $d_{min} = 8$ bits. It can correct three errors. In the end, we get a regular one-dimensional Hadamard Code but the code words can be represented as images that open a new way to consider this code, as we see later.

3 CNN Approach for Decoding Procedure of 2D-Hadamard Code

The main idea of this paper is to apply Artificial Intelligence techniques for error correction. Because the 2D Hadamard Code consists of images, it is obvious to apply a Convolutional Neuronal Network to detect these images. It is well known, that CNN is well adapted for image recognition and classification. By this approach, we reduce the error correction, to the problem of image recognition and classification.

The theory of CNN is well described in [16]. In this chapter, we give a short overview about the functionality of CNN used in our experiments. For more detailed information refer to [17].

A convolutional neural network consists of the following layers:

- Convolutional layer
- Pooling layer
- Fully connected layer

The convolutional layer has the task to recognize characteristics and edges of the objects and serves as a feature extractor. The result of the convolutional layer is a features map of an image. The pooling layer has the task to reduce the resolution of the features map. The result of the pooling layer feeds into fully connected layer, where all information is used to interpret the feature representations and reaches the classification and decision.

For our work, we used the open source Software CNN "TensorFlow 2.0.0" and Phyton 3.7.5. As training images where used 1024 basis images of 2D Hadamard Code. The sizes of the images are (32 × 32) (Fig. 3).

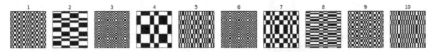

Fig. 3. Samples of loaded basis images

To these images, noise has been added and it is used to feed the CNN. In Fig. 4 the noisy basis images (noise factor 0.2) are depicted.

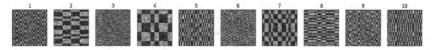

Fig. 4. Noisy basis images

The number of images that have been used for training varied between 1024 and 10240 in the experiments, when using 1024 images, each code only occurred once, in the case of 10240 each code occurred 10 times.

The total scheme of CNN processing is depicted in Fig. 5.

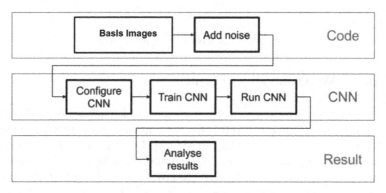

Fig. 5. Working scheme of CNN

The results of the experiments are shown in the Fig. 6. As we can see from the diagram all Basis Images that are corrupted by 30% noise (it corresponds to 307 bit errors in a 1024 bit long code word) can be recovered completely. If the amount of noise increases to the level of 50% only 30% of the whole 1024 Basis Images can be recovered. It is a very good result, because according the classical error correcting capability of Hadamard Code (1024, 11,512), as we can see from Eq. (1), the number of correcting errors is $t = 255$. In our case by using the CNN, we can overcome the burden of the Hamming distance by 20%.

It seems that CNN can better recover the corrupted code words, than the classical Hadamard decoding method.

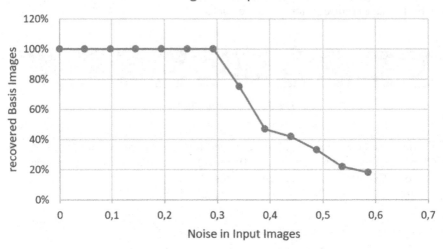

Fig. 6. Recovered basis images versus noise

4 Proposed Watermarking Scheme

The proposed watermarking scheme works in the spectral domain and uses an Interframe Discrete Wavelet Transform (DWT) [10] of video sequences and an Intraframe Discrete Cosine Transform (DCT) for embedding procedure [11, 12]. In Fig. 6, the whole encoding process is illustrated. The raw format of the luminance channel of the original video stream is decomposed by multi-level Interframe DWT with Haar Wavelet. This low pass filtered part of the video stream undergoes a block-wise DCT Transform. From DCT spectrum, special coefficients are selected and used for embedding procedure with 2D Hadamard coded watermarks. The embedding procedure itself is realized through QIM (Quadrature Index Modulation) techniques [13] (Fig. 7).

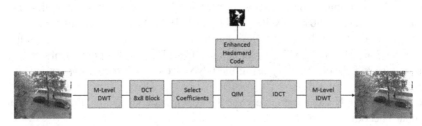

Fig. 7. Watermarking encoding process

The decoder procedure is depicted in Fig. 8. At the beginning of the decoding procedure, the embedded video sequence undergoes the same multi-level Interframe DWT and Intraframe DCT transforms as on the encoder side.

Fig. 8. Watermarking decoding procedure

After the selection of the proper DCT coefficients, the inverse QIM (IQIM) is applied. It delivers the decoded code words (pulse stream). Through the help of Enhanced Hadamard Error Correcting Code, the original watermark is extracted.

4.1 Multi-level DWT

As mentioned above a multi-Level Interframe DWT with Haar Wavelet was used to deliver a low pass filtered video. The Fig. 9 illustrates the operating principle of this transform. In the first level, the two consecutive frames are averaged. In the second level, the frames from level one are averaged and so forth. In this watermarking schemes, we used DWT levels from 12 till 16.

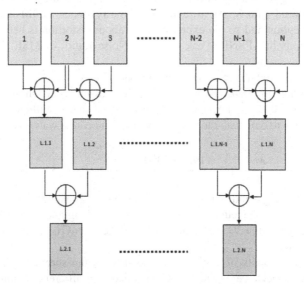

Fig. 9. Multi-Level Interframe DWT. At the first level, the two consecutive frames are averaged. At level two the consecutive frames from level one are averaged and so forth.

To realize the embedding procedure, some coefficients from the DCT spectrum of DWT filtered video sequence must be selected. The Fig. 10 shows which coefficients are qualified for watermarking. These are mostly from the yellow area.

1	9	17	25	33	41	49	57
2	10	18	26	34	42	50	58
3	11	19	27	35	43	51	59
4	12	20	28	36	44	52	60
5	13	21	29	37	45	53	61
6	14	22	30	38	46	54	62
7	15	23	31	39	47	55	63
8	16	24	32	40	48	56	64

Fig. 10. Coefficients of DCT Spectrum which fits for embedding (Color figure online)

5 Investigation of 2D Hadamard ECC with CNN Decoder

The investigation was done with HDTV video sequence with the resolution of 1080 × 1920 and 25 fps. The video was captured with an AVCHD Camera. The watermarking processing was performed only for the luminance channel (after converting RGB into YCrCb color space) because it is more robust against distortions than any other channels. It was investigated how many embedded watermark bits survive compression attacks without causing significant impairments. The degradation of the watermarked output video was measured with SSIM (Structural Similarity) index. SSIM is based on the human eye perception and so the expressiveness about distortion is better than in the traditional methods like PSNR (Peak Signal to Noise Ratio) or MSE (Mean Square Error) [14].

It was chosen the Enhanced 2D Hadamard Code of the size of 32 × 32, which means the code word length of 1024 bits. This implies the message code length of 11 bit. The DCT block size was 8 × 8 and from each block were selected 9 coefficients. With these, information is easy to calculate the total number of embedded watermark bits for each frame.

$$E = \frac{H \cdot W}{B^2} \cdot \frac{M}{W} \cdot C = \frac{1920 \cdot 1080}{8^2} \cdot \frac{11}{1024} \cdot 9 = 3132 \text{ Bit/Frame}$$

Where H is the height and W is the width of the frame. The letter B denotes the block size of DCT transform; the letter M is the message code length; the letter W represents the code word length of the 2D Hadamard Code and the letter C is the number of selected spectral coefficients.

In Table 3, the results of capacity and robustness measurements are presented. The compression attacks were done by H.264 codec with different compression ratios. Because the method works in the raw video, the original data rate is 1.2 Gbit/s. As a watermark was used a chessboard pattern of the size of 30 × 30 pixel. The watermarks were inserted successively into the frames.

The embedded video sequence was compressed with different compression ratios. In case of compression to 5 Mbit/s, which corresponds to a compression ratio of 1:240, it is still possible to extract all watermarks error free with both methods. However with the increasing of compression rate the CNN Decoding has better performance. With the data rate of 4 Mbit/s CNN-Decoding can still recover the watermarks error free, in contrast to standard Hadamard Coding, which has an error of 1,7%.

Table 3. Results for Hadamard Code with CNN Decoding

Data Rate	Compression Rate	DWT-Level	Selected Coefficients	Embedded Bits	Hadamard Code	Errors %	Hadamard Code with CNN	Errors %
5 Mbit/s	1:240	4	9	3132		0		0
4 Mbit/s	1:300	4	9	3132		1,7		0
3 Mbit/s	1:400	4	9	3132		7		1,5
2 Mbit/s	1:600	4	9	3132		37		28,6

6 Conclusion

In this paper a new type of 2D Hadamard Error Correcting Code with CNN based decoder, was introduced. It has remarkable property; it can overcome the limit of $\frac{n}{4} - 1$ correctable bit errors of a standard Hadamard Code. The application of this Code in Video Watermarking gives also a strong prove of its effectiveness.

Compared to standard Hadamard Code CNN based decoding seems to be more effective.

Watermarks protected by CNN based Hadamard Code can be easily recovered error-free from a video with a compression ratio of 1:240, which corresponds to a data rate of 4 Mbit/s.

All these results are very promising, and they show that the new CNN based Hadamard Code is a very powerful tool. Further investigation of this new error coding method can surely improve the ability of this error correcting approach method.

References

1. Plotkin, M.: Binary code with specified minimum distance. IRE Trans. IT-**6**, 445–450 (1960)
2. Bose, R.C., Shrikhande, S.S.: A note on the result in the theory of code construction. Inf. Control **2**, 183–194 (1965)
3. Peterson, W.W.: Error Correcting Codes. The M.I.T. Press, Massachusetts Institute of Technology & Wiley, Cambridge, New York (1961)
4. Levenshtein, V.I.: Application of Hadamard matrices to a problem in coding. Probl. Cybern. **5**, 166–184 (1964)
5. Combinatoric in Space, The Mariner 9 Telemetry System. http://www.math.cuden.edu/~wch erowi/courses/m6409/mariner9talk.pdf
6. Swanson, M.D., Kobayashi, M., Tewfik, A.: Multimedia data-embedding and watermarking technologies. Proc. IEEE **86**, 1064–1087 (1998)
7. Lin, S.D., Chen, C.-F.: A robust DCT-based watermarking for copyright protection. IEEE Trans. Consum. Electron. **46**, 415 (2000)

8. Shu, L., Costello Jr., D.J.: Error Control Coding. Prentice-Hall, Inc., Englewood Cliffs (1983)
9. MacWilliams, F.J., Sloane, N.J.A.: The Theory of Error-Correcting Codes. North Holland, New York (1977)
10. Chan, P.W., Lyu, M.R.: A DWT-based digital video watermarking scheme with error correcting code. In: Qing, S., Gollmann, D., Zhou, J. (eds.) ICICS 2003. LNCS, vol. 2836, pp. 202–213. Springer, Heidelberg (2003). https://doi.org/10.1007/978-3-540-39927-8_19
11. Dawei, Z., Guanrong, C., Wenbo, L.: A chaos-based robust wavelet-domain watermarking algorithm. Chaos Solutions Fractals 22, 792 (2004)
12. Cox, I.J., Kilian, J., Leighton, F., Shamoon, T.: Secure spread spectrum watermarking for multimedia. IEEE Trans. Image Process. 6, 1673–1687 (1997)
13. Chen, B., Wornell, G.W.: Quantization index modulation for digital watermarking and information embedding of multimedia. J. VLSI Sig. Process. 27, 7–33 (2001). https://doi.org/10.1023/A:1008107127819
14. Hartung, F., Kutter, M.: Multimedia watermarking techniques. Proc. IEEE 87, 1079–1107 (1999)
15. Ho, A.T.S., Shen, J., Tan, S.H., Kot, A.C.: Digital image-in-image watermarking for copyright protection of satellite images using the fast Hadamard transform. Geosci. Remote Sensing Symp. 6, 3311–3313 (2002)
16. Goodfellow, I., Bengio, Y., Courville, A.: Deep Learning. MIT Press, Cambridge (2016)
17. Huang, K., Hussain, A., Wang, Q.-F., Zhang, R.: Deep-Learning: Fundamentals, Theory and Applications. Springer, Cham (2019). https://doi.org/10.1007/978-3-030-06073-2

Crowd Density Estimation Based on Face Detection Under Significant Occlusions and Head Pose Variations

Rouhollah Kian Ara and Andrzej Matiolanski[✉]

AGH University of Science and Technology, Mickiewicza 30, 30-059 Kraków, Poland
matiolanski@kt.edu.pl
http://www.agh.edu.pl

Abstract. Counting and detecting occluded faces in the crowd is a challenging task in computer vision. In this paper, we propose a new approach to crowd estimation based on face detection under significant occlusion and head pose variations. Most of the state-of-the-art face detectors are unable to detect occluded faces. To address the problem, a novel approach for training various detectors is described. In order to obtain a reasonable evaluation of our solution, we trained and tested the model on our substantially occluded data-set. Images of the face up to 90° out-of-plane rotation and the faces with 25%, 50%, and 75% occlusion level. In this study, we trained the proposed model on 48,000 images obtained from our data-set consisting of 19 crowd scenes. To evaluate the model, 109 images with the face counts ranging from 21 to 905 and with an average of 145 individuals per image are utilized. Detecting faces in the crowded scenes with the underlying challenges cannot be addressed using a single face detection method. In this paper, by incorporating different traditional machine learning (ML) and the state-of-the-art convolutional neural network (CNN) algorithms, a robust method for counting faces visible in the crowd is proposed. Utilizing a compact variant of the VGG neural network [21], the proposed algorithm outperforms various state-of-the-art algorithms in detecting faces 'in-the-wild'.

Keywords: Crowd Density Estimation · Face detection · Convolutional neural network

1 Introduction

The huge growth in the world population has lead to an increased number of social events such as concerts, sports events, pilgrimage, political rallies, etc. All of those assemblies can lead to mass panic, riots or violent protests. Therefore, employing the automated or semi-automated crowd supervision techniques such as the approximation of crowds' density, queue management, detecting and counting people and detecting crowd flaws, play an essential role in human safety. Crowd density estimation and people counting problems are generally categorized into direct and indirect approaches [5].

© Springer Nature Switzerland AG 2020
A. Dziech et al. (Eds.): MCSS 2020, CCIS 1284, pp. 209–222, 2020.
https://doi.org/10.1007/978-3-030-59000-0_16

Detecting human faces in a crowd scene is a fundamental problem in computer vision, which has been made significant progress after seminal work by Paul Viola and Michael Jones [23]. The primary, task of modern face detectors which are widely used in real-world applications, is to identify whether there is a certain frontal face in an image. Recent research in this area focuses on face detection challenges, such as variations in scale, head pose, exaggerated facial expression, significant occlusion, and different lighting conditions.

In recent years, deep learning architectures such as convolutional neural networks (CNN) has become the most popular algorithm for face detection as a special type of object detection task in computer vision, overshadowing classical computer vision approaches. In contrast to traditional Machine Learning algorithms, CNN extracts, crucial and meaningful features such as edges in its first layers and combine them to detect shapes in the next layers and further fully connected layers learn how to utilize all these features in order to detect or classify objects in the scene. Although CNNs, are computationally expensive and usually require more data in comparison with the ML algorithms, it is effective in detecting the most sophisticated feature of images. Detecting faces in the crowded scenes with the underlying challenges cannot be addressed using a single face detection method. In this paper, by combining various traditional machine learning (ML) and the state-of-the-art CNN algorithms, a robust face counting in crowd method is proposed.

First, we employ a well-known traditional machine learning algorithms such as a histogram of oriented gradient (HOG) with support vector machines (SVM), Haar feature-based cascade classifier to obtain the size of faces in the crowd images. Afterward, the obtained sizes are utilized to specify the step size between the window patches. Finally, CNN is employed to classify and count faces in each patch. Counting of faces in small patches achieves, the number of all detected faces in the entire crowd image.

The rest of this paper is organized as follows. Section 2 briefly reviews the related work. Section 3 describes the proposed approach to face detection. Section 4 discuss our experiments and empirical results. Lastly, Sect. 5 concludes this paper.

2   Related Work

Face detection and recognition have evolved as one of the most widely used biometric techniques in many areas, such as public security, finance, crowd management and safety in recent years. Viola and Jones's idea was the first face detection framework that proposed rectangular Haar features in a cascaded Adaboost classifier to detect the faces in real-time with promising accuracy and efficiency [23]. Its drawbacks such as large feature size and incapable to detect faces in wild, motivated researchers to address the problems with more complicated features like HOG [18], scale-invariant feature transform (SIFT) and speeded up robust features (SURF) [13].

Some researchers, improved the accuracy of detectors, by separately training the several models for different head poses and scenes [10,14]. Chen et al.

Introduced a model to perform face detection combined with face alignment to improve the accuracy and speed of the object detector in challenging datasets [3].

In recent years, the deep convolutional neural networks (CNN) have achieved remarkable success in face detection applications. [9] investigate applying the Faster R-CNN [19], a state-of-the-art generic object detector, and achieved considerable performance in both speed and accuracy. Combining Faster R-CNN with hard negative mining and ResNet, [24] achieved remarkable performance on the FDDB face detection benchmark. Sun et al. [22] improved the performance of the Faster R-CNN algorithm by proposing several strategies such as feature contention, multi-scale training, and hard negative mining. Although many studies focused on occluded face detection [16,17,25], the performance of face detectors are imperfect in severely occluded faces and pose variations. In the next section, we will describe our approach in more detail, which can overcome the limitations of the existing studies.

3   Proposed Method

Many algorithms have been evaluated on low-density crowds, such as UCSD, Mall, PETS data-sets with a density of 11–46, 13–53, 3–40 people per image respectively [2,4,6]. Some other researches have been principally focused on counting people in extremely dense crowd images that each individual in the image may occupy a few pixels [8]. The proposed face-based algorithm in this study has been evaluated on medium density crowds, images consist of 21 and 905 faces per image. To obtain a reasonable evaluation of our solution, we trained and tested the model on our substantially occluded data-set (AGH Crowd Density Estimation Database (ACD)) [11]. Face-based algorithms such as face detection can be attributed to variations in pose, scale, exaggerated facial expression, severe occlusion, low resolution, and lighting condition.

Our goal is to estimate the number of people based on faces in crowd scenes under significant occlusion. To address the problem of occlusion and variation in poses, we involve occlusion in the model. By segmenting images into the several random sections in the training procedure of the CNN algorithm, the model learn various features of faces and can mitigate the negative effects of occlusion and variations in pose, on face detection. We train the CNN model on our medium crowd images data set. We further use different data set to evaluate the model accuracy.

In contrast to many state-of-the-art detection and classification approaches, which utilize windows of varied sizes and time-consuming pyramid structure, in object detection [7,15,26], we propose a novel sliding-window technique. We firstly divide images into 50 by 50 patches and perform CNN for each of them. Counting of the number of detected faces in each patch results in the final estimation. To prevent twice or several counting of the faces, which may appear in the border between patches, we employed a combination of several approaches such as Haar-cascade detection, SVM classifier with HOG features, to obtain the size of each head. According to the information achieved by detectors, a novel sliding-window technique proposed to specify the step size between patches. The flowchart of the proposed algorithm is shown in Fig. 1.

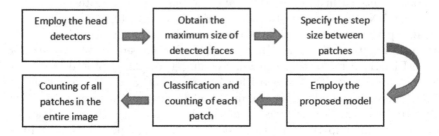

Fig. 1. Flowchart of the proposed algorithm.

3.1 Data Preparation

We trained and tested proposed model on our dataset [11] with 48K and 109 images respectively. The total number of individuals in the training dataset images was 2181 while it was 16501 in the testing dataset images.

Before feeding the dataset into the model, images manually are labelled. Firstly, database images are converted to the grayscale images and the position of faces in each image is specified by marking with a single red dot on each face. To train the most significant and meaningful part of faces, red dots are put in the middle of the eyes and the noise triangle. Subtracting of images with red points from grayscale images, obtained the number of all labels in each image automatically. Furthermore, it has been used to randomly segment the images, to generate a 40,000 training dataset of four classes:

- Class 0: negative images (patches without any faces)
- Class 1: positive images (patches consist of one face)
- Class 2: positive images (patches consist of two faces)
- Class 3: positive images (patches consist of three faces)

Proposed segmenting, labelling and classifying of the data-set, enable our CNN model to observe and learn faces (features) from different aspects which makes the model significantly robust in detecting of severely occluded faces.

3.2 Proposed VGG Network

Our Convolutional Neural Network training data-set consists of 40,000 images of faces, in 4 classes. We train CNN to recognize and classify each of these classes. The proposed Convolutional Neural Network architecture is a smaller and more compact variant of the state-of-the-art VGG model, which has been trained on ImageNet, the most comprehensive hand-annotated visual dataset [21]. Among the best performing CNN models, VGG is remarkable due to its simplicity and uniform architecture. In contrast with the 16 layers VGG network, with a 7.3% error rate (submission of ILSVRC 2014), there are much more complicated models such as Microsoft's ResNet model with a 3.6% error rate, but many more layers (152 layers) [21]. Notwithstanding its benefits, VGG neural network has few drawbacks. VGG is very slow in the training phase, and its weights are extremely large, which makes deploying VGG an exhausting task.

In order to save the computational costs, we reduced the number of features in many layers of our proposed model. The first convolutional layer consists of 32 kernels of size 3 * 3 applied with a stride of 1 and padding of 0. ReLU the activation function followed by batch normalization has been utilized in the first layer. The max-pooling is performed over a 3 * 3-pixel window to reduce its dimensionality. In order to reduce over-fitting caused by the adaption of the model on training data, the most popular regularization technique, dropout (drop out of 25% in this layer) applied to hidden layer nodes [20].

In order to learn the most sophisticated features of faces, the number of filters are increased from 32 to 64 in the second phase of the model structure. To prevent down-sampling the image into a smaller dimension very quickly, Max-pooling size is reduced from 3 * 3 to 2 * 2. A dropout of 25% of nodes is again performed at this stage.

The next phase of the proposed model is similar to the second phase except increasing the number of filters to 128 kernels.

Finally, to attain predicted probabilities for each class label (label 0 = negative image, label 1 = one face, label 2 = two faces, label 3 = three faces), fully-connected layers with a dropout of 50% of nodes are followed by a Softmax classifier at the end of the model structure.

To avoid over-fitting, another regularization technique, such as data augmentation is employed during the training phase. Data augmentation is a technique to generate more training data from the existing data-set by applying random transformations such as rotations, variations in the brightness of images, horizontal/vertical shifts, horizontal/vertical flips, etc. (Fig. 2). The rest of the model's parameters are listed as: The total number of Epoches = 300, The initial learning rate for Adam optimizer = 1e−3, Batch size = 32.

The proposed model is trained on 80% of randomly selected images and afterward tested on the 20% of subsequent images. As illustrated in Fig. 3, our Convolutional Neural Network obtained 84.41% classification accuracy on the training set and 84.36% accuracy on the testing set. In order to increase the classification accuracy of the model, 8000 images with the classification confidence score of greater than 0.95 are appended to the source data set. Afterward, the proposed model retrained on the new data-set and improved its classification accuracy by 3% (Fig. 3).

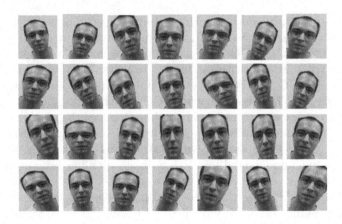

Fig. 2. Data augmentation on the faces.

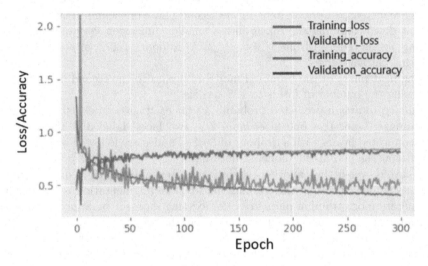

Fig. 3. Training loss and accuracy of the model.

3.3   Sliding-Window and Occlusion Solutions

In order to address the problem of occlusion and variation in head poses, we involve occlusion in the training phase of the model. The proposed model has been trained on the images of faces with an occluded area up to 75% where faces are 50% occluded in both vertical and horizontal directions. Figure 4, demonstrates how the proposed method evades counting faces, twice or more, where part of faces can appear in more than one patch.

For estimating the number of people in the crowd scenes, images are divided into the 50 * 50 patches. Feeding each patch into the model, performs, classification results of each specific patch. Counting the classification result of all patches achieves the final estimation result. To prevent overlapping between faces and

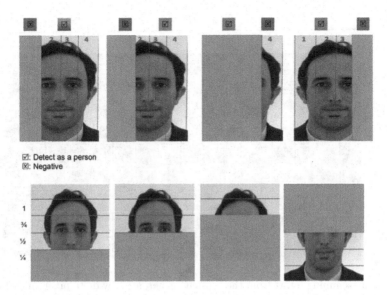

Fig. 4. The proposed algorithm recognizes faces with an occluded area of up to 75%.

patches, where some parts of faces can appear in two or even more patches, by combining different methods and algorithms we proposed a novel sliding-window technique.

In the proposed technique, fixed-size windows are a slide from left to right, and from up to down to identify faces using classification (see Fig. 5). In this method, firstly the size of the detected head is specified by various approaches, afterward based on achieved sizes, step size between each window is calculated by:

$$\Delta = L + \frac{M}{4} \tag{1}$$

where, $L = 50$ is the length of the window and M is the maximum length of the detected face with various approaches such as Haar-cascade detection, SVM classifier with HOG features, etc.

Since we have trained the model on images of faces up to 75% occlusion level, it is possible to disregard 25% of appeared faces in the subsequent patches, which prevent the counting of the number of detected faces twice or even more.

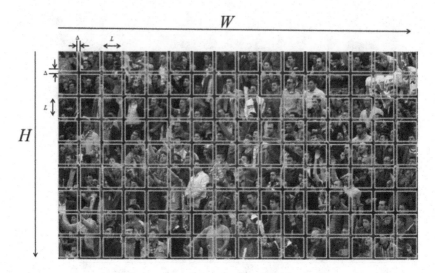

Fig. 5. Scene-scanning (start from the top-left corner, shift by delta pixels and classify sliding window).

4 Experiments and Evaluation

As mentioned before in this paper, we collected 109 images with count ranging between 21 and 905 with an average of 145 individuals per image from different sources. Some of the examples of images with the associated ground truth count are illustrated in Fig. 6.

4.1 Comparison of Methods Under Pose Variations and Severe Occlusion

The studies involving face detection, are different in terms of the objects, and the training and testing data set. Therefore, the accurate comparison of this study with these works may not be appropriate and significant. Hence in this study, the only comparison of face pose variations, such as rotation of faces from −90 to 90 and detection under various occlusion levels such as faces with 25%, 50%, and 75% occlusion are assessed.

In order to evaluate the comparison of different methods in real-world applications, we utilize our data set (AGH Crowd Density Estimation Database (ACD)), which is a more challenging benchmark compared to the existing datasets.

In this study, the Sum of Absolute Difference (SAD) and the Mean of Absolute Error (MAE), are utilized to evaluate the performance of different face detectors by the following formulas:

$$SAD = \sum_{i=1}^{N} |y_i - x_i| \tag{2}$$

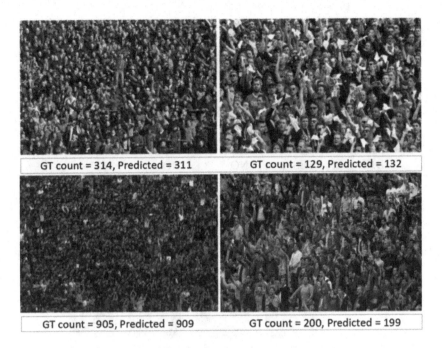

Fig. 6. Estimation results of our proposed method.

$$MAE = \frac{1}{N} \sum_{i=1}^{N} |y_i - x_i| \qquad (3)$$

where N is number of test samples, y and x are estimated count and ground truth respectively.

In the first scenario, empirical comparison of performance of proposed approach and the well-known face detection libraries and toolkits such as Haar Cascade Face Detector, Deep learning face detector in OpenCV [1], and the histogram of oriented gradients (HOG) with linear SVM, and Maximum-Margin Object Detector (MMOD) with CNN based features in Dlib [12], in the most challenging conditions is demonstrated in the Table 1 and Table 2.

Since each of these algorithms are trained on images with specific sizes, a reasonable caparison of these methods may not be appropriate. Therefore, the algorithms are evaluated based on their desired sizes. As shown in Table 1 and Table 2, the proposed approach is able to recognize faces in a variation of poses and the faces with the occluded area up to 75%. The DNN and MMOD methods outperform the Haar, LBP, and HOG based Face detectors, especially in pose variations. HOG based detectors are more accurate than LBP and Haar cascades, with less false positives (FP). However, false positive (FP), is the major drawback of Haar Cascade Face Detector, appropriate thresholding is used to overcome this problem. In this study discarding of faces greater than twice of average detected faces size, we overcome false-positive errors.

Table 1. Successful detections with face occlusion are indicated by YES

HAAR	NO	NO	NO	NO
LBP	YES	NO	NO	NO
DNN	YES	NO	NO	NO
HOG-SVM	YES	NO	NO	NO
MMOD	YES	NO	NO	NO
Proposed	YES	YES	YES	NO

Table 2. Successful detections with head pose variations are indicated by YES

HAAR	NO	NO	YES	NO
LBP	NO	NO	YES	NO
DNN	YES	YES	YES	NO
HOG-SVM	NO	NO	YES	NO
MMOD	YES	YES	YES	NO
Proposed	YES	YES	YES	YES

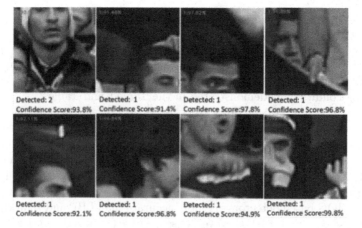

Fig. 7. The face detection result of the proposed method on our data set. The evaluation has been examined on 50 * 50 images. Displayed images resized to 400 * 400 images.

HOG and Haar Feature-based Cascade Classifiers are less robust to occlusion, which has been utilized in the first phase of the proposed approach, where, we would like to obtain the full size of the human face (Fig. 7).

4.2   Proposed Method Results

In this section, a combination of different methods is compared and presented in Table 3. For comparison, we used 109 images containing between 21 and 905 individuals per image. Size of each faces in the images varying from 18 * 18 to 162 * 162 pixels.

Table 3. Comparison of different methods

Methods	SAD	MAE
Haar cascade + Proposed model	1237	11.34
HOG with SVM + Proposed model	676	6.2
HOG with SVM + HAAR + Proposed model	873	8
HOG with SVM + DNN-OpenCV	1754	16.09

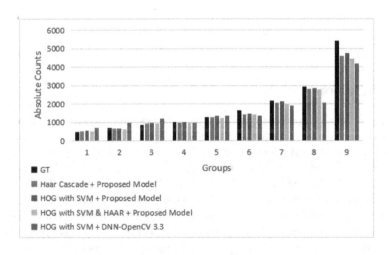

Fig. 8. Comparison of the absolute counts.

The first row in Table 3 shows the results of using only Haar cascade for specifying the size of faces and it achieves SAD of 1237 and MAE of 11.34. The second row shows that using HOG with SVM reduces MAE interestingly to 6.2. A combination of HOG with SVM and Haar cascade does not improve the accuracy of the model. As can be perceived from Table 3, a combination of HOG with SVM for specifying the size of faces and proposed CNN model outperforms other combinations and the state-of-the-art face detection algorithm presented in OpenCV. In Fig. 8 and Fig. 9, we demonstrate a comparison of the Absolute Counts (AC) for nine groups of 109 images each, which are sorted by ground truth counts values from the smallest to the largest. In contrast to the DNN face detector which does not correspond well to the density changes, our proposed method has a uniform error in various densities.

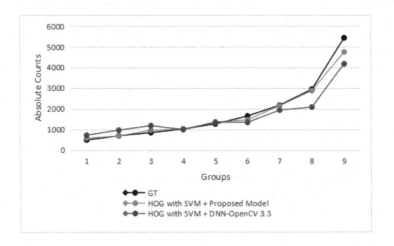

Fig. 9. Comparison of the absolute counts.

5   Conclusion

In this paper, we proposed an approach to crowd estimation based on face detection under significant occlusion and pose variation. To improve the robustness of the CNN model, several effective strategies are proposed. By segmenting images into the random sections in the training phase of the CNN algorithm, the model is able to learn various features of faces and mitigate the negative effects of occlusion and head pose variations in face detection. The proposed method combines the well-known traditional machine learning algorithm and the state-of-the-art CNN algorithm to estimate faces in the crowd scenes. Using a compact variant of the VGG neural network, the proposed algorithm outperforms various face detection algorithms on our challenging data-set.

References

1. Open Source Computer Vision Library (2019). https://github.com/opencv/opencv
2. Chan, A.B., Liang, Z.-S.J., Vasconcelos, N.: Privacy preserving crowd monitoring: counting people without people models or tracking. In: 2008 IEEE Conference on Computer Vision and Pattern Recognition, pp. 1–7 (June 2008). https://doi.org/10.1109/CVPR.2008.4587569

3. Chen, D., Ren, S., Wei, Y., Cao, X., Sun, J.: Joint cascade face detection and alignment. In: Fleet, D., Pajdla, T., Schiele, B., Tuytelaars, T. (eds.) ECCV 2014. LNCS, vol. 8694, pp. 109–122. Springer, Cham (2014). https://doi.org/10.1007/978-3-319-10599-4_8

4. Chen, K., Loy, C.C., Gong, S., Xiang, T.: Feature mining for localised crowd counting. In: BMVC (2012)

5. Conte, D., Foggia, P., Percannella, G., Tufano, F., Vento, M.: A method for counting people in crowded scenes. In: 2010 7th IEEE International Conference on Advanced Video and Signal Based Surveillance, pp. 225–232 (August 2010). https://doi.org/10.1109/AVSS.2010.78

6. Ferryman, J., Ellis, A.L.: Pets 2010: dataset and challenge, pp. 143–150 (October 2010). https://doi.org/10.1109/AVSS.2010.90

7. Han, D., Kim, J., Ju, J., Lee, I., Cha, J., Kim, J.: Efficient and fast multi-view face detection based on feature transformation. In: 16th International Conference on Advanced Communication Technology, pp. 682–686 (February 2014). https://doi.org/10.1109/ICACT.2014.6779050

8. Idrees, H., Saleemi, I., Seibert, C., Shah, M.: Multi-source multi-scale counting in extremely dense crowd images, pp. 2547–2554 (June 2013). https://doi.org/10.1109/CVPR.2013.329

9. Jiang, H., Learned-Miller, E.: Face detection with the faster R-CNN. In: 2017 12th IEEE International Conference on Automatic Face Gesture Recognition (FG 2017), pp. 650–657 (May 2017). https://doi.org/10.1109/FG.2017.82

10. Jones, M., Viola, P.: Fast multi-view face detection. Tech. rep. TR2003-96, MERL - Mitsubishi Electric Research Laboratories, Cambridge, MA 02139 (August 2003). http://www.merl.com/publications/TR2003-96/

11. Ara, R.K., Matiolanski, A.: Crowd counting based on face detection database (2019). http://kt.agh.edu.pl/matiolanski/CrowdDensityEstimationDatabase/

12. King, D.E.: DLIB-ML: a machine learning toolkit. J. Mach. Learn. Res. **10**, 1755–1758 (2009)

13. Li, J., Zhang, Y.: Learning surf cascade for fast and accurate object detection. In: 2013 IEEE Conference on Computer Vision and Pattern Recognition, pp. 3468–3475 (June 2013). https://doi.org/10.1109/CVPR.2013.445

14. Li, S.Z., Zhu, L., Zhang, Z.Q., Blake, A., Zhang, H.J., Shum, H.: Statistical learning of multi-view face detection. In: Heyden, A., Sparr, G., Nielsen, M., Johansen, P. (eds.) ECCV 2002. LNCS, vol. 2353, pp. 67–81. Springer, Heidelberg (2002). https://doi.org/10.1007/3-540-47979-1_5

15. Liu, S., Dong, Y., Liu, W., Zhao, J.: Multi-view face detection based on cascade classifier and skin color. In: 2012 IEEE 2nd International Conference on Cloud Computing and Intelligence Systems, vol. 01, pp. 56–60 (October 2012). https://doi.org/10.1109/CCIS.2012.6664367

16. Mahbub, U., Patel, V., Chandre, D., Barbello, B., Chellappa, R.: Partial face detection for continuous authentication, pp. 2991–2995 (September 2016). https://doi.org/10.1109/ICIP.2016.7532908

17. Opitz, M., Waltner, G., Poier, G., Possegger, H., Bischof, H.: Grid loss: detecting occluded faces. CoRR abs/1609.00129. http://arxiv.org/abs/1609.00129 (2016)

18. Zhu, Q., Yeh, M.-C., Cheng, K.-T., Avidan, S.: Fast human detection using a cascade of histograms of oriented gradients. In: 2006 IEEE Computer Society Conference on Computer Vision and Pattern Recognition (CVPR 2006), vol. 2, pp. 1491–1498 (June 2006). https://doi.org/10.1109/CVPR.2006.119

19. Ren, S., He, K., Girshick, R.B., Sun, J.: Faster R-CNN: towards real-time object detection with region proposal networks. CoRR abs/1506.01497. http://arxiv.org/abs/1506.01497 (2015)
20. Rosebrock, A.: Keras and convolutional neural networks (2018). https://www.pyimagesearch.com/2018/04/16/keras-and-convolutional-neural-networks-cnns/
21. Simonyan, K., Zisserman, A.: Very deep convolutional networks for large-scale image recognition. arXiv 1409.1556 (2014)
22. Sun, X., Wu, P., Hoi, S.: Face detection using deep learning: an improved faster RCNN approach. Neurocomputing **299**, 42–50 (2017). https://doi.org/10.1016/j.neucom.2018.03.030
23. Viola, P., Jones, M.J.: Robust real-time face detection. Int. J. Comput. Vis. **57**(2), 137–154 (2004). https://doi.org/10.1023/B:VISI.0000013087.49260.fb
24. Wan, S., Chen, Z., Zhang, T., Zhang, B., Wong, K.: Bootstrapping face detection with hard negative examples. CoRR abs/1608.02236. http://arxiv.org/abs/1608.02236 (2016)
25. Yang, S., Luo, P., Loy, C., Tang, X.: From facial parts responses to face detection: a deep learning approach. In: 2015 IEEE International Conference on Computer Vision (ICCV), pp. 3676–3684 (December 2015). https://doi.org/10.1109/ICCV.2015.419
26. You-Jia, F., Jian-Wei, L.: Rotation invariant multi-view color face detection based on skin color and Adaboost algorithm (April 2010). https://doi.org/10.1109/ICBECS.2010.5462517

A Hybrid Data Fusion Architecture for BINDI: A Wearable Solution to Combat Gender-Based Violence

Esther Rituerto-González[1] , Jose Angel Miranda[2(✉)] ,
Manuel Felipe Canabal[2] , José M. Lanza-Gutiérrez[2] ,
Carmen Peláez-Moreno[1] , and Celia López-Ongil[2]

[1] Departamento de Teoría de la Señal y Comunicacionones,
Universidad Carlos III de Madrid, 28911 Leganés, Spain
{erituert,cpelaez}@ing.uc3m.es
[2] Departamento de Tecnología Electrónica,
Universidad Carlos III de Madrid, 28911 Leganés, Spain
{jmiranda,mcanabal,jlanza,celia}@ing.uc3m.es
http://portal.uc3m.es/portal/page/portal/inst_estudios_genero/
proyectos/UC3M4Safety

Abstract. Currently, most of the affective computing research is about modifying and adapting the machine behavior based on the human emotional state. Although, the use of the affective state inference can be extended to provide a tool for other fields more society related such as gender violence detection, which is a real global emergency. Based on the World Health Organization (WHO) statistics, one in three women worldwide experiences gender-based violence, often from an intimate partner. Due to this motivation, the authors developed BINDI, which is a wearable solution for detecting automatically those situations. It uses affective computing together with short-term physiological and physical observations. It represents a step toward an autonomous, embedded, non-intrusive, and wearable system for detecting those situations and connecting the victim with a trusted circle. In this work, and as a response for improving the detection capability of BINDI, a novel hybrid data fusion architecture is proposed. This new architecture is intended to improve the already implemented decision level fusion architecture. Further details of the uni-modal systems and the different approaches needed to be explored in the future are given.

Keywords: Gender violence · Machine learning · Physiological signals · Speech · Data fusion · Cognitive computing

1 Introduction

Gender-based violence is one of the biggest social problems in the world, whose cultural origins make it an invisible phenomenon still tolerated by part of the

E. Rituerto-González and J. A. Miranda—These authors contributed equally to this work.

society. Thus, statistics say that 35% of women worldwide have experienced either physical and/or sexual violence at some point in their lives [33].

Women are subject to different types of violence caused by their sentimental couples and even by the social environment, ranging from psychological control and disrespect to physical and sexual aggression. Thus, gender violence affects women of any religion, age, as well as economic and social conditions, taking place anywhere, such as their homes, workplaces, and public places.

This situation means that combating gender-based violence is a real global emergency, which needs to be fought with actions, such as making prevention campaigns, changing school education for future generations, and providing help and resources to victims. These educational actions could be also combined with technological solutions, which could help to detect and resolve assault or assault attempts, providing a quick response mechanism for security forces.

On this basis, the research conducted in this paper is within a project called BINDI, by the UC3M4Safety group at University Carlos III Madrid, Spain. We aim at providing a smart technological solution to the gender-based violence problem adopting a multidisciplinary perspective, combining knowledge from several fields such as gender studies, electronics, telematics, speech & audio technologies, and artificial intelligence [1].

Specifically, the final goal of BINDI is to develop a non-intrusive wearable solution, able to automatically detect and alert when a user is under an intense emotional state (e.g., panic, fear, or stress as their moderate relative) potentially caused by a gender violence situation so that help could be supplied accordingly [18]. To this end, the system draws on physiological and speech data, which is later processed by a hierarchical intelligent decision engine based on artificial intelligence.

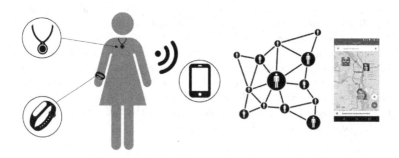

Fig. 1. Conceptualization of the BINDI system [26]

Figure 1 shows a conceptualization of BINDI, composed of two wearable devices, a bracelet and a pendant, and a smartphone application. The bracelet measures physiological data, specifically blood volume pulse (BVP), galvanic skin response (GSR), and skin temperature (SKT) [16,19]. The pendant records audio and speech, mainly from the user wearing it, but also from the environment and other people around [26]. Based on these data, the intelligent decision engine should be able to automatically trigger an alarm in the case that a warning situation is detected. Additionally, the system also allows to manually trigger an alarm by the physical buttons in both wearable devices. The initial architecture for the hierarchical intelligent decision engine in BINDI is as follows.

The bracelet acts as the first layer in the decision engine, following a low-power conception to maximize the battery duration. This device periodically captures BVP, GSR, and SKT data, which are preprocessed to improve the overall signal quality. Next, features of interest are extracted so that a lightweight classification machine learning algorithm predicts if the user is under an emotion of significance [19]. The response of this first layer acts as a low-cost moderate-precision switch for activating the next layer, which is located in the pendant.

The pendant captures audio-on-demand, which is sent via low-power Bluetooth to the smartphone. The audio signal is analyzed based on a neural network approach so that sound events, voice levels, and distinctive noises could be detected. In this process, there are two main tasks to perform: stress detection [15] and speaker identification [25]. The first one consists in the detection of stress in the victim's voice. The second one relies on the identification of the victim's voice. If the analysis results in the detection of a gender-based violence situation, the system triggers an alarm to law enforcement agencies and/or a previously selected group of people. The audio recorded is also stored in a read-only cloud protected by encryption so that it could be used as legal evidence in case of need. The BINDI cloud architecture is detailed in [5].

This initial architecture in BINDI is based on a late uni-modal data fusion strategy, which is executed following a two-layer cascade, where each layer has an intelligence model associated. The model in the first layer acts as a low-cost switch to activate a more demanding second layer, which is also related to a more powerful detection capability. This initial low-power strategy is useful for deciding when the more powerful and costly audio capture in the pendant should be carried out. However, the usage of the data captured in the bracelet only for switching purposes could imply that the intelligent decision engine is not considering all the information available.

On this basis, this paper aims to propose a novel hybrid data fusion architecture to strengthen the reliability and robustness of BINDI, so that physiological and audio data could be jointly considered in the decision to trigger the alarm. Our main contributions are as follows:

- The two independent uni-modal systems are described together with their performance.
- A decision level approach or late fusion based on both uni-modal systems is described.
- A novel hybrid data fusion architecture by combining late and early fusion approaches is proposed able to cope with the constraints of lightweight wearables and battery consumption considerations.

The rest of the paper is organized as follows. Section 2 discusses related works within the field. Section 3 describes the architectures used for the intelligent sub-systems in BINDI and proposes data fusion models. Section 4 outlines some conclusions and future research lines.

2   Related Work

In the following sections, the state-of-the-art in emotion recognition and identification, both using speech and physiological signals, is reviewed.

2.1   Speech Emotion and Speaker Recognition

In recent years, the interest in detecting and interpreting emotions in speech, as well as the recognition of speakers from their speech, has grown in parallel for a variety of applications.

The research work done on emotions in speech is very extensive [4]. Specifically, speech emotion recognition (SER) is the collection of methodologies that processes and classifies speech signals to detect emotions and affective states embedded in them. SER has applications in human-computer interaction, as well as robots, mobile services, computer games, and psychological assessments, among others. In spite of its many applications and the substantial progress due to the advent of deep learning techniques [12], emotion recognition is still a challenging task, mainly due to the subjectivity involved in emotions. That means that there is no consensus on how to categorize or measure them. Thus, emotions are evaluated by their perception in other humans, and sometimes even humans are known to misinterpret them.

On the other hand, speaker recognition (SR) is the task of authenticating or recognizing a speaker based on the unique features captured from their speech waveforms that characterize them. Characteristics or features which are unique to an individual such as speaking style or pitch are used as distinguishing components of the human speech signal [21]. Within SR, there are two main tasks, speaker identification (SI) and speaker verification (SV). For a system trained for a set of speakers, SI is the task of determining which amongst the set of speakers is speaking, which is a multi-class problem setting. SV is the task of determining whether the speakers are the ones whom they claim to be, which is a binary problem setting [23].

Speech in real-life conditions is distorted by intrinsic and extrinsic factors, which are difficult to predict. Usually, this problem of variability affects speech systems due to their reliance on probabilistic models trained from clean training corpora. That means that there is a need to develop robust systems that can handle variability without a degradation in performance. Some examples of extrinsic factors are noise, music or the reverberation present in the environment or in the transmission channel. Some examples of extrinsic factors are the speaker's accent, emotions, speaking rate, and style. The mismatch problem between the statistical features of the training utterances and those of real-life can lead to very different characteristics on the speaker's voice, causing speaker recognition models to lose some of their precision and predictive power.

In our case, the alert detection system triggers an alert when a dangerous situation is detected. This information is provided by the physiological and speech signals that correlate the state of the user that wears BINDI. Among the intense emotional states that the user could experience in such situations are fear, panic, or even stress. This fact implies that one important problem when designing a system as BINDI is the lack of databases recorded with an emotional speech. Those existing are either recorded by acted speech under emotions, or by people to whom different emotions were elicited. This last option is truly complicated to conduct, particularly for negative emotions. The ideal case takes place when there is a match between the signals used to train the models and the test speech signals. Thus, there is a need to use a speech from real-life conditions to improve the performance of the systems.

Literature is scarce on databases containing real-life speech under panic or fear conditions, but there are a few in which stressed speech is either simulated or recorded under real conditions, such as SUSAS [9], VOCE [3], and UT-Scope [10]. Stress is intimately related to anxiety and nervousness. It can be defined as a state of mental or emotional tension resulting from adverse or demanding circumstances. Among the physiological consequences of stress are respiratory changes, increased heart rate, skin perspiration and increased muscle tension of the vocal cords and vocal tract. All of these factors may, directly or indirectly, adversely affect the quality of speech. And due to the difficulty to find databases containing real elicited panic or fear in speech, we decide to use stress because of its close relationship. The main difficulty with these data relies on the labeling process because, again, there is no universal agreement on how to categorize or measure emotions.

Some works proposed multi-modal approaches combining visual and speech data to improve and strengthen emotion recognition [11,32] and speaker diarization systems [20,24]. This conception is not possible in BINDI because there is not a visual component. Thus, the additional information will come from physiological variables as will be explained next.

2.2 Emotion Recognition Through Physiological Signals

In the last decades, physiological signals have been proven to be a valuable source of information regarding emotion recognition. Unlike other signals, physiological ones are controlled by the autonomous nervous system (ANS), which works without being consciously manipulated by humans. Variations of SKT, GSR, BVP, and other physiological signals have been experimentally connected with human emotional changes, which have led up to the design and implementation of affective computing systems based on physiological information [29].

Most of the research presented across the literature, related to emotion recognition, is based on well-known and accepted emotion theories and models. There are two main types of emotion models: discrete and dimensional. The discrete emotion model was proposed by Ekman [8] and the dimensional one was stated by Russell [27]. The first one defines a set of basic emotions. The second one numerically quantifies emotions in three dimensions, which are arousal (i.e., excitement over external stimuli), valence (i.e., pleasure over external stimuli), and dominance (i.e., the control over what feels). This third dimension is useful for distinguishing between two close emotions, such as fear and anger. In this line, the authors in [6] analyzed the fear-anger distinction and affirmed that a three-factor model or PAD model (arousal or pleasure, valence, and dominance) is required to identify the affective state adequately. However, these emotion models do not contain any assumption regarding the physiological-emotion relationship, thus, different methodologies to accomplish this connection were performed [29].

There are open available datasets dealing with emotion recognition by physiological signals. The authors highlight six of them: Eight-Emotion [22], DEAP [14], MAHNOB-HCI [30], DECAF [2], ASCERTAIN [31], and WESAD [7]. These databases were recorded in a lab environment, i.e., the physiological signals were captured while different audiovisual stimuli evoked some emotions of interest. Most of these databases include details about the same three stages of their experiments, which are the pre-tagging stage (i.e., the stimuli are labeled by a set of experts regarding the expected emotion to be evoked), the on-going experiment stage (i.e., the methodology for capturing the physiological signals, as well as a report from the patients about the emotion evoked), and machine learning stage (i.e., the algorithms considered for predicting the emotions in the patients). However, there are some open questions, such as the labeling methodology and the number of patients required for the study. The work in [17] provided a detailed review of these databases and gave some insights about key factors for designing an emotion recognition database using physiological data.

As stated previously regarding the shortage of real-life speech datasets, data collection in the wild is essential and needed for designing and implementing affective computing systems. In our case, BINDI is conceived to operate in day-to-day real-life situations. Thus, the training of the system requires considering not only those physiological variations in a laboratory set-up but also all the factors that affect the quality of the signals. As stated in [28], more databases based on field studies are needed to go towards real-life affective computing systems, which could be embedded into wearable-ready devices.

2.3   Multi-modal Fusion Techniques

Multi-modality is a natural concept for living beings as a means of interacting with the outside world. In living beings, the acquired information comes from internal and external sensors. This information is combined and fused to provide rapid responses to the external constantly changing environment.

Focusing on affective computing, handling more than one modality is challenging because data differ in aspects as origin, structure, and relevance. However, the diversity within a multi-modal emotion recognition system (e.g., combining both physiological and physical signals) usually allows improving the insights in a way that cannot be achieved by a single modality [4]. In the literature, there are four main techniques for data fusion: feature level, decision level, model level, and hybrid fusion [34].

In feature level fusion or early fusion, the different synthetic metrics or features obtained from each input sensor are combined into another feature vector before classification. The main drawback of this method is the high dimensionality of the combined feature vector, which could lead to the well-known curse of dimensionality.

Unlike early fusion, decision level fusion or late fusion requires multiple training stages (e.g., one training stage for only physiological signals and one for only physical signals). In this case, each of the modalities can be modeled more precisely by their classifiers, but the system does not handle in any way the interactions or correlations between modalities. This fusion mechanism is based on the uni-modal recognition results late combination by some criterion. As already commented before, the initial version of BINDI considered a decision level fusion technique according to the uni-modal inference outputs based on physiological and speech data.

Two other fusion methodologies can be applied to deal with the interaction problem from the decision level fusion technique: hybrid and model level fusion approaches. Both combine aspects from the two techniques already commented (early and late fusion). Level fusion is based on the mutual correlation between the different streams from the modalities in the system. Level fusion is usually considered to explore the temporal correlation between those streams. The hybrid fusion implements more than one fusion level within the same system (e.g., combining feature and decision level approaches), which usually provides better recognition results than applying solely one fusion technique alone.

3   Uni-Modal and Multi-modal Architectures for BINDI

This section discusses each of the uni-modal systems implemented and the databases used in the development of each. A detailed description of the initial multi-modal data fusion implemented in BINDI is provided. The section concludes with the proposed hybrid data fusion architecture in this paper, combining late and early fusion.

3.1   The Uni-Modal Speech-Based System

Since BINDI will be used in real-life to detect dangerous situations it is necessary to 1) work with databases containing speech in real-life conditions and 2) that those include real fear, panic, or anxiety feelings, which could be evoked in the type of situations to be detected in the use case.

The condition in 1) is relatively easy to obtain in the literature, but not the one in 2). As a result, the authors opted for selecting a database generated in real-life conditions but studying a relatively close feeling as stress. Specifically, the authors selected the VOCE Corpus Database [3] because of two main reasons, i) it includes data captured in real stress conditions and ii) some sensors used during the capturing stage are similar to those present in the bracelet for getting additional heart rate measurements.

The last version of VOCE includes 135 voice recordings that result from a set of 45 Portuguese-speaking people. The voice files correspond to three different recording settings labeled as recording (free speaking from a public event of free duration), pre-baseline (reading a standard text at least 24 h before a public event), and baseline (reading the same text as in the pre-baseline setting approximately 30 min before the public event). Together with the audio data, two measured physiological variables are provided and used to estimate the heart rate (HR) every second with an electrocardiogram (ECG) device. Unfortunately, the database only gathers complete information (the three audio files and the corresponding HR values) from 21 individuals.

VOCE speech recordings were originally labeled in terms of the type of event (reading or public speaking) with a stressful or neutral mark. Each of these recordings can last up to an hour, which results in only one label throughout the whole event, which is too coarse information for the alarm detection application. As a solution, the authors chose to generate one-second stress/non-stress labels based on the HR provided in the database by establishing an adapted basal threshold for each speaker. This methodology was inspired by the work done in [15], where the feasibility of relating HR metrics with stress in speech is confirmed. Thus, the proper HR threshold for the stress/non-stress labels relative to each of the users was empirically determined by employing a subset of the data. As a result of this methodology, every second of the speech signal is labeled as stressed or neutral.

A pre-processing stage was applied to all speech signals for better handling: conversion from stereo to mono, down-sampling, and normalization in amplitude. The authors also applied a voice activity detector (VAD) module to avoid silent frames from which no relevant information regarding stress could be extracted. Next, some features of interest were extracted. Specifically, the set of features includes the pitch, the mel-frequency cepstral coefficients (MFCC), the formants, and the energy of the speech signals.

For the feature extraction, an analysis window of 20 ms with a 10 ms delay over the speech signals was applied. However, the dimensions of the feature vectors obtained with this analysis window do not correspond to those needed, which are one-second-long. To adapt the dimensions of these vectors some statistics, such as mean and variance were computed throughout a second for each of the feature dimensions.

Based on the features extracted, the classification stage discriminates between neutral and stressed using a multi-layer perceptron (MLP) approach, a precursor of deep neural networks, to achieve a balance between simplicity and performance. F-scores in the range of 85–90% and 80–85% where obtained for speaker-dependent and speaker-independent experiments, respectively.

Additionally, to detect the stress in the voice of the user there is a need to track the user's voice separating it from the rest of the speakers in the acoustic scenario. However, the fact that the voice of the victim could be influenced by her emotional state constitutes a challenge for any speaker identification system. Moreover, we think that opens an interesting possibility for situations, where it would be desirable to identify all the speakers involved in the scene, e.g., in case of legal evidence required.

Though still being under integration in the second version of BINDI, we have developed a speaker identification module tailored for a stress-distorted speech by making use of the speaker labels in VOCE. To this end, we have considered the same feature vectors extracted for stress detection, as well as the classifier type used for that task. To deal with the development of a speaker identification system robust to emotional bias, we focused on addressing the problem of data scarcity under emotional or stress conditions. Due to the inherent complexity of collecting this type of data in real-life conditions with BINDI, the authors analyzed the viability of applying synthetic data augmentation techniques to address the problem.

Preliminary results show that the best performance is obtained when naturally stressed samples are included in the training dataset together with neutral speech. However, when naturally stressed samples are not available, data augmentation can improve the performance of the system by generating a stressed speech modifying its pitch and speed reaching up to 99.45% of speaker identification accuracy for the VOCE dataset with 21 speakers [25]. Furthermore, as a noise mitigation procedure, data augmentation techniques could increase the generalization capability of the algorithms during the training stage. Thus, the authors aim to create synthetic noisy signals by additively contaminating the database with real-life environment noise, both for hand-crafted and bottleneck features.

3.2   The Uni-Modal Biosignal-Based System

As mentioned previously, BINDI includes a physiological data analysis based on BVP, GSK, and SKT. This subsystem is embedded in the wristband, which imposes some design constraints in terms of computational load, memory requirements, and energy efficiency.

This physiological data analysis consists of a pre-processing and prediction stage. During the preprocessing stage, different techniques for signal noise removal are applied. In this stage, there is no feature extraction as such. Instead, the average value of a 10-second temporary window is calculated for each raw signal to keep low the computational complexity. This information is later considered in a lightweight k-nearest neighbors (KNN) supervised classification algorithm. KNN predicts the label of a future sample based on the k nearest samples in the multidimensional space defined during the training stage.

The uni-modal bio-signal system was tested using a freely available dataset: DEAP [14]. This database contains physiological information from a total of 40 trials, one-minute duration each (e.g. audiovisual content), of 32 participants captured during an emotion elicitation experiment. Only the same three physiological signals used in BINDI were taken from DEAP. The labels of the experiments for the different participants were mapped into a binary representation based on arousal, valence and dominance self-reported scores. This binary mapping was performed based on the fear detection necessity and, following the PAD model commented in Sect. 2.2, the positive class was selected as low arousal, high valence, and low dominance, which fear, panic, and related emotions reside.

In this stage of BINDI, the authors preferred to trigger a false alarm than missing a real alert, even though accuracy could be lowered. Thus, the key parameters for this first version of BINDI were the miss-classification costs and the hold-out. The latter defines the amount of data used for training and testing, e.g., a hold-out value of 0.80 means that 20% of data is used for training the system and 80% is used for testing. This value has a direct impact on memory usage because of the KNN strategy followed, as the training set must be stored in the device. The miss-classification cost represents a penalty for false negatives, leading up to a cost-sensitive learning approach. The results for a user-dependent approach data shown, on average, an accuracy, sensitivity, and specificity of 85%, 99%, and 81%, respectively, with hold-out set to 0.99 and a miss-classification cost of 8 [19].

3.3 A Decision-Based Multi-modal Automatic Alert Generation

As an initial approach in BINDI, both the speech and the bio-signal alert detection systems were fused by following a decision level approach, also called late fusion. To this end, the authors considered a cascade approach in which the two systems were run one after the other.

The system starts by running the bio-signal system, which analyzes the data captured in the bracelet and decides if the user is in a dangerous situation or not. As discussed before, this bio-signal system is based on a KNN classification algorithm, which is run in the processor inside the bracelet. If the bio-signal system results in a positive detection, it communicates with the smartphone, which triggers a request to the speech system to analyze the current situation. The speech system captures audio data for a while, which is sent to the smartphone with a previous compression process. In the smartphone, the audio data is analyzed as described before, which includes an MLP approach running in the smartphone microprocessor, being the prediction done by the speech system the global prediction reached in BINDI.

Thus, the bio-signal system acts as a trigger for activating the next stage in the cascade. This design decision was assumed because the energy cost of the bracelet capturing such physiological data, as well as the lightweight machine learning algorithms inside the processor, allows the device to work during hours (at least two days). On the contrary, capturing audio data and comprising the information for sending it is costly, and then it should be reduced as much as possible. In addition, many times running the audio data analysis is also costly for the smartphone in terms of battery. For all these reasons, the speech system was decided to be in the second stage of the cascade.

3.4 A Novel Hybrid Multi-modal Automatic Alert Generation

As discussed before, the initial fusion architecture in BINDI is done at the decision level. This strategy is easy to implement, but it includes the disadvantage of not considering the possible relationships between the different modalities in the system, i.e., the possible correlations between physiological and physical (audio) information. Moreover, another disadvantage is the heterogeneity among the confidence scores provided by the models from each modality. Before discussing other fusion architectures for BINDI, some key aspects should be considered:

- BINDI is a distributed system composed of three devices, a smartphone and two embedded devices (a bracelet and a pendant). It means that communications are required.
- BINDI is within a constrained cyber-physical system, meaning that both computational resources and battery are limited, especially for the two embedded devices. Focusing on battery life, data transmission consumes more energy than other usual tasks, as processing and sensing. Therefore, the less data is transmitted, the longer the battery of the devices will last.
- The initial decision level architecture implies that signals from the two modalities are misaligned in time. Thus, the physiological signals which trigger the alarm are acquired before the audio recording.

Taking into account these key aspects, and in contrast to other methods for fusing physiological and vocal information through feature-level fusion that influenced this work [13], the authors propose a hybrid data fusion architecture by combining both the decision level (late) and feature level (early) approaches. As far as the authors know, this hybrid approach was never considered before for a multimodal physiological-audio wearable system.

The authors take two main design decisions for this hybrid architecture. First, the two embedded devices cannot perform the feature level fusion due to constraints in computational capacity and battery. Therefore, the smartphone will be in charge of this task. Second, it is not possible to continuously send physiological and physical information to the smartphone to perform the feature level fusion and therefore it cannot take place at all times.

Figure 2 shows the hybrid data fusion proposed for BINDI. By default, the system is performing the late fusion already included in the initial approach of BINDI. It means that the bracelet is capturing physiological data over time (step 1). Then, the ML system in the bracelet analyzes the input data. In case it detects the targeted emotion, it generates a trigger to the smartphone (2). The smartphone requests the pendant (3) to capture audio data (4). The audio information is compressed and sent to the smartphone (5). The smartphone runs the MLP based model (6), getting the response for the late fusion architecture (7). In case that the late fusion results in a positive detection, then the early fusion architecture is performed. In such a case, the smartphone requests the physiological data from the bracelet (8), which were captured in the past (i.e., the physiological data which generated the trigger in the late fusion and the one obtained during the time the pendant got audio data). After applying some compressing sensing techniques to alleviate the battery usage, the information requested is sent to the smartphone (9) that runs a classification algorithm combining both physiological and physical data (10). The output of this early fusion architecture will be the output of the whole BINDI system. Further processing is performed in the cloud [5].

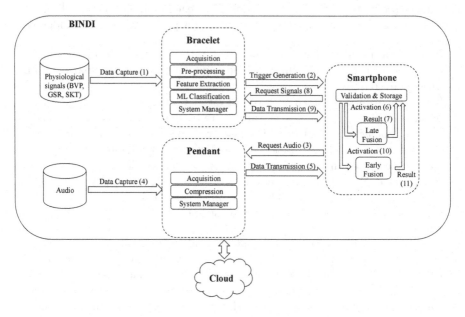

Fig. 2. A hybrid data fusion architecture for BINDI.

The design of the classification algorithm in the early fusion architecture is currently work in progress. It includes the selection of techniques for dimensionality reduction, feature selection, and classification, as well as the possibility of designing a neural network architecture.

4   Final Remarks

As a response for improving the detection capability of BINDI, a wearable cyber-physical system based on the combination of physiological signals and audio for detecting gender violence situations, a novel data fusion architecture was proposed. This novel architecture includes a third layer (i.e., early fusion) to the already implemented system in BINDI. Alternative fusion techniques are to be explored in the future specifically tailored for this problem and able to account for its inherent limitations, such as the necessary bandwidth optimization including data compression, hardware and computational constraints, and battery consumption trade-offs.

Further approaches need to be explored in the future. Related to the speech system, to include the study of audio event classification for detecting threatening sounds, the identification of other speakers' voices, and the energy variability of the signals so that considerable changes in the energy of the signals can be detected (e.g., from silence to very loud sounds).

From the physiological signals point of view, it could include the implementation of non-linear feature extraction techniques to better disentangle the emotion dynamics and the application of novel techniques for motion artifact removal. All of these methods could provide us with more insights into what is going on in a violent situation and in consequence execute a more appropriate action plan.

Acknowledgements. This work has been partially supported by the Department of Research and Innovation of Madrid Regional Authority, in the EMPATIA-CM research project (reference Y2018/TCS-5046). The authors thank the rest of the members of the UC3M4Safety for their contribution and support of the present work. We thank NVIDIA Corporation for the donation of the TITAN Xp used for this research. The authors also thank the Department of Education and Research of the Community of Madrid and the European Social Fund for the conceded Pre-doctoral Research Staff grant for Research Activities, in the CAM Youth Employment Programme (reference PEJD-2019-PRE/TIC-16295).

References

1. UC3M4Safety - Multidisciplinary team for detecting, preventing and combating violence against women (2017). https://www.linkedin.com/company/uc3m4safety/
2. Abadi, M.K., Subramanian, R., Kia, S.M., Avesani, P., Patras, I., Sebe, N.: DECAF: MEG-based multimodal database for decoding affective physiological responses. IEEE Trans. Affect. Comput. **6**(3), 209–222 (2015). https://doi.org/10.1109/TAFFC.2015.2392932
3. Aguiar, A., Kaiseler, M., Cunha, M., Silva, J., Meinedo, H., Almeida, P.: VOCE corpus: ecologically collected speech annotated with physiological and psychological stress assessments. In: LREC 2014: 9th International Conference on Language Resources and Evaluation, May 2014
4. Akçay, M.B., Oğz, K.: Speech emotion recognition: emotional models, databases, features, preprocessing methods, supporting modalities, and classifiers. Speech Commun. **116**, 56–76 (2020). https://doi.org/10.1016/j.specom.2019.12.001. http://www.sciencedirect.com/science/article/pii/S0167639319302262
5. Campos-Gaviño, M.A., Larrabeiti, D.: Toward court-admissible sensor systems to fight domestic violence. In: IEEE International Conference on Multimedia Communications, Services & Security, MCSS 2020 (2020, submitted)
6. Demaree, H., Everhart, D., Youngstrom, E., Harrison, D.: Brain lateralization of emotional processing: historical roots and a future incorporating "dominance". Behav. Cogn. Neurosci. Rev. **4**, 3–20 (2005). https://doi.org/10.1177/1534582305276837
7. Dua, D., Graff, C.: UCI Machine Learning Repository (2017). http://archive.ics.uci.edu/ml
8. Ekman, P.: Are there basic emotions? Psychol. Rev. **99**(3), 550–553 (1992). https://doi.org/10.1037/0033-295X.99.3.550
9. Hansen, J.H.L.: Speech under simulated and actual stress (SUSAS) database. Linguistic Data Consortium, Philadelphia (1999). https://catalog.ldc.upenn.edu/LDC99S78

10. Ikeno, A., Varadarajan, V., Patil, S., Hansen, J.H.L.: UT-Scope: speech under Lombard effect and cognitive stress. In: 2007 IEEE Aerospace Conference, pp. 1–7, March 2007. https://doi.org/10.1109/AERO.2007.352975

11. Kahou, S.E., et al.: EmoNets: multimodal deep learning approaches for emotion recognition in video. CoRR abs/1503.01800 (2015). http://arxiv.org/abs/1503.01800

12. Khalil, R.A., Jones, E., Babar, M.I., Jan, T., Zafar, M.H., Alhussain, T.: Speech emotion recognition using deep learning techniques: a review. IEEE Access **7**, 117327–117345 (2019)

13. Kim, J., André, E.: Emotion recognition using physiological and speech signal in short-term observation. In: André, E., Dybkjær, L., Minker, W., Neumann, H., Weber, M. (eds.) PIT 2006. LNCS (LNAI), vol. 4021, pp. 53–64. Springer, Heidelberg (2006). https://doi.org/10.1007/11768029_6

14. Koelstra, S., et al.: DEAP: a database for emotion analysis; using physiological signals. IEEE Trans. Affect. Comput. **3**(1), 18–31 (2012). https://doi.org/10.1109/T-AFFC.2011.15

15. Minguez-Sanchez, A.: Detección de estrés en señales de voz. Bachelor's thesis (2017). http://hdl.handle.net/10016/27535

16. Miranda, J.A., Canabal, M.F., Lanza, J.M., Portela-García, M., López-Ongil, C., Alcaide, T.R.: Meaningful data treatment from multiple physiological sensors in a cyber-physical system. In: DCIS 2017: XXXII Conference on Design of Circuits and Integrated Systems, November 2017. http://oa.upm.es/51130/

17. Miranda, J.A., Canabal, M.F., Lanza-Gutiérrez, J.M., García, M.P., López-Ongil, C.: Toward fear detection using affect recognition. In: 2019 XXXIV Conference on Design of Circuits and Integrated Systems (DCIS), pp. 1–4, November 2019. https://doi.org/10.1109/DCIS201949030.2019.8959852

18. Miranda, J.A., Canabal, M.F., Portela-García, M., Lopez-Ongil, C.: Embedded emotion recognition: autonomous multimodal affective internet of things. In: CPSWS 2018: Cyber Physical Systems Summer School, Designing Cyber-Physical Systems - From Concepts to Implementation, vol. 2208, pp. 22–29, September 2018

19. Miranda-Calero, J.A., Marino, R., Lanza-Gutierrez, J.M., Riesgo, T., Garcia-Valderas, M., Lopez-Ongil, C.: Embedded emotion recognition within cyber-physical systems using physiological signals. In: DCIS 2018: XXXIII Conference on Design of Circuits and Integrated Systems, November 2018

20. Noulas, A., Englebienne, G., Krose, B.J.A.: Multimodal speaker diarization. IEEE Trans. Pattern Anal. Mach. Intell. **34**(1), 79–93 (2012). https://doi.org/10.1109/TPAMI.2011.47

21. Pawar, R.V., Jalnekar, R.M., Chitode, J.S.: Review of various stages in speaker recognition system, performance measures and recognition toolkits. Analog Integr. Circuits Sig. Process. **94**(2), 247–257 (2017). https://doi.org/10.1007/s10470-017-1069-1

22. Picard, R.W., Vyzas, E., Healey, J.: Toward machine emotional intelligence: analysis of affective physiological state. IEEE Trans. Pattern Anal. Mach. Intell. **23**(10), 1175–1191 (2001). https://doi.org/10.1109/34.954607

23. Poddar, A., Sahidullah, M., Saha, G.: Speaker verification with short utterances: a review of challenges, trends and opportunities. IET Biometr. **7** (2017). https://doi.org/10.1049/iet-bmt.2017.0065

24. Ren, J.S.J., et al.: Look, listen and learn - a multimodal LSTM for speaker identification. CoRR abs/1602.04364 (2016). http://arxiv.org/abs/1602.04364

25. Rituerto-González, E., Gallardo-Antolín, A., Peláez-Moreno, C.: Speaker recognition under stress conditions. In: IBERSPEECH, pp. 15–19, November 2018. https://doi.org/10.21437/IberSPEECH.2018-4

26. Rituerto-González, E., Mínguez Sánchez, A., Gallardo-Antolín, A., Peláez-Moreno, C.: Data augmentation for speaker identification under stress conditions to combat gender-based violence. Appl. Sci. **9**, 2298 (2019). https://doi.org/10.3390/app9112298

27. Russell, J.: Core affect and the psychological construction of emotion. Psychol. Rev. **110**, 145–72 (2003). https://doi.org/10.1037//0033-295X.110.1.145

28. Schmidt, P., Reiss, A., Duerichen, R., Van Laerhoven, K.: Wearable affect and stress recognition: a review, November 2018

29. Shu, L., et al.: A review of emotion recognition using physiological signals. Sensors **18**, 2074 (2018). https://doi.org/10.3390/s18072074

30. Soleymani, M., Lichtenauer, J., Pun, T., Pantic, M.: A multimodal database for affect recognition and implicit tagging. IEEE Trans. Affect. Comput. **3**(1), 42–55 (2012)

31. Subramanian, R., Wache, J., Abadi, M.K., Vieriu, R.L., Winkler, S., Sebe, N.: ASCERTAIN: emotion and personality recognition using commercial sensors. IEEE Trans. Affect. Comput. **9**(2), 147–160 (2018). https://doi.org/10.1109/TAFFC.2016.2625250

32. Vryzas, N., Vrysis, L., Kotsakis, R., Dimoulas, C.: Speech emotion recognition adapted to multimodal semantic repositories. In: 2018 13th International Workshop on Semantic and Social Media Adaptation and Personalization (SMAP), pp. 31–35, September 2018. https://doi.org/10.1109/SMAP.2018.8501881

33. World Health Organization: Global and regional estimates of violence against women: prevalence and health effects of intimate partner violence and non-partner sexual violence (2013). https://www.who.int/reproductivehealth/publications/violence/9789241564625/en/

34. Wu, C., Lin, J., Wei, W., Cheng, K.: Emotion recognition from multi-modal information. In: 2013 Asia-Pacific Signal and Information Processing Association Annual Summit and Conference, pp. 1–8, October 2013. https://doi.org/10.1109/APSIPA.2013.6694347

Dangerous Tool Detection for CCTV Systems

Paweł Donath, Michał Grega$^{(\boxtimes)}$ ⓘ, Piotr Guzik ⓘ, Jakub Król,
Andrzej Matiolański ⓘ, and Krzysztof Rusek ⓘ

AGH University of Science and Technology, Kraków, Poland
grega@kt.agh.edu.pl

Abstract. In this paper we present our work towards an effective solution for detection of dangerous objects, such as firearms or knives in a Closed Circuit Television System. We have gathered a large, manually annotated dataset of recordings supplemented by our original artificial sample generation method. We have used this dataset for training of a convolutional neural network. We present our approach and training results. We have also implemented and present software architecture that implements the neural network. We have shown, that the convolutional neural networks are well suited even for such complex object detection task, when provided with enough training samples.

Keywords: Machine learning · Convolutional neural networks · Dangerous tools · Data analysis · Object detection

Both in the United States and in the rest of the world the crimes with use of weapons are on the rise. For the US the Mother Jones project [13] monitors Mass Shootings (or Active Shooter Incidents). The database held by the project shows significant rise of both the number of such attacks and the number of fatalities. In the EU such events are more commonly classified as terrorist attacks. And while the number of terrorist attacks is slowly declining over the last 40 years, the fraction of attacks with use of dangerous tools is on the rise.

In this paper we propose an effective and fully automated system that is capable of raising of an alarm if a person holding a dangerous object (a pistol, revolver, rifle or a knife) is visible in the CCTV image. Our solution has novel features that make it interesting not only for the scientific community but also for the market use. First, we have trained our algorithms using a large and custom created dataset (which is made available for the scientific community). Second, we have consulted the requirements for the system with the end users and have focused on limiting the amount of false alarms raised, which comes at the cost of sensitivity. This assumption might be surprising, but the justification is that if a system detects only a part of events – it is still more effective than a bare

This work was supported by the Polish National Center for Research and Development under the LIDER Grant (No. LIDER/354/L-6/14/NCBR/2015).

CCTV solution without any automation. On the other hand – a system that raises too many false alarms is useless as it overloads the operator. Finally, in order to construct our solution we have utilized state-of-the-art techniques such as convolutional neural networks, GPU based computing and genetic algorithms making it, to our best knowledge, one of the most advanced systems of its kind.

The rest of the paper is structured as follows. Section 1 provides a description of the research problem. Section 2 covers the related work in the filed. Section 3 describes our dataset and methods used for artificial sample generation. It is followed by Sect. 4, that provides information on our software solution and neural networks. Section 5 presents the performance of the system. The paper is concluded in Sect. 6.

1   Problem Statement

The goal of the presented research is to develop and test an algorithm that raises an alarm in case a dangerous tool is visible in the CTTV camera image. While our system is supposed to work in a fully automated manner, we expect each of the alarms to be verified by a human operator.

Presented paper is a continuation of our work in the filed of dangerous object detection. The first proof of concept for detection of pistols was presented by the authors in [7] while a broader approach covering more types of dangerous objects was presented in [8]. The presented paper shows a mature solution, that can be easily integrated into existing digital attended and unattended CCTV systems.

From the scientific point of view we aim to create a classifier that takes, as an input, a stream from a CCTV camera and as output provides information raised alarms. From the functional point of view we have to minimize the amount of the false alarms (specificity of the system) by retaining the acceptable level of detected events (sensitivity of the system). We define a "single detection" when a dangerous tool is detected in a single frame and a "detected event" when we detect that a person is holding a dangerous tool over numerous frames.

From the applicability point of view we have assumed that our system is supposed to detect no less than 70% of events and raise no more than 1 alarm for every 24 h of the video stream. There is an obvious trade off between sensitivity and specificity of the system, and the broad goal of our research was to find the 'sweet spot' between those two.

Taking into consideration the aim of our research we have identified several research tasks that had to be fulfilled. First, we performed a search and identified potential sources of video data for the research. Unfortunately, none of the available material was long enough nor of acceptable quality. We have created a large and unique dataset of recordings containing acted and not acted scenes wit dangerous tools. For those recordings we have manually created ground truth – information on temporal (frame number) and spatial (coordinates) location of dangerous tools in the recordings. We have decided to use convolutional, deep neural networks, as a recent advancement in object recognition for the detection task. As such a system requires huge amounts of learning samples we have developed a unique method of generation of artificial samples based on green box technique. Finally, while our neural networks detect dangerous objects on individual frames – we have proposed a spatial and temporal algorithm for event detection.

2   Related Work

The idea of automatic detection of dangerous tools in CCTV data appeared first in 2007 when Darker et al. raised the question, whether is it possible to detect (and possibly prevent) gun crime using CCTV [3] as a part of the MEDUSA project. The authors suggested, that there are some cues in video data that may help to prepare an automatic system for gun crime detection. Next year, the same team proceeded with the research on visual cues indicating that a person visible in CCTV is carrying concealed or unconcealed firearm. Darker et al. concluded, that their human-derived performance indicates that it is possible to built an effective automatic system for the detection of a firearm that is not concealed [1] but dedicated image processing algorithms are needed to complete the task.

At the beginning of the past decade several proofs of concept algorithms were presented for the detection of knives and firearms in optical imaging. Those algorithms used approaches that earlier proved to work well in other machine vision applications. In 2011 Haar cascade classifier was used to detect knives in still images [19] with promising results on a limited database. Active Appearance Models were also considered a possible approach for the detection of knives in optical images [5] but its performance strongly depends on proper landmark initialization and object segmentation and may work properly only in some arranged situations (e.g. on X-Ray images of luggage at the airport). Tiwari and Verma proposed a solution based on SURF algorithm supported with color-based segmentation [18] for automatic firearm detection, though most research on that is concentrated mainly on the use of Artificial Neural Networks [7], the last utilizing simple convolutional neural network, trained however on a very small dataset of still images. Deep learning, especially in case of convolutional neural networks, needs a lot of computing power. The usage of GPU units is a natural choice here [12].

Recently another, ontology-based, approach for the detection of guns has emerged [16]. Recognizing parts of a gun may help to detect it even if it is partially occluded [10]. The method works however only for some predefined weapon models and to be effective, it should be accompanied by other computer vision techniques.

Though some of the approaches (especially those most recent) gave promising results, their applicability in real CCTV system is questionable because of unacceptably high false alarm rates if we consider the fact that CCTV stream corresponds to hundreds of images generated per every minute, not to mention, that there may be more than one false alarm per image.

3   Dataset

Deep Learning solutions need a lot of data that is used to train the algorithm. Since we could not find a sufficiently large and diverse public database designed for the detection of dangerous tools in video sequences, we decided to create such a database.

3.1   Natural Samples

We recorded about 300 video sequences of total length of almost 18 h. Most of the images were obtained using a typical CCTV camera, however we got also a substantial amount of data with the use of thermographic camera and some with near infrared device. The video sequences were obtained both indoor and outdoor. To make the dataset diverse they were recorded in various housings and under different lighting conditions and with various dangerous tools.

Additionally we recorded some video sequences where a dangerous tool was visible against a homogeneous, green background. We refer to those recordings as the 'greenbox recordings'. They were used to create additional artificial training samples by background substitution. More than 10 h of recordings are labeled as "background". Those video sequences do not contain any dangerous objects though there are often people holding various items, that may resemble firearms or knives. The database statistics are presented in Table 1. Columns represent type of video sequence, while rows correspond to the type of a dangerous tool.

These recordings were later used to prepare samples to train the Deep Neural Network. We took video sequences that contain dangerous tools and cut out the positive samples (guns, knives etc.) from them. We use only a subset of frames from each video sequence in such a way that the subset is visually diverse (i.e. if there is no or little change in a set of frames, only one of them is used to prepare a positive sample). We mark every case of a dangerous tool with the smallest square that contains the whole tool with the tool situated as close to the center of the square as possible.

3.2   Artificial Samples

Since a Deep Neural Network needs hundreds of thousands or even millions of different, labeled samples, it is practically impossible to prepare such a set manually. To overcome that problem, one may want to multiply the number of samples using simple image transformations. To apply this idea, we cut every manually labeled sample with some additional margin in such a way, that a new sample contained the whole original sample and some background (especially the arm holding the dangerous tool). The object (e.g. gun) was selected by a square bounding box and d_b was as small as possible. During the training, this labeled object was a prototype for family training samples at various scales. The scale was determined by the final window w whose size was in range $(1.1d_b, 2.5d_b)$. An image used for training was a random patch of size w containing tight bounding box. We used five different window sizes placed at quantiles of the tight box distribution, e.g. $w \in \{128, 160, 190, 230, 300\}$. Such procedure serves two purposes. The first is to increase the number of training samples and the second is to introduce scale variation. We additionally randomly flipped samples along vertical axis and randomly modified their saturation in order to introduce even more variation to the training dataset.

Artificial samples prepared in such a way are still strongly correlated though - they all share virtually the same background. What is more, the recordings were obtained in a limited number of visually different places when compared to all possible implementation locations. To battle this problem we decided to record additional video sequences (greenbox recordings), this time with a human holding a dangerous tool against the background that was homogeneous in color (different than that of a human and that of a dangerous tool) and with smooth texture. We prepared the samples following the same pipeline as previously, but this time we also segmented the object from the sample, using logistic regression to predict pixels' attribution to either the background or the object. That allowed us to accurately separate the object and substitute in into another background images. We call the samples obtained by this procedure greenbox samples. The method was described in detail in [6].

Table 1. Duration of recordings

	Optical	IR	Thermovision	Greenbox	Sum
Non-object	8 h 51 min 59 s	1 min 7 s	1 h 16 min 12 s	3 min 51 s	10 h 13 min 07 s
Gun	1 h 54 min 05 s	9 min 17 s	27 min 48 s	7 min 20 s	2 h 38 min 29 s
Knife	1 h 16 min 37 s	9 min 7 s	29 min 07 s	25 min 02 s	2 h 19 min 52 s
Long	1 h 09 min 37 s	9 min 14 s	27 min 50 s	21 min 42 s	2 h 08 min 23 s
Cold steel	0 h 15 min 08 s	0	0	0	0 h 15 min 08 s
Mixed	0 h 19 min 56 s	0	0	0	0 h 19 min 56 s
Sum	13 h 47 min 21 s	28 min 45 s	2 h 40 min 57 s	57 min 54 s	17 h 54 min 57 s

4   Methods

4.1   Convolutional Neural Network for Dangerous Tool Detection

Dangerous tools detection is challenging in two aspects. The first one is that typically training sets are imbalanced. Images containing a dangerous tool are highly outnumbered by scenes without a gun or a knife. The second problem arises from the fact, that it is quite easy to classify an image as either a gun or a knife provided the object of interest occupies a large portion of the image. However, if the object is small compared to dimensions of the frame a location proposal is needed and it is a problem general to every object detection task. In theory, an end-to-end approach of classifying the entire frame could work.

It would require a lot of training samples and the processing of high resolution frame would be computationally expensive.

In the presented project we addressed the first problem by a special training procedure of a deep convolution neural network being the key component of the system. For the object region proposal we used a proven sliding window technique, commonly used in computer vision and image processing. The algorithm divides the entire frame into overlapping squares of size d shifted by a stride d_s in both directions. The neural network classifies the image (video frame) regions as either background class (no dangerous tool) or one of the specified dangerous tool classes (gun, knife). This is a simple mechanism compared to the state of the art object detectors like YOLO [14] or RNN [2] based ones. However, it has some advantages when the assumptions of presented research are taken into account. Key assumption is that we expect an object in a given range from the camera. Analysis of training set statistics revealed that multi-scale object detection is unnecessary as the single scale is enough for that range. Minor scale variations are handled by training samples preparation, as described in Sect. 4.

Introducing scale range during the training, allowed for a single window size in the inference phase what implicates great performance benefits. The sliding window algorithm creates another opportunity for performance optimization. Stacking all the patches into a large batch of images makes inference numerically efficient and it is easy to drop some patches if the performance is not satisfactory. The classifier can interleave between lines on consecutive frames, just like the raster scan worked for analog television.

A sliding window detector is designed to work with the image classifier. Since deep neural networks are state-of-the-art image classifiers, our first approach was a custom neural net inspired by AlexNet [11] and VGGNet [15] architectures. The network was trained from scratch thus the nets like Inception [17] or ResNet [9] were too complex for both the real time application and training on a limited dataset.

Class imbalance can be a huge problem when training a classifier from scratch. We trained the first model using uniform class distribution in the batch, however the best results we obtained using transfer learning and special batch construction we called *diluting training*.

The idea behind diluting training is to use uniform class distribution at the beginning of the epoch and gradually reduce the amount of object examples in the batch while learning rate decays. At the beginning, learning rate is high and classes are properly balanced, thus the weights are updated towards the optimal values. When one class (non object) starts dominating batch distribution, typical network would over-fit to that particular class. However, since we defer most of samples to the time when learning rate is low, the network does not over-fit and only gets slightly biased towards dominating class. We discovered that such a training policy fulfills exactly the goals of our project, as the resulting classifier has a very low rate of false alarms (high precision at the cost of recall).

Besides diluting training, the artificial training samples can be used to improve the balance in class distribution. We observed that feeding the network with additional information about the type of training sample (real or greenbox) improves accuracy. Therefore among the image embedding obtained from transfer learning we introduced a binary feature named greenbox. This feature was set to 1 for each synthetic positive training example. Non-objects were always real (not artificially generated). In order to avoid learning that greenbox feature of 1 implicates a dangerous tool, for each non-object the feature was randomly set to 0 or 1 with equal probabilities. Greenbox feature was concatenated with the output from the convolutional part of the network (image embedding) and the resulting vector was an input to the final classifier being a fully connected neural network. Regularization was provided by a dropout in a layer. We observed that a substantial dropout made the training more stable. In the case of sufficient computational power, dropout can also be used to approximate Bayesian inference [4] and estimate network prediction confidence. The final layer in the network has softmax activation function and outputs a vector of probabilities of each class.

4.2   Software Modules for Dangerous Tool Detection

In order to reliably test the possibility of detecting dangerous tools using deep neural networks, a prototype software was developed. The software uses open source solutions and is divided into modules in which each is responsible for part of the data processing. The software is scalable, and long-term tests proved its stability. The data processing scheme using the described software has been presented in Fig. 1. Dangerous tools detection software consists of six modules which work together in data processing chain. H_CORE is the main module of the system responsible for managing the other modules. It is setting up the configuration which is loaded from the configuration files.

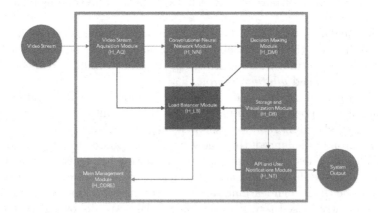

Fig. 1. Module dependences in the prototype.

H_AQ acquires a frame from the data source such as a video stream from a camera, URL or file. Data sources can be interchanged during the normal operation without the need of restarting. In an absence of an input image the module is suspended. The acquired frame is checked in order to to match the required image parameters (e.g. resolution). In the other case frame is put into the data queue between H_AQ and H_NN.

Frame from the H_AQ module is processed by the H_NN module. This module firstly divides the frame into overlapping square sub-regions of its size not less than 100 px. The stride of the sub-region must be less than a half of it size. Each sub-region is later processed by a deep convolutional neural network (described in Sect. 4.1) trained to output probability of dangerous tool in the image sub-region.

Frame and output from H_NN are sent to the H_DM module where final decision about raising the alarm is made. The module uses two methods to distinguish if the detection is in relation to the previous ones and if it is a part of the same event. First is the Kalman Filter method with a set of given parameters which predicts the coordinates of the next detection. If the distance between prediction and current detection is smaller than the configured parameter the detection is classified as the belonging to the same event. The second method used is based on distance calculated between positions of consecutive detections. If the distance is smaller than the configured the detection is classified as belonging to the same event.

Frame and output from H_DM are send to H_DB where the data is stored in the database. The module saves all the alarms and video sequences which caused those alarms.

H_NT uses data stored in the database and provides a user notification service.

H_LB is a load balancer module. It aggregates load data from each of the processing modules and temporally reconfigures the analysis process by sending the request to the H_CORE.

5   Results

5.1   Image Classifier

We have trained two types of image classification neural networks whose architectures are depicted in Fig. 2. The first was a custom deep convolutional neural network inspired by AlexNet and VGG referred to as Simple. The second was implemented by means of transfer learning using MobileNet V2 as image embedding. Both networks were implemented in TensorFlow with MobileNet provided by the tfhub library. The simple network was trained on input images of size 128 × 128 px, thus a 128 px MobileNet fits perfectly into our setup. MobileNet 100% is the largest in the 128 px family and in our task it substantially outperforms (in terms of accuracy) smaller versions. See Fig. 3 for accuracy comparison, where error is lowest for the larges MobileNet network. Smaller versions on the other hand are better in term of inference time.

The networks were trained using diluting training as described in the previous Section. The simplest and efficient way to implement the procedure is to split

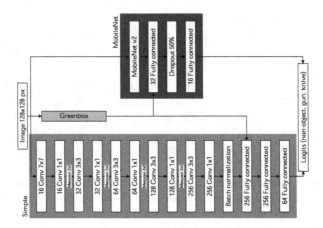

Fig. 2. Neural network architectures used in the experiments. Logits are calculated either by a custom network or by transfer learning.

training samples across multiple per class files. Because of class imbalance, the non-object files will be the largest. During the training we are reading samples from all files simultaneously, thus at the end of an epoch, the samples from the largest file will dominate in the batch. The distribution of labels in the batch can be easily controlled by allowing n_r repeated reads from object files during one epoch of negative samples (non-object). In the experiments we used $n_r \in \{1, 3, \infty\}$. Infinity means that the objects were repeated without the limit resulting in a class balance in every batch. Setting $n_r = 1$ is the most aggressive of diluting training because at the end of an epoch the batch contains almost non-object classes as depicted in Fig. 4. For $n_r > 1$ non-object percentage is almost the same however, the fractions of knives and guns are equalized. Figure 5 shows the typical loss pattern in diluting training. Note that the training is working quite well despite unusual periodic behavior of a train loss (peaks at the beginning of each epoch), the evaluation loss is constantly decreasing from epoch to epoch.

We observed a few properties of diluting training. The key observation is that the low number of repetitions n_r biases the nets towards non-object class and the resulting classifier has very high precision at the cost of a very low recall. On the other hand, full batch balance biases the network towards object class and the network has very high recall while precision is sacrificed. This precision-recall trade off is depicted in Figs. 7 and 6 (notice that trade-off for MobileNet is lower when compared to our simple network).

The best results in terms of accuracy (Fig. 8) and both precision and recall are obtained using three repetitions (five or more are similar to infinity for our training set). However, setting $n_r = 1$ also leads to highly accurate networks, but the training is not more random and the results are not as reproducible as for $n_r = 3$.

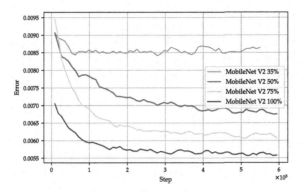

Fig. 3. Exponentially smoothed accuracy for different MobileNet V2 image embeddings.

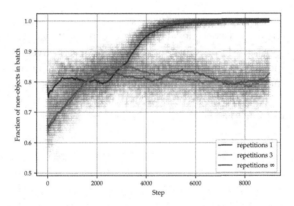

Fig. 4. Non-object fraction in batch during diluting training. Exponentially smoothed sample path.

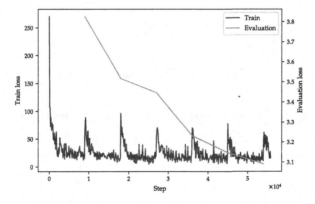

Fig. 5. Loss in diluting training (One epoch is approx. 10,000 steps)

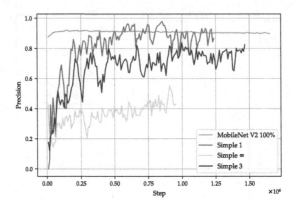

Fig. 6. Total precision for object detection (no distinction among gun or knives).

The most accurate network developed in the project was trained using one repetition strategy for a long training lasting for about five million iterations (more than 550 epochs). The final confusion matrix for this network is presented in Table 3. The network is highly accurate but still does not meet our high accuracy standard, thus on top of this network a decision maker is used to further reduce false alarms (Table 2).

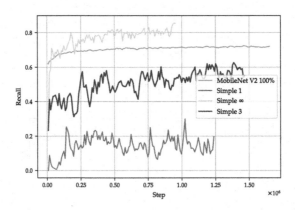

Fig. 7. Total recall for object detection (no distinction among gun or knives).

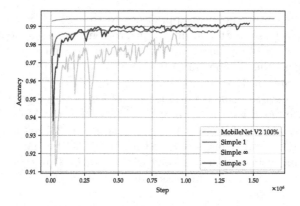

Fig. 8. Accuracy for different training

Table 2. Confusion matrix (Mobilenet, $n_r = 3$), baseline 0.9859

		Predicted label			
		Non object	Gun	Knife	Per class recall
True label	Non object	**286493**	76	261	0,9988
	Gun	824	**2126**	73	0,7033
	Knife	312	76	**703**	0,6444
	Per class precision	0,9961	0,9333	0,6779	**0,9944**

Table 3. Confusion matrix for final network baseline acc 0.9859

		Predicted label			
		Non object	Gun	Knife	Per class recall
True label	Non object	**286652**	62	116	0,9994
	Gun	725	**2248**	50	0,7436
	Knife	325	108	**658**	0,6031
	Per class precision	0,9964	0,9297	0,7985	**0,9952**

6   Conclusions and Further Work

In this paper we have presented a mature and effective solution for dangerous tool
detection. The developed system is major progress in our research on video analysis systems for CCTV. We have created a large dataset, developed a method of
generation of artificial samples, developed and conducted neural network training procedure and created a software suite, that can be easily integrated with
existing CCTV systems.

While our trained neural networks excel at detection of firearms on individual frames, we also aim at utilizing spatial and temporal relationships between
consecutive frames.

We are investigating possible approaches to the H_DM design. One of the research paths is to solve the optimization problem, in which we aim to select the best possible set of parameters, which minimize the number of false alarms while maximizing the number of event detections. We are comparing use of genetic algorithms and Bayesian optimization.

A separate research topic is optimization of the performance of the system. On a system equipped with a GeForce GTX 970 GPU the MobileNet achieves average analysis speed of 242 ms per frame, of which 237 ms is consumed by the H_NN module, while 6 ms is required by the H_AQ for data acquisition for a FullHD stream, using a 160 px sliding window with 80 px stride. This allows analyzing 4 FPS in a real time operation of the system. Time required by other modules is insignificant.

We have planned several approaches to the problem of optimization. First, we plan to limit the amount of analyzed data using motion detection algorithms. Second, we plan to check the impact of the video resolution and FPS on detection accuracy. Finally, we will investigate the impact of less complex NN architectures on the performance of our system.

6.1   Intellectual Property Rights Protection.

Presented invention was submitted as a patent application to the European Patent Office (application number EP18159762.6)

References

1. Blechko, A., Darker, I., Gale, A.: Skills in detecting gun carrying from CCTV. In: 2008 42nd Annual IEEE International Carnahan Conference on Security Technology, pp. 265–271, October 2008. https://doi.org/10.1109/CCST.2008.4751312
2. Cao, Y., Niu, X., Dou, Y.: Region-based convolutional neural networks for object detection in very high resolution remote sensing images. In: 2016 12th International Conference on Natural Computation, Fuzzy Systems and Knowledge Discovery (ICNC-FSKD), pp. 548–554. IEEE, August 2016. https://doi.org/10.1109/FSKD.2016.7603232. http://ieeexplore.ieee.org/document/7603232/
3. Darker, I., Gale, A., Ward, L., Blechko, A.: Can CCTV reliably detect gun crime? In: 2007 41st Annual IEEE International Carnahan Conference on Security Technology, pp. 264–271, October 2007. https://doi.org/10.1109/CCST.2007.4373499
4. Gal, Y., Ghahramani, Z.: Dropout as a Bayesian approximation: representing model uncertainty in deep learning, June 2015. http://arxiv.org/abs/1506.02142
5. Glowacz, A., Kmieć, M., Dziech, A.: Visual detection of knives insecurity applications using active appearance models. Multimedia Tools Appl. **74**(12), 4253–4267 (2015). https://doi.org/10.1007/s11042-013-1537-2
6. Grega, M., et al.: Application of logistic regression for background substitution. In: Dziech, A., Czyżewski, A. (eds.) MCSS 2017. CCIS, vol. 785, pp. 33–46. Springer, Cham (2017). https://doi.org/10.1007/978-3-319-69911-0_3
7. Grega, M., Łach, S., Sieradzki, R.: Automated recognition of firearms in surveillance video. In: 2013 IEEE International Multi-Disciplinary Conference on Cognitive Methods in Situation Awareness and Decision Support (CogSIMA), pp. 45–50, February 2013. https://doi.org/10.1109/CogSIMA.2013.6523822

8. Grega, M., Matiolański, A., Guzik, P., Leszczuk, M.: Automated detection offirearms and knives in a CCTV image. Sensors **16** (2016). https://doi.org/10. 3390/s16010047

9. He, K., Zhang, X., Ren, S., Sun, J.: Deep residual learning for image recognition, December 2015. http://arxiv.org/abs/1512.03385

10. Hempelmann, C.F., Arslan, A.N., Attardo, S., Blount, G.P., Sirakov, N.M.: Real life identification of partially occluded weapons in video frames. In: SPIE conference (2016)

11. Krizhevsky, A., Sutskever, I., Geoffrey E.H.: ImageNet classification with deep convolutional neural networks. In: Advances in Neural Information Processing Systems 25 (NIPS 2012), pp. 1–9 (2012). https://doi.org/10.1109/5.726791. https:// www.nvidia.cn/content/tesla/pdf/machine-learning/imagenet-classification-with-deep-convolutional-nn.pdfpapers.nips.cc/paper/4824-imagenet-classification-with-deep-convolutional-neural-networks.pdf

12. Martínez-Díaz, S., Palacios-Alvarado, C.A., Chavelas, S.M.: Accelerated pistols recognition by using a GPU device. In: 2017 IEEE XXIV International Conference on Electronics, Electrical Engineering and Computing (INTERCON), pp. 1–4, August 2017. https://doi.org/10.1109/INTERCON.2017.8079659

13. Pan, D., Follman, M., Aronsen, G.: US mass shootings, 1982–2018: data from Mother Jones' investigation, June 2018. https://www.motherjones.com/politics/2012/12/mass-shootings-mother-jones-full-data/

14. Redmon, J., Divvala, S., Girshick, R., Farhadi, A.: You only look once: unified, real-time object detection, June 2015. http://arxiv.org/abs/1506.02640

15. Simonyan, K., Zisserman, A.: Very deep convolutional networks for large-scale image recognition, September 2014. http://arxiv.org/abs/1409.1556

16. Sirakov, N.M., Arslan, A.N., Hempelmann, C.F., Attardo, S., Blount, G.P.: Firearms identification through partonomy. In: SPIE conference (2015)

17. Szegedy, C., Vanhoucke, V., Ioffe, S., Shlens, J., Wojna, Z.: Rethinking the Inception Architecture for Computer Vision, December 2015. http://arxiv.org/abs/1512.00567

18. Tiwari, R.K., Verma, G.K.: Notice of retraction a computer vision based framework for visual gun detection using surf. In: 2015 International Conference on Electrical, Electronics, Signals, Communication and Optimization (EESCO), pp. 1–5, January 2015. https://doi.org/10.1109/EESCO.2015.7253863

19. Żywicki, M., Matiolański, A., Orzechowski, T., Dziech, A.: Knife detection as a subset of object detection approach based on Haar cascades. In: Proceedings of the 11th International Conference on Pattern Recognition and Information Processing, Minsk, Republic of Belarus, May 2011

Isolated Word Automatic Speech Recognition System

Martina Slívová$^{(\boxtimes)}$, Pavol Partila$^{(\boxtimes)}$ ⓘ, Jaromír Továrek$^{(\boxtimes)}$ ⓘ, and Miroslav Vozňák$^{(\boxtimes)}$ ⓘ

VSB–Technical University of Ostrava, 17. listopadu 2172/15, 708 00 Ostrava, Czechia
{martina.slivova,pavol.partila,jaromir.tovarek,miroslav.voznak}@vsb.cz

Abstract. The paper is devoted to an isolated word automatic speech recognition. The first part deals with a theoretical description of methods for speech signal processing and algorithms which can be used for automatic speech recognition such as a dynamic time warping, hidden Markov models and deep neural networks. The practical part is focused on the description of the proposal which is based on convolutional neural networks (CNN). The system was designed and implemented in Python using Keras and TensorFlow frameworks. An open audio dataset of spoken words was used for training and testing. A contribution of the paper lies in the specific proposal using CNN for automatic speech recognition and its validation. The presented results show that the proposed approach is able to achieve 94% accuracy.

Keywords: Automatic speech recognition · Machine learning · Hidden Markov models · Dynamic Time Warping · Deep neural networks

1 Introduction

A noticeable trend today is the effort to simplify communication between man and machine. For this purpose, there are automatic speech recognition (ASR) systems that are able to extract information from a speech signal [1]. The speech signal is very complex so that automatic speech recognition is not an easy task. Speech is an acoustic signal with various levels of information (for example phonemes, syllables, words, sentences, etc.). In addition to information content, the speech also transmits clues about the speaker and the environment, which can complicate the decoding of the signal. ASR system can be speaker-dependent or more complicated speaker-independent [2].

These systems can be widely used not only in the personal and industrial field but also for military and defense forces, where voice control and speaker identification will make the configuration and operation of partial services and applications more efficient. The aim of this work is to design and implement a speaker-independent isolated word automatic speech recognition system.

A. Dziech et al. (Eds.): MCSS 2020, CCIS 1284, pp. 252–264, 2020.
https://doi.org/10.1007/978-3-030-59000-0_19

2   State of the Art

There are various methods that can be used for ASR. For example, methods that operate on the principle of comparing with the references, statistical methods or Artificial Neural Network (ANN). In literature [3] authors focused on isolated word recognition in an acoustically balanced, noise-free environment. For feature extraction is used Mel-Frequency Cepstral Coefficients (MFCC) and for a classification Dynamic Time Warping (DTW) and K-Nearest Neighbor (KNN) is used. Results are showed in the confusion matrix, the accuracy of this system is 98.4%. DTW algorithm was used in [4,5] too.

Another possibility is a method called Vector Quantization (VQ) which is used in [6]. The result of a training phase VQ is a codebook. The experiment in this paper showed that increasing the size of the codebook increase the accuracy of the system.

The authors of [11] focus on automatic recognition of connected words in English and Hindi. During preprocessing, noise reduction was performed, and VAD (Voice Activity Detector) was modified to split sentences into words. Parameterization was performed using the MFCC method. The authors compare DTW and Hidden Markov Model (HMM) classifiers. The results show that the HMM method has a lower error rate for English than the DTW method. Hindi showed the same average error rates for both methods.

HMM algorithm is used in [8–10]. In [7] is a combination of deep neural network (DNN) and HMM. The vector of features is produced by MFCC. The results were evaluated on the TI digits database. The recognition accuracy increased with the quantity of the hidden layers in the network. As a result of this comparison, the authors found that when shifting convolution filters in the frequency domain, the relative performance improvement was over 27% compared to DNN in both pure and noisy conditions. When limiting the parameters, the relative improvement was over 41%.

In the literature [12], the authors focused on searching for keywords with small memory footprint, low computational cost, and high precision, and designed a system based on deep neural networks. They compared this system with the commonly used HMM classification technique and focused on significantly simpler implementation. The authors used a feed-forward fully connected neural network. Experimental results have shown that the proposed system outperformed standard HMM in both noisy and noise-free conditions.

3   Applied Digital Speech Processing

In this chapter, we describe individual steps mostly used in the speech processing. The speech is the easiest communication method for most people, although speech as a signal is very complex. Speech is an acoustic signal with many levels of information like phonemes, syllables, words, sentences and more. Besides the information about content, there is information about the speaker and its surroundings. Systems for automatic speech recognition require mathematical models of speech (Eq. 1) [13].

$$s(t) = g(t) \star h(t) = \int_{-\infty}^{\infty} g(\tau)h(t - \tau)d\tau, \tag{1}$$

where $s(t)$ is signal, $g(t)$ is excitation function and $h(t)$ is impulse response.

$$S(f) = G(f)H(f), \tag{2}$$

where $S(f)$ is spectrum of a signal, $G(f)$ is spectrum of a excitation function, and $H(f)$ is spectrum of a impulse response.

3.1 Preprocessing

Preprocessing is supposed to prepare the signal for feature extraction, it consists of four basic steps - removing Direct Current (DC) offset, preemphasis, segmentation, and windowing (see Fig. 1).

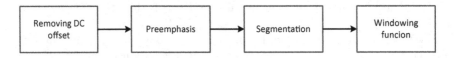

Fig. 1. Preprocessing

Removing DC Offset

DC offset is a part of a signal which can negatively affect signal processing. It is mean value from all samples of the signal and it needs to be removed by simple deduction. Calculation of the DC offset:

$$\mu_s = \frac{1}{N} \sum_{n=1}^{N} s[n], \tag{3}$$

where μ_s is mean value and $s[n]$ is input discrete signal. Then removing it from the signal:

$$s'[n] = s[n] - \mu_s, \tag{4}$$

where $s'[n]$ is signal without DC offset, $s[n]$ is input discrete signal and μ_s is mean value. For real-time application (for example when a signal is captured from a microphone) it can be calculated:

$$\mu_s[n] = \gamma\mu_s[n - 1] + (1 - \gamma)s[n], \tag{5}$$

where $\mu_s[n - 1]$ is mean value of a previous sample, $\mu_s[n]$ is mean value of a current sample and $s[n]$ is real value of a current sample [14].

Preemphasis

The preemphasis is performed for the purpose of equalizing the frequency response of the signal and it is supposed to compensate signal attenuation at higher frequencies [15]. This is done by applying a basic first-order FIR (Finite Impulse Response) filter, where the filtration is given by:

$$s''[n] = s'[n] - ks'[n - 1], \tag{6}$$

where $s'[n]$ is input discrete signal. Values from 0.9 to 1 are selected for parameter k.

Segmentation

Speech is an unstable non-stationary signal. However, it is assumed that speech is stationary in the short term and therefore we divide it into short sections where we can analyze. These sections (frames) are usually 20 to 30 ms long with an overlap to smooth the time change of parameters. In Fig. 2 is shown segmentation and N is a total number of samples, l_{ram} is length of a segment, s_{ram} is shift of a segment and p_{ram} is an overlap.

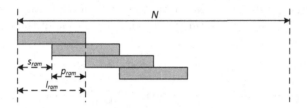

Fig. 2. Segmentation [14]

Windowing Function

The windowing function is used for the elimination of sharp transition between frames which can be developed during segmentation and can cause further problems. The most common is the Hamming window:

$$w[n] = 0.54 - 0.46 \cos\left(\frac{2\pi n}{L - 1}\right) \quad \text{for} \quad 0 \leq n \leq L - 1, \tag{7}$$

where L is the number of samples selected by the window.

3.2 Feature Extraction

Linear Predictive Coding (LPC)

Linear Predictive Coding (LPC) is an audio signal analysis method that estimates speech parameters by assuming that each signal sample can be described by a linear combination of the previous samples and the excitation function. LPC can be used to calculate power spectral density estimates and can also be used for formant speech analysis.

LPC calculation is based on homomorphic speech processing. The speech generation model can be described by the transfer function [13]:

$$H(z) = \frac{G}{1 + \sum_{i=1}^{Q} a_i z^{-i}},$$ (8)

where G is gain and Q is the order of the model.

Mel-Frequency Cepstral Coefficients (MFCC)

The MFCC tries to respect the non-linear perception of sound by the human ear - at lower frequencies the resolution is higher than at high frequencies, which can be used in speech recognition. Non-linearity is compensated by using triangular filters with a linear distribution of frequencies on mel scale, which is defined by [16]:

$$f_m = 2595 \log_{10} \left(1 + \frac{f}{700} \right),$$ (9)

where f[Hz] is linear scale frequency and f_m[mel] is corresponding frequency in mel scale [13].

In Fig. 3, is a block scheme of MFCC process. It consists of preprocessing, fast Fourier transform (FFT), Mel filtration (with filter bank), logarithm calculation, discrete cosine transform (DCT) and calculation of the dynamic delta coefficients.

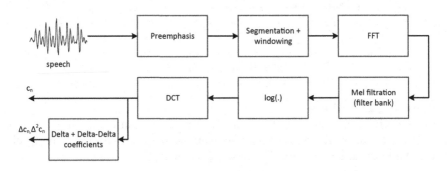

Fig. 3. MFCC calculation

3.3   Classification

Automatic speech recognition is a difficult task for several reasons. The voice of each person is different. It can also change in different situations depending on the emotional state of the speaker. Another problem may be background noise, which may affect recognition. Basic classification of ASR according to the complexity of the recognizer design:

- isolated word automatic speech recognition
- connected word speech recognition
- continuous speech recognition

Dynamic Time Warping

The DTW method is based on a direct comparison of words with references (computing distances between the speaker speaking words and words stored in the dictionary) [3]. Words can vary in time and space. This method is used for recognizing isolated words with a small dictionary - large dictionaries present a problem with high computing and memory requirements. DTW is used in speaker-dependent systems with small dictionaries.

This method can logically be divided into two phases. In the first phase, a pattern reference matrix is created for each word in the database. In the second phase, after the feature extraction from speech, the shortest path between the reference and test sequence of feature is sought.

Hidden Markov Model

The Markov Chain based approach is widely used in many research fields such as in modeling channel in wireless networks [17,18], in prediction schemes for resource reservation [19], and so on. HMM is a statistical method used for speech recognition. The basic prerequisite of statistical modeling is that the signal is random and can be characterized by a parametric random process. These parameters can then be accurately determined. Hidden Markov models are sources of probability function for Markov chains [20]. The Hidden Markov model is a model of a statistical process that is represented by a probabilistic finite state machine [21]. The HMM structure for ASR is usually the left-right Markov models, an example of this model is shown in Fig. 4.

When recognizing isolated words, we can assume that we have a dictionary of size N words and each word is modeled by a different HMM. Suppose we have a training set for each word that contains K occurrences of each spoken word and each occurrence has a sequence of features. To recognize isolated words, we first need to create an HMM model for each word in the dictionary and estimate its parameters. Next, you need to analyze the features for each unknown word and calculate the maximum similarity to the models that are in the dictionary. The determination of the maximum probability can be done, for example, by the Viterbi algorithm. The continuous speech recognition system is usually more complex and its structure includes, in addition to acoustic modeling, lexical decoding, syntactic and semantic analysis.

Deep Neural Network (DNN)

Deep learning is a part of machine learning based on a particular type of learning algorithm, which is characterized by an effort to create a learning model with several levels of which the deepest levels have the output of previous levels as input [23]. This view of layering levels of learning is inspired by the way the human brain processes information and learns to respond to external stimulation.

Deep neural networks are neural networks that have more complex models with large numbers of neurons, hidden layers, and connections. They apply to problems of machine learning with supervised learning. DNNs work in parallel to process large amounts of data and require training to correctly determine the weights of connections between individual neurons.

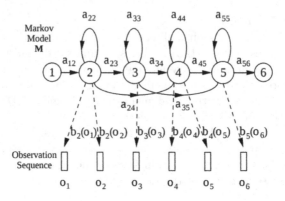

Fig. 4. Example of HMM structure [22]

Convolutional Neural Network (CNN)

Convolutional neural networks are primarily used for image processing [24], but can also be used for other types of input data such as audio processing. Spectrogram analysis is one of the ways to use it for speech recognition. Instead of fully interconnected hidden layers, which are used in standard DNN, there are used special layers called convolutional and pooling layers.

In order to use CNN for pattern recognition input data must be organized into feature maps. This name is derived from image processing applications where the input data is organized into a two-dimensional array of pixels. For color images, RGB values can then be displayed as 3 different feature maps, each indicating a color. CNN moves a small window (filter) across the input image for both training and testing so that weights within the network using this filter can learn from the various features of the input data independently of their absolute position [28]. The CNN architecture typically consists of convolutional layers, activation ReLU layers, pooling layers, and at least one fully connected layer should always be the end of the model. One popular method is to use a spectrogram as input for CNN. In this case, the convolutional filters are applied to the two-dimensional image of the spectrogram. This use of CNN is described in [25–27].

4   Implementation and Results

The created system for isolated word ASR is based on MFCC feature extraction. MFCC coefficients represent the input for recognition. These parameters were chosen because of the non-linear perception of sound by the human ear. A convolutional neural network is used for classification. The system was developed in Python with TensorFlow and Keras. The Speech commands dataset version 2 was used for training and testing the NN.

4.1   Dataset

This dataset is designed to help design, train, and evaluate simple speech recognition systems. It contains a total of 105,829 recordings of 35 words from 2618 different speakers (both women and men) in different environments. The individual words and their numbers are listed in the Table 1 and are composed of commands and other short words that cover many different phonemes. Single-word recordings are in wav format with PCM encoding and 16 kHz sampling rate, each file is 1 s or less [29].

Table 1. An overview of the words of the dataset

Word	Number of recordings	Word	Number of recordings
Backward	1 664	No	3 941
Bed	2 014	Off	3 745
Bird	2 064	On	3 845
Cat	2 031	One	3 890
Dog	2 128	Right	3 778
Down	3 917	Seven	3 998
Eight	3 787	Shiela	2 022
Five	4052	Six	3 860
Folow	1579	Stop	3 872
Forward	1 557	Three	3 727
Four	3 728	Tree	1 759
Go	3 880	Two	3 880
Happy	2 054	Up	3 723
House	2 113	Visual	1 592
Learn	1 575	Wow	2 123
Left	3 801	Yes	4 044
Marvin	2 100	Zero	4 052
Nine	3 934		

The following 15 words were selected to train the designed system: 'Down', 'Five', 'Four', 'Go', 'Left', 'No', 'Off', 'On', 'Right', 'Seven', 'Stop', 'Two', 'Up', 'Yes', 'Zero' (see Table 1). These words were chosen because of the largest number of recordings in the dataset. The entire dataset was not used due to computational complexity.

4.2 Proposed Solution and Results

The database of recording was randomly split into training and testing sets. Training data contains 80% of recordings and the remaining 20% is for testing. In the preprocessing phase, the DC offset was removed and preemphasis was performed. The next step is segmentation, where each word was divided into 25 ms long sections with 10 ms overlap. The length of each recording is 1 s, resulting in 98 frames for each word. The last step of the preprocessing was weighing by Hamming's window. MFCC with delta coefficients was used for feature extraction. 12 MFCC features and 12 delta coefficients were extracted from each frame which means a matrix of 98 × 24 features was created for each word.

After that several different models of the neural network were created to achieve the highest recognition accuracy. The final neural network model includes 6 convolution layers, 11 ReLu layers, 10 dropout layers, 3 pooling layers, 3 noise layers, 1 flatten layer, and 2 fully connected layers. The structure of the neural network is shown in Appendix A. The created model starts with a convolution layer, followed by activation and dropout layers - this is twice in a row. Then there is the pooling layer, after which noise is added to increase the robustness of the recognition, followed by the activation and dropout layers again. This whole structure is repeated three times. At the end of the model, there is a flatten layer, a fully connected layer, activation, and dropout layers, the last one is a fully connected layer, which has the same number of neurons as the number of recognized classes (words), followed by another activation layer.

Figure 5 illustrates neural network learning for 50 epochs. Training of 50 epochs was chosen as a compromise between the length of training and the resulting accuracy. With more than 50 epochs, accuracy no longer increased. A total of 46,604 words for training and 5,826 words for testing were used. The resulting model accuracy was 91.35% for the training set and 94.08% for the testing set.

In Table 2 is a confusion matrix where the results of the recognition can be seen. The use of the trained model is possible with the application that captures sound from the microphone. The app can send recognized word to any other voice-controlled system or device.

The results showed that the proposal can be used for ASR. Another goal will be to train the model on the entire dataset or modify the CNN model to achieve higher accuracy in training compared to testing. With the availability of other datasets, the design could be adapted for other languages, or extended and redesigned for continuous speech recognition.

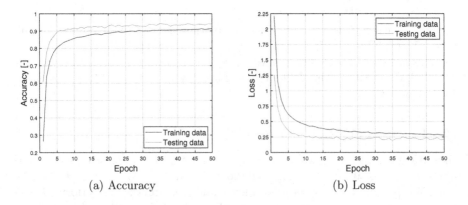

(a) Accuracy   (b) Loss

Fig. 5. Training in 50 epochs

Table 2. Confusion matrix for testing dataset

Predicted / Actual	Down	Five	Four	Go	Left	No	Off	On	Right	Seven	Stop	Two	Up	Yes	Zero	Sum
Down	394	1	0	3	4	3	0	0	0	0	0	1	1	1	0	408
Five	1	376	1	0	2	3	0	2	2	1	1	0	2	0	0	391
Four	2	2	352	0	3	3	3	5	0	1	1	0	0	0	2	374
Go	7	1	1	339	1	9	1	0	0	0	2	3	1	2	0	367
Left	0	3	0	0	379	5	0	0	1	1	0	2	2	8	0	401
No	9	0	0	2	3	368	0	0	0	0	0	0	0	0	0	382
Off	1	3	2	1	2	4	312	7	0	0	3	0	9	1	0	345
On	4	8	3	1	0	1	2	366	0	0	1	0	2	0	0	388
Right	3	6	0	0	4	3	0	0	371	0	0	1	3	1	1	393
Seven	2	0	0	0	1	2	0	0	1	383	7	1	1	0	1	399
Stop	4	1	1	2	1	1	1	1	0	1	365	1	3	0	1	383
Two	0	1	1	3	2	2	0	0	0	4	1	386	1	0	3	404
Up	2	6	1	8	0	6	39	8	0	0	5	0	253	0	0	328
Yes	0	0	0	1	6	3	0	0	0	0	0	0	2	407	0	419
Zero	0	0	0	0	1	1	0	0	0	2	0	8	1	1	430	444
Sum	429	408	362	360	409	414	358	389	375	393	386	403	281	421	438	5826

5 Conclusion

The paper describes a proposed system for isolated word automatic speech recognition, which is based on MFCC feature extraction and using a convolutional neural network for classification. The developed system demonstrates a way how CNN can be used for ASR. The presented proposal in this paper belongs to the better approaches for its accuracy 94% which is comparable with existing solutions mentioned in Sect. 2 achieving their best accuracy between 80–98%. The described proposal in this paper is promising and its development and improvement make sense. Of course, there is a possibility of extending the system for continuous ASR, nevertheless, the issue is a computational complexity of such a solution due to the dimension of dataset and the internal structure of CNN.

Acknowledgment. The research was supported by the Czech Ministry of Education, Youth and Sports from the Large Infrastructures for Research, Experimental Development and Innovations project reg. no. LM2015070 at the IT4Innovations - National Supercomputing Center, where a computational time was provided by the projects OPEN-19-38, and partly by the institutional grant SGS reg. no. SP2020/65 conducted at VSB - Technical University of Ostrava.

A   Neural network diagram

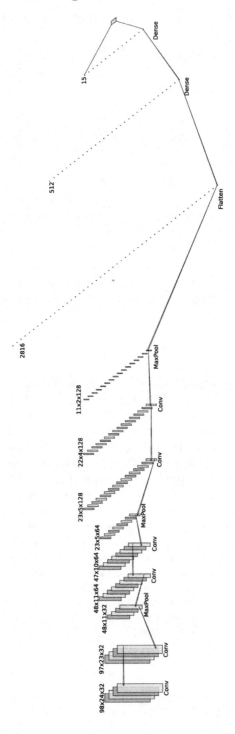

References

1. Benzeghiba, M., et al.: Automatic speech recognition and speech variability: a review. Speech Commun. **49**(10–11), 763–786 (2017)
2. Petkar, H.: A review of challenges in automatic speech recognition. Int. J. Comput. Appl. **151**(3), 23–26 (2016)
3. Imtiaz, M.A., Raja, G.: Isolated word Automatic Speech Recognition (ASR) system using MFCC, DTW & KNN. In: 2016 Asia Pacific Conference on Multimedia and Broadcasting (APMediaCast), pp. 106–110 (2016). https://doi.org/10.1109/APMediaCast.2016.7878163
4. Senthildevi, K.A., Chandra, E.: Keyword spotting system for Tamil isolated words using Multidimensional MFCC and DTW algorithm. In: 2015 International Conference on Communication and Signal Processing, ICCSP 2015, pp. 550–554 (2015). https://doi.org/10.1109/ICCSP.2015.7322545. Article No. 7322545
5. Xu, L., Ke, M.: Research on isolated word recognition with DTW-based. In: ICCSE 2012 - Proceedings of 2012 7th International Conference on Computer Science and Education, pp. 139–141 (2012). https://doi.org/10.1109/ICCSE.2012.6295044. Article No. 6295044
6. Abu Shariah, M.A.M., Ainon, R.N., Zainuddin, R., Khalifa, O.O.: Human computer interaction using isolated-words speech recognition technology. In: 2007 International Conference on Intelligent and Advanced Systems, ICIAS 2007, pp. 1173–1178 (2007). https://doi.org/10.1109/ICIAS.2007.4658569. Article No. 4658569
7. Dhanashri, D., Dhonde, S.B.: Isolated word speech recognition system using deep neural networks. In: Satapathy, S., Bhateja, V., Joshi, A. (eds.) Proceedings of the International Conference on Data Engineering and Communication Technology. AISC, vol. 468, pp. 9–17. (2017). https://doi.org/10.1007/978-981-10-1675-2_2
8. Ranjan, R., Dubey, R.K.: Isolated word recognition using HMM for Maithili dialect. In: 2016 International Conference on Signal Processing and Communication, ICSC 2016, pp. 323–327 (2016). https://doi.org/10.1109/ICSPCom.2016.7980600. Article No. 7980600
9. Frangoulis, E.: Isolated word recognition in noisy environment by vector quantization of the HMM and noise distributions. In: Proceedings of ICASSP 1991: 1991 International Conference on Acoustics, Speech, and Signal Processing, pp. 413–416 (1997). https://doi.org/10.1109/ICASSP.1991.150364
10. Zhao, L., Han, Z.: Speech recognition system based on integrating feature and HMM. In: 2010 International Conference on Measuring Technology and Mechatronics Automation, ICMTMA 2010, vol. 3, pp. 449–452 (2010). https://doi.org/10.1109/ICMTMA.2010.298. Article No. 5458876
11. Singhal, S., Dubey, R.K.: Automatic speech recognition for connected words using DTW/HMM for English/Hindi languages. In: International Conference Communication, Control and Intelligent Systems, CCIS 2015, pp. 199–203 (2016). https://doi.org/10.1109/CCIntelS.2015.7437908. Article No. 7437908
12. Chen, G., Parada, C., Heigold, G.: Small-footprint keyword spotting using deep neural networks. In: 2014 IEEE International Conference on Acoustics, Speech and Signal Processing (ICASSP), Florence, pp. 4087–4091 (2014). https://doi.org/10.1109/ICASSP.2014.6854370
13. Psutka, J.: Mluvíme s počítačem česky. Academia, Praha (2006)
14. Partila, P., Voznak, M., Mikulec, M., Zdralek, J.: Fundamental frequency extraction method using central clipping and its importance for the classification of emotional state. Adv. Electr. Electron. Eng. **10**(4), 270–275 (2012)

15. Ibrahim, Y.A., Odiketa, J.C., Ibiyemi, T.S.: Preprocessing technique in automatic speech recognition for human computer interaction: an overview. Ann. Comput. Sci. Ser. **15**(1), 186–191 (2017)
16. Bou-Ghazale, S.E., Hansen, J.H.L.: A comparative study of traditional and newly proposed features for recognition of speech under stress. IEEE Trans. Speech Audio Process. **8**(4), 429–442 (2000)
17. Fazio, P., Tropea, M., Sottile, C., Lupia, A.: Vehicular networking and channel modeling: a new Markovian approach. In: 2015 12th Annual IEEE Consumer Communications and Networking Conference (CCNC), pp. 702–707 (2015)
18. Tropea, M., Fazio, P., Veltri, F., Marano, S.: A new DVB-RCS satellite channel model based on Discrete Time Markov Chain and Quality Degree. In: 2013 IEEE Wireless Communications and Networking Conference (WCNC), pp. 2615–2619 (2013)
19. Fazio, P., Tropea, M.: A new Markovian prediction scheme for resource reservations in wireless networks with mobile hosts. Adv. Electr. Electron. Eng. **10**(4), 204–210 (2012)
20. Rabiner, L.R.: A tutorial on hidden Markov models and selected applications in speech recognition. Proc. IEEE **77**(2), 257–286 (2016). https://doi.org/10.1109/5.18626
21. Cooke, M., Green, P., Josifovski, V., Vizinho, A.: Robust automatic speech recognition with missing and unreliable acoustic data. Speech Commun. **34**(3), 267–285 (2001). https://doi.org/10.1016/S0167-6393(00)00034-0. Accessed 26 Feb 2020
22. Young, S., et al.: The HTK Book. HTK Version 3.4. B.m.: Cambridge University Engineering Department (2006)
23. Zaccone, G., Karim, M.R., Mensha, A.: Deep Learning with TensorFlow. Packt Publishing, Birmingham (2017)
24. Tropea, M., Fedele, G.: Classifiers comparison for Convolutional Neural Networks (CNNs) in image classification. In: 2019 IEEE/ACM 23rd International Symposium on Distributed Simulation and Real Time Applications (DS-RT), pp. 1–4 (2019). https://doi.org/10.1109/DS-RT47707.2019.8958662
25. Dorfler, M., Bammer, R., Grill, T.: Inside the spectrogram: Convolutional Neural Networks in audio processing. In: 2017 International Conference on Sampling Theory and Applications (SampTA), pp. 152–155 (2017). https://doi.org/10.1109/SAMPTA.2017.8024472
26. Gouda, S.K., et al.: Speech recognition: keyword spotting through image recognition. arXiv preprint arXiv:1803.03759 (2018)
27. Fu, S.-W., Hu, T.-Y., Tsao, Y., Lu, X.: Complex spectrogram enhancement by convolutional neural network with multi-metrics learning. In: IEEE International Workshop on Machine Learning for Signal Processing, MLSP, pp. 1–6 (2017). https://doi.org/10.1109/MLSP.2017.8168119
28. Abdel-Hamid, O., Mohamed, A.-R., Jiang, H., Deng, L., Penn, G., Yu, D.: Convolutional neural networks for speech recognition. IEEE Trans. Audio Speech Lang. Process. **22**(10), 1533–1545 (2014). Article No. 2339736
29. Warden, P.: Speech commands: a dataset for limited-vocabulary speech recognition. http://arxiv.org/abs/1804.03209. Accessed 09 Mar 2019

Audio Feature Analysis for Precise Vocalic Segments Classification in English

Szymon Zaporowski[1]([⊠]) [iD] and Andrzej Czyżewski[2] [iD]

[1] Audio Acoustic Laboratory, Faculty of Electronics, Telecommunications and Informatics, Gdansk University of Technology, Narutowicza 11/12, 80-233 Gdansk, Poland
smck@multimed.org
[2] Multimedia Systems Department, Faculty of Electronics, Telecommunications and Informatics, Gdansk University of Technology, Narutowicza 11/12, 80-233 Gdansk, Poland
ac@pg.edu.pl

Abstract. An approach to identifying the most meaningful Mel-Frequency Cepstral Coefficients representing selected allophones and vocalic segments for their classification is presented in the paper. For this purpose, experiments were carried out using algorithms such as Principal Component Analysis, Feature Importance, and Recursive Parameter Elimination. The data used were recordings made within the ALOFON corpus containing audio signal recorded employing 7 speakers who spoke English at the native or near-native speaker level withing a Standard Southern British English variety accent. The recordings were analyzed by specialists from the field of phonology in order to extract vocalic segments and selected allophones. Then parameterization was made using Mel Frequency Cepstral Coefficients, Delta MFCC, and Delta Delta MFCC. In the next stage, feature vectors were passed to the input of individual algorithms utilized to reduce the size of the vector by previously mentioned algorithms. The vectors prepared in this way have been used for classifying allophones and vocalic segments employing simple Artificial Neural Network (ANN) and Support Vector Machine (SVM). The classification results using both classifiers and methods applied for reducing the number of parameters were presented. The results of the reduction are also shown explicitly, by indicating parameters proven to be significant and those rejected by particular algorithms. Factors influencing the obtained results were discussed. Difficulties associated with obtaining the data set, its labeling, and research on allophones were also analyzed.

Keywords: Allophone classification · Feature Importance · Random forest

1 Introduction

In recent years the growing interest of scientists and specialists from the industrial sector in technologies related to speech signal processing can be observed [1, 2]. According to

---

Dataset employed in this research available at website: https://modality-corpus.org in ALOFON corpus section.

A. Dziech et al. (Eds.): MCSS 2020, CCIS 1284, pp. 265–277, 2020.
https://doi.org/10.1007/978-3-030-59000-0_20

some predictions, it is possible that more than 50% of all search queries over the internet will be utilized by voice; also, mobile device communication can be done the same way [3]. As voice assistants increase in popularity, in particular the solutions proposed by Amazon, Apple, and Google, the use of voice communication with devices will require the development of finer solutions to better understand voice commands. Finding better solutions for voice communication with computer devices will probably require not only the development of solutions related to machine learning or deep learning but also analysis of speech itself in a deeper context and meaning. Approaching the problem in this way could be more challenging due to the fact that the allophone articulation is not a simple process in terms of its analysis. First of all, an allophone is any of the various phonetic realizations of a phoneme in a language, which do not contribute to distinctions of meaning. For example, realization of "p" in word "sip" is different in word "seep". Each of realization of "p" in these words are different allophones. Especially, the dependence on the preceding sounds, context, short duration time and individual features require a change in the approach popular in the literature. In practice, speech is quite rarely analyzed in such a detailed way as to go to the allophonic level. Works on analysis aspects related to the level of allophones are usually conducted by linguists and they are not strictly related to the application in the broadly understood machine learning.

The analysis of allophones is mainly used in relation to the quality of pronunciation in a given language. There are some relationships, such as the difference between dark /l/ and light /l/ in English, for example, as in Recasens's paper [4]. Based on the implementation of such an allophone analysis, it is possible to determine whether a given person who speaks English comes, for example, from England or from Scotland [5]. This topic, in particular, the recognition of the speakers' accent, has potential applications in security technologies. There are also many different fields where allophone recognition and analysis can be beneficial e.g., for biometrics with a speaker identification system, where allophone analysis can determine the identity of a person [6]. Also, allophones can help in the early detection of dyslexia. However, this issue concerns allophonic perception and its disorders [7].

The plan of this article is as follows, in the second section, an overview of works related to the topic of speech research at the allophonic level, the parameterization process, parameter reduction, and classification of allophones and vocalic segments are presented. The third section concerns the methodology, a description of the used corpus, and its most important features. Then the parameterization method is briefly described. Next, three selected algorithms that were used to reduce and to indicate the significance of parameters in the obtained feature vector are presented. These algorithms applied are Extremely Randomized Trees, Principal Component Analysis, and Recursive Feature Elimination. The fourth section contains the description and results of the experiments. The fifth and final section includes discussion and conclusions.

2   Related Work

Several works have been found in the literature related to the classification of allophones. Most of this work was written as part of a larger project on the multimodal methodology for allophone research [3, 8–10]. In most cases, simple artificial neural network architectures consisting of at least one hidden layer were used for classification. Algorithms K-Nearest Neighbors, Support Vector Machines, Self-Organizing Maps, Convolutional Neural Networks were also used [3, 8]. In the case of clustering, Gaussian Mixture Models and Hidden Markov Networks were employed [11, 12].

In the parameterization of the speech signal, various parameters are used. Based on the experiments carried out as part of the study of allophones [13, 14], a set of features consisting of acoustic descriptors, their derivatives, and statistical values, which carry information, was created. Such a feature vector includes parameters in both time and frequency domain. Time-domain parameters include the center of gravity (Temporal Centroid - TC), number of zero crossings (Zero Crossing - ZC), RMS energy (Root Mean Square Energy), and peak value to RMS value (Peak to RMS). Frequency domain-related parameters were obtained by transforming the time domain signal using a Discrete Fourier Transform. The following spectral characteristics were used: the power density spectral center (Audio Spectrum Centroid - ASC), the power density gravity center variance (Variance of Audio Spectrum Centroid - varASC), the mean square power deviation (Audio Spectrum Spread - ASSp), the mean square deviation variance power density spectra (Variance of Audio Spectrum Spread - varASSp), the skewness of the mean square power density spectrum (Audio Spectrum Skewness ASSk), the variance of the mean square power spectrum deviation (Variance of Audio Spectrum Skewness - varASSk) [15, 16]. Since Mel Frequency Cepstral Coefficients are most often used in speech signal recognition [17, 18], that is why the focus in this paper is put on this type of feature.

3 Methodology

3.1 Data Acquisition

The recordings were made in a room prepared for voice recordings with the two acoustic dampers. They were used to reduce unwanted sounds. Two microphones, a super-directional microphone, and a lavalier microphone and an external recorder were employed to record the audio signal. The signal from microphones was recorded with a 16-bit resolution and 48 kHz/s sampling rate. Also, video and Facial Motion Capture (FMC) modalities were recorded using Six Vicon Vue cameras, Vicon reference Camera, digital camera, and sports camera. However, it must be noted that those modalities are not subject to this research. Other authors' work describes an approach that uses FMC and combined audio modality with FMC to classify allophones and vocalic segments. The arrangement of the equipment in the room used in the context of wider experimental research is presented in Fig. 1.

The recording sessions lasted two days. Seven speakers were recorded. Audio recordings acquired during these sessions were used in the experiments described in this Each speaker uttered 300 short expressions or words. The recorded subjects were native or near-native speakers speaking with varying pronunciation (with Standard Southern British English variety). The level of English pronunciation, gender, and accent of each

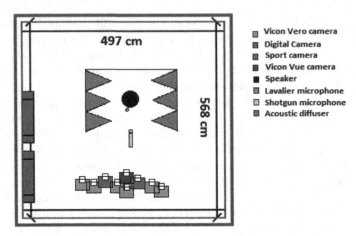

Fig. 1. Schematics of room arrangement for a recording session

speaker is presented in Table 1. It is worth noting that two speakers are English phonology specialists and both are of Polish origin. Classes that were obtained from recording sessions are highly imbalanced in cardinality, which is shown in Table 2.

Table 1. List of recorded speakers

Speaker ID	Gender	English pronunciation level	Accent
1	Female	Near-native	British
2	Male	Native	British
3	Male	Native	British (Estuary)
4	Male	Native	South African
5	Female	Near-native	British
6	Male	Native	British
7	Female	Native	British

Only selected vowels and diphthongs were used for the presented study. The list of recorded utterances contains about 2100 items for all speakers that constitute a set of English pure vowels and consonants placed in various consonantal context.

The prepared recordings were used by phonology specialists for the process of manual labeling of allophonic sounds. The labeling took about two months, which means it was nearly a week of manual processing for each speaker. There was no possibility to automate the process. This is probably one of the reasons why there is a lack of this kind of research employing a deep learning approach since it is a time-consuming labeling process necessary.

Table 2. List and number of vocalic segments recorded for all speakers

Segment	Quantity	Segment	Quantity
ae	420	I	273
e	266	A	252
ei	203	O	182
i:	182	ai	154
eu	126	a:	119
u:	91	3:	70
o:	70	U	35
au	35	aiE	7
oi	7	ir	7
eE	7	ie	7

Another problem is the difference in the duration of each segment; it could last less than 40 ms for pure vowels to almost 400 ms for diphthongs. Due to highly imbalanced classes, there was a decision to reject from classification all classes with a number of elements smaller than 35.

Dataset presented in this research is available to download from the MODALITY corpus webpage available in the ALOFON corpus tab [19]. Detailed information about the above corpora is mentioned in the authors' previous works [8, 20].

3.2 Parameterization

This research presented in this paper uses the first 40 MFCCs – 20 first MFCC's average values, 20 first MFCC's variance values, and 20 delta MFCC and 20 delta-delta MFCC Coefficients. Using the formula (1) it is possible to calculate the first and second-order derivatives of MFCC:

$$d_t = \frac{\sum_{n=1}^{2} n(c_t + n - c_t - n)}{2 \sum_{n=1}^{2} n^2} \tag{1}$$

where c is the nth cepstral coefficient and first-order dynamic coefficient, and t stands for time.

The MFCC parameters were calculated for 512 samples of speech frames (with an overlap of 50%) and then the average and the variance values were calculated, which results in an 80-dimensional vector of parameters.

3.3 Feature Selection and Reduction Algorithms

Principal Component Analysis is one of the most popular and widely used algorithms for dimension reduction [21, 22]. PCA algorithm is used when there is a need for extracting crucial information from the data, compressing the size of the data vector and clarify the dataset description. One of the advantages of this algorithm is the fact that is one of the easiest ways to analyze the structure of the observations and the variables. PCA was used to reduce the dimension of gathered data with minimal loss of accuracy in classification.

Extremely Randomized Trees (ERT) algorithm is deriving concept from the random forest algorithm [23]. It provides a combination of tree predictors such that each tree depends on the values of a random vector sampled independently and is also characterized by the same distribution for all trees in the forest. The error connected with generalization for forests converges to a limit as the number of trees in the forest grows. The generalization error of a forest of tree classifiers depends on the correlation between trees in the forest and on the strength of the individual trees in the whole set [24, 25]. The algorithm was implemented using scikit python library [26]. ERT algorithm was used with 10 estimators, entropy criterion, minimum sample split equal two, minimum samples per leaf equal one, a maximum number of features equal twenty and with balanced class weight to balance an uneven number of examples for classes of classified vocalic segments. Bootstrap and warm start settings were not used. The biggest advantage of the ERT is obtaining detailed information about the most important parameters forming the data vector.

The goal of the Recursive Feature Elimination (RFE) algorithm is to sort out features using recursive reduction of the dataset content. It uses an external estimator, which allocate weight for each feature. The algorithm works as follows. In the first step, the initial set of features is used to train the estimator. The importance of feature is received for the given attributes. In the next step, the less important feature is pruned out of the current set of features. This procedure is repeated recursively until the desired number of features is reached [27]. RFE model was implemented using scikit library [26].

3.4 Classification

A simple feedforward architecture was used as an artificial neural network classifier. It was a neural network used with three hidden layers consisting of 80 neurons, each with a Relu activation function and softmax functions on the last layer, which size is determined by the size of the classes being the object of classification. The network was implemented with the use of Keras library in the Python programming language [28]. For the training, the Stochastic Gradient Descent (SGD) algorithm with the learning rate 0.05 was used, and also a categorical cross-entropy loss function has been applied with 10 times cross-validation of data.

The classifier using the Support Vector Machine algorithm used in this work was implemented using the scikit-learn library in the Python programming language [26]. The data processing module used was identical to the one used for neural networks. Two types of the kernel were used: the polynomial kernel and the RBF (Radial Basis Function) kernel. In addition, it was decided to use weights for the classes used due to their heterogeneous number in order to balance them. The automatically selected gamma coefficient was also employed, while the shape of the decision function was adopted as one vs the rest. Data were split into 60/40 for training and testing sets.

For both classifications presented in this section, there were used 3 algorithms presented in Sect. 3.3. The results of the classification are presented in the next section.

4 Results

In Table 3, 4 and 5 results for ANN classification are presented employing ERT, RFE and PCA algorithm. Training took 1500 epochs for each validation. The number of features selected for each algorithm was 39 for ERT and 20 for both PCA and RFE. This number of coefficients was chosen according to obtained results. Presented results are average from 10 classification algorithm executions.

The data are presented by showing values for specific speakers instead of the average value for the whole set, because otherwise it would not be possible to see differences between individual speakers.

Table 6, 7 and 8 consists of results for SVM combined with ERT, RFE and PCA algorithms respectively. The number of features selected for each algorithm was the same as in the ANN approach. Results are also the average of 10 classification attempts for each algorithm. Figure 2 presents the results of the Feature Importance algorithm for the top 20 coefficients. Figure 3 shows the results of Feature Importance algorithm for each speaker separately.

Table 3. Results of data classification using ERT algorithm with ANN

Speaker ID	Accuracy	Precision	Recall
1	0.943	0.969	0.969
2	0.971	0.984	0.984
3	0.943	0.969	0.969
4	0.857	0.769	0.755
5	0.886	0.952	0.938
6	0.829	0.906	0.906
7	0.829	0.769	0.755

Table 4. Results of data classification using RFE algorithm and ANN

Speaker ID	Accuracy	Precision	Recall
1	0.943	0.936	0.969
2	0.914	0.964	0.953
3	0.971	0.964	0.984
4	0.914	0.805	0.802
5	0.943	0.956	0.969
6	0.914	0.955	0.953
7	0.857	0.923	0.922

Table 5. Results of data classification using PCA algorithm and ANN

Speaker ID	Accuracy	Precision	Recall
1	1	1	1
2	0.914	0.817	0.787
3	0.914	0.968	0.787
4	0.943	0.984	0.969
5	0.886	0.952	0.938
6	0.371	–	–
7	0.8	0.931	0.724

Table 6. Results of data classification using ERT algorithm and SVM

Speaker ID	Accuracy	MSE
1	0.857	0.517
2	0.857	1.025
3	0.828	0.907
4	0.771	0.841
5	0.857	1.204
6	0.457	0.041
7	0.914	0.954

Table 7. Results of data classification using RFE algorithm and SVM

Speaker ID	Accuracy	MSE
1	0.857	0.471
2	0.886	0.897
3	0.886	0.4661
4	0.743	0.798
5	0.886	0.90
6	0.8	1.19
7	0.857	0.74

Table 8. Results of data classification using PCA algorithm and SVM

Speaker ID	Accuracy	MSE
1	0.857	0.591
2	0.886	1.075
3	0.914	0.491
4	0.829	0.751
5	0.743	1.549
6	0.457	0
7	0.886	1.025

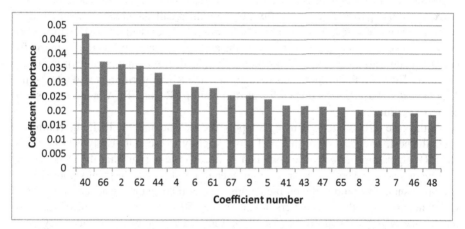

Fig. 2. Results of Feature Selection algorithm for all speakers – mean value for top 20 coefficients

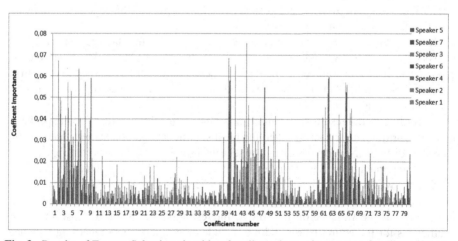

Fig. 3. Results of Feature Selection algorithm for all speakers – importance for all coefficients according to each speaker

5 Discussion

In the vast majority of scientific papers on subjects related to allophones, too little importance is attached to the significance of parameters found in the vector, which is directed to the classifier input. In the overwhelming majority of cases, the Principal Component Analysis (PCA) method is used, while not paying attention to which of the parameters considered by the algorithm are significant, thus they should be transferred to the classifier input, and which ones were treated as noise to be removed.

In the case of classification using neural networks, the RFE algorithm performed best, slightly behind the solution using Extremely Randomized Trees. The PCA algorithm worked the worst. It is puzzling that the results are unstable for the speaker ID 6. In the case of RFE and ERT algorithms, the results do not differ significantly from the results obtained for other speakers. However, the case of the PCA algorithm could not be exceeded by up to 50% accuracy. Furthermore, the recall and precision metrics could not be calculated due to the significant number of errors in classification. However, even in the absence of counting speaker ID 6 to the average value of the accuracy metric for individual algorithms, PCA performs the worst. The decrease in the value of the recall metric for ERT and PCA algorithms in relation to the RFE algorithm is also interesting. This indicates that the selection of features made for ERT and PCA is not necessarily the most optimal.

In the case of classification using Support Vector Machine, the RFE algorithm was again the best. The PCA algorithm performed slightly worse, but visibly weaker, while the ERF algorithm performed worse than it did. It is important that the same hyper-parameter settings were used for each speaker in order to enable results comparison. Attention should be paid to the problem with speaker ID 6 again, the accuracy results of which in two out of three classifiers did not exceed 50%. Moreover, the MSE value for this speaker was divergent. In the case of the ERF algorithm, where the accuracy score was 80%, MSE indicates the possibility of under-training the algorithm. For PCA and RFE, MSE values are overfitting. For speakers ID 2 and ID 5, MSE values also indicate the possibility of matching hyperparameters.

Based on the conducted experiments, it was observed that the classifier using a neural network is more effective and more universal than the Support Vector Machine. In most cases, recall and precision metrics indicate the actual classifier has learned to recognize individual allophones but does not try to always guess the same etiquette, which is common for unbalanced classes.

According to the results of Feature Importance algorithm applied for all speakers, it is noteworthy that for each speaker, the most significant coefficients indicated by the algorithm differed. Nevertheless, it can be seen which coefficients most often appeared as the most important ones. Based on these results, a ranking of the top 20 most significant coefficients was created by calculating the average value for each coefficient.

Information on Feature Importance for all speakers indicates that the most important parameter was the variance of the MFCC. Interestingly, the list of 20 most important coefficients for the entire dataset did not include other coefficients regarding variance (positions 21–40). The list includes 5 delta MFCC coefficients (66 and 62 in second and fourth place), 8 coefficients constituting average MFCC values (2 in third place, 4 in sixth place, 6 in seventh place) and 5 delta MFCC coefficients (44 in fourth place). Based on the results obtained from the Feature Importance algorithm, it cannot be clearly stated that one of the categories of coefficients is redundant. However, it can be observed that the MFCC coefficients with the highest indices and their derivatives are not as important as the coefficients with the lower indices. It indicates that it is not worth making parameterization using more than 15 factors. The only exception is the aforementioned variance parameter, which came from a factor of 20 and was the only one to represent the variance of MFCC coefficients in the prepared statement.

One of the things that are worth mentioning is the fact that the speaker's accent did not significantly affect the results of the classification. Also, the pronunciation level cannot be clearly linked to the quality of the classification.

6 Conclusions

In this paper, an approach to the classification of allophones and the significance of vocalic segments parameters using the Artificial Neural Network and Support Vector Machine is presented. Using the Extremely Randomized Trees, Principal Component Analysis and Recursive Feature Elimination algorithms, efforts were made to obtain the resulting feature vector to obtain the best classification result for both types of classifiers and at the same time check which coefficients in the feature vector are the most important using the Feature Importance algorithm. The obtained results indicate that the Recursive Feature Elimination algorithm works best, ahead of the Extremely Randomized Trees algorithm. It was found using the Feature Importance algorithm that it may not be clearly indicated which group of features is the most important. However, there are indications that features above MFCC and its derivatives do not affect classification. The same happens with the variance of MFCC coefficients.

It should be noted that the tests were carried out on a relatively small group of speakers. In order to conduct research on a larger scale, it would be necessary to solve the biggest problem associated with the classification of allophones, i.e., to develop automatic labeling and detection of allophones in recordings.

Further work related to the classification of allophones can be used, for example, in voice biometry, to verify users, because as is seen in the significance ranking of features, each speaker has a different set of the most important features, which can be used as a unique feature.

Acknowledgment. Research sponsored by the Polish National Science Centre, Dec. No. 2015/17/B/ST6/01874.

References

1. Karpagavalli, S., Chandra, E.: A review on automatic speech recognition architecture and approaches. Int. J. Sig. Process. Image Process. Pattern Recogn. **9**(4), 393–404 (2016)
2. Xu, D., Qian, H., Xu, Y.: The state of the art in human–robot interaction for household services (chap. 6.1). In: Xu, D., Qian, H., Xu, Y. (eds.) Household Service Robotics, pp. 457–465. Academic Press, Oxford (2015)

3. Piotrowska, M., Korvel, G., Kurowski, A., Kostek, B., Czyzewski, A.: Machine learning applied to aspirated and non-aspirated allophone classification—An approach based on audio 'Fingerprinting'. In: 145 Audio Engineering Society Convention (2018)

4. Recasens, D.: A cross-language acoustic study of initial and final allophones of /l/. Speech Commun. **54**(3), 368–383 (2012)

5. German, J.S., Carlson, K., Pierrehumbert, J.B.: Reassignment of consonant allophones in rapid dialect acquisition. J. Phon. **41**(3–4), 228–248 (2013)

6. Drahanský, M., Orság, F.: Fingerprints and speech recognition as parts of the biometry. In: Proceedings of 36th International Conference MOSIS, pp. 177–183 (2002)

7. Noordenbos, M.W., Segers, E., Serniclaes, W., Mitterer, H., Verhoeven, L.: Allophonic mode of speech perception in Dutch children at risk for dyslexia: a longitudinal study. Res. Dev. Disabil. **33**(5), 1469–1483 (2012)

8. Zaporowski, S., Cygert, S., Szwoch, G., Korvel, G., Czyżewski, A.: Rejestracja, parametryzacja i klasyfikacja alofonów z wykorzystaniem bimodalności (2018)

9. Piotrowska, M., Korvel, G., Kostek, B., Ciszewski, T., Czyzewski, A.: Machine learning-based analysis of English lateral allophones. Int. J. Appl. Math. Comput. Sci. **29**(2), 393–405 (2019)

10. Zaporowski, S., Czyżewski, A.: Selection of features for multimodal vocalic segments classification. In: Choroś, K., Kopel, M., Kukla, E., Siemiński, A. (eds.) MISSI 2018. AISC, vol. 833, pp. 490–500. Springer, Cham (2019). https://doi.org/10.1007/978-3-319-98678-4_49

11. Jeevan, M., Dhingra, A., Hanmandlu, M., Panigrahi, B.K.: Robust speaker verification using GFCC based *i*-vectors. In: Lobiyal, D., Mohapatra, D.P., Nagar, A., Sahoo, M. (eds.) Proceedings of the International Conference on Signal, Networks, Computing, and Systems. LNEE, vol. 395, pp. 85–91. Springer, New Delhi (2017). https://doi.org/10.1007/978-81-322-3592-7_9

12. Xu, J., Si, Y., Pan, J., Yan, Y.: Automatic allophone deriving for Korean speech recognition. In: Proceedings - 9th International Conference on Computational Intelligence and Security, CIS 2013, pp. 776–779 (2013)

13. Korvel, G., Kostek, B.: Examining feature vector for phoneme recognition. In: 2017 IEEE International Symposium on Signal Processing and Information Technology (ISSPIT), pp. 394–398 (2017)

14. Kostek, B., Piotrowska, M., Ciszewski, T., Czyzewski, A.: No comparative study of self-organizing maps vs subjective evaluation of quality of allophone pronunciation for non-native English speakers. In: Audio Engineering Society Convention 143 (2017)

15. Kostek, B., et al.: Report of the ISMIS 2011 contest: music information retrieval. In: Kryszkiewicz, M., Rybinski, H., Skowron, A., Raś, Z.W. (eds.) ISMIS 2011. LNCS (LNAI), vol. 6804, pp. 715–724. Springer, Heidelberg (2011). https://doi.org/10.1007/978-3-642-21916-0_75

16. Sikora, T., Kim, H.G., Moreau N.: MPEG-7 Audio and Beyond: Audio Content Indexing and Retrieval. Wiley, Hoboken (2005)

17. Eringis, D., Tamulevičius, G.: Modified filterbank analysis features for speech recognition. Baltic J. Mod. Comput. **3**(1), 29–42 (2015)

18. Zheng, F., Zhang, G., Song, Z.: Comparison of different implementations of MFCC. J. Comput. Sci. Technol. **16**, 582–589 (2001). https://doi.org/10.1007/BF02943243

19. Multimedia Systems Department: Modality Corpus (2018). http://modality-corpus.org/. Accessed 13 Feb 2020

20. Cygert, S., Szwoch, G., Zaporowski, S., Czyzewski, A.: Vocalic segments classification assisted by mouth motion capture. In: 2018 11th International Conference on Human System Interaction (HSI), pp. 318–324 (2018)

21. Bro, R., Smilde, A.K.: Principal component analysis. Anal. Methods **6**, 2812–2831 (2014)

22. Abdi, H., Williams, L.J.: Principal component analysis. Wiley Interdiscip. Rev. Comput. Stat. **2**(4), 433–459 (2010)
23. Geurts, P., Ernst, D., Wehenkel, L.: Extremely randomized trees. Mach. Learn. **63**(1), 3–42 (2006). https://doi.org/10.1007/s10994-006-6226-1
24. Louppe, G., Wehenkel, L., Sutera, A., Geurts, P.: Understanding variable importances in forests of randomized trees. Adv. Neural. Inf. Process. Syst. **26**, 431–439 (2013)
25. Svetnik, V., Liaw, A., Tong, C., Culberson, J.C., Sheridan, R.P., Feuston, B.P.: Random forest: a classification and regression tool for compound classification and QSAR modeling. J. Chem. Inf. Comput. Sci. **43**(6), 1947–1958 (2003)
26. Pedregosa, F., et al.: Scikit-learn: machine learning in Python. J. Mach. Learn. Res. **12**, 2825–2830 (2012)
27. Mao, Y., Pi, D., Liu, Y., Sun, Y.: Accelerated recursive feature elimination based on support vector machine for key variable identification. Chin. J. Chem. Eng. **14**, 65–72 (2006)
28. Chollet, F.: Keras (2015). https://keras.io. Accessed 10 Sept 2018

Toward Court-Admissible Sensor Systems to Fight Domestic Violence

Miguel Ángel Campos Gaviño[✉] and David Larrabeiti López[✉]

University Carlos III of Madrid, Av. Universidad, 30, 28911 Leganés (Madrid), Spain
miguel.angelcg1996@gmail.com, dlarra@it.uc3m.es

Abstract. Gender-based violence is an important problem in nowadays society. A huge number of women are killed every year, and those who survive often live in constant danger because of potential retaliation. In an effort to deal with this problem from a technological perspective, the UC3M4Safety task force has developed an innovative solution to detect stress or violence based on data obtained from smart wearable sensors. The goal is to use that information to trigger alarms and to be used as an admissible evidence in a court of law. The goal of this paper is to design a security architecture for the sensor system addressing all relevant security issues according to the European regulation in terms of data privacy and data protection (General Data Protection Regulation). The design tries to preserve the chain of custody of the data in order to facilitate its consideration as admissible evidence in court.

Keywords: Chain of custody · Data privacy · Gender-based violence

1 Introduction

The goal of this paper is to propose a security architecture for a networked system of wearable sensors called *Bindi*, whose purpose is protecting women from domestic violence, although the solution is applicable to a wide variety of other applications with a common denominator of personal data management with the purpose of generating alarms and digital evidence. Bindi security scheme preserves the chain of custody of all the data collected from the users in such a way that this information has the maximum chances of being regarded as valid evidence in a judicial process. In order to achieve this, several data protection techniques are going to be applied to the system in order to guarantee confidentiality, integrity and availability during the entire data life cycle.

The paper is structured as follows. In Sect. 2 we overview different systems that deal with personal safety application. In Sect. 3 we describe Bindi, the target system to be secured. Then, in Sects. 4 and 5 we present the proposed security

This work has been partially supported by the Department of Research and Innovation of Madrid Regional Authority, through the EMPATIA-CM research project (reference Y2018/TCS-5046).

© Springer Nature Switzerland AG 2020
A. Dziech et al. (Eds.): MCSS 2020, CCIS 1284, pp. 278–291, 2020.
https://doi.org/10.1007/978-3-030-59000-0_21

architecture and its prototype, respectively. As the goal is to create a realistic lawful system legally usable in a wide range of nations, we align the design with the corresponding regulation regarding data privacy and data protection, in particular, the European General Data Protection Regulation (GDPR) [1]. Finally, Sect. 6 is devoted to analyse different security and privacy aspects of this architecture and Sect. 7 draws conclusions.

2   Related Work

Personal safety technology and applications have been multiplying along with the use of smart devices and IoT. The possibility to measure different kind of data with just a smart band and a smartphone, which acts as a centralized data processing unit, has given people the opportunity to infer the overall health status of a person without the need for costly medical equipment. Of course, this information may not be extremely accurate but is precise enough to detect anomalies and emergency situations.

We can see this approach in the two biggest companies that control the smartphone market: Google and Apple. They both have created their own solution to help users when an emergency is detected and to warn emergency services if this situation is confirmed. These are the Personal Safety App [7], developed by Google, and the fall detection functionality [4], which is present in modern Apple Watches. The Personal Safety App uses the GPS localization of the user to detect potential car crashes. Thanks to the algorithms and information provided by the phone, the app is able to detect if a user is travelling by vehicle or on foot. If the car crash detection option is enabled, the smartphone is going to constantly track the user and whenever it detects a strong variation in the speed of the vehicle, it displays an alarm screen. Then, the user has 30 s to cancel the alarm. If not, the smartphone is going to assume there has been an accident and automatically send an alert to emergency services along with its location. Regarding the fall detection functionality, the Apple watch is able to detect strong movements of the user and assume he has fallen, triggering the corresponding alarm. If no response from the user is detected, it will alert emergency services too.

There are also a number of safety applications that incorporate a panic button to trigger emergency calls, including location communication. Some more sophisticated applications also include chat facilities to manage user's own protection contacts, like Guardian Circle [3], featuring different levels of emergency needs. However, to the date, only lawful interception systems run by Law Enforcing Authorities have been designed with a chain of custody guarantees. On the other hand, this does not mean that data generated by other devices, such as smartphones, is not admissible as evidence. Many cases admit recordings, chat conversations (e.g. Whatsapp, Telegram, Messenger) and exchanged pictures as valid, given the authentication implications that are common in a mobile phone. However, seeing the problem from another perspective, it should be clearly stated that technologically-obtained evidence without proper real time witnessing of the data generation process, can not be considered the only basis to prove a crime, as digital information is intrinsically manipulable. Nevertheless, all contextual digital information (location, recordings, sensor data, etc.) can become relevant in court to prove the declaration of what witnesses saw and to help locate the scene, time and people present during a crime. This is the context of our target system.

3 Bindi

3.1 System Overview

Bindi is a wearable system that aims to monitor, record and recognize panic and high-fear-stress emotions in the user, due to sexual or violent attacks, and subsequently trigger a set of alarms. These alarms are going to be triggered through an application installed in the smartphone of the user and will alert emergency services as well as a group of people, called Guardian Circle, chosen by her.

Bindi is composed of two different smart devices connected to the phone via Bluetooth Low Energy (BLE), a lightweight protocol that provides a good autonomy in terms of battery life and bandwidth. Both are equipped with a panic button that the user can press when she feels she is in a dangerous situation. In addition to this, the set of sensors are able to detect fear or stress emotions automatically and trigger an alarm if she is unable to push the panic button. These alarms, as well as the information received from sensors, are going to be managed by an app called Smart Sensor Guard (SSG). When an alarm is triggered, the SSG will alert the Guardian Circle and emergency services, if possible. At the same time, sensors are going to record audio and other information related to the user and its environment. This is going to be properly secured and stored in order to use it as evidence in case a crime is committed.

All the information collected from the user is going to be uploaded to a server and is going to be analyzed by a machine-learning algorithm. This algorithm will train the system in order to improve the detection of high-stress or panic emotions in the user as well as dangerous situations.

3.2 System Components

An overview of system's components is shown in Fig. 1. The system is composed of three different entities:

- Smart Bracelet (SB): used to monitor physiological variables from the user and to detect panic or high-stress emotions due to violent situations.
- Smart Pendant (SP): used for detecting stress or panic situations with the help of audio recordings.
- Smart Sensor Guard (SSG) App: installed in the smartphone of the user, it is connected with both the SB and the SP in order to receive the information. It is going to process the data and classify the emotion being felt by the user, triggering an alarm if an emergency is detected. If that was the case, it would alert the corresponding people with the location of the user.

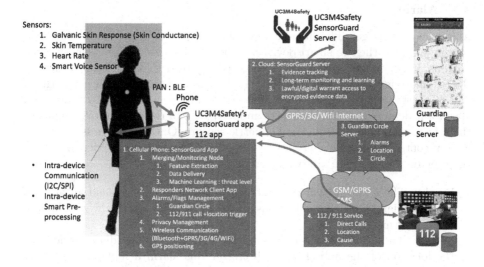

Fig. 1. Communication scheme of Bindi (Source: UC3M4Safety Bindi Software Specification. Anu and Naveen Jain women's safety XPRIZE)

The two devices of Bindi can work either separately or together. The highest degree of safety is achieved when both the SB an the SP are operating together. However, a reasonable degree of safety is assured when only a single device is active, apart from the smartphone.

3.3 Communication System

We are able to differentiate three different communication procedures involved in Bindi. A full communication scheme is previously shown in Fig. 1. Each one uses a different channel:

- Smart devices and Smartphone: Both the SP and the SB are going to be connected to the smartphone via a wireless BLE connection. All the information received from the physiological sensors is going to be sent to the smartphone through this link. The BLE protocol provides better performance than other wireless protocols. Regarding power consumption, it offers a better ratio power/transmitted bits with a higher transmission efficiency. In addition to this, the market offers low-cost implementation, even for wearable-oriented products.
- Smartphone and Bindi's servers: All the information sent from smart devices to the phone and the data generated by the phone is going to be uploaded to the server through Internet. In addition to this, alarms sent to the Guardian Circle are going to be sent to Bindi's servers too.
- Smartphone and Emergency services: They are going to contact emergency services over GSM/GPRS/SMS and will also send the exact location of the user with the help of the official 112 app.

3.4   Alarms

Alarms can be triggered in different ways. The simplest way is to press the panic button in any of the two smart devices. If the user is unable to press those panic buttons, it is possible to say a preconfigured keyword that will be recorded by the SP and trigger an alarm immediately. However, if the user can not perform any of those actions, it is still possible for Bindi to automatically trigger an alarm if it detects that the user fears and may be in a risky situation, thanks to the information coming from the biometric sensors. Once an alarm is triggered, it may contact emergency services or only the Guardian Circle, depending on the type of alarm. There are two types of alarms:

– Level 0: These alarms will call emergency services and also send an alert to the Guardian Circle. Panic buttons and alarm keywords will always generate level 0 alarms.
– Level 1: These alarms will only send an alert to the Guardian Circle with the location of the user. Bindi will trigger this alarm if it detects panic or high-stress emotions in the user. The user then will have a limited amount of time to enter the deactivation code. If this action is not performed, this will turn into a Level 0 alarm.

An alarm can be deactivated through a previously configured deactivation keyword or a deactivation code that has to be input in the smartphone. If not, the SSG is going to send the alert to the Guardian Circle and the emergency services depending on the alarm. In the meantime, the microphone present in the SP is going to record audio of the enviroment and store it securely for its later use during the trial.

4   Proposed Data Management Design

The proposed architecture is shown in Fig. 2. It is composed of five different main actors:

– User: client of Bindi and user of the SSG app. Bindi is going to process biometric data obtained from her sensors.
– Machine Learning: machine learning process that will read the information stored in the database in order to improve the fear detection algorithm for each client.
– Judge: corresponding authority in charge of the judicial investigation who requests access to evidences stored in the user's database.

– Bindi Server: The server will act as an intermediary between clients and the database. It is going to authenticate users, process the data and store it in the database.

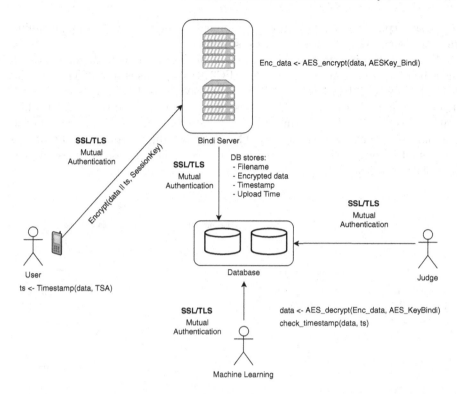

Fig. 2. Proposed communication system

- <u>Database</u>: The information obtained from clients as well as the data generated by Bindi is going to be stored here. The database is placed inside a Virtual Private Network (VPN) in order to isolate it from the Internet and not to expose it to external attacks. Additionally, it will make use of SFTP to make the data available to the judge.

The communication among all these entities is going to be protected through a TLS session. For that reason, we are creating our own Certification Authority (CA) that will issue and sign every certificate involved in the communication. Each entity is going to be given a certificate and use it to create the secure channel.

4.1 Data Life Cycle

A summary of this process is shown in Fig. 3. First, information is captured by sensors. If these are either the necklace sensor or the smartwatch sensor, the data is sent to the smartphone through the Bluetooth Low Energy (BLE) link. This protocol includes data encryption during transmission, and thus the information is protected against eavesdropping attacks. Some sensors are located in the smartphone and data is directly obtained by the SSG application, meaning that no transmission between devices is needed.

When all the information is received, a process of a trusted timestamping must be carried out. According to the RFC3161 [11], this is to be done with the help of a Trusted Third Party (TTP). Nowadays, this TTP role is taken by a Time Stamping Authority (TSA). These entities will receive the hash of a file, concatenate it with the datetime when the data has been received and sign the outcome with their own private key. The result is a digital time stamp that can be trusted as long as the TSA is trusted. The complete process of timestamping is explained in Sect. 4.2.

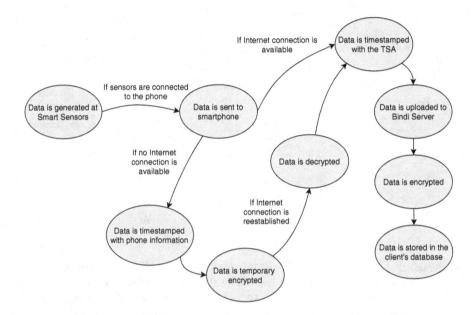

Fig. 3. Overview of the data life cycle from its collection to its storage

At this point, we have considered two possible scenarios: the phone is able to reach the server and upload the information or the device has no Internet connection, hence can not upload the data. If no connectivity is available, information is going to be stored until the connection is reestablished and then uploaded. The impossibility to connect to the server is not desirable, as evidences may never reach the server and could not be used during the trial. If that was the case, it would still be possible to present the phone as an evidence and retrieve the information kept in it. Consequently, it is reasonable to secure the data and store it for later purposes. Therefore, data is going to be encrypted and stored in the internal memory of the smartphone. This procedure is shown in Sect. 4.3. However, if the device is lost or destroyed, evidences will also be lost.

When favorable internet conditions are met, data is uploaded to the server through the secure channel created by the TLS session. The server is going to receive the generated file and check its integrity with the signature. If everything is correct, data is going to be encrypted and stored it in the personal database created for the client. This is going to be done with the help of the user associated to the client. This user only has permissions to insert new data in the database, in other words, it is not able to read or modify previously existing information in the database. Once the information is correctly uploaded, it is only going to be decrypted and accessible under two different cases:

1. The machine learning algorithm needs to access the data in order to update parameters for the fear detection algorithm created for the client.
2. A judge wants to retrieve evidences for the judicial investigation.

Client information is going to be stored in the database during the time the client uses the service provided. Once she decides to delete her account, the information is also going to be deleted. However, due to legal reasons, biometric data and audio recordings are going to be stored a maximum of 30 days.

4.2   Data Timestamping

Once the data is retrieved, we have considered two possible scenarios for implementing the trusted timestamping procedure. In the first one, the phone has internet connectivity and is able to contact the TSA in order to create the time stamp without problem. In the second one, no connection is available and it is impossible for the client to create a trusted time stamp for the file. We are going to discuss the approach taken for the second scenario.

There are different options that can be taken. It may seem reasonable to simply wait for connection and query the TSA as soon as it is reestablished. However, it could be the case that it is never reestablished. This assumption fits perfectly under our scenario. Whenever a crime has been committed, phones are usually stolen or destroyed. Nonetheless, they may still receive information from the biometric devices and store evidences of a potential crime, if they are in range to keep the Bluetooth connection alive. Therefore, we must take into account the chain of custody: securely store this information in the device and provide a trusted timestamping for files.

It is difficult to obtain a trusted time stamp without the possibility of querying a TTP and there are many reasons for that. First of all, we can not trust the system's datetime, as it may be misconfigured or even modified by a third person in order to create fake time stamps. In the case of a crime, it would be possible for the attacker to manipulate the datetime of the system, making this way impossible for us to determine the exact time when the data was created. Another option would be to manually set a timer within the application to keep track of the creation of each file. However, this idea was also discarded because as soon as the phone is restarted or powered off, every running process will be terminated and the timer would stop.

The proposed solution aims to delimit the time stamp in a time lapse where the data has been created and that can be trusted. The SSG application is going to store the last trusted time stamp that was returned by the TSA, which will provide us a lower boundary of the data creation time. Then, as soon as the connectivity is restored, the TSA is going to be queried again and a second trusted time stamp is going to be issued. The result is a trusted time frame when the file has been created. However, we need to keep in mind that several files can be generated while the phone is not connected. Therefore, it is necessary to establish an order among them. For this reason, we are going to set a counter in every file that will show us the creation sequence of all the data. Finally, if the phone is never coming back online and we need to determine the exact time when a file has been created, it would be useful to determine a precise time reference for the data. The lower boundary time offered by the last saved time stamp of the TSA and the ordered sequence of files are not enough in the trial to prove the exact creation time of a file. Hence, we have taken the date of the system to accomplish this and we have created another time stamp with it. Even though this last time stamp can not be fully trusted, the date of the system seems a reasonable time reference in this particular scenario. If the phone is retrieved, a forensic analysis could easily determine whether this time source can be trusted or not.

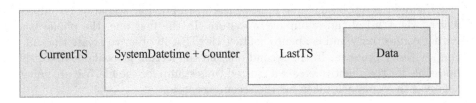

Fig. 4. Data timestamping scheme of a file if no Internet connection was available

As a summary, the first time stamp is going to be created with the time reference of the last time stamp retrieved by the TSA. The private key of the user is going to be used in this process. Then, the second time stamp is going to be generated with the current system date and a counter. Lastly, if the phone restores connection to the Internet, a third time stamp issued by the TSA is going to be created and the data is going to be updated to the server of Bindi. The resulting schema is represented in Fig. 4.

The proposed solution offers the following advantages in a worst-case scenario:

1. We are able to delimit the time when a file was created thanks to the two trusted time references as soon as the phone reconnects to the Internet.
2. If several files are created while the phone is offline, we have a time reference of its creation obtained from the system's datetime. This can be trusted if we prove that no time manipulation has been carried out in the phone.
3. Even if the system's datetime is not valid or has been manipulated, it is still possible to establish an order relation among every file while the phone was offline.

4.3 Data Encryption

There are two main phases where encryption should be focused on: during transmission and during storage. The encryption during transmission aims to prevent third parties from gaining information while data is being exchanged between two entities. On the other side, storage encryption tries to prevent information gaining when files are compromised due to security breaches or data leakages.

Transmission. The Secure Socket Layer (SSL) [6] and the Transport Layer Security (TLS) [9] are cryptographic protocols that provide authentication, data integrity and data encryption between two parties. A secure communication channel is established and all the exchanged data is protected with the session key that has been previously agreed by both parties. Before the session is established, a handshake is performed. During this handshake, different aspects like the cryptographic algorithm used for encrypting the data are agreed and the authentication is carried out.

However, under a classic TLS session the client does not authenticate against the server. Because of this, an additional step is required and a mutual authentication procedure is carried out. This means, the client sends her own digital certificate to the server and it and checks its signature. If everything is correct, the client is authenticated. For this reason, we have developed our own CA in Bindi. This CA is going to issue and send every client a signed digital certificate so that mutual authentication can be carried out. Each time a client wants to connect to the server, she is first going to present a valid certificate to establish a TLS session and then encrypt the information with the session key.

Storage. Files received by phone are usually uploaded as soon as they are processed so there is no need for encryption at that point. However, if no connection is available, data need to be securely stored. Therefore, every file is going to be encrypted with a symmetric encryption algorithm like AES and stored in the internal memory of the phone. The key used for this is going to be derived from the private key of the user with the help of a Key Derivation Function (KDF), an algorithm that is able to create a cryptographic key from a passphrase. Once the phone reconnects to the Internet, data is going to decrypted and uploaded to the server.

In the case of the database, data containing sensitive information of the user is going to be encrypted with a symmetric encryption algorithm and an encryption key property of Bindi. This information is only going to be decrypted in two scenarios: when the machine learning process needs to read the database in order to improve the detection algorithm, and when the judge is carrying out an investigation.

5 Prototype

At the moment, the UC3M team is developing a prototype version of Bindi, both in the hardware and the software side. The front-end of the SSG app is on its first version and now the backend is being produced. In order to create a demo version of the security architecture, we have created a group of scripts that emulates the client, the server and the timestamp service. These can be found in the following repository[1], along with instructions. There are three main scripts:

- client.py: This script is going to take a file and its time stamp, connect to the server and upload them. This script corresponds to the SSG app in the smartphone of the client
- server.py: This script is going to receive files from the client, encrypt them and upload them to the personal database of the client. It corresponds to the Bindi Server.
- timestamp.py: This script receives a file as a parameter and timestamps it with the help of a trusted third party called freeTSA [5] (Fig. 5).

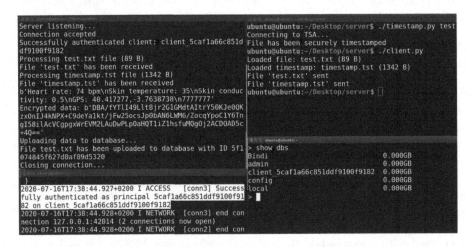

Fig. 5. Demo scripts for the prototype. Top left: Bindi server. Top right: timestamping and client script. Bottom left: MongoDB logs. Bottom right: MongoDB structure

The database has been created using MongoDB and filled with sample data. User authentication and access control have been implemented with the help of the custom root CA created for Bindi. Each actor has been given a certificate in order to create the TLS session and secure the communication.

6   Security Analysis

6.1   Risk Assessment

According to the Article 30 of the GDPR, it is mandatory for every data controller and data processor to document the treatments applied to the personal

---

[1] https://github.com/MaxPowell/Bindi.

information in the Records of Processing Activities. After that, in the Article 35.1, it is stated that the controller must perform a risk analysis in case there is a treatment of information that falls into the special category data or if there is a high risk situation for the subject. This analysis must be documented in the Data Protection Impact Assessment (DPIA). As Bindi works with biometric data, which is categorized as special category data, both documents have been written and the main findings of the risk analysis are the following:

- **Compromise of the information stored in the phone**: The smartphone of the user acts as a centralized point for all the information that is going to be uploaded to the server. Therefore, it is a weak spot for obtaining the information. There are two main ways to achieve this: the smartphone is rooted and the user can bypass most security measures implemented or the smartphone gets infected with malware and takes advantage of a vulnerability to steal the information.

  In order to mitigate this risk, we are preventing the user from installing the SSG app in a rooted device and recommend her to follow good security practices when using her device.

- **Compromise of the Bindi server infraestructure**: The server deployed for intercepting all the clients' requests acts as a bottleneck and could compromise the service in case of failure. In addition to this, it is the entry door to all the information stored in the database, as it has valid credentials for the VPN. As a result, countermeasures to prevent this from happenning must be applied.

  Apart from duplicating the number of servers and databases for adding redundancy, perimetral security has to be implemented. Firewalls and load balancers will be placed between the Internet and Bindi. In addition to this, different tools such as Fail2Ban [2] or SSHGuard [10] are recommended to prevent brute-force attacks and hardenize the host. At the database side, it is important to have a robust access control mechanism with defined roles and to perform exhaustive logging and monitoring to prevent potential threats.

6.2 Possible Improvements

During the development of Bindi several decisions both from the technical side and from the regulatory side had to be taken in order to comply with the European legislation and to provide a secure service for the user. However, there are still some aspects of the security of Bindi that may require an improvement.

Certification Authority for Bindi. The main purpose for creating a self-signed Certification Authority for Bindi is to establish mutual authentication TLS session between each actor that is going to either send or receive the data. This mutual authentication procedure would add more consistency and trust to the investigation in case a crime is commited and user information is requested to Bindi. However, in order to provide a trustable service, it would be mandatory to get the Bindi's Root certificate signed by a CA. According to this article written by Microsoft [8], this represents a considerable amount of money and could put at risk the whole project. Consequently, low-budget implementation should be explored.

The solution for this could be divided into client authentication and host authentication. In order to authenticate the client without the use of a certificate, another passwordless mobile oriented solution could be implemented, like FIDO. Once the user is authenticated, the procedure would be the same as the one explained in Sect. 4 taking into account that under this scenario only servers would be able to authenticate during the TLS session. When it comes to host authentication, it could still be posible to use a self-signed certificate to create a mutual authentication TLS session, as most part of the communication involved is going to be internal in the Bindi private network.

On Premise vs Cloud. Even though the original idea is to deploy an On Premise solution for Bindi, there are several challenges that need to be solved in order to reach a considerable level of security in the infrastructure. These can be the monitoring, logging, availability, at-rest encryption or even the escalability of the system. Spending a considerable amount of money necessary for developing all security measures on local could not be optimal and as a result different cloud solutions like AWS or GCP should also be explored.

The problematic point of the cloud approach would be that we are trusting highly sensitive personal information to a third party. This decision could lead to a rejection from the user due to its growing online privacy awareness and online bad security practices concern. Therefore, this decision should be carefully analyzed before the market launch.

7   Conclusions

The focus of this paper was the design of a security architecture for Bindi that could make collected biometric and recorded audio information be accepted as evidence in a trial, by preserving integrity of data and the chain of custody throughout its entire lifecycle. Data collection and management is also performed in compliance with the current regulation in terms of data protection and data privacy. Security principles such as confidentiality, integrity and availability have been taken into acount in the design and subsequent security analysis. The non-repudiation principle plays also a very important role for the project as the attribution of a crime depends directly on it.

References

1. Regulation (EU) 2016/679 of the European parliament and of the council of 27 April 2016 on the protection of natural persons with regard to the processing of personal data and on the free movement of such data, and repealing directive 95/46/ec (general data protection regulation). OJ L 119, pp. 1–88, 4 May 2016. http://data.europa.eu/eli/reg/2016/679/oj

2. Fail2ban. https://www.fail2ban.org/wiki/index.php/Main_Page. Accessed 09 Feb 2020
3. Guardian circle. https://guardiancircle.com/. Accessed 09 Feb 2020
4. Apple: fall detection functionality. https://support.apple.com/en-us/HT208944. Accessed 09 Feb 2020
5. FreeTSA.org: Freetsa. https://www.freetsa.org/index_en.php. Accessed 09 Feb 2020
6. Freier, A.O., Karlton, P., Kocher, P.C.: The secure sockets layer (SSL) protocol version 3.0. RFC 6101, August 2011. https://doi.org/10.17487/RFC6101, https://rfc-editor.org/rfc/rfc6101.txt
7. Google: personal safety app. https://play.google.com/store/apps/details?id=com.google.android.apps.safetyhub. Accessed 09 Feb 2020
8. Microsoft: certification authority root signing. https://social.technet.microsoft.com/wiki/contents/articles/5973.certification-authority-root-signing.aspx. Accessed 09 Feb 2020
9. Rescorla, E.: The transport layer security (TLS) protocol version 1.3. RFC 8446, August 2018. https://doi.org/10.17487/RFC8446. https://rfc-editor.org/rfc/rfc8446.txt
10. SSHGuard: SSHGuard. https://sshguard.net/. Accessed 09 Feb 2020
11. Zuccherato, R., Cain, P., Adams, D.C., Pinkas, D.: Internet X.509 public key infrastructure time-stamp protocol (TSP). RFC 3161, August 2001. https://doi.org/10.17487/RFC3161. https://rfc-editor.org/rfc/rfc3161.txt

A VCA-Based Approach to Enhance Learning Data Sets for Object Classification

Remigiusz Baran[1]([⊠]) [iD] and Andrzej Zeja[2] [iD]

[1] Department of Computer Science, Electronics and Electrical Engineering, Kielce University of Technology, Kielce, Poland
r.baran@tu.kielce.pl
[2] Department of Teleinformatics, University of Computer Engineering and Telecommunications, Kielce, Poland
a.Zeja@Wstkt.Pl

Abstract. This paper presents a novel approach to solving the problem of poor learning data in complex object classification task. It efficiently combines the Visual Content Analysis technique known as the Scalable Vocabulary Tree (SVT) and contour-based descriptors to recommend new training samples. The SVT technique uses the SIFT features to identify and accurately localize objects of interest within the visual content of the processed query images. Despite the small learning data set its classification accuracy is pretty good and matches the accuracy of a dedicated CNN network trained under the same conditions. However, due to the ability of fast and effective incremental learning, it overcomes the convnet type networks. Contour-based classification based on Point Distance Histogram (PDH) is utilized then to increase the classification certainty. During this stage, the PDH descriptors representing a given object of interest are matched against descriptors stored in the pattern database, where each object is represented by a collection of 360 pattern outlines extracted from its 3D model. As finally reported, such an exact pattern representation allows for achieving a high classification accuracy of the entire approach.

Keywords: Poor dataset quality · CNN · SVT · Incremental learning · Shape descriptor · 3D models

1 Introduction

The amount of data stored in and transferred over the Internet is increasing rapidly. As reported in [1] the storage capacity of the Internet "is doubling in size every two years". This hard to imagine a source of data, especially visual data, which is the most rapidly-growing type of media on the Internet, gives nowadays pretty real opportunities to build intelligent computer vision systems where intelligence, in general, comes from content analysis of this visual data.

Facebook's face recognition service, which is capable of automatically tag persons on added photos in an example of a successful solution of this type which helps Facebook users to manage their photos and protect them against Facebook stalking. Namely, it is

© Springer Nature Switzerland AG 2020
A. Dziech et al. (Eds.): MCSS 2020, CCIS 1284, pp. 292–306, 2020.
https://doi.org/10.1007/978-3-030-59000-0_22

based on the DeepFace - a deep learning facial recognition system, which was created by the Facebook AI Research (FAIR) team in 2014[1]. According to [2], 4 million facial images taken from Facebook, with the permission of around 4,000 Facebook users, were used to train the DeepFace network.

Another pretty successful and promising visual content analysis engine has been created by Google LLC. Its admirable abilities can be verified by using the Google Lens mobile app[2], which uses the phone's camera to scan the camera view and identify elements of its content. Its standard facilities include recognizing text, plants, animals, and popular landmarks to show then information relevant to recognized objects provided as a result of searching the Internet.

The companies mentioned above – Facebook Inc. Google LCC, are not the only leaders in implementing solutions in the field of artificial intelligence based on content analysis of visual data. In addition to them, the leading role in this field also play such enterprises as IBM, Microsoft Corporation, Clarifai, Inc., Amazon.com Inc., CloudSight, Inc., and many others. A common feature of the listed companies is serving a cloud-based image analysis, including object and scene recognition, facial detection and recognition[3], explicit content, logo, and landmark detection, tagging images, categorizing them and identifying image types[4], etc.

Good quality image databases on which the above solutions have been trained and tested are the main and the obvious sources of their success. It is because the accuracy of a given predictive model depends mainly on the quality of the historical data used to train it. Quality standards that the historical data must meet are exceptionally broad and high. First of all, the historical data set need to be right, what means that it has to be unbiased, free of duplicates, properly labeled and must take into account the entire range of possible inputs.

The development of qualitatively good data for deep learning systems is difficult and complex. This requires a very good understanding of the needs of the predictive model being built, well-defined image registration and labeling procedures, elimination of human errors, and so forth. Therefore, still, the most common way to ensure good data quality is to look through large and chaotic sets and selecting the right data manually by data scientists who are directly involved in building the predictive model. Since, however, the set of even several thousand samples (images) is usually considered too small and insufficient [3], such a manual approach, due to its time-consuming and arduous nature, "is the problem data scientists complain about most"[5] - it usually takes up to 80% of their time[6].

A solution, based on Visual Content Analysis techniques [4], that is capable to minimize the above defects of the right data preparation is presented in the paper. An intelligent data enhancement architecture known also as Content Discovery and Enrichment Engine (CD&EE), is the main element of this solution.

---

[1] https://ai.facebook.com/.

[2] https://lens.google.com/.

[3] https://aws.amazon.com/rekognition/.

[4] https://cloudsight.ai/.

[5] https://hbr.org/2018/04/if-your-data-is-bad-your-machine-learning-tools-are-useless.

[6] https://hbr.org/2016/12/breaking-down-data-silos?autocomplete=true.

More detailed information on the CD&EE engine and its data recommendation capabilities will be given in the remainder of this paper which is structured as follows. Background information together with a clear description of requirements and methodologies of processing visual data by the CD&EE engine is provided in Sect. 2. The problem of low data quality along with an example of a deep learning approach to recognizing a given category of objects of interest, trained under the conditions of this problem, is also discussed in this Section. The proposed "VCA-based approach to enhance learning data sets for object classification" as well as the way of generating contour patterns based on 3D models of objects, which is an essential element of the proposed approach, are presented, in turn, in Sect. 3. The effectiveness of the proposed method, examined with the use of selected sample test objects, is reported, in turn, in Sect. 4. The summary of the paper, including directions of future works, is finally given in Sect. 5.

2 Background and Motivation for the Research

The CD&EE engine mentioned above operates both as object recognition and data recommendation system for the needs of the Knowledge Base Processes Management Platform (KBPMP) of the INRED system, where the INRED system is an expected outcome of the B&R project of the same name, the subject of which is: "An intelligent system for effective analysis of diagnostic and repair work of industrial devices using mobile units and advanced image analysis". More specifically, the development of an innovative system supporting employees in the implementation of repair and repair works, as well as diagnostic services for industrial devices, as well as ensuring a significant increase in work safety while increasing quality is the main objective of this project[7].

One of the most important tasks to be implemented by the INRED system is the automation of supervision over ongoing works with the ability to quickly respond to life-threatening events due to the integration of all system components through the developed Knowledge Base Processes Management Platform (KBPMP), where providing automation of decision-making and renovation processes is, in general, the goal of the KBPMP platform. The KMPMP platform integrates many different specialized modules, including inter alia:

- Knowledge Base Repository (KBR) and Semantic Search Engine – modules aimed to add and manage knowledge for accumulating all repair and renovation procedures, which will allow for accelerating employee training in the implementation of complex repair tasks,
- Object and Threat Recognition Module - an intelligent system of object recognition and threat detection and prediction during renovation and diagnostic works,
- Video and Data Stream Management Platform – a platform designated, in general, as a source of pre-processed (e.g. abstracted – in the case of video streams) visual data for Knowledge Base Repository, documenting, for example, the repair procedures (a source of historical data for predictive models build for the needs of e.g. Semantic Search Engine and Object and Threat Recognition Module).

---

[7] http://www.doosanbabcock.com/pl/intro/projekt-inred/.

The arrangement of the above modules in the entire organizational structure of the INRED system is depicted in Fig. 1. According to this Fig. 1, the KBPMP platform enables the integration of all system modules. It uses the KBR repository which stores repair scenarios and renovation procedures devoted to various devices, equipment, and industrial valves, constituting the subject of the INRED system recipients' activities.

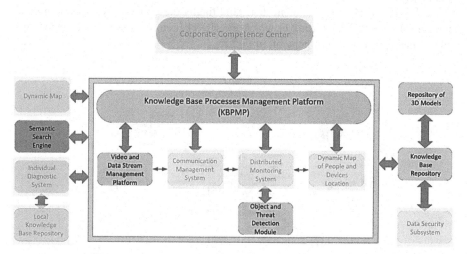

Fig. 1. An overall organizational chart of the INRED system.

The repository is also (and perhaps above all) a source of all additional complementary documentation, i.e. technical drawings, 3D models, photos, instructional films, recordings of previously performed repairs, etc., which may help develop (prepare) new renovation procedures. To fulfill this requirement, the above documents are made available to contractors via the Semantic Search Engine. This means, however, that any documents that are to be truly accessible must first be indexed, including the content of the visual data. In general, multimedia indexing is the process that allows efficiently and accurately retrieve different multimedia content items: images, videos, animated gifs, 3D objects, etc., at the required granularity level. Automatic indexing of visual data is the domain of Visual Content Analysis (VCA) [4], that, in general, may be based on various machine learning techniques, including neural networks, deep learning, Bayes networks, decision trees, rule systems, soft computing methods, etc. The component of the Knowledge Base Repository, which is responsible for the VCA tasks is known as the Content Discovery and Enrichment Engine.

2.1 Content Discovery and Enrichment Engine

The Discovery and Enrichment Engine (CD&EE) has been designed and implemented as a system based on microservices. According to the above, all its components, known, in general, as Metadata Enhancement (MES) Services [5], their properties, capabilities, etc. must fit the microservices architecture specifications [6]. For this reason, it gains versatility and flexibility and also ensures long-term agility in all areas of its possible applications. The CD&EE engine has been implemented as a distributed system based on Service-Oriented Architecture (SOA) while its MES services are RESTful web services with their REST-based interfaces. Based on their RESTful API, MES services are capable to exchange messages between each other as well as with other parts of the INRED system, including e.g. the repository of 3D models. This allows them to access and process different multimedia content items and finally enrich them by expanding their metadata. The concept according to which the CD&EE engine has been designed and implemented is illustrated, in general, in Fig. 2.

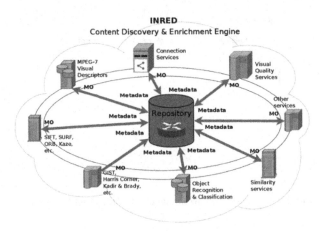

Fig. 2. Content discovery and enrichment engine of the INRED system.

The CD&EE engine is fully scalable, which means that it can be combined with many different MES services. It is also fully reconfigurable, which, in turn, means that its MES services can be called according to specific processing requirements.

At the moment many different MES services have been implemented and incorporated into the CD&EE engine. Most of them address the tasks of Visual Content Analysis. These include inter-alia, general-purpose services, for example, services that apply selected feature transformations (SIFT, ORB, MSER, etc.) or MPEG-7 Visual Descriptors applications to images and video frames and extract their visual descriptions. There are also more specialized VCA services, which e.g. implement different approaches to object detection and classification, including approaches based directly on selected image features as well as on deep learning techniques. The small amount and low quality of test data available at the moment is the reason for using both of the above-mentioned machine learning methodologies. As will be shown later in the paper, they can complement each other pretty well under such restrictions.

2.2   CNN-Based Service for Object Detection and Classification

MES services are dedicated applications or processes that are fully independent of each other but they can work together using the API communication interface. They can be implemented using different frameworks and languages, and run on different operating systems and platforms, and can benefit from different APIs, as illustrated, in general, in Fig. 3.

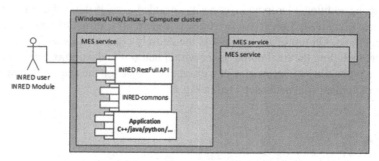

Fig. 3. Activity diagram of INRED's MES services

The example CNN-based object detection and classification service described in this sub-section has been implemented using the Keras library[8] with the TensorFlow framework[9] as its backend. The data set for learning and testing its convolutional neural network (known also as the convnet network) was collected as a set of video frames extracted from the sample recordings of the renovation procedures of five different types of devices and industrial valves that are elements of power station equipment. Examples of images from this set are shown in Fig. 4.

Fig. 4. Sample input images for CNN-based object detection and classification service.

As shown in Fig. 4 recordings that were made accessible, were recorded in conditions typical for the interiors of the power plants, i.e. in low light and the presence of a large number of different details forming the background. Besides, the duration of these recordings allowed the selection of only 67 frames in total for all 5 categories (classes) of elements. The above collection has been finally split into train and test sets, with 46 and 21 images, respectively. To meet such a challenge and mitigate overfitting, a data augmentation technique has been used, consisting of shifting initial dataset images along both axes (by a maximum of 20% of their original width or height) and zooming them out or zooming in (by 10%). Given that the total number of epochs the model was trained

---

[8] https://keras.io/.

[9] https://www.tensorflow.org/neural_structured_learning/framework.

for was 30, the size of the training set has been increased in this way to 1380 color (three channels) images with dimensions 224 × 224.

The modeled convnet is a stack of alternated Conv2D and MaxPooling2D layers with stride value 2. All layers, except the last one, are with ReLU activation. To further reduce overfitting, an additional Dropout layer has been added to scale down the output by the dropout rate equal to 0.3 or, in other words, to ignore 30% of neuron outputs during a particular pass. On top of the convent is the densely connected classifier consisting of 2 layers including the final output layer with 5 neurons and softmax activation, that returns the probability of occurrence of a given class object on the analyzed image. The topology of applied convnet is depicted in Fig. 5.

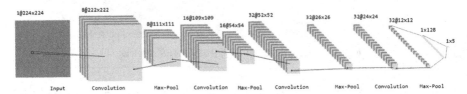

Fig. 5. The topology of applied convnet.

Since the presented problem assumes multi-class single-label classification, a categorical cross-entropy was chosen as a function of the model's loss. For the first 20 epochs, the learning rate was 1e−4 and then, for the next 10 epochs, it was reduced to 1e−5. Because the network solves the problem for a very small amount of data, 50 models were trained and their results were averaged. The average classification accuracy achieved in this way is 0.7533 while the average loss is 0.7904. The graphs depicted in Fig. 6 show the average values of the loss function (Fig. 6a) and the classification accuracy for all 50 models (Fig. 6b).

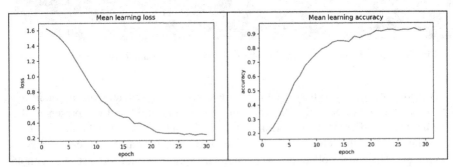

Fig. 6. The average values of a) the loss function and b) the classification accuracy for all 50 models.

Obtained classification accuracy is obviously insufficient, especially due to the much larger expected number of object categories to be recognized in the implemented version of the INRED system. This suggests the need for the capability of automatic or at least semi-automatic improvement of the input dataset quality. To improve its quality, the input dataset must be first enriched by adding new, right, not duplicated, and correctly labeled data. This, in turn, requires some kind of recommendation that CD&EE can successfully provide. A solution that can provide it is introduced in the next section.

3 Proposed Recommendation Approach

The problem of detection and classification of objects presented so far relates directly to situations known from the real world, in which information (educational data) is hardly available in its entirety at the same time. The scenario according to which data is collected gradually, incrementally over time, is much more common. This is also the scenario that applies to the INRED project.

Although convnet networks have become in recent years state-of-the-art for image classification tasks, their training on gradually collected data is still an unresolved problem. Due to the issue referred to as hyperparameter tuning or the tendency of catastrophic forgetting, which leads to a sudden and complete loss of taught knowledge after learning new data, re-training of the model from scratch, using the entire available dataset (containing both old and new data) is still a standard approach [7]. However, training the model from scratch, especially for large scale classification tasks, is computationally expensive and time-consuming. For example, it takes up to 2 weeks to train a 50-layer ResNet on ImageNet[10] from scratch on an NVIDIA M40 (GPU) graphics processor [8]. Of course, a large number of GPUs and highly parallel training, as well as distributed computing with extreme scalability, can significantly reduce this time. Other techniques, referred e.g. to as model compression [9] are also able to accelerate the training process. Nevertheless, such approaches require huge computer resources or additional efforts that increase software development costs. Therefore, pretty different approaches, known as incremental learning methods, are gaining popularity recently. They provide, in general, solutions to learn additional information only from new data with leveraging past knowledge [10]. Still, however, finding a good compromise between accuracy and required resources remains a challenge.

The last of the cited works, however, brought us associations with the technique known as Scalable Vocabulary Tree (SVT) [11] from the category of object recognition methods based on intentionally selected features, which we have already used successfully in our research [12]. In general, the SVT technique is used to create a hierarchy of features, which are organized as tree nodes. The SVT algorithm has evolved from the Bag-of-Features (BoF) method with the k-mean clustering algorithm as the base. It outperforms the BoF method due to its ability to generate a large codebook of centroids with light calculations. Besides, the SVT tree is a very compact representation of image patches. It is "simply one or two integers which should be contrasted to the hundreds of bytes or floats used for descriptor vectors" [11]. However, the most important advantage of the SVT technique is that it truly allows updating the model only by adding new data or classes [11]. That is why we finally decided to base the approach for improving learning data sets for object classification precisely on this technique.

---

[10] http://www.image-net.org/.

3.1 The SVT Algorithm

A multilevel hierarchy of features, known as the vocabulary tree **VT**, is initiated by k-means clustering that is carried out over the "bag" of visual words extracted from the dataset of training images – **TD**, which can be described as follows:

$$TD = \{TI_1, TI_2, \ldots, TI_{NC}\} \tag{1}$$

where:

TI_i – set of training images of class i,
$TI_i = \{TI_1, \ldots TI_m\}$, where m is fixed for all classes,
NC – number of classes.

The "bag" of visual words can be, in turn, described by a set of feature vectors **F**, extracted from **TI** images belonging to the dataset **TD**, given as follows:

$$F = \{F_{T1}, F_{T2}, \ldots, F_{TNC}\} \tag{2}$$

where:

F_{Ti}, – set of feature vectors extracted from training images of a given set TI_i,
$F_{Ti} = \{s_1, \ldots s_n\}$, where n varies across F_{Ti} instances.

The k-means algorithm is used then also to iteratively subdivide these initial clusters into smaller groups, which centroids, after a predetermined number of iterations, create the final codebook. In other words, k stands in that case for the SVT parameter known as "branching_factor" B, which determines the number of children of each node of the vocabulary tree. Next, distinct clusters of features are assigned to such children nodes, wherein tree nodes are getting smaller (after successive subdivisions), clusters of features assigned to these nodes are also getting smaller. The "depth" parameter L determines, in turn, the number of levels (the depth) of the created tree. In parallel, visual features **F** extracted from the training data set **TD** are propagated down the **VT**, along with references to training images of their origin. Summing the above up, the vocabulary tree **VT** is created using hierarchical k-means clustering and consists of:

$$C = B^L \text{ codewords } v_{l,h} \in VT \tag{3}$$

where:

B – branch factor, L – the depth of VT,
$l \in \{0, 1 \ldots, L\}$ – level of the codeword,
$h \in \{1, 2 \ldots, B^L\}$ – index of the codeword (at particular l).

The number of feature vectors assigned to each cluster builds weighted relations between tree nodes and training images. These relations form an object known as "image database" where references to training images are stored in an indexed manner. This type of indexing makes it possible to very fast retrieve or classify images according to their visual content.

To predict a class of a given query image QI, its descriptors $\mathbf{F}_{QI} = \{\mathbf{d}_1, \ldots \mathbf{d}_z\}$, where z varies from one QI image to another, must be first quantized. This is done in the same way as when the **VT** is created. Next, the Term Frequency – Inverse Document Frequency (TF-IDF) [11] scoring scheme is applied to determine which item in the "image database" **I** is most relevant to the query image QI. The FQI descriptors, which are the most common for a given image and at the same time rarely "appear" in other images got higher TF-IDF scores s that are defined as follows:

$$s(QI, \mathbf{I}) = \left\| \frac{QI}{\|QI\|} - \frac{\mathbf{I}}{\|\mathbf{I}\|} \right\| \tag{4}$$

3.2 Flowchart of the Approach

For the above reasons, we suggest using the SVT algorithm to detect and classify images and video frames that are successively added to the Knowledge Base Repository of the INRED system, especially that, as our research has shown, the classification accuracy of this algorithm, in the case of small amounts of learning data, does not differ from the accuracy of the convnet-type network presented for example in Subsect. 2.2. To verify this accuracy, a dataset has been used that contained very few images (13 or 14) representing the five selected classes of devices or industrial valves, as shown in Fig. 4. Selected images were then divided into training and test sets, consisting of 9 (10) and 4 images for each class, respectively. The study was based on two different types of local features extracted from images: the Scale Invariant Feature Transform (SIFT) [13] and the Oriented FAST and Rotated BRIEF (ORB) [14, 15], respectively. The results of this study referred to the classification accuracy depending on the "depth" parameter and for the "branching_factor" equal to 3 are presented in Fig. 7.

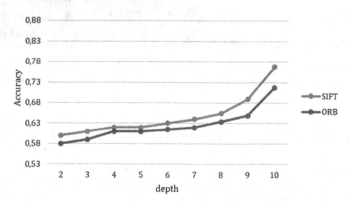

Fig. 7. The classification accuracy of the SVT algorithm based on the SIFT and ORB features.

The SVT algorithm is applied in the first stage of the proposed approach. Taking, however, into account, that the classification accuracy at the level of 0.77 (as shown in

Fig. 7) is not satisfactory at all, we suggest to utilize also another classifier, but based on quite different contour features of recognized objects.

Getting an Outline of an Object

To extract those features, that are currently limited only to object outlines, the objects detected using the SVT algorithm must be extracted from a given query image using a bounding box that covers the entire object and at the same time contains as little remaining image content as possible, as depicted for example in Fig. 8a.

Fig. 8. An exemplary query image with a) a bounding box drawn around the object of interest and sub-images being effects b) of extraction the bounding box, c) segmentation, d) binarization and e) contour extraction.

To mark such a bounding box around the object of interest, the DescriptorMatcher method (namely, the FlannBasedMatcher) from the OpenCV library[11] is utilized. This lets us extract the object of interest, as shown for example in Fig. 8b. After that, to remove from an obtained image all the background elements that are not parts of the object of interest, the GrabCut algorithm [16], that segments image into foreground and background using iterative graph-based segmentation, is applied. The result is an image as in Fig. 8c which is then binarized using the standard Otsu's binarization method [17].

---

[11] https://docs.opencv.org/master/db/d39/classcv_1_1DescriptorMatcher.html.

A binary image (as shown in Fig. 8d) being an effect of this step is then carried out with the use of the SSPCE and the MAE algorithms [19] that extracts, approximates, and finally returns the outline of an object (as depicted in Fig. 8e).

Pattern Database

Outlines of objects obtained as results of processes described so far are then compared against contour patterns stored in the pattern database. Of course, contour patterns are also outlines of objects of interest. However, unlike typical solutions of this type, they have not been extracted from the training set, which, as mentioned, may be too small to be representative, but from 3D models of these objects.

At the moment, 3D CAD modeling is becoming a standard in design engineering in many different sectors, including architecture and construction[12], power energy[13], and various other industries[14]. Reducing the production time, streamlining maintenance procedures, improving design flexibility, mapping accuracy are just only some selected advantages of 3D modeling. Therefore, manufacturers of specialized devices, e.g. in the field of power plant equipment as well as companies dealing with maintenance and servicing of such devices, now also implement 3D technologies[15]. This is why, the Repository of 3D Models is, as shown in Fig. 1, one of the main components of the INRED system. A 3D model of sample INRED's object of interest (a power boiler) and its outlines (marked with a blue line) giving contour representation of this object from two selected view angles, is depicted in Fig. 9.

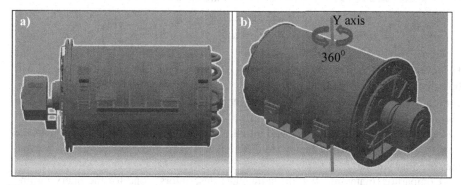

Fig. 9. Sample 3D model of power boiler (an object of interest) and their contours (marked with a blue line) seen from two selected angles (Color figure online).

To get a comprehensive contour representation of a given object using its 3D model, we propose to extract its outline every 1° during a full rotation of this object around the Y-axis of its symmetry, as shown in Fig. 9b. Besides, the object should be viewed from a certain angle from above during these extractions, as is usually the case when creating

---

[12] https://www.autodesk.co.uk/.

[13] .https://www.power-technology.com/features/featurebuilding-a-giant-3d-power-plant-design/.

[14] https://3dprintingcenter.net/.

[15] http://www.doosanheavy.com/en/intro/digital-transformation/plannbuild/.

video documentation of repair procedures. As a result, each object is represented by a collection of 360 outlines, giving its detailed contour representation from every possible viewpoint. That gives the pattern database as a collection of records indexed accordingly to tags given to objects and viewing angles of their extraction.

4 Contour-Based Classification

As previously described, outlines of objects obtained as results of processing a given query image are then compared against contour patterns stored in the pattern database. Contours are compared with the use of their Point Distance Histogram (PDH) [19] descriptors. The PDH is a contour shape descriptor given as a histogram that bins the radii coordinates of the polar contour representation (r, φ) calculated regarding the centroid O of the contour shape. Assuming that coordinates of the centroid O in the Cartesian coordinate system are given as follows:

$$x_O = \frac{1}{N} \sum_{i=0}^{N-1} x_i, \qquad y_O = \frac{1}{N} \sum_{i=0}^{N-1} y_i \tag{5}$$

where:

N – the number of contour vertices,
x_i, y_i – Cartesian coordinates of the i-th contour vertex.

the polar coordinates of the i-th contour vertex are expressed by a formula:

$$r_i = \sqrt{(x_i - x_O)^2 + (y_i - y_O)^2}, \varphi_i = atan\left(\frac{y_i - y_O}{x_i - x_O}\right) \tag{6}$$

However, vector r has to be rearranged and normalized before the final histogram will be calculated. Rearrangement of vector r is carried out as follows. First of all, the φ_i coordinates are rounded to the nearest integer values. The r_i coordinates are sorted then according to the increasing values of φ_i. After that, they are normalized by dividing them by the greatest r_i value and quantized into the assumed number of bins. That gives the final PDH histogram that is capable to differentiate between contour shapes even when they are very similar.

Comparing (matching) two different PDH descriptors - one for the query outline and one for the j-th contour pattern from the pattern database can be carried out with the use of any distance measures, e.g. the Euclidean L2 norm. The effectiveness of the PDH descriptor within the range of contour matching has been confirmed in numerous applications [20], including this described in this paper.

Results of Performed Experiments
Analysis of the classification accuracy of the approach presented in the previous section has been performed according to the Overall Success Rate measure (OSR) defined as follows:

$$OSR = \frac{1}{N} \sum_{i=1}^{k} n_{i,i} \tag{7}$$

where:

N - is the number of test (query) images,

k - is the number of classes to which processed query images were assigned,

$n_{i,i}$ - entries of the main diagonal of the confusion matrix.

The total number of test images selected for the experiments was 54. They belonged to 4 different classes of objects of interest, represented, in turn, by 1440 contour patterns in the pattern database. The confusion matrix obtained as a result of carried out experiments is given in Table 1. The true classes and classes assigned to query images by the contour-based classifier are noted as C_i and $\hat{C}_i$, respectively.

Table 1. Confusion matrix for the case of 4 class contour-based classification.

	C_1	C_2	C_3	C_4
$\hat{C}_1$	**15**	0	0	0
$\hat{C}_2$	0	**14**	0	0
$\hat{C}_3$	0	0	**10**	0
$\hat{C}_4$	0	4	0	**11**

According to the true- and miss-classifications reported in Table 1, the Overall Success Rate for the case of 4 class contour-based classification is 0.93.

5 Summary

A novel approach to the problem of poor learning data in the complex object classification task, that efficiently combines the Scalable Vocabulary Tree (SVT) technique and contour-based descriptors to recommend new training samples is presented in the paper. It outperforms other approaches of this type because it enables rapid model updates, as in the CNN-based incremental learning techniques, but without their typical drawbacks. By using 3D models and classification methods based on contour-oriented features, it also ensures high classification accuracy of objects being the subjects of interest. Nevertheless, further work is required to raise the certainty of the above classification. Supplementing the outlines of objects with a more detailed description based on their internal contour features will be one of the main directions of future work.

Acknowledgments. This work was supported by the Polish National Centre for Research and Development under the Smart Growth Operational Programme, INRED project no. POIR.01.01.01-00-0170/17. We want also to address our special thanks to our colleagues Iwo Ryszkowski and Krzysztof Nowakowski from AGH University of Science and Technology (Poland) for their valuable contributions to this work.

References

1. http://www.live-counter.com/how-big-is-the-internet/. Accessed 26 Feb 2020
2. Taigman, Y., Yang, M., Ranzato, M., Wolf, L.: DeepFace: closing the gap to human-level performance in face verification. In: 2014 IEEE Conference on Computer Vision and Pattern Recognition, Columbus, OH, pp. 1701–1708 (2014). https://doi.org/10.1109/cvpr.2014.220
3. Chollet, F.: Deep Learning with Python. Manning Publications Co., New York (2018)
4. Worring, M., Snoek, C.: Visual content analysis. In: Liu, L., Özsu, M.T. (eds.) Encyclopedia of Database Systems, pp 3360–3365. Springer, Boston (2009). https://doi.org/10.1007/978-0-387-39940-9_1019
5. Baran, R., Zeja, A.: The IMCOP system for data enrichment and content discovery and delivery. In: Proceedings of the 2015 International Conference on Computational Science and Computational Intelligence (CSCI 2015), pp 143–146, Las Vegas, USA (2015)
6. Wolff, E.: Microservices: Flexible Software Architectures. Addison-Wesley, Boston (2016)
7. Li, Z., Hoiem, D.: Learning without forgetting. PAMI **40**, 2935–2947 (2018)
8. Tao, Y., Tu Y., Shyu, M..: Efficient incremental training for deep convolutional neural networks. In: 2019 IEEE Conference on Multimedia Information Processing and Retrieval (MIPR), San Jose, CA, USA, pp. 286–291 (2019)
9. Cheng, Y., Wang, D., Zhou, P., Zhang, T.: A survey of model compression and acceleration for deep neural networks, CoRR, vol. abs/1710.09282 (2017)
10. Roy, D., Panda, P., Roy, K.: Tree-CNN: a hierarchical deep convolutional neural network for incremental learning. Neural Netw. **121**, 148–160 (2018)
11. Nister, D., Stewenius, H.: Scalable recognition with a vocabulary tree. In: Conference on Computer Vision and Pattern Recognition, New York, NY, USA, pp. 2161–2168 (2006)
12. Baran, R.: Efficiency investigation of BoF, SVT and pyramid match algorithms in practical recognition applications. In: Proceedings of the 2017 IEEE International Conference on Mathematics and Computers in Sciences and in Industry (MCSI), pp 171–178, Corfu Island, Greece (2017)
13. Lowe, D.G.: Object recognition from local scale-invariant features. In: Proceedings of the ICCV 1999, vol 2, pp 1150–1157. IEEE Computer Society (1999)
14. Rublee, E., Rabaud, V., Konolige, K., Bradski, G. R.: ORB: an efficient alternative to SIFT or SURF. In: ICCV 2011, pp. 2564–2571 (2011)
15. Baran, R., Rudziński, F., Zeja, A.: Face recognition for movie character and actor discrimination based on similarity scores. In: Proceedings of the 2016 IEEE International Conference on Computational Science and Computational Intelligence (CSCI), pp 1333–1338, Las Vegas, USA (2016)
16. Rother, C., Kolmogorov, V., Blake, A.: GrabCut - interactive foreground extraction using iterated graph cuts. ACM Trans. Graph. **23**(3), 309–314 (2004)
17. Otsu, N.: A threshold selection method from gray-level histograms. IEEE Trans. Syst. Man Cybern. **9**(1), 62–66 (1979)
18. Baran, R., Kleszcz, A.: The efficient spatial methods of contour approximation. In: Proceedings of the 2014 IEEE International Conference on Signal Processing: Algorithms, Architectures, Arrangements, and Applications (SPA 2014), pp. 116–121, Poznań, Poland (2014)
19. Frejlichowski, D.: Shape representation using point distance histogram. Polish J. Environ. Stud. **16**(4A), 90–93 (2007)
20. Frejlichowski, D.: application of the point distance histogram to the automatic identification of people by means of digital dental radiographic images. In: Chmielewski, L.J., Datta, A., Kozera, R., Wojciechowski, K. (eds.) ICCVG 2016. LNCS, vol. 9972, pp. 387–394. Springer, Cham (2016). https://doi.org/10.1007/978-3-319-46418-3_34

Symbol Error Probability of Secondary User in Underlay Cognitive Radio Networks with Adaptive Transmit Power Constraint

Hoang-Sy Nguyen[1]([✉]) [ID], N. X. Huy Nguyen[2], Q.-P. Ma[3], Jakub Jalowiczor[3], and Miroslav Voznak[3] [ID]

[1] Faculty of Information Technology, Robotics and Artificial Intelligence, Binh Duong University, Thu Dau Mot City, Binh Duong Province, Vietnam
nhsy@bdu.edu.vn
[2] Faculty of Electrical and Electronics Engineering, Binh Duong University, Thu Dau Mot City, Binh Duong Province, Vietnam
nnxhuy@bdu.edu.vn
[3] VSB - Technical University of Ostrava, 17. listopadu 2172/15, 708 00 Ostrava, Czech Republic
{phu.ma,jakub.jalowiczor,miroslav.voznak}@vsb.cz

Abstract. The objective of this paper is to study the performance of a cognitive radio network (CRN) under the influence of an eavesdropper (EAV) which can wiretap the primary user (PU) communication. In this CRN, the secondary transmitter (SU)'s transmit power is susceptible to the collaborative constraint of its peak transmit power. Consequently, the author groups derive an adaptive transmit power policy and analytical expression of symbol error probability for the SU. From the numerical results that were obtained, it can be concluded that as the SU presents in the CRN, the primary network security is enhanced. Readers as operators or system designers may find this paper useful as it provides information about the cooperation of the PU and SU in a spectrum sharing CRN to prevent security attack.

Keywords: Physical layer security · Cognitive radio networks · Symbol error probability · Eavesdropper

1 Introduction

Recent years have witnessed significant developments in the field of radio spectrum resulted from the increasing demand for wireless devices. Cognitive radio (CR), as cited in [1–6], is among the most efficient technologies utilized for spectrum utilization. A CR network allows unlicensed secondary users (SUs) to get access to the spectrum without causing interference for the licensed primary users (PUs). Moreover, the underlay CR can grant permission for concurrent information transmission to the SUs provided that it does not violate the PUs'

© Springer Nature Switzerland AG 2020
A. Dziech et al. (Eds.): MCSS 2020, CCIS 1284, pp. 307–319, 2020.
https://doi.org/10.1007/978-3-030-59000-0_23

interference constraints [7,8]. Nevertheless, the primary network constraints can greatly influence the performance of the secondary network. So as to overcome this issue and protect the PUs' communication, a diverse number of constraints namely peak or average interference power constraints, outage constraints, and different power allocation strategies have been explored in [9–12]. Thanks to the application of those constraints and strategies, the utilization of the spectrum can be greatly improved. However, ones may inevitably face security problems from the primary and secondary networks upon utilizing the spectrum underlay method because of the wireless signal broadcasting essence [13]. Despite being one of the most utilized methods to defend network eavesdropping in wireless communications, the upper layer cryptographic still has its drawback of being not cost-effective and unreliable for confidential data transmission [14,15]. Thus, the physical layer security (PLS) was deployed to further protect the data transmission process in cooperation with the currently in-used cryptographic protocols [16,17]. For this concept, the PLS will adopt the wireless channel characteristics to protect the confidential data from the risk of being wiretapped [18,19].

In the context of a wireless channel with an eavesdropper (EAV), ones can deploy the information-theoretic security and the channel's physical characteristics to measure the amount of safely delivered information [20]. Indeed, a so-called secrecy capacity which is used to assess the transmitted data security level, namely physical layer authentication (PLA) protocol, was introduced in [21–23]. Particularly, the secrecy capacity determines the maximum transmission rate of messages which are successfully and securely sent to a legitimate receiver remaining hidden from the EAV.

PUs and SUs, in a CRN, operate in the same bandwidth. This potentially leads to mutual interference, should there be any missed detection or missed power control in the network. Maintaining network security is, thus, more challenging. Researchers in [24,25] listed several different cyberattack types to the CRN aiming at its physical layer. They analyzed as well the PU's secrecy capacity and its outage probability. Another group of researchers in [26] conducted a cooperative experiment between PU and SU, whereas the two cooperate and autonomously do adjustments to their transmitting power to maximize the information rates and secrecy. The cooperation is considered successful provided that the PU can achieve higher secrecy rate afterwards. If not, there is no cooperation. Nevertheless, since the SU's interference constraints was not considered in [26–31], the primary network can not guarantee the quality of the service (QoS).

The objective of this paper is to improve the security of the CRN by investigating into the secondary network performance which subjects to the PU interference. This is inspired from the analyses conducted on the symbol error probability (SEP) whereas the SU transmit power control is put through its peak and the maximum acceptable PU outage constraint presented in [32–34].

Following the introduction in this Sect. 1, readers will find the descriptions of the system and channel models in Sect. 2. Section 3 presents the system's exact close-form expression analysis. Numerical simulations utilizing Monte-Carlo methods were done to confirm the correctness of the former analyses and are described in Sect. 4. This paper is concluded in Sect. 5. *Notation:* As stated above, the secondary transmitter transmit power is studied under the collaborative influence of the PU outage and its maximum transmit power limit. Moreover, there are a number of different inputs provided along with their notations to study: the probability density function (PDF), the cumulative distribution function (CDF) of the random variables (RVs) Z with exponential distribution are respectively denoted as $f_Z(x) = \frac{1}{\lambda}e^{-\frac{x}{\lambda}}$, and $F_Z(x) = 1 - e^{-\frac{x}{\lambda}}$. The signal-to-interference-plus-noise ratio (SINR) is denoted as γ. $Pr(.)$ is the probability function.

2   System Model

First of all, the system model is introduced as a foundation for further study.

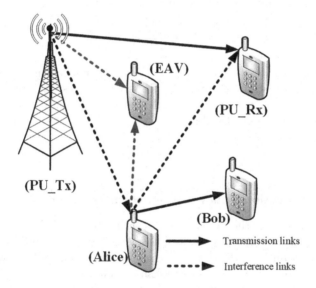

Fig. 1. System model

A typical CRN is shown in Fig. 1. There are SU-Tx as *Alice user, A* and the secondary receiver (SU-Rx) as *Bob user, B*. The communication between them occurs as A exploits the PU's licensed frequency band to transmit data to B. There is an *EAV user, E* whose role is to observe the channel output then eavesdrop the signal from the primary transmitter (PU-Tx). Indeed, there would be joint interference from the A user and PU-Tx, respectively, to the primary receiver (PU-Rx) and the B user. This study is conducted on a typical D2D communication model whereas the A user → B user is a D2D link, and the PU-Tx → PU-Rx link plays the role of the uplink or downlink of a cellular network [35].

In the considered system, the channel power gain of the PU-Tx $\rightarrow$ PU-Rx, A $\rightarrow$ PU-Rx, A $\rightarrow$ B, PU-Tx $\rightarrow$ A, PU-Tx $\rightarrow$ E, and A $\rightarrow$ E links are denoted respectively as a, b, c, d, e, and f. Those links are self-sufficient, allocated identically, and under Rayleigh fading condition. The channel gains, for $X = \{a, b, c, d, e, f\}$, are exponentially distributed with λ_X. Moreover, the PU-Tx's transmit power, the A user, and the noise power are denoted as P_P, P_A, and N_0.

The formula for the signal-to-interference-plus-noise ratio (SINR) at the PU-Rx, whereas the two PU-Tx and PU-Rx communication links are under the influence of the A user's interference link, is defined as

$$\gamma_P = \frac{P_P a}{P_A b + N_0}. \tag{1}$$

Correspondingly, the B user's SINR whereas A $\rightarrow$ B and A $\rightarrow$ PU-Tx are the communication and interference links, is defined as

$$\gamma_B = \frac{P_A c}{P_P d + N_0}. \tag{2}$$

Utilizing the broadcasted signal in wireless communication, the E user can eavesdrop the information that the PU-Tx sends to PU-Rx. Interestingly, the information the E user receives is as well interfered by the A user. Hence, the SINR of the E user is formulated as

$$\gamma_E = \frac{P_P e}{P_A f + N_0}. \tag{3}$$

2.1 Power Allocation Policy of the Secondary User

In the system model, as the SU attempts to utilize the PU's licensed frequency band for data transmission, it can cause a severe effect on the PU's QoS which is unacceptable from the PU's perspective. To avoid harmful interference for the PU-Rx, system designers must establish the interference constraints for the PU, as well as an appropriate power allocation policy for SU to make sure that the interference at the PU-Rx can be kept under a desired threshold value. Subsequently, ones can interpret the PU's interference constraint to the outage probability constraint as given in [36]

$$OP_P = \Pr\{B\log_2(1 + \gamma_P) < r_P\} \le \theta_{th}, \tag{4}$$

whereas B, r_P, and $0 \le \theta_{th} \le 1$, respectively, stand for the system bandwidth, the target min-rate of the primary network, and its desired outage probability.

It can be interpreted from the Eq. (4) that as the outage probability of the PU capacity remains below the threshold value θ_{th}, the A user can still be able to access the licensed frequency band of the PU and bring about limited interference to the PU. Practice wise, the transmit power is subject to some limitations. Hence, the A user transmits the power which is formulated with an additional constraint namely the peak transmit power, or the maximum transmit power limit, P_{pk}

$$P_A^* \leq P_{pk}. \tag{5}$$

It is assumed that the c_1 and c_2 are constant and positive. Independent variables Z_1 and Z_2, whose mean values are λ_1 and λ_2, are exponentially distributed RVs. Thus, the function can be derived as

$$Z = \frac{c_1 Z_1}{c_2 Z_2 + 1}. \tag{6}$$

The formulas of the CDF and PDF of Z are given as follows:

$$F_Z(x) = 1 - \frac{1}{1 + x\delta_1} e^{-x\delta_2}, \tag{7}$$

and

$$f_Z(x) = \delta_1 \frac{e^{-x\delta_2}}{(1 + x\delta_1)^2} + \delta_2 \frac{e^{-x\delta_2}}{(1 + x\delta_1)}, \tag{8}$$

whereas $\delta_1 = \frac{c_2\lambda_2}{c_1\lambda_1}$, and $\delta_2 = \frac{1}{c_1\lambda_1}$.

Proof. As stated in the probability definition, ones can utilize the corresponding approach [12] to derive the CDF of the RB Z

$$\begin{aligned} F_Z(x) &= \Pr\{Z \leq x\} \\ &= \int_0^{y=\infty} \Pr\left\{Z_1 < x\frac{(c_2 y + 1)}{c_1}\right\} f_{Z_2}(y)\, dy. \end{aligned} \tag{9}$$

Given that Z_1 and Z_2 are independent exponentially distributed RVs, rewriting of the Eq. (9) can be done as follows

$$F_Z(x) = \int_0^{y=\infty} \frac{1}{\lambda_2} \left\{1 - e^{\left(-x\frac{(c_2 y + 1)}{c_1\lambda_1}\right)}\right\} e^{-\frac{y}{\lambda_2}}\, dy. \tag{10}$$

With integration, the CDF of the Z can be acquired as in (7). Additionally, as the (7) is differentiated with respect to variable x, the PDF of Z can be obtained, as in (8).
This is the end of the proof.

In this context, the SU is allowed to access the PU's licensed frequency band. Hence, the A user must possess a transmit power policy which is flexible to keep the PU's interference below a predefined threshold value. The PU's outage probability can be derived from (4) to obtain the transmit power expression for the SU network as follows

$$OP_P = \Pr\left\{\frac{P_P a}{P_A b + N_0}\right\} \leq \gamma_{th}, \tag{11}$$

whereas $\gamma_{th} = 2^{r_P} - 1$.

Utilizing *Lemma* 1, the PU outage probability can be expressed as

$$OP_P = 1 - \frac{P_P \lambda_a}{\gamma_{th} P_A \lambda_b + P_P \lambda_a} e^{-\frac{\gamma_{th}}{\rho \lambda_a}}, \tag{12}$$

whereas $\rho = \frac{P_P}{N_0}$

After substituting (12) into (4), the product is then combined with (5) to form an adaptive transmit power policy for the A user in signal transmission to the B user, given as

$$P_A^* = \min\left\{\frac{P_P \lambda_a}{\gamma_{th} \lambda_b} \chi, P_{pk}\right\}, \tag{13}$$

whereas $\chi = \frac{1}{1-\theta_{th}} e^{-\frac{\gamma_{th}}{\rho \lambda_a}} - 1 > 0$.

2.2   The CDF and PDF for Different SINR

Before continuing with this section, it should be noted that the CDF and PDF for the SINR at the PU-Rx, A, and E were obtained already in (1), (2), and (3).

Utilizing *Lemma* 1, the CDF and PDF of γ_P are given respectively by

$$F_{\gamma_P}(u) = 1 - \frac{1}{1 + u\psi_{1a}} e^{-\frac{u}{\psi_{1b}}}, \tag{14}$$

and

$$f_{\gamma_P}(u) = e^{-\frac{u}{\psi_{1b}}} \left[\frac{\psi_{1a}}{(1 + u\psi_{1a})^2} + \frac{1}{\psi_{1b}(1 + u\psi_{1a})}\right], \tag{15}$$

whereas $\psi_{1a} = \frac{P_A^* \lambda_b}{P_P \lambda_a}$, and $\psi_{1b} = \rho \lambda_a$.

Likewise, the CDF and PDF of γ_B can be calculated from

$$F_{\gamma_B}(v) = 1 - \frac{1}{1 + v\psi_{2a}} e^{-\frac{v}{\psi_{2b}}}, \tag{16}$$

and

$$f_{\gamma_B}(v) = e^{-\frac{v}{\psi_{2b}}} \left[\frac{\psi_{2a}}{(1 + v\psi_{2a})^2} + \frac{1}{\psi_{2b}(1 + v\psi_{2a})}\right], \tag{17}$$

whereas $\psi_{2a} = \frac{P_P \lambda_d}{P_A^* \lambda_c}$, and $\psi_{2b} = \frac{P_A^*}{N_0} \lambda_c$.

The CDF and PDF of γ_E can be easily obtained as

$$F_{\gamma_E}(w) = 1 - \frac{1}{1 + w\psi_{3a}} e^{-\frac{w}{\psi_{3b}}}, \tag{18}$$

and

$$f_{\gamma_E}(w) = e^{-\frac{w}{\psi_{3b}}} \left[\frac{\psi_{3a}}{(1 + w\psi_{3a})^2} + \frac{1}{\psi_{3b}(1 + w\psi_{3a})}\right], \tag{19}$$

whereas $\psi_{3a} = \frac{P_A^* \lambda_f}{P_P \lambda_e}$, and $\psi_{3b} = \rho \lambda_e$.

3   Performance Analysis

Having based on the transmit power constraint from the PU and SU, the system performance of the CRN was studied. This is possible by evaluating the channel capacity among the communication links under the interference links, along with the effect of the Symbol Error Probability (SEP) on the SU.

By invoking the Shannon theorem, ones can formulate the channel capacity between the PU-Tx and the PU-Rx link, the A user and B user link, and the PU-Tx and E user link over the wiretapped channel as follows

$$C_i = B\log_2\left(1 + \gamma_i\right), \tag{20}$$

given that $i \in (P, B, E)$ at the PU-Tx, A and E user, respectively.

As can be observed in [37], η and ε are constant and dependent in the particular modulation scheme. As the M-phase shift keying (M-PSK) modulation scheme is assigned with $\eta = 2$, $\varepsilon = sin^2(\pi/M)$, and $M = 4$, the SEP of the SU can be described as

$$OP_{sep} = \frac{\varepsilon\sqrt{\eta}}{2\sqrt{\pi}} \int_0^\infty \frac{e^{-\eta\gamma}}{\sqrt{\gamma}} F_{\gamma_B}\left(\gamma\right) d\gamma. \tag{21}$$

Theorem 1. *The analytical expression of the SU SEP is given by*

$$OP_{sep} = \frac{\varepsilon}{2}\left[1 - \sqrt{\eta\pi A_2}e^{A_1 A_2}\left(1 - Q(A_1 A_2)\right)\right], \tag{22}$$

whereas $Q(.)$ is the error function, $A_1 = \frac{N_0}{P_A^*\lambda_c} + \eta$, and $A_2 = \frac{P_A^*\lambda_c}{P_P\lambda_d}$.

Proof. As the (16) is substituted into the (21), the SU SEP expression can be formulated as

$$OP_{sep} = \frac{\varepsilon\sqrt{\eta}}{2\sqrt{\pi}} \int_0^{\gamma=\infty} \frac{e^{-\eta\gamma}}{\sqrt{\gamma}}d\gamma - \frac{\varepsilon\sqrt{\eta}}{2\sqrt{\pi}} \int_0^{\gamma=\infty} \frac{1}{(1 + \psi_{2a}\gamma)\sqrt{\gamma}}e^{-A_1\gamma}d\gamma, \tag{23}$$

whereas $A_1 = \frac{N_0}{P_A^*\lambda_c} + \eta$.

Furthermore, by utilizing the [[38], Eq.(3.361.2)], the Eq. (23) can be rewritten as

$$OP_{sep} = \frac{\varepsilon}{2} - \frac{\varepsilon\sqrt{\eta}}{2\sqrt{\pi}} \int_0^{\gamma=\infty} \frac{1}{(1 + \psi_{2a}\gamma)\sqrt{\gamma}}e^{-A_1\gamma}d\gamma, \tag{24}$$

Last but not least, by doing variable change and assigning $t = \gamma + \frac{1}{\psi_{2a}}$, this formula is obtained

$$OP_{sep} = \frac{\varepsilon}{2} - \frac{\varepsilon\sqrt{\eta}}{2\sqrt{\pi}} A_2 e^{A_1 A_2} \int_{A_2}^\infty \frac{1}{t\sqrt{t - A_2}}e^{-A_1 t}dt, \tag{25}$$

whereas $A_2 = \frac{1}{\psi_{2a}}$.

Ones can obtain their desired result from (22) with the help of the error function $Q(.)$, with $Q\left(x\right) = \frac{2}{\sqrt{\pi}}\int_0^x e^{-t^2}dt$, and [[38], Eq.(3.363.2)]. The proof ends here.

4   Numerical Results

This section presents the numerical results obtained from studying how the system performance is influenced by a certain number of primary network parameters. Moreover, the SU is introduced into the primary network and its effect was studied. For better understanding, the primary simulated parameters along with their default values are provided below in Table 1.

Table 1. Simulation parameters

Primary Parameters	Values
The channel Bandwidth, B	5 MHz
The maximum transmit SU, $\rho^* = P_A^*/N_0$	15 dB
The channel power gain, λ_b, λ_d	2
The channel power gain, λ_a, λ_c, λ_e,λ_f	4
The target rate primary network, r_P	20 Kbps
The OP threshold primary network, θ_{th}	1%

Figure 2 depicts the relation between the PU power transmission, with different values of the SU maximum transmit SNR, ρ^*, and the SU capacity transmission secondary user. The increase of the ρ^* leads to the raise of the SU capacity transmission secondary user A. This is because the A transmit SNR increase will lead to the rise of the ρ^*. Notwithstanding, the A user SNR is impossible to grow further from its limit boundary exerted by the ρ^*. Consequently, the SU capacity transmission secondary user is decreased because of the strong interference from the PU transmit SNR to the SU.

Figure 3 illustrates the SU SEP versus the PU transmit SNR for the BPSK modulation, with different PU target rate impact values denoted as r_P. It can be observed that the SU SEP is inversely proportional to the PU transmit SNR, ρ (dB), given that the ρ and the SU-Tx transmit SNR increase with respect to each other. Subsequently, the PU transmit SNR can strongly interfere with the SU causing the SU SEP to increase. As a result, system performance is decreased. This is because the rise in r_P brings up higher SINR value at the PU-Rx. Thus, to satisfy the PU outage constraint, the SU transmit SNR is compulsorily decreased. This leads to the SU SEP being degraded.

Figure 4 plots the SU SE versus the PU transmit SNR relation with different values of the SU maximum transmit SNR, $\rho^* = P_{Pk}/N_0 = 5, 10, 15$(dB). The changes in the resulted SEP were recorded and compared. It can be easily observed that the SEP drops to reach its optimal value first, then sharply increases as the PU transmit SNR increases, correspondingly, at $\rho^* > -3, 2, 6$. It can be concluded that the higher the ρ^*, the lower the degradation of the SEP.

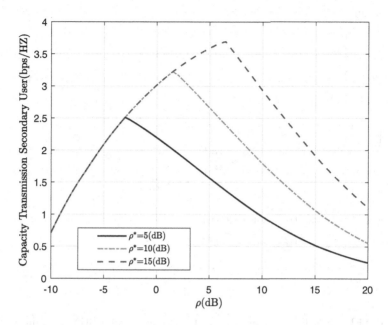

Fig. 2. Capacity transmission versus PU transmit SNR with different values of SU maximum transmit SNR

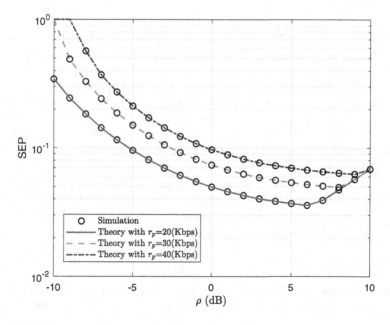

Fig. 3. SU SEP versus PU transmit SNR with different values of PU target transmission rate

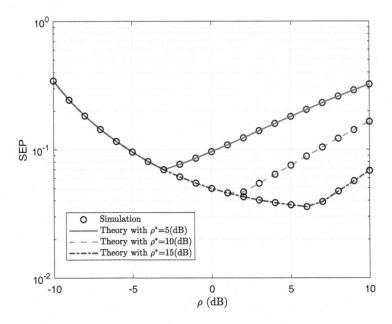

Fig. 4. SU SEP versus PU transmit SNR with different values of SU maximum transmit SNR

5   Conclusion

In summary, the CRN's performance under the influence of the collaborative constraint from the PU outage and the SU maximum transmit power limit was studied. The investigated model typically represents a D2D communication model whereas the PU-Tx → PU-Rx link plays the role of an uplink or a downlink of a cellular network, A → B link as a D2D communication link. According to this, formulas for the adaptive transmit power of the A user and the SU SEP were derived. Moreover, further investigation was made on how the PU transmit SNR and the SU peak transmit power affect the system performance. Essentially, it can be drawn from this study that there is a strong dependency of the primary network security on the A → E link's channel condition and the SU transmit power policy. The primary network security is also under the strong influence of the channel mean power between the primary and the secondary networks, the A → E link's channel condition, and the A user's transmit power policy.

Acknowledgements. The research leading to these results received funding from the Czech Ministry of Education under grant No. SP2020/65 conducted at VSB - Technical University of Ostrava and computational time was provided within projects OPEN-19-38 and OPEN-16-32 in the National Supercomputing Centre IT4Innovations.

References

1. Suriano, F., De Rango, F., Popovski, P. Opportunistic interference cancellation evaluation in cognitive radios under power control strategies. In: 2013 9th International Wireless Communications and Mobile Computing Conference (IWCMC), pp. 609–614 (2013)
2. Zou, Y., Yao, Y., Zheng, B.: Cooperative relay techniques for cognitive radio systems: spectrum sensing and secondary user transmission. IEEE Commun. Magazine **50**(4), 98–103 (2012)
3. Mitola, J., Maguire, G.Q.: Cognitive radio: making software radios more personal. IEEE Personal Commun. **6**(4), 13–18 (1999)
4. Yang, Y., Zhang, Q., Wang, Y., Emoto, T., Akutagawa, M., Konaka, S.: Multi-strategy dynamic spectrum access in cognitive radio networks: modeling, analysis and optimization. China Commun. **16**(3), 103–121 (2019)
5. Huynh, V.-V., Nguyen, H.-S., Hoc, L.T.T., Nguyen, T.S., Voznak, M.: Optimization issues for data rate in energy harvesting relay-enabled cognitive sensor networks. Comput. Netw. **157**(5), 29–40 (2019)
6. Huynh, V.-V., Tan-Loc, N., Quoc-Phu, M., Sevcik, L., Nguyen, H.-S., Voznak, M.: Energy efficiency maximization of two-time-slot and three-time-slot two-way relay-assisted device-to-device underlaying cellular networks. Energies **13**, 3422 (2020)
7. Andreotti, R., Wang, T., Lottici, V., Giannetti, L.F., Vandendorpe, L.: Resource allocation via max-min goodput optimization for BIC-OFDMA systems. IEEE Trans. Commun. **64**(6), 2412–2426 (2016)
8. Nguyen, H.S., Nguyen, T.S., Voznak, M.: Wireless powered D2D communications underlaying cellular networks: design and performance of the extended coverage. Automatika **58**(4), 391–399 (2018)
9. Zhang, R.: On peak versus average interference power constraints for protecting primary users in cognitive radio networks. IEEE Trans. Wireless Commun. **8**(4), 2112–2120 (2009)
10. Smith, P.J., Dmochowski, P.A., Suraweera, H.A., Shafi, M.: The effects of limited channel knowledge on cognitive radio system capacity. IEEE Trans. Vehicular Technol. **62**(2), 927–933 (2013)
11. Zhou, F., Beaulieu, N.C., Li, Z., Si, J., Qi, P.: Energy-efficient optimal power allocation for fading cognitive radio channels: ergodic capacity, outage capacity, and minimum-rate capacity. IEEE Trans. Wireless Commun. **15**(4), 2741–2755 (2016)
12. Nguyen, H.-S., Nguyen, T.-S., Nguyen, M.-T., Voznak, M.: Optimal time switching-based policies for efficient transmit power in wireless energy harvesting small cell cognitive relaying networks. Wireless Personal Commun. **99**(4), 1605–1624 (2018). https://doi.org/10.1007/s11277-018-5296-2
13. Nguyen, T.N., Minh, T.H.Q., Tran, P.T., Voznak, M.: Adaptive energy harvesting relaying protocol for two-way half-duplex system network over rician fading channels. Wireless Communications and Mobile Computing, 2018, art. no. 7693016 (2018)
14. Rodriguez, L.J., Tran, N.H., Duong, T.Q., Le, N.T., Elkashlan, M., Shetty, S.: Physical layer security in wireless cooperative relay networks: state of the art and beyond. IEEE Commun. Magazine **53**(12), 32–39 (2015)
15. De Rango, F., Potrino, G., Tropea, M., Fazio, P.: Energy-aware dynamic internet of things security system based on elliptic curve cryptography and message queue telemetry transport protocol for mitigating replay attacks. Pervasive Mob. Comput. **61**, 101105 (2020)

16. Poor, H.V.: Information and inference in the wireless physical layer. IEEE Commun. Magazine **19**(1), 40–47 (2012)
17. Yang, N., Wang, L., Geraci, G., Elkashlan, M., Yuan, J., Di Renzo, M.: Safeguarding 5G wireless communication networks using physical layer security. IEEE Commun. Magazine **53**(4), 20–27 (2015)
18. Dai, B., Yu, L., Luo, Y.: New results on the wire-tap channel with noiseless feedback. In: IEEE Information Theory Workshop (ITW), pp. 1–5, Guangzhou (2018)
19. Fazio, P., Tropea, M., Marano, S., Voznak, M.: Meaningful attack graph reconstruction through stochastic marking analysis. In: Proceedings of the 2016 International Symposium on Performance Evaluation of Computer and Telecommunication Systems, SPECTS 2016 - Part of SummerSim 2016 Multi conference, art. no. 7570519 (2016)
20. Nguyen, T.N., et al.: Performance enhancement for energy harvesting based two-way relay protocols in wireless ad-hoc networks with partial and full relay selection methods. Ad Hoc Netw. **84**, 178–187 (2019)
21. Forssell, H., Thobaben, R., Al-Zubaidy, H., Gross, J.: Physical layer authentication in mission-critical MTC networks: a security and delay performance analysis. IEEE J. Selected Areas Commun. **37**(4), 795–808 (2019)
22. Liu, X.: Outage probability of secrecy capacity over correlated log-normal fading channels. IEEE Commun. Lett. **17**(2), 289–292 (2013)
23. Karmakar, S., Ghosh, A.: Secrecy capacity region of fading binary Z interference channel with statistical CSIT. IEEE Trans. Inf. Forensics Secur. **14**(4), 848–857 (2019)
24. Tran, H., Kaddoum, G., Gagnon, F.: Cognitive radio network with secrecy and interference constraints. Phys. Commun. **22**, 32–41 (2017)
25. Bouabdellah, M., Kaabouch, N., Bouanani, F.E., Ben-Azza, H.: Network layer attacks and countermeasures in cognitive radio networks: a survey. J. Inf. Secur. Appl. **38**, 40–49 (2018)
26. Al-Talabani, A., Deng, Y., Nallanathan, A., Nguyen, H.X.: Enhancing secrecy rate in cognitive radio networks via stackelberg game. IEEE Trans. Commun. **64**(11), 4764–4775 (2016)
27. Quach, T.X., Tran, H., Uhlemann, E., Truc, M.T.: Secrecy performance of cooperative cognitive radio networks under joint secrecy outage and primary user interference constraints. IEEE Access **8**, 18442–18455 (2020)
28. Huynh, V.-V., et al.: Optimization issues for data rate in energy harvesting relay-enabled cognitive sensor networks. Comput. Netw. **157**, 29–40 (2019)
29. Nguyen, H.-S., et al.: Wireless powered D2D communications underlying cellular networks: design and performance of the extended coverage. Automatika **58**, 391–0399 (2018)
30. Nguyen, H.-S., et al.: Outage performance analysis and SWIPT optimization in energy-harvesting wireless sensor network deploying NOMA. Sensors **19**, 613 (2019)
31. Huynh, V.-V., et al.: Energy efficiency maximization of two-time-slot and three-time-slot two-way relay-assisted device-to-device underlaying cellular networks. Energies **13**(13), 3422 (2020)
32. Sibomana, L., Tran, H., Zepernick, Kabiri, C.: On non-zero secrecy capacity and outage probability of cognitive radio networks. In: Proceedings of the IEEE International Symposium Wireless Personal Multimedia Communications (WPMC), pp. 1—-6, Atlantic City, USA (2013)

33. Zhang, J., Kundu, C., Dobre, O.A., Garcia-Palacios, E., Vo, N.: Secrecy performance of small-cell networks with transmitter selection and unreliable backhaul under spectrum sharing environment. IEEE Trans. Vehicular Technol. **68**(11), 10895–10908 (2019)

34. Erdogan, E., Birol, A., Gucluoglu, T.: Error probability performance of channel estimation error on cognitive multi relay networks. In Proceedings of the 25th Signal Processing and Communications Applications Conference (SIU), pp. 1–4. Antalya (2017)

35. Liu, Y., Wang, L., Raza Zaidi, S.A., Elkashlan, M., Duong, T.Q.: Secure D2D communication in large-scale cognitive cellular networks: a wireless power transfer model. IEEE Trans. Commun. **64**(1), 329–342 (2016)

36. Kalamkar, S.S., Majhi, S., Banerjee, A.: Outage analysis of spectrum sharing energy harvesting cognitive relays in Nakagami-m channels. In: Proceedings of the IEEE Global Telecommunications Conference (GLOBECOM), pp. 1–6, San Diego, CA, USA (2015)

37. McKay, M.R., Grant, A.J., Collings, I.B.: Performance analysis of MIMO-MRC in double-correlated rayleigh environments. IEEE Trans. Commun. **55**(3), 497–507 (2007)

38. Gradshteyn, I.S., Ryzhik, I.M.: Table of Integrals, Series, and Products, 7th edn. Academic Press, New York (2007)

Evaluation of Improved Components of AMIS Project for Speech Recognition, Machine Translation and Video/Audio/Text Summarization

Aritz Badiola[1], Amaia Méndez Zorrilla[1], Begonya Garcia-Zapirain Soto[1], Michał Grega[2], Mikołaj Leszczuk[2(✉)] (iD), and Kamel Smaïli[3]

[1] University of Deusto, Bilbao, Spain
[2] AGH University of Science and Technology, Kraków, Poland
leszczuk@agh.edu.pl
[3] University of Lorraine, Nancy, France

Abstract. To evaluate a system that automatically summarizes video files (image and audio) and text, how the system works, and the quality of the results should be considered. With this objective, the authors have performed two types of evaluation: objective and subjective. The actual assessment is performed mainly automatically, while the individual assessment is based directly on the opinion of people, who evaluate the system by answering a set of questions, which are then processed to obtain the targeted conclusions. One of the purposes of the described research is to try to narrow the space of possible summarization scenarios.

Meanwhile, in the light of individual results obtained, the researchers cannot unambiguously indicate one single scenario, recommended as the only one for further development. However, the researchers can state with certainty that the new development of scene 1, which has received many negative evaluations among professionals, should be discontinued. Considering the results of the set of questions about the quality of the complete system, the end-users have evaluated the scenario 3, and they think that the quality is excellent, obtaining results over 70% on a scale of 0 to 100.

Keywords: Subjective evaluation · Summarization system · Summarized videos · AMIS project

1 Introduction

Nowadays, information is widely available in different media: TV, social networks, newspapers, etc. in foreign languages. When the video does not necessitate any understanding, there does not have great difficulty. In the opposite, when the information requires understanding the word, a human being is limited in terms of mastering a foreign language. One of the main objectives of the AMIS project is to make available a system, helping people to understand the content of a source video by presenting its main ideas in a target understandable language. Some scholars believe that the best way

© Springer Nature Switzerland AG 2020
A. Dziech et al. (Eds.): MCSS 2020, CCIS 1284, pp. 320–331, 2020.
https://doi.org/10.1007/978-3-030-59000-0_24

to do that is to summaries the video for having access to the essential information. AMIS focuses on the most relevant information by synthesizing it and by translating it to the user if necessary.

Several capabilities are necessary to achieve this objective: video summarization, automatic speech recognition, machine translation, text summarization, etc.

In this article, we will present the first results of the subjective evaluation of the proposed architectures of AMIS [1], and personal assessment of the whole system with videos in Arabic.

The research team decided that it is a waste of resources to develop several scenarios at the same time, so the researchers should determine what scene will be used for further development.

The research team decided that the language of the recorded source video sentences would be Arabic and French.

2 Objective

As presented in the previous section, the problem to be solved is the development of an evaluation procedure for the developed video summarizer in the project AMIS. The development of this evaluation procedure is considered necessary, as there is not a standardized way of evaluating the summarizer systems, so, developing a tested and complete evaluation procedure for video summarizes is the objective of this project.

To develop this evaluation procedure, it has been used the already developed video summarization system in the project AMIS as a use case. The used method to develop this evaluation procedure is presented in the next sections, including the subjective evaluation procedure, the actual evaluation procedure and the obtained results with each system.

3 Subjective Evaluation

In this section, the Materials and methods used for the different evaluations made in the AMIS project are described.

3.1 Methodology

Methods for Subjective Video Evaluation of the Generated Scenarios. To evaluate the three scenarios generated by AMIS project methods, a set of 9 video sequences manually taken to represent diversified content have been used. From the source video sequences, 27 sequences were subsequently generated (for each source sequence, three series summarized, in scenarios 1, 3 and 4). In the next step, file names were randomized, in such a way that the outsider could only learn the source sequence number, but not the amount of the summary scenario used for the sequence summarization. The research team distributed the thus prepared video sequence packet within the project consortium and students. Members of the AMIS consortium was asked to rank, for each of the nine source video sequences, generated three summaries (from the best to the worst) – of course, without knowing the assignment of a specific video summary file to the number of the summary scenario. We addressed two groups of respondents: students (pre-teenagers) and professionals (scientists, academic teachers, technical workers – generally adults, working full-time). Sixty-two people (51 students and 11 professionals) responded to the call, generating a total of 558 sets of data, fed to the following analyses.

First, collective analysis of all answers was carried out. Then (for reasons that we will give later), separately in the groups of students and professionals.

Methods for Subjective Video Evaluation of the Generated Scenarios. After selecting the best scenario for video summarization considering the obtained results from the evaluation of the different scenarios, a subjective evaluation of the summaries generated but that scenario has been performed, to evaluate the final system performance.

The only applied inclusion criteria when selecting the users for the evaluation is that the user must be a native speaker of the language spoken in the video and have a right level of English, at least a B2 level to understand the questions of the questionnaire.

The age of most of the users that took part in the evaluation was between 18 and 35 years old, and their mother language was French or Arabic, and their nationality French or Arab. The maximum level of education of most of them was a bachelor's degree, but there were some with an elementary school, high school, master or doctoral degree.

As said, the objective of this evaluation process is to analyze how good the summarization system performs with Arabic and French videos. With this purpose, an evaluation section has been created on the web page of the project, where the users can register themselves and evaluate different videos.

The evaluation section of the web page has been structured in the following way:

- An introduction, explaining to the user the purpose of the evaluation and the steps to do it.
- The video summarization generated by the system.
- Questionnaire part:

  - Five questions about the critical points of the original video to ensure that the summary video includes the main ideas and the user can get these ideas from the summary. Three possible answers per question are provided to the user.
  - Two generic questions about the quality of the video summary. The possible answers are from 0 to 4, "Not fulfilled", "Fair", "Good", "Very good", "Excellent". The questions are the following ones:

    - "Is the summary understandable?".
    - "Doesn't the video contain any part out of context, or it does not affect the main expressed ideas?".

3.2   Results of Subjective Evaluation of the Different Scenarios

Subjective Evaluation of All People. The first approach analyzed the percentage distribution of "winners" (see Fig. 1). By winners, we mean scenarios indicated as the best during the evaluation. The consortium members expected a definite answer at this stage, but this did not happen.

Scenarios

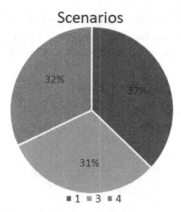

Fig. 1. Subjective evaluation winners.

The result significantly surprised the experimenters. As one can see, the differences are negligible. All scenarios achieve a similar effect, dividing the "pie" by approximately 1/3. Differences between individual scenes are in practice different percentage points, which does not allow to draw firm conclusions.

Since the research team could not unequivocally set the best scenario, the researchers asked a research question differently: is it possible to at least indicate the worst-case scenario (or the worst scenarios)? So, reject this scenario (these scenarios)? Therefore, such an analysis of "losers" was carried out (see Fig. 2).

Scenarios

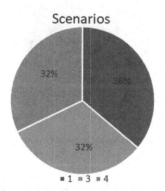

Fig. 2. Subjective evaluation of losers.

Nevertheless, again, as one can see, the differences are rather negligible. All scenarios achieve a similar result, dividing the "pie" by approximately 1/3. It was somewhat surprising because, in the subjective opinion of the project members, the differences between the scenarios were quite visible and significant.

Subjective Evaluation of Students. In the case of the group of students, the result was still not decisive. Practically repeated the scheme of results previously known during the analysis of the entire group of respondents.

The analysis of winners (see Fig. 3) have not provided precise results. All scenarios achieve a similar effect, dividing the "pie" by approximately 1/3. So, students pointed to each scene as the best, more or less in the same number of cases.

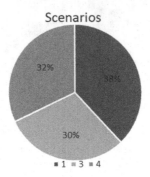

Fig. 3. Subjective evaluation winners among students.

Moreover, similarly, the analysis of losers (see Fig. 4) was not decisive. All scenarios achieve a similar result, dividing the "pie" by approximately 1/3. So, students pointed to each scene as the worst, more or less in the same number of cases.

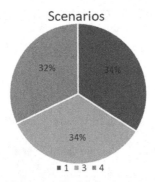

Fig. 4. Subjective evaluation losers among students.

Subjective Evaluation of Professionals. In the case of a group of professionals, the result still turned out to be very interesting. As for the winners, he was still not decisive (see Fig. 5). All scenarios achieve a similar result, dividing the "pie" by approximately 1/3. So, professionals pointed to each scene as the best, more or less in the same number of cases.

However, regarding the losers, this time, it is evident that the testers indicated scenario number 1 as the worst in almost 1/2 of cases. The other two scenarios (3 and 4) divide the "pie" more or less equally, with no visible indication of any of the remaining scenes (see Fig. 6). However, at least, this time, differences between individual scenario one and the two remaining ones are in practice over a dozen percentage points, which finally does allow to draw firm conclusions.

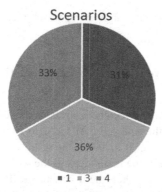

Fig. 5. Subjective evaluation winners among professionals.

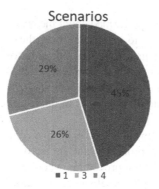

Fig. 6. Subjective evaluation losers among professionals.

Why are these two groups so different in terms of pointing out the worst-case scenario? It is not known precisely. Indeed, professionals were well motivated to perform the test reliably: either they worked on the project themselves, or the persons working on the project personally asked other professionals to do the test. Meanwhile, students did not have a similar motivation. At the same time, it is worth noting that differences can also result from one or a combination of a more significant number of entirely different, partly independent reasons, such as age, education, knowledge or experience.

Conclusions. As mentioned, the purpose of the described research was to try to narrow the space of possible scenarios. Therefore, in the light of individual results obtained, the researchers cannot unambiguously indicate one single scene, recommended as the only one for further development. However, the researchers can state with certainty that the new development of scenario 1, which has received many negative evaluations among professionals, should be discontinued.

Along with all the possible scenarios, it has been selected the scene 3 for the final system evaluation. It is true that in most of the assessment of the situations performed by all the participants, the results of the three scenarios are similar. However, in the case of the evaluations by the professionals, the results of scene 3 are prominently better than the ones obtained for the rest of the scenarios.

More information about the methods using which these results were obtained has been provided in [1].

3.3 Results of the Subjective Comprehension-Evaluation of Scenario Three Videos

This section includes the obtained results from the tests performed by the users about the summaries produced by the selected best scenario from the previously performed evaluation, which is ranged from 0 to 100. This score is the result of the answers to the five specific questions about the main ideas of the video. Each correct answer is 20 points, so, if the five are correct, then the user will get 100 points (being acceptable from 70). It is included another information that is considered attractive too, such as the number of videos, users, answers, standard deviation and the results of the generic questions.

There is not too much work performed about the evaluation of this type of systems. Still, there is a perfect example to understand how the review should be approached inside the publication Multimedia summarization using social media content [4]. In this paper, the evaluators see the multimedia content. Then they are asked to summaries all the content in two distinct triples of keywords and two different sets of summaries, each one containing 15, 25 and 50 images from the list of candidates computed by the algorithm.

In the case of the system being analyzed in this paper, it has been considered to apply a more complex and flexible approach for the subjective evaluation by users, as established by [5] as extrinsic evaluation procedure, where the quality of the summarization based on how it affects the completion of some other tasks, such as question-answering and comprehension tasks. Considering that the summary task more complicated due to the multilingual content and the duration of the videos and that the final objective of summarization is giving to the user the necessary information to understand the original content, it has been considered the extrinsic Q&A method as the best one for this case, with some extra details that will be explained in the next paragraphs. Other papers such as the challenging task of summary evaluation: an overview [6] analyses different ways of evaluating summarization systems too, including questionnaires answered by users about the quality and the content of the summaries about the original content, in a similar way it is done into this case.

Some users from different cultures and nationalities summaries the original videos in a set of 5 questions that include the main ideas of the video, so, then, other users can answer the questions only watching the summarized videos, evaluating in this way the quality of the system (Figs. 7, 8, 9, 10, 11 and 12).

Arabic Video Summarization System Evaluation Result.

Number of videos	Number of users	Number of answers	AVG score	AVG SD	GQ_AVG[a]
8	20	35	80.56	15.71	2.46 (between good and very good)

Fig. 7. Overall results of the evaluation of the Arabic video summarization system (a. Generic Question Average: as explained before, there are 2 generic questions about the quality of the video summary included in the questionnaire, which range from 0 to 4: "Not fulfilled","Fair", "Good", "Very good", "Excellent").

Video ID	Number of users	AVG	SD	GQ_AVG
1	4	60	28.28	2.5
2	2	66.66	11.55	2.16
40	5	80	12.65	1.58
41	3	95	10	3
42	5	90	10.95	2.83
43	4	76	16.73	2.4
44	8	88.88	17.64	2.39
45	4	88	17.89	2.8

Fig. 8. Results per video of the evaluation of the Arabic video summarization system.

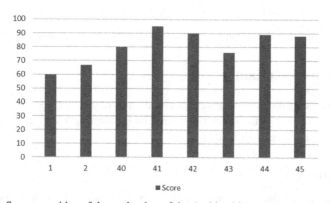

Fig. 9. Score per video of the evaluation of the Arabic video summarization system.

French Video Summarization System Evaluation Result.

Number of videos	Number of users	Number of answers	AVG score	AVG SD	GQ_AVG
10	6	11	64	2.82	1.93 (near good)

Fig. 10. Overall results of the evaluation of the French video summarization system.

Video ID	Number of users	AVG	SD	GQ_AVG
17	1	80	0	2
18	1	40	0	1
19	1	80	0	3
20	1	20	0	0.5
21	1	80	0	3
26	1	60	0	3.5
27	1	40	0	0.5
31	1	80	0	1.5
32	1	80	0	3
33	2	80	28.28	1.25

Fig. 11. Results per video of the evaluation of the French video summarization system.

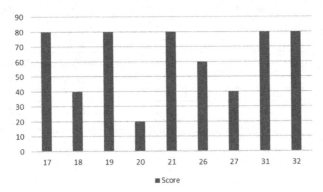

Fig. 12. Score per video of the evaluation of the French video summarization system.

4   Objective Evaluation

This section presents the evaluation results based on an objective (tag-based) evaluation procedure [2]. The aim of the objective evaluation is selecting a summarizing scenario based on the quality of different situations.

4.1   Input Data

This Subsection describes the input data that has been used. The video sequences are described separately, and the tag selection independently.

Video Sequences. The objective evaluation used the set of 27 video sequences, manually chosen to represent diversified content. From the source video sequences, 81 sequences were subsequently generated (for each source sequence, three series summarized, in scenarios 1, 3 and 4).

Tag Selection. For the tag-based evaluation procedure, the most critical data used were YouTube tags. We used YouTube tags for every selected video sequence. Tags used there, summaries the given newscast/report video sequence. Tickets are, depending on the particular video sequences, written in different languages. Here are some examples:
    RT, Russia Today, FSA kicks out US special forces troops, FSA, Free Syrian Army, US special forces soldiers, withdraw, kicked out, Syria, war, troops, us-backed.

4.2   Evaluation Algorithm

Every video sequence used has its own set of tags. They are in different languages. The algorithm for each video sequence is:

1.   Retrieve the audio track from the original video sequence.
2.   Use an Automatic Speech Recognition (ASR) system engine [3]. It is a system created with two parts: an acoustic model and language model—the system bases on KALDI ASR toolkit. The acoustic model uses a Deep Neural Network (DNN), which has an input layer of 440 neurons, six hidden layers of 2048 neurons each. The output layer has around 4000 neurons. ASR returns a set of words with timecodes. We use it to obtain a textual transcription of the original video sequence. Precise mathematical description and handling of the neural network approach has been provided in [1] and [3].
3.   Retrieve tags. If a tab contains more than one word, split it. Create a set without duplicates.
4.   Check which tags appear in the textual transcription of the original video sequence. Limit the set of cards to these tags that occur in the textual transcription of the original video sequence.
5.   Create a summary of the original video sequence.
6.   Retrieve an audio track from the recently created summary [7].
7.   Use the ASR engine to obtain a textual transcription of the summarized video sequence.
8.   Check which tags appear in the textual transcription of the summarized video sequence. Create a set of cards that occur in the textual transcription of the synthesized video sequence.
9.   Check the tags that occur in the summarized and the original video sequence. Calculate statistics.

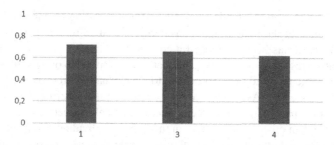

Fig. 13. Objective (tag-based) evaluation procedure results per scenario.

4.3   Experiment Results

This Subsection presents results for the objective, tag-based method. In Fig. 13, one can observe the relative number of tags in the summarized video sequences and the number of cards in the original video sequences – for all tested video sequences, grouped by scenarios.

As we can see, for most of the selected video sequences, the percentage of occurring tags in summaries is above 60. It means that they contain most of the content described in tags. It is a valuable check.

Regarding the winning scenario, it is not evident which one the responders indicated as the best one. All three scenarios gave more or less similar results; however, with a slightly visible indication of scene 1.

The difference between scenario one and the next scenario 3 is in practice five percentage points, which finally does allow to draw some slight conclusions.

The relatively high position of scenario 1 for objective evaluation is puzzling. While in the case of subjective assessment, the choice of a particular version of the summary is mostly a result of the respondent's taste, the objective evaluation, after all, includes the content of critical words in the review. Moreover, if so, it would be logical that the scenarios three and four should be the winning ones (which work just on the principle of focusing on compelling content), rather than ssituation1 (which only considers the visual aspect). In the meantime, it is not happening. So, the question is, wherefrom does this delicate advantage of Scenario 1 come?

Perhaps the answer stems from a particular feature of scenario 1, which does not appear in scenes 3 and 4. Now, in the scene, the first shot is rigorously included in the summary (in which, in the case of news and reports, it is not uncommon to find most valuable, crucial words). It naturally raises statistics in the case of objective evaluation. Meanwhile, scenario three and scenario four do not include such a rule, based solely on the analysis of the text. Consequently, the summary in inch consists first shot only in about 20% of cases. Perhaps, then, the quality of the summarizations generated in scenarios three and four could be increased using the rigid rule of incorporating the first shot, straight from scene.

5 Conclusion

Considering the performed evaluation about the different existing scenarios of the system and the assessment of the final system considering the situation that performed better, it is believed that it has been developed a complete evaluation procedure, which has provided exciting results for our policy, and that can be applied to other similar systems.

This deliverable reported two approached to the evaluation procedures, a subjective one and an objective one. As mentioned, the purpose of the described research was to try to narrow the space of possible scenarios. The actual evaluation did not indicate situations worse than others. Meanwhile, in the light of individual results obtained, the researches cannot unambiguously indicate one single scenario, recommended as the only one for further development. However, the researchers can state with certainty that the new development of scene 1, which has received many negative evaluations among professionals, should be discontinued. At the same time, as said, there is not a precise winner scenario. Still, considering the results obtained by the evaluations by the professionals, scene three has been considered as best scenario because of the obtained better results, even if the difference is little.

As a final subjective evaluation, scenario three has been used to generate the summaries of some videos, and different users have performed some tests to know how well the system functions. The obtained results, with an average above 70 out of 100, indicate that the performance of the system is excellent. It must be considered that the results of the tests, apart from the quality of the summary, depending on the understanding and individual capabilities of the evaluators.

It is considered that the objective of the project has been fulfilled and the value of the developed system is deemed to be high, as, it includes two different ways of evaluating a video summarization system evaluation, one that reflects the physical quality and other that reflects the real quality considered by the final users. It has been tested with a real project, getting promising results. So, the developed evaluation procedure can be used for the evaluation of any video summaries system, as a general use evaluation procedure has been established.

Acknowledgement. Research work funded by CHIST-ERA call 2014 (project AMIS under the topic Human Language Understanding: Grounding Language Learning). Research work by Michał Grega and Mikołaj Leszczuk funded by the National Science Center, Poland (project registration number 2015/16/Z/ST7/00559).

References

1. Smaïli, K., et al.: Summarizing videos into a target language: methodology, architectures and evaluation. J. Intell. Fuzzy Syst., 1–2 (2019)
2. Smaïli, K., et al.: A first summarization system of a video in a target language. In: Choroś, K., Kopel, M., Kukla, E., Siemiński, A. (eds.) MISSI 2018. AISC, vol. 833, pp. 77–88. Springer, Cham (2019). https://doi.org/10.1007/978-3-319-98678-4_10
3. Komorowski, A., Janowski, L., Leszczuk, M.: Evaluation of multimedia content summarization algorithms. In: Choroś, K., Kopel, M., Kukla, E., Siemiński, A. (eds.) MISSI 2018. AISC, vol. 833, pp. 424–433. Springer, Cham (2019). https://doi.org/10.1007/978-3-319-98678-4_43
4. Amato, F., Castiglione, A., Moscato, V., Picadillo, A.: Giancarlo Sperlì. Multimedia summarization using social media content, Multimedia Tools Appl. (2018)
5. Mani, I., House, D., Klein, G., Hirschman, L., Firmin, T., Sondheim, B.: The TIPSTER SUMAC Text Summarization Evaluation. In: Proceedings of EACL '99 (1999)
6. Lloret, E., Plaza, L., Aker, A.: The challenging task of summary evaluation: an overview. Lang. Resour. Eval. **52**(1), 101–148 (2017). https://doi.org/10.1007/s10579-017-9399-2
7. Jouvet, D., Langlois, D., Menacer, M.A., Fohr, D., Mella, O., Smaïli, K.: About vocabulary adaptation for automatic speech recognition of video data. In: ICNLSSP'2017 - International Conference on Natural Language, Signal and Speech Processing, Casablanca, Morocco, pp. 1–5, December 2017

Survey on the State-Of-The-Art Methods for Objective Video Quality Assessment in Recognition Tasks

Kamil Kawa[1], Mikołaj Leszczuk[1(✉)] [iD], and Atanas Boev[2]

[1] AGH University of Science and Technology, 30059 Kraków, Poland
vq@kt.agh.edu.pl, leszczuk@agh.edu.pl
[2] Huawei Technologies Duesseldorf GmbH, 40549 Duesseldorf, Germany
atanas.boev@huawei.com
http://vq.kt.agh.edu.pl

Abstract. This paper is a technical report, presenting a survey on the state-of-the-art methods for objective video quality assessment in recognition tasks. It bases on the most up-to-date solutions, developed by various research teams. The study considers, among others, solutions developed by the AGH University research team, including the contributions to ITU-T Recommendation P.912 (dealing with video quality assessment methods for recognition tasks) as well as the video quality indicators (available at http://vq.kt.agh.edu.pl/). In particular, we consider evaluation metrics based on a trade-off between computer vision performance and compression efficiency.

Keywords: Closed-Circuit Television (CCTV) · Video surveillance · Advanced Driver Assistance System (ADAS) · Self-driving systems · Robot-based industrial production · Quality of Experience (QoE) · Quality of Service (QoS) · Metrics · Evaluation · Performance · Target Recognition Video (TRV) · Computer Vision (CV) · Video Quality Indicators (VQI) · Key Performance Indicators (KPI).

1 Problem Introduction

Nowadays, we have many metrics for overall Quality of Experience (QoE), both Full-Reference ones, like Peak Signal–to–Noise Ratio – PSNR or Structural Similarity – SSIM and No–Reference ones, like video quality indicators, successfully used in video processing systems for video quality evaluation. However, they are not appropriate for recognition tasks analytics (Target Recognition Video, TRV).

Given the use of TRV, qualitative tests do not focus on the subject's satisfaction with the video sequence quality, but instead, they measure how the subject uses TRV to accomplish certain tasks [14]. Purposes of this may include:

Supported by Huawei Innovation Research Program (HIRP).

- video surveillance – recognition of vehicle license plate numbers,
- telemedicine/remote diagnostics – correct diagnosis,
- fire safety – fire detection,
- rear backup cameras – parking the car,
- games – spotting and correctly reacting to a virtual enemy,
- video newscasts and reports editing – video summarization [6,7].

Since the number of for example surveillance cameras is growing extremely fast, the likelihood that automatic systems will be used to carry out this task is increasing as well. As presented in many scientific publications, automatic recognition algorithms are the clue to handle recognition tasks. Concerning the entertainment video, there were performed researches into the content parameters that most affect perceptual quality. These parameters form a framework creating predictors, and thus developing objective measurements, through the use of subjective testing. However, this framework is not appropriate for the recognition task. Due to that, one has to develop a new set of rules. The problem is not only limited to methods of examining the quality of a video. The condition when and how the video is collected is also crucial. One has to take into consideration the exposure, ISO, weather conditions, acuity, bit rate and many more to perform a valid experiment.

Moreover, a security surveillance system often produces weak – quality video, so it can not be relevant evidence in, for example, criminal cases. Based on that, some standards were established. By selecting components complies with the standard, a user achieves fully operable CCTV (Closed Circuit Television) system. Technical regulations affect different parts of a CCTV system like storage and playback of surveillance video, lenses, cameras, monitors, video motion detection equipment, local and primary control units, recording and hard copy equipment, video transmission. Of course, law regulations cover all the above [13]. For a long time, optimizing Visual QoE meant reducing the visibility of artefacts (e.g. noise or other disturbing factors) that occur due to technical limitations. Such a view based on the assumption that the sole appearance of artefacts would disrupt the whole visual experience. Some research has shown that, the type of device through which they access multimedia or the content type of the media influence the QoE. In other words, the visibility of an artefact alone is not the sole factor determining user satisfaction with media experiences anymore [27].

The traditional approach to video quality assessment mostly focuses on Quality of Service (QoS) techniques. However, it is now an obsolete method. To prepare a more accurate assessment of the video quality, one has to take into account the perception of the user. Based on the limitation of QoS for video applications, the QoE describes the performance of the whole, end-to-end video delivery system from the user's point of view. According to [21], several essential factors affect the perceived video quality of experience:

- quality degradation during the content production phase;
- artefact introduced by lossy compression;
- network transmission errors;

– application and display device-specific parameters;
– end user's preferences and perception model.

moreover, metrics, that fulfills the expectations:

– in-service applicable;
– no-reference quality assessment;
– high performance for diverse video content;
– coverage of all the mentioned factors contributing to the overall QoE;
– the mapping between measured parameters (QoS, artefacts level) and QoE.

Referring to [13], many parameters impact the ability to achieve a recognition task, but we can select five of them as the most important ones:

1. Usage time frame. It specifies if one needs to analyze the video in real-time or will be stored and analyzed later.
2. Discrimination level. It specifies a fine level of detail sought from the video.
3. Target size. Specifies whether the predicted region of interest in the video occupies a relatively small or large percentage of the video.
4. Lightning level. It specifies the anticipated lighting level of the scene.
5. Level of motion. It specifies the anticipated motion level in the video scene.

2   Assessments Environment

General viewing condition for subjective assessments has to be met. The conditions are divided into home and laboratory environment [8]

2.1   General Viewing Conditions for Subjective Assessments in Laboratory Environment

The assessors' viewing conditions should be arranged as follows (Tables 1 and 2):

Table 1. Viewing condition for subjective assessments in laboratory environment. The original source: [8]

Ratio of luminance of inactive screen to peak luminance:	$<=0.02$
Ratio of the luminance of the screen, when displaying only black level in a completely dark room, to that corresponding to peak white:	≈ 0.01
Maximum observation angle relative to the normal	30
Ratio of luminance of background behind picture monitor to peak luminance of picture	≈ 0.15
Chromaticity of background	D_{65}
Other room illumination	Low

Table 2. Viewing condition for subjective assessments in home environment. The original source: [8]

Inactive screen vs. peak luminance	<=0.02
Maximum relative vs. normal observation angle	30°
Screen size for a 4/3 format ratio	Screen size should satisfy PVD rules
Screen size for a 16/9 format ratio	Screen size should satisfy PVD rules
Monitor processing	Without digital processing
Peak luminance	200 cd/m²
Environmental illuminance on the screen	200 lux

2.2   General Viewing Conditions for Subjective Assessments in Home Environment

The viewing distance and the screen size have to be selected in order to satisfy PVD (preferred viewing distance). In Fig. 1, the PVD in the function of the screen size is shown. The information in the table and the function are recommending the PVD related screen size that should be used (Table 3).

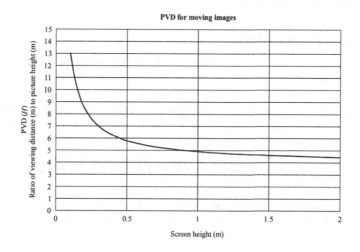

Fig. 1. PVD for moving images. The original source: [8]

3   Methods

ITU-T P.912 [18] introduces a lot of useful methods for the recognition task. This scientific paper defines subjective assessment methods for evaluating the quality of one-way video used for the target recognition task. Target refers to an object on video that the tester needs to identify (e.g. face, object, number). Target Recognition Video (TRV) is a video used as a tool that checks the ability

Table 3. Information on the PVD and related screen sizes. The original source: [8]

Screen diagonal (in)		Screen height (H)	PVD
4/3 ratio	16/9 ratio	(m)	(H)
12	15	0.18	9
15	18	0.23	8
20	24	0.30	7
29	36	0.45	6
60	73	0.91	5
>100	>120	>1.53	3–5

to recognize specific targets of interests in the video stream. TRV is applicable in various services such as surveillance, licence place identification, human identification, telemedicine and more. According to [18], one can divide the target into three categories:

1. Human identification (including facial recognition)
2. Object identification
3. Alphanumeric identification

3.1 Single Choice Method

As the title implies, it is a single answer method. One may use it if there is an unambiguous answer to the identification question. This technique is utilizable for alphanumeric character recognition scenarios. The test driver asks a tester which letter(s), or number(s) was/were appearing in specific are of the video. The answer can be evaluated only as a binary one (correct or incorrect). According to that, Yes or No test is also acceptable. For example, one may ask a viewer if a certain object was present in the scene. In such a method, it is essential to ensure that the available answers are easy to understand. Care must also be taken to avoid terminology differences. The use of "unsure" answer is allowed, but not recommended. The reason for that is the fact that testers overuse this option, which leads to contamination of the experiment result.

3.2 Multiple Choice Method

This method is especially appropriate for all discrimination class levels (introduced in ITU–T P.912 [18]) and target categories. For this method, the test driver shows the video, and the list of possible answers is listed below. After presenting the video, the viewers must choose the label that is the closest to what they recognize on the clip. The use of fixed multiple choices eliminates any possible misunderstanding that could arise from open questions. Due to that, more accurate measurements are possible. The number of choices offered to the tester depends on the number of alternative scenes presented. As in the previous method, one must take special care when "unsure" is one of the listed choices.

3.3   Timed Task Method

A viewer may be asked to watch for a particular action or object that the viewer is about to recognize in the video clip. When the tester perceives that the target occurs, one can push a timer. In the timed task, the experimenter can determine whether the time falls within an acceptable time-frame for decision making. This time-frames are applicable for example in video scenarios: a tester is responding to a violent situation and needs to identify whether crowd members have real weapons versus a person who is chasing a vehicle and needs to read the license plate.

3.4   Scenes

TRV is used to perform a recognition task. Scenes should contain targets consistent with the application under study. Measurement of the test mostly focused on a subject's ability to identify objects and actions. Here the problem may be that a viewer may memorize the scene content and use other visual clues to remember the identity of the target. Therefore, a set of scenes containing multiple version may replace a particular scene. It is the best way to control the differences between the versions. The example scenario: a person walks across the field of view carrying objects. The set of videos would consist of multiple shots using different object and different people. The number of scenarios in the set should be large enough to reduce the likelihood of scene memorization. Of course, the experts should determine the content of each scene. The difference could be, for example, an object that a person on the video is carrying. Experts should identify critical tasks or parameters of the scenes. One should base a set of multiple-choice answer and experiment design on these parameters. One should create the scene in a way that, the object of interest appears in the video at a resolution realistically expected in practice.

3.5   Image Semantic Recognition

As [11] presents, this is one of the most challenging problems in the field of computer vision. Much effort has been put by the research community to improve image scene and object recognition performances: creating a larger data set, designing better features, training more robust machines. Due to the wider availability of "supercomputers," the more complicated algorithms could be applied. That allowed for the growth of Convolutional Neural Networks (CNNs) and resulted in enormous progress in the field of image semantic recognition. The pioneering efforts of using CNNs for target identification was AlexNet by Krizhevsky et al. [11]. Based on five convolutional and three fully connected layers, the AlexNet processes 224×224 pictures to map them into a 1000-dimensional vector, the components of which describe the likelihood rates that the input picture refers to either of a thousand predefined target classes. Simultaneously with target identification, scene identification has also had its part of dynamic growth with the arrival of CNNs. An example of recently proposed trained CNN for scene recognition is trained on the Places image data-set, which contains 2.5 million images with a scene category label. There were 205 scenes category defined. The system outputs a 205-dimensional vector with components describing the likelihood that the input picture refers to any of the 205 scene classes.

3.6   Machine Learning

It is a new technique to quantify the correlation between QoS and QoE. Machine learning algorithms are used to predict the QoE, based on inference rules extracted from a set of measurements reflecting the network state and the user's perception. In [17], the authors present a Machine Learning–based bitrate estimation system. It parses the bitrate information from IP packet level measurements. In a presented model, a decision tree classifier is used to assess the QoE based on the bitrate of video segments. In the first step, YouTube traffic is identified based on the DNS Lookup method. Then, one identified the HTTPS adaptive streaming protocol. Finally, one extracts the bitrate identifier, and the suitable metrics are computed to assess the video QoE. The other, commonly used classification machine learning algorithms to predict QoE are Naïve Bayes, OneR, Random Forest, Sequential Minimal Optimization.

3.7   The Double-Stimulus Impairment Scale (DSIS) Method (the EBU Method)

The double-stimulus (EBU) cyclic method. The tester is firstly presented with an unimpaired reference, then with the same picture impaired. Then the person is asked to vote on the second, keeping in mind the first one. A full session lasts up to a half-hour. In that time the assessor is presented with a series of pictures or sequences in random order. The series are ordered randomly with impairments covering all required combinations. The unimpaired picture is included in the set ready for assessment. At the end of the session, the mean score for each test condition and the test picture is measured. The result obtained using this method shows that the stability of the results is higher for small impairments than for large ones. There are two variants to the structure of presentations:

1. The reference picture or sequence and the test picture/sequence are presented only on time
2. The reference picture or sequence and the test picture/sequence are presented two times

Of course, the second variant is more time - consuming, but it may be applied if the discrimination of minimal impairments is required. Finally, there is a five-grade impairment scale:

5   imperceptible
4   perceptible, but not annoying
3   slightly annoying
2   annoying
1   very annoying.

4   Metrics

Referring to [9] and [12] some subjective and objective recognition metrics have to be mentioned. The listed ones are not contexted specific. Moreover, these do not apply video surveillance-oriented standardized discrimination levels.

4.1   Peak Signal-to-Noise Ratio (PSNR)

It is one of the best-known and most often used methods for measuring the video quality. The result is the ratio of the maximum signal power to the noise power distorting the signal. Usually, one expresses it in the logarithmic decibel scale. It is used to determine the visual similarity of the reference and distorted image. One usually derives PSNR via the mean squared error (MSE) between the two signals about the maximum possible value of the luminance of the images. The bigger the PSNR, the better.

4.2   Structural Similarity Index Metric (SSIM)

SSIM is designed to improve on methods such as a PSNR. This metric does not compare pixels but the elements of the scene visible by the human eye. So, it uses a functional model of the HVS (Human Visual System). One divides performance of quality of video sequences using SSIM into three layers: the local layer of a block-shaped region, the distortion map obtained at the frame level and the layer are spanning the complete video sequence. Firstly an $8times8$-pixel blocks are extracted both from the original and the distorted video sequence. At this Level, SSIM is calculated separately for each block. Next, the local quality values are combined to form a value for the quality level of the frame. The Level of brightness calculates the quality of the local regions. Finally, one calculates quality for the whole video sequence. The quality level of each frame is weighted using frame motion vectors due to some types of distortion (e.g. blur) do not affect the quality of the scenes in the presence of motion. SSIM method focuses on the texture components of each frame.

4.3   Video Quality Metric (VQM)

The Institute for Telecommunication Science originally developed this method. It is implemented in several different ways, depending on the area. It measures the perceptual effects of video impairments including blurring, globe nose, block distortion and colour distortion, and combine them into a single metric, by using a linear combination of these parameters. VQM's task, in general, is to assess the quality of an image, so the degree of distortion seen by a human being. Usually, the Video Quality Metric values highly correlate with tester's subjective opinions. Value of 0 means no difference between images. The higher the value, the worse quality and the values over-perform ones from PSNR.

4.4   No-Reference Blockiness Metric

This metric explains the pixel blocking. It bases on the property of a Discrete Cosine Transform (DCT). The use of lossy compression often causes blockiness Block artefacts. It is a result of the independent coding of pixel blocks (like 8×8 pixels) in most of the currently used video coding algorithms including H.261 – H.265, MPEG-4 Part 2 and Part 10 or MPEG-2. These algorithms use a quantization of DCT for each block separately, which cause noise sharpening. Such a scenario leads to coding artefacts in the form discontinuities for coded block boundary.

4.5   No-Reference Blur Metric

It is one of the most common approaches toward image blur estimation. It utilizes the fact that blur makes the image edges less sharp. Referring to [4], this metric is based only on an average width of sharp edges. It terms of prediction accuracy sharp edges selection is the most important part. First of all, strong edges are detected. Then, one measures their width as number neighbouring pixels that fulfil specified in [4] criteria. In general approach, Blur Metric measures the luminance change in the neighbourhood of each pixel. The bigger the value, the smaller the blur level, so the better the quality. The primary source of blur in compression techniques is the truncation of high-frequency components in the transform domain of an image. Other possible reasons for the blurring of an image or video can be out-of-focus capturing, relative motion between the camera and the object being captured or limitations in the optical system.

4.6   BRISQUE

It is a shortcut that stands for Blind/Referenceless Image Spatial Quality Evaluator. It is a statistical model of pair-wise products of neighbouring luminance values. The model's parameters are further used to quantify the naturalness of the image. It was proven in [16], that characterizing locally normalized luminance coefficients in this way is sufficient for both, to quantify naturalness and to quantify quality in the presence of distortion.

Regarding paper, BRISQUE performs well on an independent database, analyze its complexity and produce as good results as other NR IQA approaches. BRISQUE requires a training procedure to calibrate the regressor module. It is a good practice to divide the database into two randomly chosen subsets 80% training and 20% testing. It is done to ensure that the reported results do not depend on features extracted from known spatial content. Such a situation can artificially improve performance and is hard to discover. To produce reliable results, this random train-test procedure could be repeated many times (1000 times in the mentioned paper). One calculates the reported result as a median of the performance across those iterations. To assess performance between the predicted algorithm's score and DMOS, one used the Spearman's rank-ordered correlation coefficient (SROCC) and Pearson's (linear) correlation coefficient (LCC).

Moreover, this algorithm is applicable for real-time blind assessment of visual quality due to its low complexity. This method is computational efficiency and obtains excellent quality prediction performance. It all makes BRISQUE an attractive option for practical applications. Exemplary utilization could be the usage of a quality measure to increment the performance of image repair algorithms. The performance of BRISQUE remains stable in terms of variation in the window size used to compute the mean and variances. The obtained results from Brovik's experiments show that BRISQUE is height competitive with all no reference algorithms tested and statistically better than the full reference algorithms PSNR and SSIM [16].

4.7 BLIINDS-II

It is a single-stage framework that relies on a statistical model of local discrete cosine transform (DCT) coefficients. Firstly, one extracts a set of features from an image Then Bayesian approach is used to predict quality scores. One used model parameters to design features appropriate for perceptual image quality score prediction. As the image quality changes, the statistics of DCT features adjust predictably. BLIINDS-II differs from other NR-IQA algorithms that it is non-distortion-specific. Experiments performed in [24] have shown that DCT coefficients have a symmetrical distribution. Their approach relies on the IQA algorithm. Ground meaning is performing learning on how the NSS parameters vary across the perception of different Level of image distortion. One derives features, necessary to training phase from a statistical model of original image DCT coefficients versus various perceptual levels of image distortion. One trains the algorithm on such features, and the model's output is the prediction of perceptual image quality scores (Fig. 2).

In the first step, an image is entering the IQA pipeline. Next, one computes the 2-dimensional DCT-transform coefficient. In this stage, the image is partitioning into equally sized blocks. The next step of the flow applies generalized Gaussian modelling to each block of DCT coefficients. The third step is related to computing the derived generalized Gaussian model parameters. These are the key features used to predict image quality score. The final stage of the pipeline is a prediction quality score for the image. As a prediction algorithm, one used a simple Bayesian model. This approach maximizes the probability that the image has a certain quality score [24], taking into consideration the model-based features extracted from the image.

4.8 Transform Domain Measure of Enhancement - TDME

The quality of the images captured from security application is most of the time highly susceptible to environmental lighting conditions such as poor or non-uniform illumination. In [23] authors present a metric for independent evaluation

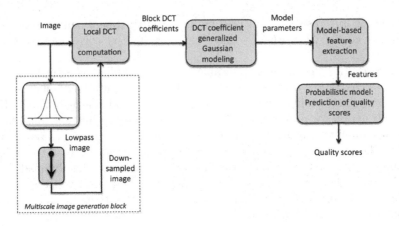

Fig. 2. High-level overview of the BLIINDS-II framework. The original picture source: [24]

that enables the security system to determine the best human vision quality image automatically. The metric is not dependent on the algorithm. Due to that, it can be utilized for a diversity of enhancement algorithms. TDME belongs to a category where the measure of image enhancement is the transform domain measures. These measures are calculated by analyzing the transformation of the image (DCT, DFT, DTW) [25] and [28]. The main advantage in comparison to measures operated in the spatial domain is that transform domain processes are less dependent on image attributes. An image attribute that is present at a certain part of an image would be scrambled in the transform of image based on its frequency contents.

Moreover, these measures reduce the processing time for the enhancement systems that operate in transform domains since the image transform has already been computed during the enhancement process. Proposed TDME measure is based on the idea that enhancing the contrast of an image would create more high-frequency content in the enhanced image compared to the original image. In other words, if considering a block of k-by-k in the lower frequency section of the image, after contrast enhancement some of the energy from this region will be transferred to the higher frequency region of the 2D spectrum as explained in Fig. 3.

The whole process begins with taking a two-dimensional DCT of grey-scale image. A sliding block of k-by-k pixels (k = 1, 2, 3, ..., minimum of rows and columns) is used to separate the low frequency and the high-frequency region of the image. The average magnitude of DCT coefficients for the high-frequency region normalized by the average magnitude of DCT coefficients for the entire image would calculate the TDME measure for the current sliding k-by-k block 1. Equation originally published at: [25]

$$TDME_k \frac{\frac{1}{MN-k^2} \sum_{i=k}^{M} \sum_{j=k}^{N} Mag(DCT(i,j))}{\frac{1}{MN} \sum_{i=1}^{M} \sum_{j=1}^{N} Mag(DCT(i,j))} \tag{1}$$

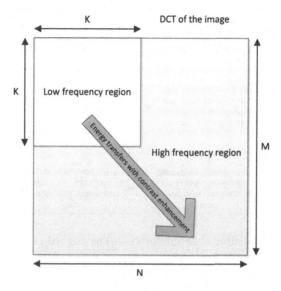

Fig. 3. The enhancement process presenting energy transfer from low to high frequency region of the image DCT. The original picture source: [25]

The numerator denotes the average magnitude in the high-frequency region, and the denominator shows the average magnitude over the entire 2-D spectrum. The general algorithm process is presented in Fig. 5:

The result presented in [23] confirmed that this method is suitable for real-time autonomous security system imaging applications, due to it does not require a reference, nor has parameters to select or optimize (Fig. 4).

Fig. 4. (1) DCT Transform of original image, (2) DCT Transform of enhanced image using unsharp masking. The original picture source: [25]

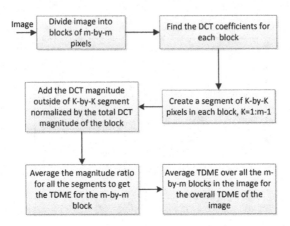

Fig. 5. TDME generator algorithm process. The original picture source: [25]

4.9   Neural Networks - CNN

The recent researches are keen on developing a new, no-reference image quality metric. As an example, one has to present Convolutional Neural Networks (CNNs) [22]. The network structure already includes parts that extract features from input images and a regression part to output a prediction for the corresponding input. Then the training is performed. This process optimizes not only the prediction model but also the layers responsible for extracting characteristic features for the problem at hand. This study [10] shows that such an approach brings promising results. Although, while using neural network users should be aware that, the high dimensionality of learnable CNN could lead to overfitting of the training data.

On the other hand, the key problem in non-reference image quality assessment is how to effectively model the human visual system in a computer understandable manner. The proposed model [19] is based on a novel framework which consists of a fully convolutional neural network (FCNN) and a pooling network to solve this problem. FCNN can predict pixel-by-pixel similar quality map using only distortion image as an output. To do so, it utilizes the intermediate similarity maps derived from conventional full-reference image quality assessment methods. At the process end, a deep network maps the quality map into a score. The Fig. 6 represents the proposed BPSQM framework. As an input, the network is given an index map label. One used the predicted quality map as a measurement reflection for describing distorted images. Then the fully convolutional neural network simulates the process of FR-IQA methods. In case of success, as an output, it generates a similarity index map. Next, with the known score label (individual result), pooling strategies predict a global image quality score based on the predicted quality map. The main advantage of this model is the fact that FCNN is learning pixel distortion features in intermediate layers by adding similarity map labels.

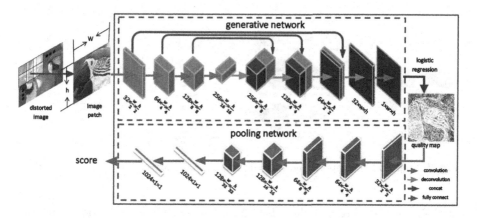

Fig. 6. Architecture of BPSQM framework. The original picture source: [19]

4.10   Single-Image Super-Resolution (SR)

These algorithms aim to construct a high-quality high-resolution (HR) image from a single low-resolution source. Most SR methods are focused on generating sharper edges with more vibrant textures. Edges are evaluated by measuring the relationship between super-resolved HR and images using full-reference metrics like the mean squared error (MSE), peak signal-to-noise ratio (PSNR) and structural similarity (SSIM) index. Proposed solution in [15] in the first step human subject studies using a broad set of SR images should be performed. As an output, one collects perceptual scores. With these scores for training, no-reference quality assessment algorithms that match visual perception well are suggested as the best option. The approach uses the same methodology as that of general image quality assessment (IQA) approaches. However, the difference is that evaluation of the effectiveness of the signal reconstruction by SR algorithms is essential rather than analyzing noise and distortions (e.g., compression and fading) as in existing IQA methods. The proposed algorithm utilizes three types of statistical properties as features: local and global frequency variations and spatial discontinuity. It has been done to quantify artefacts and assess the quality of SR images. Figure 7 shows the main steps of algorithm learning.

Since one generates SR images from LR inputs, the task is a restoration of high-frequency components on LR images. To quantify the high-frequency artefacts introduced by SR restoration, the proposed solution in [15] is to transform SR images into the DCT domain and fit the DCT coefficients by the generalized Gaussian distribution (GGD) as in [24]. The chosen model for the features of local frequency, global frequency and spatial discontinuity with three independent with regression forests [2]. The outputs are linearly regressed on perceptual scores to predict the quality of evaluated SR images. Since the [15] contains detailed results, the main one reflects that the proposed metric regress three types of low-level statistical features extracted from SR images to perceptual scores. Experimental results demonstrate that the proposed metric performs

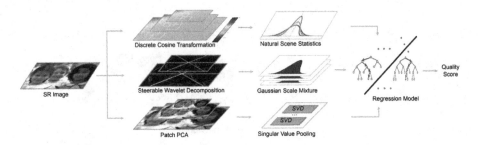

Fig. 7. Steps of the proposed no-reference metric. The original picture source: [15].

favourably against state-of-the-art quality assessment methods for SR performance evaluation.

4.11 Deep Neural Networks for No-Reference and Full-Reference Image Quality Assessment

A deep neural network is going to be more useful due to the easy availability of enormous data amount and computation power. The one solution proposed in [1] based on deep CNN (convolutional neural network) with architecture, comprising ten convolutional layers and five pooling layers for feature extraction, and two fully connected layers for regression. In a general IQA setting, CNN shows that network depth has an essential impact on performance. As first, one has addressed the FR IQA problem. To handle it the Siamese networks know from classification tasks [5] was used. One extracts the features from both, the reference and the distortion image. In general, the number of parameters that need to be trained in deep networks is significant, so the training set has to contain enough data samples in order to avoid overfitting.

In comparison to most data-driven IQA approaches, patches input to the network are unnormalized. It enables the proposed method to deal with distortions introduced by luminance and contrast changes. To this end, global image quality is derived by pooling local patch qualities only by averaging and, for convenience, this method's name is Deep Image QuAlity Measure for FR IQA (DIQaM-FR). Nevertheless, the abolishment of one of the feature extraction paths in the Siamese network allows applying the network within an NR context as well. Technical details of the built network establish that Siamese networks are used to learn similarity relations between two inputs.

For this, the inputs are processed in parallel by two networks sharing their synaptic connection weights. One treats the connected features as an input to the regression part of the network. Figure 8 represents the architecture of the proposed network.

For the proposed IQA approach, one split images into 32×32 sized patches used as an input to the neural network. The choice of strategy for spatial pooling affects the training and have a deep explanation. As [1] states, the easiest way

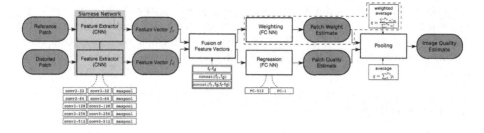

Fig. 8. Deep neural network model for FR IQA. The original picture source: [1].

to pool estimated visual qualities y_i to a global image-wise quality estimate q is to assume identical importance of every image region (every image path i) as

$$q = \tfrac{1}{N_p} \sum_i^{N_p} y_i$$

Where N denotes the number of patches sampled from the image. Commonly, one uses the MSE as a minimization criterion. As mentioned, the approach to use the deep network in NR IQA required to abolish the branch that extracts features from the reference patch from the Siamese network. Figure 9 represents the architecture of the proposed network in research for NR IQA.

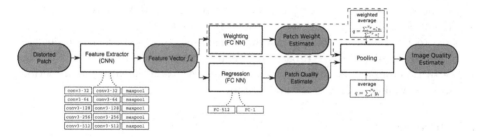

Fig. 9. Deep neural network architecture for NR IQA. The original picture source: [1].

Experiments are performed on the 3 databases: LIVE [26], TID2013 [20], CSIQ [3]. For evaluation, the networks are trained on LIVE or TID2013 database. For cross-validation, databases are randomly split by reference image. It guarantees that there are no distorted or undistorted images used in testing. To make errors and gradients comparable for different databases, one linearly maps the MOS values of TID2013 and CLIVE and the DMOS values of CSIQ to the same range as the DMOS values in LIVE. For evaluation, prediction accuracy is quantified by Pearson linear correlation coefficient (LCC), and Spearman rank-order coefficient (SROCC). For both correlation metrics, a value close to 1 indicates the high performance of a specific quality measure.

Results obtained in the experiment show that there is room for optimization in terms of feature dimensionality and balancing the ratio between network parameters. Here, prediction performance and generalization ability are essential to be studied, although there are still many obstacles and challenges for purely data-driven approaches. The whole experiment performed in [1] suggests that neural networks used for IQA have lots of potentials and are here with us to stay.

5   Conclusion

This paper included a general review of possible methods and metrics that could be used to video quality objective or subjective assessment. Based on the limitation of QoS for video applications, the QoE describes the performance of the whole end-to-end video delivery system from the user's point of view. The key point for every test session is the general viewing conditions for subjective assessments in the laboratory and home environment. Parameters are listed in 2. This Survey focuses on three possible methodologies for measuring QoE: the no – reference model without access to the original video source, the reduced-reference model, which has limited knowledge about source video and tries to combine this with real-time measurement to predict the QoE and the full-reference model with full access to the reference video. Section 3 defined various methods applicable to the recognition task. It contains a list with a brief description of used methods in scientific experiments, mostly in [18].

Furthermore, Sect. 4 introduced a range of subjective and objective recognition metrics. However, a big part is a description of NR VQA (e.g. BLINDS, BRISQUE) and ML IQA based on Neural Network (mostly on CNN), which seems to be a rising trend for measuring the quality of experience, especially assessment quality of FR/NR based on a neural network like ImageNet, AlexNet. The section showed some metrics experimenters' results measuring its performance, as well as a framework architecture.

References

1. Bosse, S., Maniry, D., Müller, K., Wiegand, T., Samek, W.: Deep neural networks for no-reference and full-reference image quality assessment. IEEE Trans. Image Process. 27(1), 206–219 (2018). https://doi.org/10.1109/TIP.2017.2760518
2. Breiman, L.: Random forests. Mach. Learn. 45(1), 5–32 (2001). https://doi.org/10.1023/A:1010933404324
3. Larson, E.C., Chandler, D.: Most apparent distortion: full-reference image quality assessment and the role of strategy. J. Electron. Imaging 19, 011006 (2010). https://doi.org/10.1117/1.3267105
4. Cerqueira, E., Janowski, L., Leszczuk, M., Papir, Z., Romaniak, P.: Video artifacts assessment for live mobile streaming applications. In: Mauthe, A., Zeadally, S., Cerqueira, E., Curado, M. (eds.) FMN 2009. LNCS, vol. 5630, pp. 242–247. Springer, Heidelberg (2009). https://doi.org/10.1007/978-3-642-02472-6_26
5. Chopra, S., Hadsell, R., LeCun, Y.: Learning a similarity metric discriminatively, with application to face verification. In: 2005 IEEE Computer Society Conference on Computer Vision and Pattern Recognition, CVPR 2005, vol. 1, pp. 539–546. IEEE (2005)

6. Garcia-Zapirain, B.: A proposed methodology for subjective evaluation of video and text summarization. In: Choroś, K., Kopel, M., Kukla, E., Siemiński, A. (eds.) MISSI 2018. AISC, vol. 833, pp. 396–404. Springer, Cham (2019). https://doi.org/10.1007/978-3-319-98678-4_40

7. Grega, M.: An integrated AMIS prototype for automated summarization and translation of newscasts and reports. In: Choroś, K., Kopel, M., Kukla, E., Siemiński, A. (eds.) MISSI 2018. AISC, vol. 833, pp. 415–423. Springer, Cham (2019). https://doi.org/10.1007/978-3-319-98678-4_42

8. ITU-R: Recommendation 500-10: Methodology for the subjective assessment of the quality of television pictures. ITU-R Rec. BT.500 (2000)

9. Janowski, L., Leszczuk, M., Larabi, M.-C., Ukhanova, A.: Recognition tasks. In: Möller, S., Raake, A. (eds.) Quality of Experience. TSTS, pp. 383–394. Springer, Cham (2014). https://doi.org/10.1007/978-3-319-02681-7_26

10. Kang, L., Ye, P., Li, Y., Doermann, D.: Convolutional neural networks for no-reference image quality assessment. In: Proceedings of the IEEE Conference on Computer Vision and Pattern Recognition, pp. 1733–1740 (2014)

11. Krizhevsky, A., Sutskever, I., Hinton, G.E.: Imagenet classification with deep convolutional neural networks. Commun. ACM **60**(6), 84–90 (2017). https://doi.org/10.1145/3065386

12. Leszczuk, M., Janowski, L., Barkowsky, M.: Freely available large-scale video quality assessment database in full-hd resolution with h.264 coding. In: 2013 IEEE Globecom Workshops (GC Wkshps), pp. 1162–1167 (December 2013). https://doi.org/10.1109/GLOCOMW.2013.6825150

13. Leszczuk, M.I., Stange, I., Ford, C.: Determining image quality requirements for recognition tasks in generalized public safety video applications: definitions, testing, standardization, and current trends. In: 2011 IEEE International Symposium on Broadband Multimedia Systems and Broadcasting (BMSB), pp. 1–5 (June 2011). https://doi.org/10.1109/BMSB.2011.5954938

14. Leszczuk, M.: Revising and improving the ITU-T recommendation p.912. J. Telecommun. Inf. Technol. **2015**, 10–14 (2015)

15. Ma, C., Yang, C.Y., Yang, X., Yang, M.H.: Learning a no-reference quality metric for single-image super-resolution. Comput. Vis. Image Underst. **158**, 1–16 (2017)

16. Mittal, A., Moorthy, A.K., Bovik, A.C.: No-reference image quality assessment in the spatial domain. IEEE Trans. Image Process. **21**(12), 4695–4708 (2012)

17. Orsolic, I., Pevec, D., Suznjevic, M., Skorin-Kapov, L.: A machine learning approach to classifying YouTube QoE based on encrypted network traffic. Multimedia Tools Appl., 1–35 (2017). https://doi.org/10.1007/s11042-017-4728-4

18. ITU-T P.910: Subjective video quality assessment methods for recognition tasks (2016)

19. Pan, D., Shi, P., Hou, M., Ying, Z., Fu, S., Zhang, Y.: Blind predicting similar quality map for image quality assessment. In: Proceedings of the IEEE Conference on Computer Vision and Pattern Recognition, pp. 6373–6382 (2018)

20. Ponomarenko, N., et al.: Color image database tid2013: peculiarities and preliminary results. In: European workshop on visual information processing (EUVIP), pp. 106–111. IEEE (2013)

21. Romaniak, P.: Towards realization of a framework for integrated video quality of experience assessment. In: 2009 IEEE INFOCOM Workshops, pp. 1–2 (2009). https://doi.org/10.1109/INFCOMW.2009.5072201

22. Russakovsky, O.: Imagenet large scale visual recognition challenge. Int. J. Comput. Vis. **115**(3), 211–252 (2015)

23. Saad, M.A., Bovik, A.C.: Natural motion statistics for no-reference video quality assessment. In: 2009 International Workshop on Quality of Multimedia Experience. pp. 163–167 (July 2009). https://doi.org/10.1109/QOMEX.2009.5246957

24. Saad, M.A., Bovik, A.C., Charrier, C.: Blind image quality assessment: a natural scene statistics approach in the DCT domain. IEEE Trans. Image Process. **21**(8), 3339–3352 (2012)

25. Samani, A., Panetta, K., Agaian, S.: Transform domain measure of enhancement-TDME - for security imaging applications. In: 2013 IEEE International Conferenceon Technologies for Homeland Security (HST), pp. 265–270 (November 2013). https://doi.org/10.1109/THS.2013.6699012

26. Sheikh, H.R., Sabir, M.F., Bovik, A.C.: A statistical evaluation of recent full reference image quality assessment algorithms. IEEE Trans. Image Process. **15**(11), 3440–3451 (2006)

27. Siahaan, E., Hanjalic, A.: Visual Quality of Experience: A Metric Driven Perspective. TU Delft (2018). https://books.google.pl/books?id=JrLzwQEACAAJ

28. Tang, J., Peli, E., Acton, S.: Image enhancement using a contrast measure in the compressed domain. IEEE Sig. Process. Lett. **10**(10), 289–292 (2003)

Three-Dimensional Operating Room with Unlimited Perspective

Klaudia Proniewska[1]($\boxtimes$) (iD), Agnieszka Pręgowska[2] (iD), Damian Dolega-Dolegowski[1], Jakub Chmiel[3], and Dariusz Dudek[4,5]

[1] Department of Bioinformatics and Telemedicine, Jagiellonian University Medical College, Lazarza 16, 31-530 Krakow, Poland
klaudia.proniewska@uj.edu.pl

[2] Institute of Fundamental Technological Research, Polish Academy of Sciences, Pawinskiego 5B, 02-106 Warsaw, Poland

[3] Department of Cardiac and Vascular Diseases, Jagiellonian University Medical College, John Paul II Hospital, Pradnicka 80, 31-202 Krakow, Poland

[4] Jagiellonian University Medical College, Institute of Cardiology, University Hospital, Jakubowskiego 2, 30-688 Kraków, Poland

[5] Maria Cecilia Hospital, Gvm Care & Research, Cotignola, RA, Italy

Abstract. Apart from operating tables and modern surgical instruments, the modern operating rooms are equipped with displays and video surveillance systems. The three-dimensional operating room allows users to watch medics perform surgery from different, individually chosen, points of view. For the first time, it is possible to reproduce/repeat the course of the operations and change the perspective or position, from which it is observed. Here, we proposed a solution based on Microsoft HoloLens and Azure Kinect DK devices as remote support to patient management. The operating room is transferred to the digital form in real-time using Augmented Reality based technologies. Users can move around the digital place like a ghost in real space. The approach proposed allows users to see observe surgery from any point of view they want without disturbing the surgeon's workflow. They can change their positions, angle, and place of observation. All environmental restrictions disappear. The presented solution gives trainees a convenient opportunity to learn. It may make a significant contribution to improving the surgeon training, patients' outcomes, and may allow virtual medical consultations during the surgery between specialists without them leaving their workplace.

Keywords: 3D operating room · Augmented Reality · HoloLens

1 Introduction

Over the years, image and sound recording systems have evolved. Starting from static black and white motion blurred pictures, through color photos, silent films, digital pictures, and movies ending with 360° ones. There are still limited with the position, from which camera records pictures and/or movies. The proposed solution changes diametrically the bounds of users' visual perception. Virtual Reality (VR) and its variation,

© Springer Nature Switzerland AG 2020
A. Dziech et al. (Eds.): MCSS 2020, CCIS 1284, pp. 351–361, 2020.
https://doi.org/10.1007/978-3-030-59000-0_26

Augmented Reality (AR) are technologies that allow changing the recording perspective and show users pictures from a different visual angle. Both begin with one of the most time-consuming processes, i.e. generating 3D models, which later can be a review on AR or VR devices. At present, this process could not be done, both quickly and automatically simultaneously. Using depth cameras we can create more/less detailed 3D models with the colored structure in real-time. Thanks to Azure Kinect DK devices and specially designed applications we can create not only static 3D models but also replicate their movement within seconds.

VR and AR devices are increasingly used in medical practice [1–4]. In 2015 interventional cardiologist Maksymilian Opolski tested Google Glass as an assistant in course of the percutaneous coronary intervention (PCI). Instead of visualizing the patient's hearts on monitors, they were projected onto glasses worn by the surgeon [5]. In turn, in July 2017, neuroradiologist Wendell Gibby performed surgery on the lumbar spine in assistance Microsoft HoloLens [6]. To precisely locate the damage disk, magnetic resonance imaging (MRI) and computed tomography (CT) images of the patient were loaded to OpenSight software and then visualized in a 3D spine image. After applying HoloLens, the doctor could see the patient's spine displayed/visualized like a film on his body. HoloLens followed the vision patch of the surgeon and allowed to navigate the anatomy with greater accuracy. Thus, in March 2018, cardiologist Dariusz Dudek performed percutaneous repair of Atrial Septal Defect (ASD) in the assistance of Augmented Reality goggles [7]. The projection was based on data read from computed tomography and it was possible to precisely locate the heart defect. In [8–10] the plastic surgical procedures using VR devices, i.e. Google Glass are reported. Disadvantages of this solution were accessed to the critical data in speakerphones and technical limitations of glasses. Thus, [11] proposed Microsoft HoloLens to improved decision-making and plastic surgical workflow. Surgical navigation system based on HoloLens in presented in [12]. Operative protocol from the point of the surgeon view is displayed in the internet browser Microsoft Edge in the form of a 2D dimension window. An interesting HoloLens application for clinical and nonclinical pathology is also shown in [13]. In turn, in [14] the idea of application of HoloLens and Azure Kinect DK as doctor assistance to meet the General Data Protection Regulation was shown.

Scientific units began to use VR and AR devices also in education. In 2016 Case Western Reserve University School of Medicine (Cleveland, Ohio) with cooperation with Cleveland Clinic (Cleveland, Ohio) started a course of the 3D holographic human anatomy with HoloLens, HoloAnatomy [15]. The most advanced anatomy application for medical learning, i.e. HoloHuman, was provided by Pearson and powered by 3D4Medical [16]. In [17] an application that allows students to visualize the geometry of 3D objects is shown. In turn, [18] presented anatomy learning with Microsoft googles. The accuracy of proposed gesture recognition was improved by an updated deep convolutional neural network. Birt ane co-authors [19] have presented two Australian higher education classrooms in physiology and anatomy, concentrating on student's perceptions. It turned out that AR and VR supported learning lessons are equivalent to the more expensive, cumbersome, and less accessible PC courses.

In this paper, the solution based on the Microsoft Azure Kinect DK and HoloLenes are to use in the operating room is widely considered. The main goal of the proposed approach is to allow users to observe surgery from any point of view they want without disturbing the surgeon's workflow. The users have, for the first time, the opportunity to replay the recorded event and select other positions/perspectives of observation. Moreover, the change of position during recording is also possible. There is no more need for having hundreds of cameras to obtain different perspectives. Currently, the market does not offer a solution with similar functionality.

2 Experimental and Computational Details

In this section, we proposed the using of the Augmented Reality system (based on Microsoft HoloLens and Azure Kinect DK devices), which enables remote support to patient management, and we recall its experimental and computational details.

2.1 Augmented and Virtual Reality Technologies

In Augmented Reality, users can actively interact with virtual objects linked to real life, while Virtual Reality replaces surrounding reality with the digital world [20]. The precise AR definition proposed by [21] says that it should incorporate real and virtual objects in one environment in real-time. It provides not only the vision but also hears, touch and smell [22]. Usually, AR systems include cameras, display, and several sensors. Camera track the user's movements in relation to virtual objects. The head-mounted display (HMD) allows users to observe these virtual objects in the physical world. Virtual objects are presented in the form of a hologram being a three-dimensional virtual image. The research to obtain the best quality of holograms are still ongoing. In [23] computational highlight holography, i.e an automated conversion process of the image to a 3D computer model is considered. The way of colorizing holograms was shown. Rosen and co-authors summarized 3D imaging techniques based on incoherent digital holography [24] and coded aperture correlation holography [25]. Bruckheimer and co-authors have reported the first case of using computer-generated digital holography in clinical medical imaging [26]. In [27] deep appearance model for face rendering, which seems to be the natural direction of further development on AR and VR devices, is shown. Intensive work on holographic near-eye displays for Virtual and Augmented Reality have been also undertaken. In [28] such displays, which are based on phase-only holographic projection, are presented. In turn, in [29, 30] holographic near-eye displays with expanded eye-box were presented. Holography as a progressive revolution in medicine is shown in [31].

2.2 Hardware

The introduction of a new technique involves the need to apply the right equipment, which will be used in the surgeon and diagnostic processes [32]. Currently, the market offers several AR and VR devices like Google Glasses [33], HTC Vive PRO [34], Oculus Rift [35] and Microsoft HoloLens [36]. Here, we proposed a solution that is based on the Azure Kinect DK and HoloLens devices, while Microsoft googles are a self-contained device and do not require a separate operation space and manual controllers. The general idea of a holographic doctor assistant was described in [37].

HoloLens is the independent holographic computer, which enables human-computer interaction in Augmented Reality without wires, phones, PC connections. Holograms are visualized in the user's real environment. First-generation of Microsoft google is equipped with a 2.3-megapixel 2 HD 16:9 display, 12.4-megapixel camera, built-in sensors, 3D audio speakers, Intel 32-bit (1 GHz) processor, 2 GB RAM, and 64 GB storage. There are included sensors like accelerometer, gyroscope, magnetometer, 4 environment sensors, energy-efficient depth camera with a 120° × 120° angle of view, four-microphone array, and ambient light sensor. The device provides 802.11ac wireless networking and Bluetooth 4.1 Low Energy (LE) wireless connectivity. The whole is powered by a 16.5 mWh battery [35].

Other devices we applied are Azure Kinect DK DK been a developer kit with AI sensors. It integrates a best-in-class 1MP depth camera (65 nm BSI 320 MHz Demodulated TOF Image Sensor with 3.5 μm Global Shutter Pixels and Analog Binning), 360° spatial microphone array with a 12MP RGB video camera, orientation sensor with multiple modes, options with software development kits providing sensor handling, body tracking, speed, and vision services. Device work in the range of temperature 10–25 °C and Relative Humidity 8–90% [38].

2.3 Software

The HoloLens device is fully integrated with Microsoft Enterprise systems. Its interface is known to users working the Windows operating system on other computer platforms, which makes the first contact easier. The disadvantage of this solution is the fact that the commercial license for HoloLens has a much higher price than VIVE Pro (even including the cost of the additional computer workstation) [39]. AR applications with spatial context for multi-users are designed and implemented using cross-platform Spatial Anchors based on the cloud [39]. In this study, a spatial awareness system Microsoft Mixed Reality Toolkit (MRTK) was used [40]. It allows scanning the environment around HoloLens while the users moved. During the user's movement, MRTK enables the scanning process and creating inside device memory, a 3D model of space, in which HoloLens currently are. This is used to map the behaviors and interaction on the displayed model linked to a real-world environment, just like in the real-word. We concentrate on the implementation of the HoloLens in a surgeon environment.

2.4 Three-Dimensional Models with Unlimited Perspective

Generating 3D models which later can be a review on AV or/and VR devices is the most time-consuming process. Using Microsoft Azure Kinect DK devices and specially designed applications we can create not only static three-dimensional (3D) models but also replicate their movement so that they look like they have been developed by a 3D graphic artist in long time process. All this can be done just in a few seconds since Azure Kinect DK allows generating view use of data from many different sensors. The most important one is 1 MegaPixel depth sensor which creates a picture with information for far is each object from the camera. To present it in a more understandable format such a picture is displayed in the color gradient. Distance from the camera is displayed as a gradient of each color. For example, when we record a view of the table it will look like it was drawn in just one color but parts of a table which are closer to the camera will have a lighter color and the one which is further are darker. Each distance contains its unique color with a gradient. Thanks to such solution pictures can be split into scenes where all objects which are in the same location are marked with light green so in 3D space they will be marked in position x and the one which is marked with dark red will have position 2x. This simple solution allows creating a 3D model and place each part of the picture in the exact space where it should be. The key future of this solution is that it records views all the time and presents it as a movie.

Another important sensor is a 12 MegaPixel CMOS sensor which is a typical RGB camera that records movies/pictures. Position, angle of it is synchronized in the way that it records exactly the same view as a depth camera. This way we get data about distance/position in the space of each object/point on the recorded view extended with data from RGB camera which allows those data to be merged. Such functionality allows getting the 3D model with textures created from the RGB camera because the picture from this view is placed in 3D space according to the pattern done by the depth sensor.

Some sensors provide data about angle and movement. 3D accelerometer and 3D gyroscope. The first one provides information about the speed of camera rotation in space. The gyroscope provides exact data about the angle in X, Y, Z space. This way we can not only tell on what angle camera watch space, but also is it moving, the following space or just stay in the same place.

To better visualize all these processes we should imagine ourselves as a camera - standing in the middle of the room with tables and chairs. Depth camera allows as to tell how far is each of the points in space where we actually look. RGB camera tells us what color is table/chairs and walls. Is there any wallpaper on it or is it just one-color wall. Accelerometer tells us with what speed we rotate our head and in what direction. Gyroscope informs us where exactly are we looking. Such data can be very easily used to create remote rotational tripod for camera connected remotely to VR/AR glasses where we display in 3D what exactly is seen. The angle/speed of rotation of remote glasses can be synchronized with the rotation of AR/VR glasses thanks to what we get the remote 3D stream. The main disadvantage is the fact that such rotation will be limited to just one operator who decides what he wants to see, all the other remote glasses will fully depend on the selected view of the main operator.

Azure Kinect DK can create a 3D model in space but cannot see things that are hidden behind other objects. Hence, we can notice that on some 3D models some spaces are empty. For example, when we record a chair and rotate in the 3D created model we will see that the space behind the chair is empty, there is a lack of data. This is because the camera cannot see that space. Here comes with help second Azure Kinect DK. When we put on a camera on the left side of the chair we will see everything that is on its left side, in front and on the back, but nothing on about right side and space around that. However, another device can be placed on the right side of the chair. Both cameras will record from two sides but there will be still a shared space that we can use as points to connect both 3D models into one more detail. Such a solution allows us to create a more precise model with much less blank spaces. Without a doubt, the more cameras we use the less blank spaces we will have. Figure 1 presents different camera shots of the 3D movie created with 2 cameras. On one picture we can see standard RGB view, on all other different angles and levels of detail selected. Surgery can be seen from the right side, left side, from the top, from the top corner and the back. Details of records are visible on the pictures thanks to points in space. They are connected into one big grid.

The proposed solution allows creating a detailed model that can be displayed using AR/VR glasses and therefore allows users to walk around that 3D model when displayed on a 1:1 scale. Thanks to that we get a 3D movie, in which each watching person can decide from what point of view they want to watch it and may change it at any moment.

3   Results and Discussion

In this section, we will present the steps in which a complex image is created using Azure Kinect DK devices, and then can be observed in Augmented Reality glasses. This solution is to allow seeing what is behind and around the camera. We can replay the event and select on our own from which perspective we want to watch. Besides that, we can change position while watching the event. The need of having hundreds of cameras to achieve different perspectives is gone. There is not yet solution on the market which could return something near the presented solution. 3D view implementation process and applicated technologies tools and experimental validation of the proposed system during an interventional procedure was performed

3.1   Implementation of the 3D View

Azure Kinect DK devices can record structure, objects, and shapes. As the first step, we will present the stages at which a complex image is created, which we can then observe using HoloLens. As an example, we will consider as an object a table on which various objects have been placed, i.e. a flower pot, sunglasses and candlesticks. Figure 1 shows how the camera can record this object and how these images are connected to create a 3D image. The first picture (Fig. 1a) presents a 3D model with natural structure and colors applied from the picture taken by one of three cameras. The second one (more colorful, Fig. 1b) shows the 3D model without natural structure and colors, computed generated model from the depth camera. In Fig. 2 three-dimensions models created by the device rotates, presenting different visual angles.

Fig. 1. Process of recording a 3D image using Azure Kinect DK devices: a 3D model with natural structure and colors (left) and a 3D model without structure and colors (right). (Color figure online)

Fig. 2. Three-dimensional model rotates with a different visual angle.

Using AR technology it is possible to changes the perspective of the observations. Figure 3, which presents how just using two cameras users can create a 3D model, where preview perspective (camera position and angle) can be changed as the user wishes. Moreover, the user can see, which part of the recorded event is higher than others, in what shape, direction.

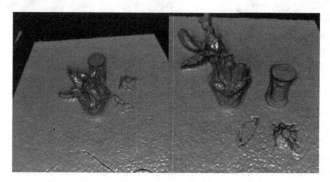

Fig. 3. A 3D model is shown from two different perspectives of the observations.

In the next step, we used the Microsoft Spatial Awareness system, which provides real-world environmental awareness in Augmented Reality applications. It enables to create the meshes to represent the geometry of the environment and interactions between real and computer-generated realities. A mesh is generated approximately every second by extracting the isosurface from the voxel volume. Spatial mapping scans in a 70-degree cone a region between 0.8 and 3.1 m—about 10 feet out. As a result, we move the entire space to the Digital Place (DP), i.e. room mapped in three dimensions should resemble a real room with people moving, light change.

This technology can be transferred to health care in many ways, eg. during the procedures in the operating room, using the proposed solution, we can create a real-time 3D model of the operating room, which can be subsequently streamed into different types of devices and viewed in the live stream.

The experimental validation was performed in the operating room by cardiologists during PFO (Patent Foramen Ovale) structural procedures. Solution based on the Microsoft Azure Kinect DK and HoloLenes, is presented in Fig. 4. It shows several perspectives from one device but few different sensors: Depth camera access and mode

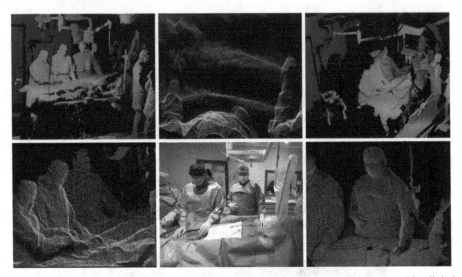

Fig. 4. Experimental validation of the proposed system in the real operating room and its digital image as well as spatial mesh.

control, RGB camera access and control and synchronized Depth-RGB camera streaming with configurable delay between cameras. We obtained multiple views at the same moment. The users can watch the operation from the surgeon position and view his work but with the option to look around, zoom in/out. In turn, with using the proposed AR system, we can not only see the operation room from the different perspectives, but also open on one of the screens a three-dimensional model of the heart and the course of the patient's electrocardiography, or other important vital signs of the patient needed during the operation.

The performed tests were quality controlled with the TPI Next (Test Process Improvement Next) audit, which takes into account:

- environmental factors,
- implementation of mapping space in the operating room during procedures, repeatability and data rate from the camera to Hololens,
- instructions and tools to support the implementation of the test process improvement,
- implementation was proposed in small steps - clusters (correlated process areas).

Changes and improvement of the tests result from the recommendation of changes resulting from the audit of the test process and significant changes in the approach to project implementation.

The testing methodology was randomly divided into two disjoint groups: test set and training set.

3.2 Possible Applications of the Technology

Thanks to the solution remote users can see ongoing surgery just like they were standing in front of the operation table, walk around in and change his/her perspective without disrupting operators who perform the procedure. "Ghost-like" participant's vision would not be limited due to, for example, the operator's hands.

First of all, this can be applied to the educational system of medical students and operators-in-training. This solution provides a theoretically unlimited number of 3D operating room participants as room size does not play a role and operators cannot be disturbed. The surgery may be recorded and reviewed afterwards and used to educate healthcare professionals with additional futures, i.e. remote pointing and painting. That may be especially useful in difficult or rare cases. Every procedure can be recorded and presented as a tutorial and used for educational purposes.

Secondly, the technology provides a tool of great use for a real-time consultation of the ongoing surgery. The operating surgeon may ask remotely more experienced operators to look and consult on the case. This may potentially reduce the number of complications and failed procedures. The solution may be especially helpful for medical centres that are short on staff or are in a great distance from a potential consultant, e.g. south pole research stations, International Space Station, container ships, 3rd world countries.

Moreover, in the future, the technology may provide better, 3D, visual systems for surgical robots and/or be the gateway to remote surgery.

4 Conclusions

Augmented Reality based technology can be implemented almost everywhere where doctors need to be in place to provide the patient with proper care. AR is already used in the operating room. When retrospectively combined with computed tomography imagining, it allows operators to see beyond human skin. In cardiology and vascular surgery, in which operators depend on 2D images, it is used to provide 3D data.

Our solution, that combines Azure Kinect DK and Microsoft HoloLens technology, allows healthcare professionals to enter the operating room regardless of their distance to it. The technology may be applied in the educational system of medical students and operators-in-training, unlimitedly and without interfering with the operator's workflow. Beyond that, it may provide the healthcare system with a powerful tool that allows "Ghost-like" supervision of the less experienced operators by the more experienced ones, that may be used where expert's help is unreachable. Moreover, the solution may have potential use in robot surgeries and be the gateway to remote surgery.

References

1. Andrews, C., Southworth, M.K., Silva, J.N.A., Silva, J.R.: Extended reality in medical practice. Curr. Treat. Options Cardiovasc. Med. **21**(4), 1–12 (2019). https://doi.org/10.1007/s11936-019-0722-7
2. Eckert, M., Volmerg, J.S., Friedrich, C.M.: Augmented reality in medicine: systematic and bibliographic review. JMIR Mhealth Uhealth **7**(4), e10967 (2019)

3. Mazurek, J., et al.: Virtual reality in medicine: a brief overview and future research directions. Hum. Mov. **20**(3), 16–22 (2019)
4. Monsky, W.L., James, R., Seslar, S.S.: Virtual and augmented reality applications in medicine and surgery-the fantastic voyage is here. Anat. Physiol. Curr. Res. **9**(1), 313 (2019)
5. Google-glass. https://lavreb.wordpress.com/2018/01/03/google-glass-surgery/
6. Dotmed. https://www.dotmed.com/news/story/38217?s=newsreg
7. Szpital Uniwersytecki w Krakowie (2018). https://en.su.krakow.pl/su.krakow.pl
8. Szpital Uniwersytecki w Krakowie Holografia. https://www.su.krakow.pl/nasz-szpital/aktual nosci/hologram-w-zabiegach-kardiologicznych
9. Sinkin, J.C., Rahman, O.F., Maurice, Y., Nahabedian, M.: Google glass in the operating room: the plastic surgeon's perspective. Plast. Reconstr. Surg. **138**, 298–302 (2016)
10. Brewer, Z.E., Fann, H.C., Ogden, D.W., Burdon, T.A., Sheikh, A.Y.: Inheriting the learner's view: a google glass-based wearable computing platform for improving surgical trainee performance. J. Surg. Educ. **73**, 682–688 (2016)
11. Tepper, O.M., et al.: Mixed reality with hololens: where virtual reality meets augmented reality in the operating room. Plast. Reconstr. Surg. **140**(5), 1066–1170 (2017)
12. Zuo, Y., et al.: A novel evaluation model for a mixed-reality surgical navigation system: where microsoft hololens meets the operating room. Surg. Innov., 1–10 (2020)
13. Hanna, M.G., Ahmed, I., Nine, J., Prajapati, S., Pantanowitz, L.: Augmented reality technology using microsoft hololens in anatomic pathology. Arch. Pathol. Lab. Med. **142**, 638–644 (2018)
14. Proniewska, K., Dołęga-Dolegowski, D., Pregowska, A., Dudek, D.: Augmented reality as a doctor support to meet the general data protection regulation in Europe, NFIC, 20th New Frontiers in Interventional Cardiology, 2019-12-11/12-13, Kraków (PL),10 (2019)
15. Case Western Reserve HoloLens. https://case.edu/hololens/
16. 3d4medical. https://3d4medical.com/apps/holohuman
17. Tang, Y.M., Leung, Y.: Comprehending products with mixed reality: geometric relationships and creativity. Int. J. Eng. Bus. Manag. **10**, 1–12 (2018)
18. Karambakhsh, A., Kamel, A., Shenga, B., Li, P., Yang, P., Feng, D.D.: Deep gesture interaction for augmented anatomy learning. Int. J. Inf. Manag. **45**, 328–336 (2019)
19. Birt, J., Stromberg, Z., Cowling, M., Moro, C.: Mobile mixed reality for experiential learning and simulation in medical and health sciences education. Information **9**(31), 2–14 (2018)
20. Slater, M., et al.: An experimental study of a virtual reality counseling paradigm using embodied self-dialogue. Sci. Rep. **9**(1), 1090321 (2019)
21. Azuma, R., Baillot, Y., Behringer, R., Feiner, S.K., Julier, S., MacIntyre, B.: Recent advances in augmented reality. IEEE Comput. Graph. Appl. **21**(6), 34–47 (2001)
22. Yu, D., Jin, J.S., Luo, S., Lai, W., Huang, Q.: A useful visualization technique: a literature review for augmented reality and its application, limitation&future direction. In: Huang, M.L., Nguyen, Q.V., Zhang, K. (eds.) Visual Information Communication, pp. 311–337. Springer, New York, NY, USA (2010)
23. Regg, C., Rusinkiewicz, S., Matusiak, W., Gross, M.: Computational highlight holography. ACM Trans. Graph. **29**(6), 170 (2010)
24. Rosen, J., Vijayakumar, A., Kumar, M., Rai, M.R., Kelner, R., Kaster, Y., Mukherjee, S.: Recent advances in self-interference incoherent digital holography. Adv. Optics Photonics **11**(1), 1–66 (2019)
25. Rosen, J., Vijayakumar, A., Ratnam, M., Mukherjee, S., Bulbul, A.: Review of 3D imaging by coded aperture correlation holography (COACH). Appl. Sci. **9**(3), 605 (2019)
26. Bruckheimer, E., et al.: Computer-generated real-time digital holography: first time use in clinical medical imaging. Eur. Heart J. Cardiovasc. Imag. **17**, 845–849 (2016)
27. Lombardi, S., Saragih, J., Simon, T., Sheikh, Y.: Deep appearance models for face rendering. ACM Trans. Graph. **37**(4), 68 (2019)

28. Maimone, A., Georgiou, A., Kollin, J.S.: Holographic near-eye displays for virtual and augmented reality. ACM Trans. Graph. **36**(4), 85 (2017)
29. Akşit, K., Kim, J., Kim, J., Shirley, P., Luebke, D.P.: Near-eye varifocal augmented reality display using see-through screens. ACM Trans. Graph. **36**(6), 189 (2017)
30. Jang, C., Bang, K., Li, G., Lee, B.: Holographic near-eye display with expanded eye-box. ACM Trans. Graph. **37**(6), 195 (2019)
31. Proniewska, K., Dołęga-Dołęgowski, D., Pregowska, A., Walecki, P., Dudek, D.: Holography as a progressive revolution in medicine in simulations in medicine computer-aided diagnostics and therapy. In: Roterman-Konieczna, I. (ed.) DeGruyter, pp. 103–116 (2020)
32. Wang, S., et al.: Augmented reality as a telemedicine platform for remote procedural training. Sensors **17**(10), 2294 (2017)
33. Google glass. https://www.google.com/glass/start/
34. HTC Vive PRO. https://www.vive.com/us/product/vive-pro/
35. Misrosoft HoloLens. https://www.microsoft.com/pl-pl/hololens
36. Oclus Rift. https://www.oculus.com/rift/?locale=pl_PL
37. Proniewska, K., Dołęga-Dołęgowski, D., Dudek, D.: A holographic doctors' assistant on the example of a wireless heart rate monitor. Bio-Algorithms Med-Syst. **14**(2), UNSP 20180007 (2018)
38. Microsoft Azure Spatial Anchors. https://azure.microsoft.com/en-us/services/spatial-anchors/
39. Orgon, D.C.: HoloLens and ViVE pro: virtual reality headsets. J. Med. Libr. Assoc. **107**(1), 118–121 (2019)
40. Microsoft Mixed Reality Toolkit. https://docs.microsoft.com/en-us/windows/mixed-reality/mrtk-getting-started

Author Index

Printed in the United States
By Bookmasters